TWO EAGLES

The History of the United States and Mexico

RICARDO SHEFFIELD

authorHOUSE®

AuthorHouse™
1663 Liberty Drive
Bloomington, IN 47403
www.authorhouse.com
Phone: 833-262-8899

Published by AuthorHouse 04/17/2023

ISBN: 979-8-8230-0064-2 (sc)
ISBN: 979-8-8230-0060-4 (hc)
ISBN: 979-8-8230-0061-1 (e)

Library of Congress Control Number: 2023902163

Print information available on the last page.

Any people depicted in stock imagery provided by Getty Images are models, and such images are being used for illustrative purposes only. Certain stock imagery © Getty Images.

This book is printed on acid-free paper.

Because of the dynamic nature of the Internet, any web addresses or links contained in this book may have changed since publication and may no longer be valid. The views expressed in this work are solely those of the author and do not necessarily reflect the views of the publisher, and the publisher hereby disclaims any responsibility for them.

Contents

Introduction

Almost two centuries of inseparable history between Mexico and the United States. Where, particularly in the past three decades, there are personal stories of millions of families interwoven between these two countries. Thousands and thousands of men and women have emigrated from Mexico to build their lives in the United States of America. A few have done it in the opposite direction, from north to south.

One of those few stories in reverse is that of my father, Frank Richard Sheffield. His story of migration began in 1958, unknown to him. Thousands of miles away, one afternoon in the Barrio Arriba neighborhood of Leon, Guanajuato, Maria de Jesus Padilla arrived home to unpleasant news. Her boyfriend, getting ahead of himself, had asked her father, Taurino, for her hand in marriage without even discussing the subject with her first.

The young lady had not the slightest intention of marrying the gentleman, even if he was a recently graduated doctor. She told Don Taurino not to count on her. She would not receive his visits, much less marry him.

Taurino was dismayed and concerned that out of ignorance he had already given his word, and with his word the honor of the family name and his family was at stake. This was not an easy dilemma to solve. The solution was to send his daughter to Los Angeles, California, for a few months with her uncle Joaquin, who had been living north of the Rio Grande for several years. By putting some distance between the two, he hoped that six months would be enough time to cool the suitor's desire for a wedding.

Taurino had lived in the United States during the three years he was in hiding during the Cristero War (a military struggle against the Mexican government for anti-Catholic measures). Like many others in central and western Mexico at the beginning of the twentieth century, he and a friend ran north to escape the armed conflict. The two, having participated in meetings of the Catholic Association of Mexican Youth in Leon during 1927, were likely to be targeted by federal soldiers. They fled for their lives, walking all night from Leon to their native San Juan de los Lagos, Jalisco. On arriving, they borrowed some horses from relatives. From there, they rode for days to Tijuana, spending several weeks off the main roads and away from the big cities, until they finally reached the border with the United States.

In those days, it was quite easy to cross the border; the hard part was actually getting there. The checkpoint was nothing more than a wooden shed on a dirt road, and the only real barrier was language. A simple wood signpost was the division between the two countries. Any kind of official identification served to register who you were. You filled out a small form by hand, and suddenly you were on the other side. Well, maybe not that fast. It used to be that you had to strip naked and have your clothes and shoes incinerated. Then you got a close shave of your beard, mustache, and hair, and your body was sprayed with insecticide, all in order to prevent pests from entering the United States. Today, this process would seem humiliating, contrary to human rights, but at that time—and for those looking to avoid death—it was just another requirement. Plus, they gave you clean, used clothes to replace the ones you had to abandon, which you could choose from some barrels next to the entry gate.

The horses had to stay on the Mexican side, but it didn't matter since there was little left of those poor animals. With your identity card in hand, the next step was to go in search of work. However, it was very difficult to find work in the border area.

The pair of friends walked north, doing small chores for a little food, until they reached the place where they were told there was work: the mines around San Francisco. Anyone who arrived would be put to work, they had been told. There was such a high turnover of workers that the two got a job within a few hours. They worked their asses off, but they got paid. The friends separated a few months later. My grandfather, Taurino, went to pick fruit south of Los Angeles. It was less pay but also less dangerous than the mines.

He bounced around California for three years, which was enough time to avoid religious persecution in his beloved Mexico. When his mother telegraphed him that things had finally calmed down, he spent many days on a return trip, shuttling on buses that passed through a few stretches of highway and many dirt roads. Sometimes he had to move on foot, or however he could, until he reached his beautiful Leon, Guanajuato. Taurino, though young and still single, returned to his roots. But many of his fellow countrymen stayed on the other side, putting down new roots in the United States.

Those memories and the fact his brother-in-law lived in Los Angeles gave him the confidence to send his daughter for a few months to that distant but neighboring land—all in order to cool off the mistaken marriage proposal.

After a long overland trip, with several stopovers, Taurino's daughter, Maria de Jesus Padilla—who was affectionately called Churra—arrived in Los Angeles. Her journey was much quicker and more civilized than the one her father had undertaken three decades earlier. At her uncle's house, a young gringo in love with Mexico, its history, its language, and its customs visited her daily. This eighteen-year-old American—of English, German, and Italian descent and who spoke Spanish quite well—knew more about the history of Mexico than all of Churra's cousins combined. He understood the customs of the land of the Aztecs better than her own uncles, even though he had only visited Tijuana for a weekend.

Churra, who had escaped marriage in Mexico, ended up finding it precisely in the United States by chance. As the saying goes, "things happen for a reason." Within two years of meeting, the young American converted from Presbyterian to Catholic, from Hollywood to proud resident of Leon, from high school teacher to leather merchant. Richard Sheffield ended up marrying Churra in the city of Leon in 1963, the city where he was buried in 2012 as he wished, with several years of dual citizenship behind him.

So, let's travel-jump to the 1970s, to a home in Leon with three sons. Where the Fourth of July was always celebrated as well as the sixteenth of September, Halloween as well as Day of the Dead, and Thanksgiving dinner preceded the traditional Mexican *posadas* in December. We had a bicultural upbringing; our mother spoke Spanish, and our father spoke English, as if they were one language. We lived in a house where it seemed normal to be born here rather than over there or over there rather than here. At that time, there was no dual nationality in Mexico, and having two or three birth certificates could be quite common.

One of those children, the oldest of the three, is me, Ricardo Sheffield, followed by my brothers, Alexander and John Arthur. Although I did not know it, I was born in Simi Valley, Los Angeles County, California. My brother Alexander was born in Leon, and John Arthur was also born in Simi Valley. We believed we were all born in Leon because that's what our documents said, and before we came of age, we never questioned them.

My parents lived in California for the first three years of their marriage. They had a bakery of traditional Mexican bread at the same time my dad was teaching theater, Spanish, and Mexican History at Simi Valley High School. Once I was born, they started living a few months each year in my maternal grandparents' house in Barrio Arriba in Leon and other months in Simi Valley, until the birth of my younger brother. When I was five years old, they moved permanently to Leon. Whether in Mexico or in the United States, in public or in private, my mother always spoke to us in Spanish, my father in English. Fortunately, we were never allowed to mix languages or mispronounce words.

I do not have many memories of my early childhood in the United States, with the exception of a forest fire in California, which reached our urban area causing serious damage, and the Sylmar earthquake of February 1971. The earthquake was the last straw that drove us out of the United States to settle permanently in Mexico. Most of my early childhood memories are of Barrio Arriba, where we were raised like all middle-class children in the Bajio—the region in Central Mexico that includes the state of Guanajuato.

With no clear memories of my childhood in the United States, my first impression of that country comes from a trip we took as a family to El Paso, Texas, when I was eleven years old. It was the first time we had returned to the United States since we moved to Mexico. For six years, my dad had not had enough money to return to his homeland, not even to visit. We traveled by train to Ciudad Juarez from Leon, crossing on foot to El Paso. The only thing I remembered about the history of the United States was the little I had studied in elementary school and the anecdotes my dad told me. I was shocked to see the disparity between walking on dirt roads on the Mexican side and the asphalt roads on the American side. And to see countless buildings more than ten stories high, while in my native Leon, there were only three. Even the air smelled different to me, as if it were cleaner, probably because of all the air-conditioning. Nobody in the Mexican Bajio had it or really used air-conditioning; the mild climate did not make it necessary. Since then, and to this day, I have read and reflected a lot about the roots of the great differences in material, infrastructure, and institutional strength that are so evident between Mexico and the United States.

I think about what the land that is now Mexico was like before the arrival of the Europeans, what Mexico was like as the viceroyalty of New Spain. I compare how it was back then for Europeans seeing those unfamiliar lands for the first time with how it is now seeing the United States of America. I cannot overlook the great transformations of the nineteenth and twentieth centuries that turned the United States into the world's leading power, while in Mexico, we are still trying to overcome extreme poverty.

After that first trip to El Paso, my mom and I returned every three months for more than six years. My mom found a way to sell *fayuca*—small contraband—and by tagging along, I learned how to do it too. *Fayuquear* consisted of buying merchandise in the United States, much of it actually from other countries, and importing it illegally into Mexico, because it was not possible to do it legally, to sell among friends. In the years prior to Mexico's entry into GATT, not one single piece of chewing gum or chocolate that was not Mexican could be obtained south of the Rio Grande. That was what was most often brought in as *fayuca*: American candy, clothing, and knickknacks.

Complementing the *fayuquero* trips, from the age of twelve, I began spending my summers in California with my paternal grandparents. During those summers, I took classes in magic, acting, dancing, and other artistic activities, and I traveled to tourist sites throughout the United States. During the week, I spent my time among English-speaking Anglos, and on Sundays, at the Catholic church with Mexican Americans. Truth be told, I didn't really identify with any of them beyond communicating naturally with one or the other in their native language, but there was no cultural identity. In my opinion, Mexican Americans were not culturally Mexican, and I was not culturally American.

All those trips ended abruptly. Dual citizenship was not allowed in Mexico until 1997, and thirteen years earlier, in 1984, when I turned eighteen, I had to choose between being an American or a Mexican citizen. Others, such as my two brothers, had not even considered it, and neither did anyone else when they came of age. Years later, they opted for dual citizenship. But my exacerbated nationalism led me to present myself at the Ministry of Foreign Affairs on the same day of my birthday, renounce my American nationality, and present the documentation at the US embassy in Mexico.

A few months later, in order to be able to travel to the United States, I needed a visa for the first time in my life. I made an appointment at the consulate in Guadalajara and went alone to complete the process. After hours of presenting my documents and visa application, I was called to a private room, where a rude and English-speaking official informed me that I would be criminally prosecuted for falsifying an official document and for lying to the US government—and that the Mexican Ministry of Foreign Affairs had already been notified of the facts.

"Are you kidding? And what document did I falsify, according to you?" I asked.

It turned out to be my birth certificate. There was no way, but according to the rude official, I was born in Los Angeles, California, not in Leon, Guanajuato. I asked her to call my parents on the phone because clearly there was a mistake. They let me use the consulate's phone. I called my dad and angrily explained the situation to him, and he said, "I'm going to put your mom on the line." I went cold. *Now it's all over,* I thought.

My mom told me that I was indeed born in Simi Valley, but after three months, they brought me to Leon. And since she had not registered my birth in the US, she registered me in Leon.

I informed my mother that, in the United States, registration is done automatically at the hospital when one is born. And although it was clear that I had not committed any crime, the US government requested that all my personal documents be invalidated, which the Mexican government did without delay. And for two years, I was left in my country without an identity. They canceled my birth certificate, my voting card, my military ID, and my renunciation of my US citizenship. I had to submit the first registration of a foreign birth certificate in the entire history of the state of Guanajuato, with a two-page attestation of facts on the back of the certificate, reprocess all my documents, and do my military service again. When my papers were finally all in order, I went to the US embassy in a rage—for so much trouble they had caused me—and again renounced my US nationality, formally, at twenty-one years of age. Several times, various embassy officials let me know that there was no longer obligatory military service in the United States, and they asked me if I had been in any encampments in Cuba or Nicaragua—countries that at that time never visited—or if I was a member of the Communist Party. *Good God! I'm just a kid from Guanajuato, for crying out loud!* I took it personally, and the more complicated they made it for me, the more I was determined to renounce my nationality, until I achieved my goal. Later, they didn't even want to give me a visa!

I went to the United States a few times between the ages of twenty and twenty-four. Then I was admitted to Harvard University (the leading university of liberalism in the United States, where Kennedy and Obama graduated) to study for a master's degree in law, which I completed in 1991.

After many travels throughout Mexico and the United States, learning about both countries' histories, and serving legal clients on both sides of the border, I have concluded that in no way do I identify with the culture of Mexican Americans—the Pochos—even though my family background and education make me an amphibian of the Rio Grande. I have cousins who are Mexican American "Pochos" and live in the United States, but it is clear to me that my cultural formation and identity are different. And the clarity of my national conviction as a Mexican is more than confirmed. So, what am I, culturally speaking? The "Pocho" celebrates cinco de mayo without knowing why, and the Mexican does not celebrate Thanksgiving … wait a minute, I know, I got it, I am a reverse Pocho, I am an "Ochop," an unorthodox definition for my unique situation of American Mexican.

Pochos or Mexican Americans are the children of Mexicans, born and raised in the United States, with US citizenship, who speak English better than Spanish because their parents did not want them to learn their native language for fear of being deported. That is why those of us who are children of parents from both sides of the border, who were educated in Mexico and who first spoke Spanish, are from a grouping without a nickname or definition. There are very few of us, and now dual citizenship allows us not to face that dilemma. Over time, I have confirmed myself as a patriotic Mexican, but culturally I consider myself an "Ochop" an American Mexican, which makes me a deep admirer of the culture of my country, Mexico, but also of the history and traditions of both countries.

I am now the fortunate father of three daughters born in Leon, Guanajuato. My wife is also a native of Leon. They have Mexican nationality, with no possibility of obtaining dual citizenship, but all their close relatives, uncles, aunts, and cousins have the dual citizenship. Some live on the other side of the border, and others live here in Mexico. With those experiences, it is even easier for me to analyze, and more intriguing to conclude, the distinctive nature of an "Ochop," of an American Mexican.

I was trained and educated in both countries, so I am bicultural and bilingual, always curious to know why there are obvious differences in the standard of living between Mexico and the United

States. I believe that in this book I can tell, in English and Spanish, the story of the two lands with a different, unheard voice—not so much as a search, but as an encounter. In the end, we will always live together, those from here, those from there, those from both sides, who already number in the millions, with an economy so integrated that even if the USMCA did not exist, we would still be one market.

And what better occasion to review our histories as great countries in the international forum than in the bicentennial of diplomatic relations between Mexico and the United States of America. I pray to heaven that from now on, it will be a history of greater mutual understanding, more mutual respect, and greater interaction. And as a popular Mexican song says, "Long live the Americas, oh blessed land of God."

Chapter 1

Here Before the Europeans

Clovis Was First

We are people of North America with a long history to share. As fate would have it, we happened to live in an area that today includes the United States and Mexico. Our history can be traced back to before the settlement of the first civilizations that domesticated corn and built temples and dwellings. We have many voices. Our heritage is complex and diverse, and we are proud of it.

It is hard to picture it in today's frenzied world, but long ago, in the backwoods of the Rio Grande, other species existed—and humans had attributes that are barely apparent today. Let's think about how life was 13,500 years ago. There are no restaurants, schools, buildings, avenues, or traffic lights, no cars, and no airplanes flying across the sky. Cell phones are unimaginable, space travel is unthinkable, at night, you can only see the light of the moon, and the only webs are the immense spider webs growing on trees or wild bushes. There are no shoes, pants, jackets, or coats of any kind; the only appropriate clothing is bison skin. Arachnids as well as various species that are hunted to survive roam freely. Remember: these are not animals that live free in a protected reserve or in captivity in a zoo; these are animals that have made humans part of their diets. But as conventional Mexican wisdom would say thousands of years later: these people were not intimidated by anyone or anything.

This following scene is told from the Clovis' perspective. Their penetrating gaze assesses the risks. They have become accustomed to getting meat from the huge beasts of the last Ice Age. Men of their clan are stalking bison for food. They work together to hunt in an organized manner, always together. Women and children wait for them in a temporary dwelling. The whole tribe is always active, ready

1

to follow the bison wherever they go. They are nomads. The bison is not alone either. It follows its herd, trying to survive as well. Their bearings, huge antlers, and bulky fur are fascinating to the Clovis people. The animal commands respect.

The following is a common scene from the period to which we have been transported. The ground shakes, a sign that another species—one that has been in continual migration from the frozen areas of the North Pole southward—is approaching. The hunters await with quartz-tipped spears ready. They know they must not make any noise, as this will decide whether or not they get food for the tribe. They wait patiently. Before their eyes, instead of bison, huge beasts with curved horns and long trunks appear, impressive hairy mammals, the mammoths. They travel in herds like the bison, and their movement produces thunderous booms that can be heard in the distance while the earth trembles.

It is likely that a member of the Clovis tribe, when seeing the formidable size of those animals, thought of backing out before such a tremendous challenge. "How do we hunt that thing? How are we going to do that? Better that we keep looking for bison."

The rest of the hunters would have tried to calm him down with a slap or two across the face. They must have reflected, *We have our spears ready, so perhaps we should use them. Let's go for it.* Of course, there are no direct witnesses to the above scene, and none of the participants wrote their testimony in a diary. Nevertheless, we should not rule out the possibility that the Clovis's behavior toward mammoths was similar to this imagined scenario.

The Clovis people venerate bison and mammoths, and they feel such devotion that they must hunt them. But the Clovis people feel much more respect for the mammoth than for the bison since taking down one of these great beasts is no easy task and will highly likely result in the death of a clan member. Mammoths are worshipped as sacred creatures, despite being hunted. And so, it could be said that at first the mammoth was not a surly beast, but they turned it into one. Now, at this point in the journey, we are with the Clovis people of New Mexico. The Clovis people are named after the town of Clovis, a small village with a population of approximately thirty-eight thousand inhabitants. Studies show that this group has lived in the American continent for twenty-two thousand years.

Like the megafauna, they came from Asia and walked across the Bering Strait. Back then, Alaska was one massive ice continent, not what is now under threat of melting due to global warming. The Clovis people traveled long distances, evading the intense cold of the last ice age, during a period we know as the Pleistocene or Ice Age. The Clovis people traveled in isolated clans. Some, such as the Naia people, were curious about distant territories and continued southward to what is currently Mexico and as far as Guatemala. Others said, "There is no reason to move; we're fine here," and remained in the north, which now includes the United States and part of Canada.

The spearheads the Clovis used are today considered priceless objects. These went on display in 2019 at the Regional Museum of Sonora, where the first exhibition on this culture was held. This discovery remained in the hands of archaeologists between 2007 and 2012.

The spearheads that helped provide sustenance for the clan are now known as "Clovis spearheads," since these are the first sign that confirms the presence of such people in the American territories. Those who have studied these ancestors report that there are approximately 12,500 to 13,500 years between the time of the Clovis culture and the present day. It is a substantial, mysterious gap. However, discoveries are gradually emerging that allow us to reconstruct the enigmas of the past, which we will discuss later on.

With regard to the period in which we describe the presence of mammoths in America, researchers from Mexico's National Institute of Anthropology and History (INAH, for the acronym in Spanish), in collaboration with some US universities, were recently able to identify eighteen hunting sites in North America. To their surprise, after laboratory studies, they determined that the mammoth was the species most frequently hunted by the Clovis people. So perhaps the mammoths would have preferred not to be venerated so much

3

by the Clovis people. The Clovis people overcame the cold climate and, using warmth from campfires, adapted to the comforts of simple caves. Whether bison or mammoth, the fact is that their existence on the American continent was possible as long as these creatures continued feeding from the vast vegetation that surrounded them. But during the last ice age, the Pleistocene, it all ended. The planet went through climate change, causing the disappearance of all densely furred species. This change was due to natural causes, resulting from the globe's evolution. Human industrial activity could not yet be blamed for such destruction. The Clovis were left with no chance of survival in the absence of their favorite animals. Gradually, over the course of a few centuries, the Clovis people disappeared from the planet.

It is true that because they were chasing the herds of large quadrupeds, they had no time to build temples and dwellings or to domesticate plant species that would lead to agriculture. On the other hand, this was not an obstacle for the Clovis culture to express themselves artistically in the graphic representations they made on rocks or on the walls inside the caves. The images of bison, mammoths, and stars, whether with flint or vegetable pigments, will remain for posterity.

This is all so far back in history that relics that might help to better understand the Clovis people remain a mystery. Still, one thing that cannot be denied is that at one time, long ago, the Clovis culture existed and ruled the continent, along with bison and mammoths. They are an essential part of our ancestral memory, although modern civilization has forgotten them.

From Naia to Cuauhtemoc

Naia was Clovis and lived in the American continent. We will continue narrating our history with her story. Naia is pregnant, undernourished, and only fifteen years old, maybe sixteen or seventeen. She wears animal skins. She does not shave and certainly does not wear perfume. Her hands and the soles of her feet are calloused, despite her youth. She has a mane of thick hair. She helps the members of her clan by working quartz crystal to make arrowheads.

Around 2007, a group of divers made a trip to inspect the underwater caves of the Yucatán Peninsula in Tulum, a region where one of the most important pre-Hispanic cultures, the Maya, prevailed for a long time. The divers extracted a small female corpse from a body of water in an underwater cave.

It took seven years before INAH decided to reveal the details of the discovery. Today, the offering of maidens to the underwater caves by the Maya is a well-known part of our culture. Perhaps because of this, what the INAH authorities were about to reveal to the public about the remains of this young woman, from approximately twelve thousand to thirteen thousand years ago, is more surprising.

The discovery of our friend Naia raised some interest momentarily but unfortunately did not transcend any further. In fact, she was even considered as the missing link of the Americas. She was named Naia after the site where she was found, referring to the aquatic nymphs of Greek mythology. In addition, divers found the skeletons of other species at the discovery site, which allowed them to elaborate on the story of the young woman. As in a police investigation, it was determined that these sites were above ground before becoming underwater caves, but due to a combination of natural phenomena, they ended up becoming flooded caves.

The top prize out of the forty-four specimens found were the remains of a saber-toothed tiger and a giant sloth. What happened at this place? Did both animals fight each other to the death and accidentally fall into the cave? Was Naia there during this fight and became trapped in the middle of it? It is impossible to know. There is no doubt that before settlement by pre-Hispanic cultures, America was the setting of countless stories such as the one we have just told.

The impact that Naia caused in the world was such that she was called the "Eve" of the American continent since this was the oldest finding of its kind. This perdurable young woman is recognized as a precursor of these lands. Naia is certainly not alone; perhaps the Clovis people could provide us with another discovery given their difficult pilgrimage from the north of Asia and through the Bering Strait. If that happens, it deserves more attention than was given to the astonishing discovery of Naia, which received only moderate interest from the media. Perhaps if she had been an influencer ...

Meanwhile, let's leave the Clovis and travel to America's northern coasts, to the Newfoundland area. A dragon's head, which locals had never seen before, appears among the waves. The beast's body approaches the beach. It stops before running aground on the sand. People quite different from the Clovis clan descend in small boats. As they descend, one can see that their skin is very red and sunburned, their hair is long and reddish. The villagers in the area, amazed, yell loudly. The men who came from the sea nickname their hosts *Skraelingar*, which means "people who shout."

The men from the sea look strong and suited for war. After overcoming their astonishment, the locals negotiate and exchange goods. There will be other vessels following this dragon-headed one. Unfortunately, the cordial relationship, as expected, will not last long. Fighting will soon begin. These reddish, bearded men will never return to American shores. The story will remain as an episode that many will doubt. Nevertheless, these explorers will return to their homeland and recount their adventures and misfortunes to the villagers who are interested in listening to them. Their confessions, in the heat of fire and wine, will inspire Scandinavian writers skilled in the pioneering literary genre of the *saga*.

Travelers from the Iberian Peninsula were long considered to be the first to arrive on this continent, ignoring the Vikings. We now know from archeological discoveries that this was not accurate. The Polynesians, who were able to take advantage of sea flows and winds to travel to the south of the continent, can also not be ignored. The lack of relics, similar to what happened with the Clovis culture, led to skepticism among locals and foreigners. The arrival of the Scandinavian Vikings in the Americas was considered fantasy. There is no way to refute it now. The story of the sagas takes place sometime around the eleventh century. Much like Skraelingar who inhabited and defended Newfoundland, a century before and to the south, pre-Hispanic cultures were already emerging. Some of them left unique traces that identify them and others, a mix of myth and legend.

From Clovis Culture to the Aztecs

The domestication of corn began in central Mexico approximately ten thousand years ago. Ancient farmers domesticated the grain when they found some peculiar seeds and sowed them to find out what would spring from the ground. A key area in the history of corn is the Tehuacan Valley, in the state of Puebla. Some time ago, researchers from the INAH found three corn specimens that were 5,300 and 4,970 years old in the Tehuacan Valley. The Olmecs even received corn from Tehuacan and expanded it to their own territories. Corn became more popular over time until it was the most widely consumed crop in Mesoamerica. Thanks to this sacred grain, the Mesoamerican cultures arose as nomads changed hunting for agriculture, becoming sedentary. They began to grow their own food instead of chasing mammoths. This transition allowed them to build great empires.

In this journey through the continent's history, we will now join a merchant from one of the most respected and venerated cities in Mesoamerica. It is not Teotihuacan or Uxmal. It is not the great Tenochtitlan either. We walk with him along one of the magnificent esplanades. The inhabitants' clothing tells us that this is an emblematic site. This ancient city is called Cuicuilco. An unusual event is about to take place. The merchant mingles among the forty thousand inhabitants in this city located to the south of the future Mexico City. He carries quetzal feathers with him to exchange them for goods. Everything is splendid on that relatively ordinary day.

We now head to the ceremonial center following our tour guide. A loud noise stops us short. A column of smoke rises toward the horizon, followed by an explosion. The nearby Xitle volcano has just erupted. Red–hot lava covers a large part of the city. The villagers run terrified while everything is reduced to rubble. The eruption destroys everything that took decades to build. The memory, our memory, is erased.

We return to the present time after the disaster. I park my vehicle in the access area of the Cuicuilco archaeological site, which can also be reached by the public metrobus route. I walk along its wide main avenue and enter its ceremonial center. I look around. The current roadway—the elevated *viaducto*—and the buildings that surround it remind me that I am on an island of time. There are few clues left after the cataclysm caused by the eruption of the Xitle to understand the culture that flourished here centuries ago. Cuicuilco represents a real enigma for experts in Mesoamerican cultures.

But the history of Cuicuilco is extraordinary. Cultures and cities disappear progressively and not suddenly. It is time for a break in this journey through time to describe the cultures that preceded and followed Cuicuilco.

In the records that we have, after the Clovis culture, Mexican territory was divided into Mesoamerica and Aridoamerica. Cuicuilco belongs to the former, while the arid zone was settled by nomadic and seminomadic peoples, such as the Tarahumara, Chichimecas, Laguneros, and Tepehuanes, among others.

The Tarahumara, or Rarámuri, which means "the light–footed," settled in the Sierra Madre Occidental, in the states of Chihuahua, Sonora, and Durango, in northeast Mexico. They live on ranches, and their main crop is corn. They still preserve rituals from their pre–Hispanic past, such as the consumption of hallucinogenic peyote. People say that they run faster than a deer, hence the meaning of their name. Their talent in races has continued to this day, and there are several Tarahumara runners who have won national and international marathons.

The Chichimecas were great strategists and warriors; they were the last tribe to fight the Spanish conquerors after the fall of Tenochtitlan. The conquerors thought they could defeat them easily, but they did not foresee that the Chichimecas were not going to let themselves be subdued without bloodshed. This brutal resistance is known as the Chichimeca War. It ended after fifty-three years, when the viceroyalty of New Spain obtained (by negotiation) the surrender of the Chichimecas in exchange for provisions and food.

The Mexicas did not sympathize with the Chichimecas. As further proof of their disdain, it is believed that they gave them the name "Chichimeca," which means "of dog lineage." They lived in the current states of Durango, Guanajuato, Queretaro, Coahuila, Zacatecas, Jalisco, and San Luis Potosi. Unfortunately, Chichimeca craftsmanship has not survived over time and has been almost completely lost.

The Laguneros, also known as the Irritila, are an ethnic group that lived in the Comarca Lagunera. They hunted hares, deer, moles, and when they were brave enough, they dared to hunt bears. Their huts were made of reeds and forage. Peyote must have something magical considering that, like the Tarahumara people, the Laguneros also used it to enliven their rituals and dances.

The Tepehuanes inhabit southern Durango and were the largest tribe in northern Mexico. Its name is of Nahuatl origin and means "owner of hills." Their main crops are corn and beans. However, they also practiced ritual cannibalism. Their religious beliefs have a strong Catholic influence. They worship both saints and the sun.

These communities are similar to the Clovis in that they did not leave a great architectural legacy, nor did they focus on developing or mastering agricultural techniques. In Mesoamerica, on the other hand, major settlements were built by the Maya, Mixtec, Olmec, Otomi, and Teotihuacan cultures, to mention a few.

The Maya civilization developed mainly in southern Mexico, in the states of Quintana Roo, Yucatán, Campeche, Chiapas, and Tabasco. Their expansion was such that their influence reached Guatemala, Belize, and part of Honduras and El Salvador. They were great architects of pyramids, observatories, acropolis, and ball courts. The most famous Maya pyramid is the Kukulkan Temple, located in Chichen Itza, Yucatán, one of the seven wonders of the modern world. They knew how to read the stillness of the stars and were great mathematicians; they were among the first to use zero in their number system. They also developed a calendar with a high level of accuracy regarding the cycles of the moon and sun, eclipses, and the movement of the planets, essential for their religious ceremonies. They practiced human sacrifices to remain in the good graces of their many gods. Only high-ranking prisoners of war were generally sacrificed, which was a relief for the rest of the captured prisoners. Their most sacred book is the *Popol Vuh*, a compilation of narratives on myths, legends, and customs that recount the creation of the Maya world and civilization. Important city-states such as Tikal, Palenque, and Chichen Itza flourished during the Classic Maya period, from AD 320 to 900. The Maya coexisted and mixed with other cultures, such as the Toltecs, at Chichen Itza. Several factors, including internal wars and droughts, led to the gradual abandonment of the cities in the fourth century. Many thousands of inhabitants must have said, "Let's get the hell out of here!" and never returned, leaving behind their great temples to stand silent. To this day, Maya beliefs, customs, handicraft production and languages endure, having survived the evangelization that almost wiped them out.

Now let's move on to the Mixtecs, "people of the rain or of the cloud." They settled in southern Mexico, in the states of Oaxaca, Puebla, and Guerrero. They had remarkable military knowledge and created their own weapons to conquer territories and defend their own from any invaders, as during the Mexica invasion. Agriculture guaranteed their survival. Besides corn, beans, chilies, and squash, they cultivated cotton and cocoa. They domesticated animals such as turkeys and the Xoloitzcuintle dog, the loyal dog that walked and guided the souls of the dead in their journey down to the Mictlan. They worshipped the sun, rain, and water. They were skilled in working gold, which they considered so sacred that they called it "the excrement of the gods." The most important Mixtec cities were San José Mogote and Monte Albán.

The Otomi people have withstood the Toltecs, the Mexicas, and the Spanish conquerors, and they are still standing fighting a tough battle against neglect. They have inhabited central Mexico since 2500 BC and share cultural traits with the Nahuas. The word *Otomi* is of Nahuatl origin and means "one who walks with arrows" since it is said that ancient Otomi hunters used to walk with a considerable number of these weapons. The Mexicas also wanted to attack the Otomi and launched several campaigns to conquer them, but they faced great resistance from the Otomi community. The Otomi language still exists, although unfortunately, it is spoken by increasingly fewer people due to migration from their communities and growing urbanization of their territories.

The groups mentioned above developed agricultural techniques, domesticated animals, and founded large cities with an architecture that continues to amaze us to this day.

In this back-and-forth through time, we will go back two thousand years from today to an era when we can already find the presence of the pre-Hispanic cultures. The Olmecs, whose name means "inhabitants of the rubber region," came into existence and flourished throughout the state of Veracruz and part of Tabasco. They are considered the mother of Mesoamerican culture. Their most emblematic works are forty-ton colossal heads that were intended to be a faithful portrait of their rulers. An interesting fact is that this name was given to them sometime later by the Mexicas, who liked to give nicknames to other people and were more generous with the Olmecs than with the Chichimecas. The Olmecs influenced the Maya culture's depiction of nature and the universe and deification of the jaguar, quetzal, and serpent. The Olmec culture is still being studied in Mexico and elsewhere, and there are many hypotheses about the exact causes of their cultural demise.

The Olmecs date back to around 3000 BC, followed by the Maya at 1800 BC, Chupicuaros at 600 BC, Zapotecs at 500 BC, Teotihuacanos at 100 BC, Totonacas at AD 100, Mixtecas at AD 300, Chalchihuites at AD 300, Toltecas at AD 900, Huastecos at AD 1000, and Mexicas at AD 1325, to name the most important cultures.

Teotihuacan means "the place where men become gods." It was the largest and most populated city in the world in its heyday. The Mexicas discovered this city when it was already abandoned.

The Mexicas, walking cautiously on deserted roads and listening to nothing but silence, believed they had arrived at the home of the gods. They believed this was the place built by giants where Tonatiuh, the Fifth Sun, gave his burning heart as a sacrifice to overcome the darkness of the world, transforming himself into the sun that shines on us today.

Teotihuacan is located northeast of the Valley of Mexico and ongoing excavations are providing more information about the city. Nevertheless, as of now, the identity of the first settlers is still unknown. What is known is that political instability, economic mismanagement, fire, and adverse weather conditions caused the decline of the city, which occurred in the seventh century. It was designated a World Heritage Site by UNESCO in 1987.

But what was the origin of the Mexicas? From this historical weaving, we will choose a thread that scholars have been following with greater certainty. We will follow a pilgrim from a tribe that has decided to find a legendary site that has been indicated as the place to build their base. This tireless traveler left the mythical Aztlan and formed a caravan with his group. He is the leader and encourages his followers to find the place promised by their divine guardian. The journey is hard and exhausting. The group's indomitable spirit makes others suspicious, and they are expelled from any place where they try to rest to recover their strength. The search is protracted and seems endless. More than one questions the purpose of the journey. Will it be worth the effort? But every cloud has a silver lining. Finally, it all pays off.

An eagle perched on a cactus devours a snake on an island. The leader who has allowed us to follow his tribe on this challenging journey, Tenoch—whose name means prickly pear cactus on stone or stone tuna—decides that this is the sacred sign. This place, surrounded by putrid waters and prone to floods, is where the mission will be fulfilled. This is the story of how Tenochtitlan was founded, which seems to have been taken from a mythological event.

Up to that time, the Mexica people—who would later become known as the Aztecs-—through determination and a spirit of survival, had developed great skills in food production and water resources. Their talent will allow them to make the most of the harsh region they decided to make their home in the Valley of Mexico. In this area, where centuries ago, the mammoths prowled with the Clovis people chasing them, there is now a large body of water made up of five tributaries. Mountain ranges and volcanoes, including the snowcapped peaks of Popocatepetl and Iztaccihuatl volcanoes, surround it. It is a flora and fauna paradise. Tenoch and his people, however, are not alone. The lordship of Azcapotzalco already occupied the site. The lords waste no time in letting the Mexicas know that they should not settle down, asking them to leave their territory as soon as possible. Nevertheless, the Mexicas managed to avoid a war and were allowed to settle down in exchange for paying a tax.

This is how they will survive, but Tenoch's days are numbered, and we have to continue this story without him. After his death, the chosen people named Acamapichtli as their ruler and first tlatoani. This did not please the lords of Azcapotzalco, who consequently imposed a double tax. This itinerant tribe will soon form an extraordinary empire. The second tlatoani, who was clever than the first, marries the daughter of one of the lords of Azcapotzalco and makes an alliance that exempts the Mexica people from paying taxes. After this alliance, both lordships subjugate the remaining towns in the Valley of Mexico. The Mexicas' efforts, despite their fierce military power, ended up enriching the tax coffers of the Azcapotzalco lords. This led to a rebellion that ended with the death of the tlatoani. His successor and third in line is betrayed by his allies. But a bold move by the Mexicas to team up with villages that are also oppressed by the Azcapotzalco regime pays enormous dividends. The rebellion is successful. Tenochtitlan became the imperial city of the Valley of Mexico.

The tribe's expansion is without precedent. They build a city in swampy areas, subjugate its lords, build a cosmopolitan center to which remote regions supply servants, and become an unprecedented military power. The Mexicas' domination parallels a complex divine pantheon that will have Tlaloc and Huitzilopochtli as guardian figures. In the Templo Mayor, symbol of Tenochtitlan, they will be equally revered.

The empire was already dominant during the period of Moctezuma I, with an agricultural structure that supplied drinking water to the inhabitants of a city, unparalleled for that time. This water comes from Chapultepec Hill, which is considered by contemporary experts as an aquifer or Tlalocan, which means place of sustenance. It was venerated by chroniclers and Hernan Cortes, but the Achilles' heel of the Mesoamerican metropolis was, indeed, water. The engineering inherited from the visionary poet Netzahualcoyotl collapses when vital sustenance is drained.

This will be the zenith of the empire's last stage. From the legacy of Moctezuma I to his successor, history was already written. Collecting a tax that was too onerous resulted in animosity toward the Mexica, just as happened with the Azcapotzalco lords. The odds for defeat were set. An alliance formed by its enemies was enough to make the imperial city decline.

Let's share the last moments of a defender of the great Tenochtitlan. The population is decimated, without water, sick, and hungry. The defender observes corpses floating in the lake the ruins of what was once the most beautiful city his eyes have ever seen. Nonetheless, he continues to defend it, such is his pride. Tenochtitlan finally falls. The magnificence of this city will be ruined and unrecognizable. Time travel brings us back to this place. We are now in the present, in what is known as Mexico City's Historic Center. We walk through the silent ruins of the Templo Mayor. All that remains of that glory are the foundations; experts continue to try to make sense of the historical memory.

From Clovis to Cherokees

The Europeans' encounter with Mesoamerican cultures was a study in contrasts. The organization, art, and government system of our continent impacted the invasive expansion plan of the Europeans.

The Spanish in particular were focused on exploiting the wealth of the subjugated empire, as happened to the south in Peru.

But this does not mean that the rest of the continent was unpopulated. Not at all. Although the saber-toothed tiger and the mammoth no longer inhabited the American continent, the bison turned out to be clever and managed to adapt and survive in the northern zones. The Spaniards, who subdued a proud and warlike empire, were not interested in conquering the great extensions of land where seminomadic groups—like our friend Naia and the Clovis peoples—continued to practice bison hunting, even though those regions had a more favorable climate than during the Pleistocene.

The adaptability of humans even enabled the Inuit population to acclimate to ice. We now know them as Eskimos and identify them by their fish-based diet and tolerance to low temperatures all year long while living in their peculiar igloos. The 1922 documentary *Nanook of the North*, by Robert J. Flaherty, is a genuine time capsule. This documentary shows us, as never before, the rough life of an Inuit family as well as the construction method for an igloo.

Moving south and keeping in mind the boundary for Aridoamerica, other peoples developed agricultural areas as well as irrigation techniques. They even domesticated animals and began farming livestock. These are the scenes corresponding to the Apache, Sioux, Cherokee ("Cherokees" or "Cheyenne"), and Kiowa tribes. Among this group of tribes, the Sioux were the most unconstrained; they became famous for the way in which they educated their children and youth. They inhabited the prairies of North America and were skilled in hunting bison. They could not settle in one place as they depended on chasing these four-footed animals. Their famous camping tents, or tepees, were made of the bison's hides and were easy to set up and take down. As for the Cherokees, they claimed territories in the southern United States as well as the northern border of Mexico. But territorial disputes with other tribes in the region forced them to migrate until they finally settled in the mountainous regions of Tennessee, Alabama, and Georgia. Their livelihood was agriculture as well as hunting deer and moose.

Other hunting tribes settled along the northern border of the US and southern border of Canada. Their conflicts with other native peoples led to their displacement until they arrived in present-day Oklahoma, where they formed strong alliances with local tribes. In general, the Aridoamerican groups were nomadic or seminomadic due to the weather and hunting conditions described above.

This review of groups that form part of the American continent's history reveals an area called Oasisamerica, which extends through part of northern Mexico and part of the southern United States. Groups here were sedentary and farmers, yet their large villages did not have the architectural durability of those farther south. For instance, from their settlements in New Mexico and Casas Grandes, Chihuahua, they left only structures and paintings before dispersing in the fourteenth century.

Furthermore, these peoples spoke different languages, and languages were even different between peoples that were divided into tribes. There are currently more than three hundred native languages in the area, indicating a vast presence in the northern part of the continent. This evidence, however, does not satisfy some historians, who do not consider these communities as civilizations. The above is in contrast to the development of science and art achieved in Mesoamerica. The exception is the cultures of the area we have previously defined as Oasisamerica.

The panorama changed for the native peoples of North America with the Europeans' arrival. Both the Apache and the Sioux domesticated horses, which allowed them to become more belligerent toward the cowboys and the US government.

Indian Wars and Jackson's Removal Act

A new player emerges in the history of North America with the arrival of the Europeans. The horse caused great astonishment among the native peoples of the region. Perhaps it also generated fear, but this was overcome because they soon learned to coexist with the species. The Europeans brought a wild horse better known as the mustang. The natives were so attracted to horses that they became an icon of identity. Horses were used for hunting different species, but it was also a vehicle of war against the settlers. Some decades later, this became a favorite plot in American films that immortalized the names of famous Apache leaders.

Although in pre-Columbian times, the native peoples of Aridoamerica were not important, during the English colonization, they played a decisive role in the development of the United States as a nation. We must not forget that although Mexico also participated in these Indian wars, it was on a smaller scale than in the neighbor to the north. These wars began with the arrival of Europeans to North American lands and culminated with the relocation of native peoples to specific areas called reservations.

Not all Europeans who got to North America had a warlike spirit or intended to seize land. Some only wanted to live in peace with the native people. The best example is the story of the *Mayflower*. The English who arrived at Plymouth on the *Mayflower* learned about planting and harvesting food from the natives. This is the origin of the traditional Thanksgiving Day celebration. But this cordiality, as we will see below, was not typical.

Europeans also brought disease that killed even more people than war. The first to reject the settlement of the colonists were the warlike Sioux; later, the Apaches would follow them.

The land over which both Native Americans and settlers traveled was a bone of contention. The new English colonies were expanding, and this made it necessary to acquire more land. However, the land was bordered by territory occupied by the Native Americans. The options were either an agreement or war. From the start, the Sioux chose the latter. The conflict lasted from the sixteenth century to the nineteenth century, during which several Native American tribal leaders became immortalized in the history of the United States.

It was after the United States Declaration of Independence that the struggle acquired a different tone; the native peoples no longer fought with civilians. Now their struggle was against the US Army.

The gradual expansion of the United States resulted in claiming territory that originally belonged to the Native Americans. The US government, in response to the combatants' tenacity, offered to relocate all the tribes to predetermined areas—the reservations—with the commitment to recognize their sovereignty and patrimony over these territories. The tribes most affected by war accepted, but the Apache and the Sioux did not.

The Apache resistance or "Apache Wars" against the US government has a key player. Now we join Geronimo, an iconic leader of this tribe born in Sonora. In fact, he belonged to the Apaches who settled on the Mexican side of the border. This geographical circumstance forced Mexico to intervene along the border as a result of the Apaches raiding the border area for supplies against the US government.

Let's go back to the moment when Geronimo decides to join this fight; the army has just murdered his wife and daughter. Geronimo will then undertake a long journey, seeking freedom for his nation and others also oppressed by the US and Mexican governments. He is a skilled strategist and conducts war operations along the southern border of the United States, and then he hides in the highlands of northern Mexico.

The US proposed an alliance to the Mexican government; they weakened and defeated the Apaches. Recognizing the respect Geronimo commanded among all native tribes, the US government offered him a home on the reservation located in Oklahoma. Geronimo surrenders and lives in peace for the rest of his life. Controversy will follow this Apache leader: for some, he was a savior and an inspiration. For others, he was a bandit, a thief, and a lawbreaker.

Now we meet another iconic figure: Red Cloud, chief of the warlike Sioux tribe. No one else could have achieved the unprecedented and rare feat of defeating the US Army. The government agrees to a truce with his tribe as a result of his victory. This was ratified when the Treaty of Laramie was signed. Unfortunately, the US government repeatedly breaks the treaty. This opens up the possibility of war once again. Sitting Bull and Crazy Horse will succeed Red Cloud.

Besides breaking the treaty, an additional factor exacerbates the Sioux's situation. Rumors of gold in the hills they considered sacred triggered the Black Hills War. On June 25 and 26, 1876, Crazy Horse and Sitting Bull led together the battle of Little Bighorn, the largest armed engagement of the Indian Wars. Colonel George Armstrong Custer was killed and the US's casualty count included more than 250 soldiers.

The US Army was able to reorganize after this great Native American victory and later defeated the Sioux forces. The Black Hills War ended when the Indian tribe signed another treaty, putting them at a complete disadvantage. Sitting Bull continued fighting and managed to run away to Canada with his most loyal supporters. He eventually returns to accept the terms of surrender imposed by the government. The scales are tipped so that the native communities and their leaders accept living on reservations. Yet the conflict continues.

On December 15, 1890, the US Army killed Sitting Bull. A group of natives led by Bigfoot, fearing the same fate, decided to flee to another reservation under the protection of Red Cloud. Their fate will be tragic and leaves a black mark on US history. The US Army intercepts the group near Wounded Knee Creek. Soldiers seize the Native Americans' weapons. Then an argument triggers a firefight against the unarmed Native Americans. About three hundred of them, mostly women and children, are killed. The official report, which is not entirely reliable, shows twenty-five casualties for the US Army.

Mexico, Lerdo Act and the War of Castes

Along this timeline on which we travel, the history of the Native Americans of both Mexico and the United States defines their current status. After dominating the continent and following the arrival of the colonists and the Spanish conquest, the dignity of our ancestors was tainted by discrimination. Some groups were even on the verge of disappearing.

Previously, we followed Geronimo and Red Cloud in their tenacious struggle to defend their territory. We found that the solution used to address conflicts that resulted in massive bloodshed were the reservations. Both Mexico and Canada played their part in the so-called Indian Wars. The reservations functioned as a dike to stop the bloodshed rather than as a happy ending. In this sense, we might think that the sovereignty granted on the reservations was a very wise move from the US government, but we should not lose sight of the history that preceded them.

We will now focus on the Mexican territory and its native peoples commonly referred to as "indigenous" in a derogatory sense. This is a misconception since the term has another connotation. In fact, it derives from Latin, which means "native to a place." The term Native Americans, however, reflects respect for the ancestors and forerunners of these nations' history. Therefore, we use this term to refer to the native or indigenous Indians, to express the deep respect they deserve.

We are in the middle of the nineteenth century. Mexico is already an independent nation and is in the process of consolidating its national identity. We are witnessing a figure who will transcend history: Benito Juarez, a descendant of Native Americans.

We are joining President Juarez on a working day and note how proud he is of his roots and how he defends them. An initiative to create indigenous municipalities, which is very similar to what the United States did with the reservations, can be found in a journal from the time Juarez was Oaxaca's state governor. If we move forward along the timeline, we will see that Benito Juarez is accused of forfeiting lands owned by Native Americans. Let's recap how these events occurred.

There is another key player: Miguel Lerdo de Tejada, the minister of finance. He is currently writing a document in which he proposes to sell some land to boost the country's economy. He signs it, and this initiative will be known in history as the Lerdo Act. This proposal assesses how to sell the land so that the Mexican economy can consequently get a reprieve. The lands that were confiscated were owned by the church and were inactive economically. In fact, these lands were known as "dead lands." However, the tricky part is that when this act was passed, Benito Juarez was not yet president; Ignacio Comonfort was the president.

The Lerdo Act was generally considered positive given that, at least in principle, it provided the opportunity for private parties to acquire land that was previously only leased or unused. This act in no way gave away land. To be accredited with any land, according to the document, a tax had to be paid to the government and the rest of the monies to the owner of the property. There was no expropriation in the technical sense. Instead, it is a sale, forced by the government, of land owned mainly by the church.

Now, let's take on the role of one of the Native Americans from anywhere in Mexico. The person in question, man or woman, knows nothing about the Lerdo Act. They live off what the communal land produces. None of the members of the community can afford to acquire a piece of land when it is for sale under the act. Those who have resources exploit this unfavorable situation. Our protagonist sees how large tracts of land suddenly belong to another family. There were no clauses in the act that prevented the acquisition of large pieces of land.

Juarez, when he became president-elect, tried to reduce the negative impact of this act; he even awarded communal lands once again to Native Americans. The fact is that, thanks to the implementation of the Lerdo Act, large estates of the type that propagated and were condemned during Porfirio Diaz's administration were created.

Another interesting episode regarding the status of Mexico's native population can be found in the Yucatán Peninsula. The testimony is from Jacinto Pat, a Maya who no longer tolerates the mistreatment he gets from the Creoles. Cecilio Chi and Manuel Antonio Ay feel the same. They will be major figures in the War of Castes.

Yucatán had already tried to become independent on several occasions, without much success, given the concentration of power in the center of Mexico. Yucatán did become independent, but only for a few hundred years during which it was called the Republic of Yucatán and even had a flag. Mexico was in the middle of its war against the United States (an invasion, actually), which made it impossible to confront the separatists. Jacinto Pat and his people used Yucatán's declaration of independence to start a confrontation in 1847. Their campaign is a success; the Maya quickly gain ground and expel both whites and Creoles from their territory. The culmination of this conflict was the appointment of Cecilio Chi as governor. By 1849, Jacinto Pat's Mayan forces controlled most of Yucatán territory. It was the rebellion's misfortune, however, that this Maya hero died that same year amid the struggle for freedom.

The leaders of the new Republic of Yucatán, finding themselves in a predicament and at such a disadvantage against the rebelling Maya, decided to ask for help from other countries. The United States was interested, but their support never materialized. The US government decides not to intervene in an internal Mexican conflict, given the recent war between the two countries.

However, Mexico offers to help the Republic of Yucatán to recover control of territory controlled by the Maya. The government of Yucatán accepted without further hesitation. The Mexican army confronted the Maya and managed to recover part of the territory. The rebelling Maya regrouped and congregated in present-day Quintana Roo. Yucatán, in gratitude, rejoins Mexico to benefit from the protection of the Mexican army.

All this happened in 1849, but the war continues with Mexican intervention. It will take more than half a century to settle, and it was not until 1901 when President Porfirio Diaz signed a treaty with the Maya people, putting an end to the conflict.

Before moving on, we should consider the context in which the War of Castes took place. It is certainly a period in which conflicts are everywhere. The Maya started to fight while the Mexican army was defending against the US invasion. Then the Reform War began, followed by the French invasion. A few years after the end of the War of Castes, the Mexican Revolution began. Mexico did not even have a chance to relax. As soon as one war ended, another war was already underway. It is true that the sum of events somewhat overshadowed the Yucatán conflict, but the latter was already a precursor to the Mexican Revolution, both for its ideals and for its emancipatory vision.

Native Americans Today

It is worth asking what has happened from Naia to the present-day inhabitants of the Americas, in particular to those who belong to the continent's native population.

We must not forget those who occupied this land before us—or lose sight of who they were. As Native Americans today, we are now protagonists.

If we look at certain data and initiatives, we could argue that there is a significant improvement for us, Apaches or Cherokees, Maya or Raramuris. The United States acknowledged our right to participate in national elections, and in Alaska, 537 tribal entities were registered. It is important to note that the government returned several territories to the Native Americans. The counterbalance is that only 1 percent of the US population falls into that category.

We now turn to Mexico, where positive changes have also been made, albeit slowly. The Zapatista National Liberation Army (EZLN for the acronym in Spanish) rose up in arms in five municipalities in the state of Chiapas on January 1, 1994, prior to implementation of the Free Trade Agreement in Mexico. The EZLN demanded better distribution of wealth as well as claiming ownership of lands that had been seized from them. In other words, they sought to be recognized as part of a country that had forgotten them. Carlos Salinas de Gortari's administration responded by sending armed troops to stop the indigenous rebellion. After twelve days of armed confrontations, the government offered a cease-fire to open a dialogue with the Zapatistas army.

It is true that, in past decades, we were completely forgotten. Over time, mistakes have been corrected. The San Andres Treaties were signed in 1996 between the Mexican government and the EZLN. The treaty committed the government to recognize indigenous peoples and grant them autonomy. The dialogue helped make the Mexican government aware of the urgent need to recognize indigenous rights in the Magna Carta. A couple of amendments to the country's constitution, as well as international treaties, now support their development and integrity—at least on paper.

The EZLN's demands have produced some valuable results. The first amendment to Article 2 of the Mexican Constitution happened on August 14, 2001, and is important because, for the first time, it recognizes the rights of indigenous people in Mexico. Article 2 states that the Mexican nation is one and indivisible, and the amendment to the article states that Native Americans must be granted autonomy and self-determination to decide on fundamental aspects of their communities, and that they must be respected in their political organization and freedom, in their economic decisions, and their normative system. The Constitution must guarantee the protection of indigenous people from any attempted discrimination, ensuring that they have the same rights to health, education, work, and welfare as other Mexicans. The amendment was harshly criticized at the time for failing to comply with all the commitments established in the San Andres Treaties. Article 2 of the Constitution was again amended on April 22, 2015, guaranteeing members of indigenous communities the right to vote and to be elected as well as the right to hold public office without discrimination of any kind. Subsequently, other amendments to the same article would follow. These were enacted on January 29, 2016, and on June 6 and August 9, 2019, and expand a wide range of indigenous rights, including gender parity and recognition of Afro-Mexican communities as part of the diverse cultures in Mexico.

However, we, as citizens of the native communities, have a question. If discrimination or segregation is to be avoided, why are we treated differently and with special laws? The fact is that these laws are about preserving the ancient culture or tradition that distinguishes us but also restricts our integrity and growth. This may be a theoretical discussion, but in reality, some disparities cannot be ignored. It is important to expand the context beyond Mexico and the United States, to have a broader view of our integrity as citizens.

According to data and surveys published in the last decade, the United Nations reports that the native populations in Latin America constitute the poorest indigenous communities in the world; this study includes the African continent and India.

Let's return to Mexico, which, despite its achievements, has the poorest native population in Latin America. Remember that native peoples lead the global statistics. Only 30 percent of Mexico's native population is above the poverty line, according to a study presented by the National Council for the Evaluation of Social Development Policy (CONEVAL for the acronym in Spanish) in 2018. There is still a long way to go, although efforts continue to make a radical change in native communities. According to UNICEF figures, 30 percent of young people from Native American communities do not complete their elementary education. The challenge is complex, and the government's efforts to change this situation must continue to be supported.

There are currently 317 Indian reservations in the United States, in almost every state. The US has approached this problem systematically and consistently over the past few decades. The reason is that recent administrations have worked decisively for the benefit of Native Americans. This serves as a benchmark for Latin America. One interesting policy is the casinos that are located on Indian reservations. Ronald Reagan's administration allowed communities with high rates of poverty to enter the gambling business as compensation for the past loss of their territories. This initiative allows them to earn millions of dollars annually and is also tax-exempt. We as citizens of the native communities have to go back to the proposal stated at the beginning. Obvious benefits are guaranteed through protective laws. But such statutes, which could be cataloged as simply laws of preservation, limit our development. So the paradox remains.

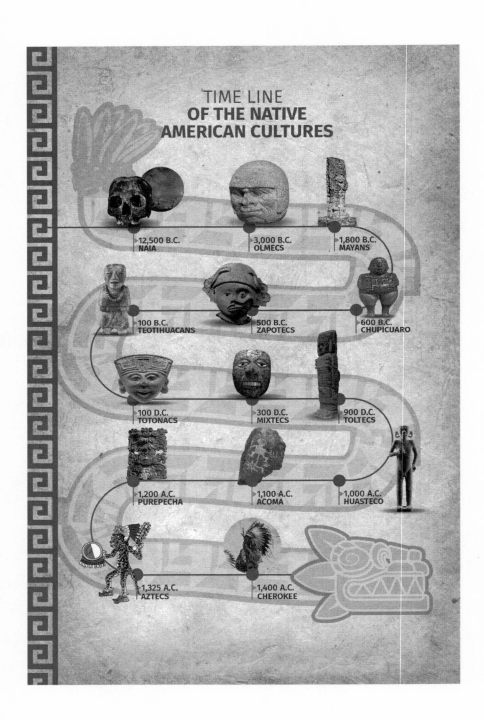

TIME LINE
OF THE NATIVE
AMERICAN CULTURES

12,500 B.C.
NAIA

3,000 B.C.
OLMECS

1,800 B.C.
MAYANS

100 B.C.
TEOTIHUACANS

500 B.C.
ZAPOTECS

600 B.C.
CHUPICUARO

100 D.C.
TOTONACS

300 D.C.
MIXTECS

900 D.C.
TOLTECS

1,200 A.C.
PUREPECHA

1,100 A.C.
ACOMA

1,000 A.C.
HUASTECO

1,325 A.C.
AZTECS

1,400 A.C.
CHEROKEE

Chapter 2

In God We Trust or Obey the Holy Church

British Paradise And Spanish Hell

America is a new world for sixteenth-century Europe. Although the discoveries of what would become Mexico and the United States occurred in different ways—Hernan Cortes reached the coast of Mexico in 1519, and the famous *Mayflower* arrived on US shores in 1620—both territories excited explorers and travelers, each with their own particular motives for leaving their homeland in pursuit of adventure.

Let's go to the moment when an English Pilgrim is about to board the *Mayflower*, taking him to North America. It is a journey of no return. His bag of belongings holds a Bible along with his hope for a life where he can freely practice his religion. The risk of such an ocean crossing does not matter, and he does not know how many months he will be at sea. The Pilgrim boards the ship and bids farewell to his homeland as it slowly fades from view.

His feelings are quite different from that of a crewmember of a Spanish ship. That voyager thinks only about the material wealth that he is going to gain—for himself and for the kingdom of Spain—by violent means, using his weapons.

For the *Mayflower* Pilgrim, both the voyage and the arrival to the new world will not be easy. But once settled in those strange lands, he will use the natural resources he finds there to build another life. The news of his experience ignites the interest of those Englishmen who practice Christianity. The migratory flow becomes a flood. While the *Mayflower* crewman—now a free colonist—devotes his time to raising crops and building his home, his example encourages new pilgrims to follow in his footsteps. These migrants are willing to save for months or years to pay for their journeys. There will even be those who offer to work as indentured servants, for up to seven years, to pay off the debt.

Once the passage is secured, the journey ahead is worthy of determined souls. No comforts. No certainties. Once they arrive in the new world, the adventure is just beginning. Most of these Englishmen engage in farming and carpentry as well as construction of boats or small houses or cabins. For both adventurer and settler, quality of life improves dramatically. They succeed in establishing settlements true to their vision of a new life based on good moral values, which shapes the formation of North American culture.

Now we'll now follow the Spanish crewman. He hears the stories of Hernan Cortes's first impressions of the American territory, especially the magnificent city of Tenochtitlan. This crewman and soldier is energized by the thought that he will easily fill his saddlebag with treasure. He and his companions share the dream of conquering the legendary El Dorado—that mythical city bathed in gold and precious stones.

This traveler reaches American territory, in what today is Mexico, but he never reaches El Dorado, which, like its treasure, will remain one of the great legends of history. Instead, the traveler finds a bountiful land whose wealth is easy to plunder and send back to Spain. This is how migrants can climb the economic ladder in what is now the viceroyalty of New Spain. And the Spanish Crown quickly became one of the great powers of that time, along with France and England.

After a period of prosperity at the cost of stolen riches, the Spanish colonist had to go to more remote areas and venture into mining. Because of the harshness of the work, he preferred to trade in spices and exotic animals, highly valued in the old continent. But whatever the case and for any of his activities, he exploits and abuses the indigenous labor force, the native population of this region.

The American Colonies and the Arrival of the Calvinist Puritans

The Catholic Church dominated the whole of Europe, and Christian elements form the basis of the English political system. Toward the last few decades of the fifteenth century, Catholicism began to gain ground. Reforms are implemented in ecclesiastical law, even within the English Christian church itself. At this point in time, religion and politics are unified to such a degree that a king obeys what the church imposes.

Given this situation, the English who still remain faithful to Christian principles begin to question such changes. Transformation begins in Switzerland, where a movement has started to purify the Christian church of Catholic influences. A group of Englishmen opts for the same ideology and are baptized as Puritans.

Firmly committed to their faith and with influence over important schools, the Puritans petition King James to grant their demands. They did not achieve their goal, but the monarch, mindful of the Puritans' strong character and looking to placate them, authorizes a new English translation of the Bible to replace the Geneva Bible. The result was the King James Bible, better known as the King James Version. Published in 1611, it is the version of the Bible most widely used in the US and England today. However, both the monarch and the church chose to follow Catholic practices. Even worse, fierce persecution against the Puritans was unleashed, and many were soon exiled.

The Toleration Act was passed in 1689 and signaled the end of the persecution of the Puritans. Its full name is "An Act to exempt their Majesties' Protestant subjects dissenting from the Church of England from the penalties of certain laws." Apparently, no one over there could find a shorter title. The statute grants freedom of worship to Nonconformists who pledge to the oaths of allegiance and supremacy and reject transubstantiation—the conversion of the whole substance of bread into the body of Christ and the whole substance of wine into that of his blood. Nonconformists were allowed their places of worship as well as to have their own teachers and preachers. In return, the law requires acceptance of certain oaths of allegiance.

The English Puritans adhere to the law, although a group of them, no longer hoping to reform the Church of England, leave the island. Here we have another person worthy of mention: Sir

Edwin Sandys, who grants them a concession to sail to the English colonies in North America. A group of English merchants, who look favorably on the Puritans, even finance part of the enterprise.

The *Mayflower* crosses the Atlantic Ocean, and passengers disembark on November 11, 1620. Let's follow its crew for a bit, shortly before arrival on American soil. Half of them had died of disease, and their bodies had to be thrown into the sea. Those who survive are weak and exhausted. After so many days of seeing nothing but the ocean, their faith keeps them alive and believing they will reach their goal. During the voyage, storms cause the ship to veer off its original course. They had intended to land at the English settlements of the Virginia Company, where they were granted the concession, but neither fate nor the sea has the final say. The change of course leads them to run aground on a shore that lies outside the king's jurisdiction, in an area not yet explored by English settlers. By chance, the community arrives at a place where there is no law to adhere to, as they had agreed with the English Crown. Faced with this situation, the travelers sign a document—the Mayflower Compact—with rules that follow the Puritan values they profess.

One more detail before we continue. Prior to their arrival at Plymouth, there were already English colonies on American soil. It is noteworthy that none showed any intention of imposing any religion on the native population.

After a rather arduous sea voyage, with the crew decimated, without the support of the English settlements, the Puritans have no choice but to produce their food themselves in order to survive. They discover that the area where they landed is suitable for growing crops. In this segment of the historical memory, we make room for an extraordinary protagonist: a Native American by the name of Squanto.

In admiration, Squanto watches as the settlers land. He does not run away. He is not afraid of these unknown people. On the contrary, he approaches the exhausted sailors and offers them his friendship. As the days go by, he becomes their guide, interpreter, and friend. He teaches them to plant corn and to fish. Squanto fosters alliances between his tribe and the pilgrims. This generosity encourages the pilgrims to forge relationships with the other tribes. Thanks to these efforts, they live in their new home peacefully.

We continue following Squanto and the Puritans. A year has passed since their arrival; it is the middle of October of 1621. The community works the land with faith and hope, always devoted to God. Their reward is an abundant harvest, which they share with Squanto and the Wampanoag tribe. From this transcendent moment, the traditional Thanksgiving commemoration is born.

Roger Williams and the Baptist Church

The Puritans who have settled in Plymouth thrive. For a decade, the population remained stable with between three and four hundred inhabitants. Its members have full freedom of religion; they meet and worship according to their high standards. However, they did not found the first Christian church.

The colony eventually grows. New colonies are authorized by New England, which is under the protectorate of the King of England. During this time, John Winthrop and Thomas Dudley, both Christians and with good economic positions in England, dream of migrating to the English colonies in America. In 1629, Charles I granted them the concession. Winthrop and Dudley hesitate. But around 1630, pressure from the Catholic Church in England against Christians increased, and this triggered their decision. The friends decide to take no chances and accept the concession.

Winthrop and Dudley do not undertake the voyage alone. A total of seventeen ships and nearly one thousand people set sail in the summer of 1630. It is the largest expedition to sail from England to New England. Once on American soil, and after settling in Massachusetts, these new colonists established Boston and seven other surrounding cities, each governed under the principles of Christianity and adhering to the laws of New England.

The leaders of the colonies, Puritans for the most part, are determined to sustain true religion based on a defined system of government. This explains the homogeneous nature of their organization and social hierarchy; this is a community that adheres to religious values with an ethical mission and progressive vision. Returns are measured against progress. This motivates the Puritans still in England, who already aspire to this model of government. Consequently, thousands of Englishmen venture to the Puritan colonies of America. Before the outbreak of the English Revolution (1642–1688), more than twenty thousand people had already arrived in New England.

Almost by accident, the Puritan government adopts a democratic form of government. They also differ from the libertarian organization of the colonies that prefer to remain independent.

We now accompany the Reverend T. Hooker, a new migrant. Around 1636, he led a group that settled near the Connecticut River. At first, his colony was organized similarly to Plymouth and Massachusetts. The community will eventually expand toward Long Island, where discord arises. These colonists began to discriminate against the natives and carry out religious practices outside the Puritan liturgy. Soon, they will be considered heretics. In response, they expel anyone who disagrees with their practices and values from the colony.

Roger Williams is a man of faith and good moral values who does not approve of Reverend Hooker's community. His egalitarian treatment of the natives earns him banishment. Faithful to his Christian convictions, he forms his own colony in Providence, which later becomes part of Rhode Island. Around 1638, he created the first Baptist Church in America. Under Roger Williams's leadership, Rhode Island became the land of opportunity for all those who are persecuted because of their faith.

The first Baptist Church in America arises from the Puritan doctrine. The reason for its transformation from Puritan to Baptist is a common occurrence in history: one generation dies off, and the next forgets its past, and the formula repeats itself endlessly. The Puritans may have succeeded in purging their church of Catholic reforms, but their own principles become distorted by the prosperity and growth of the colonies. This does not discredit Roger Williams, who will preaches his ethical and religious values in an exemplary manner.

Protestant Churches and Politics in the United States

The colonists who decide to live in New England are at no time in open rebellion against the king of England. Their motives are rooted in a desire for the freedom to practice Christianity in accordance with their principles of ethical conduct. Under orders of the monarch, the northern reaches of the continent are explored. The landing of the *Mayflower* and its pilgrims outside English jurisdiction is circumstantial. Likewise, the democratic government emerged without any previous plan within the Puritan colonies.

The settlers who followed the first migrants bring with them a land grant, as their Puritan compatriots did. The Puritans are very zealous in running their communities and always include a minister of worship or reverend as an integral part of the process. This extends even to their urban planning; the focal point for each settlement is an enclosure designated for meetings, called a meetinghouse, of course. In close proximity, they build housing for their leaders and their minister.

Local and religious matters are discussed at the meetinghouse. Education is extremely important for the community, and democracy begins to advance in the new colonies of North America.

From a distance, we can appreciate the pragmatic vision of these English colonists. For example, in Massachusetts, they proposed a representative system as a measure to streamline civic duties. In 1644, they divided their governing body into two chambers. It was a system designed for the exclusive participation of the Puritan Church. In this forum, neither the king nor Parliament had any voice or vote. Next, governors begin to be appointed, overseeing the region to which the colony belongs. It was decided that elections would have a single, fixed date when governors, delegates, and other representatives were voted into office.

At first, this does not seem to inconvenience or bother the English monarch. But it is apparent that this new system is moving toward independence from the Crown.

The point is that democratic government starts with the noble purpose of maintaining good values, preserving moral purity and, above all, an economic model that does not degrade the poor or exalt the rich. The Puritan colonists, who are greatly concerned with the education of their community, agree on this. This responsibility was placed on the shoulders of theologians from the best universities in England. The reading of the Bible was an irrefutable requirement in Puritan schools; parents are under obligation to teach their children. So that there could be no excuse, public schools are introduced and are made available to all, even to those in servitude. In Massachusetts, Harvard University is founded under these Christian principles.

Since the founding of the thirteen colonies in the United States, religion has been part of every period in the country's politics. The Christian foundation dating from this period is so solid that the phrase "In God we trust" is minted on the two-cent coin of 1864, a motto that the US Congress officially established in 1956. Once the United States became an independent nation, only two of its presidents followed the Catholic faith: John F. Kennedy and Joe Biden. Today, there are two political groups, one of which wishes to preserve or purify the form of government as it was in its earliest beginnings. However, quite apart from its Christian origins, the nation now harbors a diversity of religions and creeds.

The Spanish Invasion and the Evangelization by the Catholic Orders

The way the church arrived in Mexico is different from that of the United States. Before we continue with this historical review, it should be emphasized that the church is not a religion but an institution that represents the interests of its faithful as well as those of God.

Now let's follow the footsteps of a native of Mesoamerica. He believes in several gods and is very religious, devoted to rituals and ceremonies of appeasement to gain the protection of his divinities. He has no idea what religion his opponents profess. This person is a Mexica warrior. According to his religion's theory on the origin of the universe, blood is food for the sun and contributes to its movement. When this warrior—who will defend the great Tenochtitlan and is very faithful to his gods—is defeated and enslaved, he will find it very difficult to abandon the beliefs he has had throughout his life and will not comprehend why he must accept a new and unknown faith.

Let's look at the sequence of events. We are at the end of the fifteenth century. Europe is going through a transition from the Middle Ages to the Renaissance. This movement gives rise to monarchical absolutism; kings have divine rights with the endorsement of the church. Spain, a key player in this era, reconquered almost three-quarters of its territory that had previously been dominated by Muslims. The shift to an absolute monarchy happened because of a wedding, a marriage between Catholic kings in 1469, thereby consolidating Spain as a Catholic nation.

Decades later, in 1492, a momentous event occurred for the Spanish and for the history of humanity: Christopher Columbus arrived in America looking for a better trade route to India. As a result of evidence the explorer shows to the Spanish Crown, Spain's appetite for wealth grows, and it decides to finance many more expeditions. Ambition grows; many men dream of ruling the New World and its riches. Among these men is Hernan Cortes.

We can see Cortes is a serious and determined man, brave, a strategist with an unusual capacity for leadership. He has not yet launched his offensive against the great Tenochtitlan. We follow him as he surveys the grandeur of this city, in awe of its buildings and treasures. Cortés walks through the market together with his entourage. The Spaniards take in the stalls of birds, medicinal herbs, watercress, rabbits, deer, blankets, ointments, puppies raised as food, and slaves carrying heavy sacks full of seeds. This crowded market seems like a carnival from another planet. In the midst of so much uproar, they watch as transactions are carried out through barter or in exchange for cocoa beans. Later, still amazed by the material wealth of the Tenochtitlan markets, so different from the European ones, Cortes would relate in one of his letters to Carlos V:

> In these markets all the things that are found in the whole world are sold, there are so many and of so many kinds besides what I have already described, and because of so much detail and variety and because I do not remember them all, and furthermore because I do not know what to call them, I cannot describe it.

Now we are with Cortes in his room. He is seated at a table with burning candles and some paper that he has brought from Europe as well as a quill pen. He writes one of his letters in which he fervently recounts the splendor of the Mexica. Astonishment will combine with ambition. But he is not the only one. Other members of the expedition also spend sleepless nights thinking about the opulence of a civilization they despise as barbaric, bloodthirsty, and cruel. After the fall of Tenochtitlan, Cortes, as the new lord of the Anahuac Valley, must subdue the greed of his own people.

We return to Cortes in his room. This time, he writes a letter in which he extols his contributions to the Spanish kingdom. The Spanish Crown consents to the demands of the expeditionaries. The ships that depart from the Spanish coasts return loaded with precious metals and other valuables.

Again, we observe Cortes writing a new letter by candlelight. He asks King Carlos V to send people to the New World who can convert the natives to Catholicism. After the expulsion of Muslims from Spanish territory, the monarchs are determined to bring Catholicism to all their territories and grant the request. The legal, ethical, and political justification for the exploration and conquest of America is evangelization. The Franciscans arrived in America in 1523, the Dominicans in 1526, the Augustinians in 1533 and, finally, the Jesuits in 1572. Although each order has a different function, together they serve the same purpose: the expansion of the Catholic faith.

These missionaries are faced with a double task. In addition to converting these pagans to Catholicism, they have to intercede against the constant abuses that the Spaniards commit against the natives.

We follow this story alongside Friar Bartolome de las Casas, who observes with total disapproval the way in which the young and old, women and children, are humiliated. He devotes himself fully to their defense, advocating for Spaniards to treat all persons humanely. His philosophy is reflected in laws that he published in 1542 to safeguard the interests of the natives.

Friar Bartolome is not alone in this effort. Vasco de Quiroga joins his example and intercedes on behalf of the natives. In 1531, he even requested permission to build the so-called *pueblos hospitales* (towns constructed for native populations that also served as a shelter for travelers and missionary centers). Quiroga believes that the utopia conceived by Thomas More is possible: a community that lives from its philosophical and political ideals. In fact, Quiroga sees America as the perfect opportunity to make the concept of utopia a reality.

Along with these heroes of humanism are anonymous friars who give their lives to remind the Spanish that their mission is to civilize and evangelize the pagans. Under this directive, they set up towns with schools, where the Catholic faith is evangelized and taught; in these places, travelers are welcome.

Of course, this does not please the majority of Spaniards. Those higher up the ladder continue mistreating and violently abusing the natives. In order to improve the treatment of the indigenous population, papal bulls were published in 1537. In particular, Pope Paul III issued the bull *Sublimis deus*, which established the right of indigenous people to freedom and prohibited their enslavement. This will form the foundation for the laws that Friar Bartolome de las Casas would later publish.

In 1535, Antonio de Mendoza, the first viceroy, arrived in New Spain with a mandate from the Spanish Crown: distribute land to the conquerors and supervise the work of the Catholic Church.

Despite the efforts of missionaries who try to preach humanism by example, the Spaniards, blinded by greed, look at religion as a weapon to justify their actions. Of course, the circumstances and contexts differ, but it is worth emphasizing that the evangelization or imposition of religion in Mexico is very different from what happened with the Pilgrims and natives in the United States.

The Catholic religion was the only one that could be practiced and professed in the territories of the Spanish empire. It is entrenched in the social fabric for future generations and manifests in symbols of cultural syncretism, such as the venerated Virgin of Guadalupe. One historical example of this is the priest and insurgent Miguel Hidalgo, who takes the image of the Virgin of Guadalupe as the banner of his independence war.

When the Jesuits were expelled from all territories dominated by the Spanish Crown, including New Spain, their dedication to encouraging education had already left an indelible mark on the population. Perhaps unintentionally, they foster the seed of Mexican nationalism.

The Holy Inquisition That Came from Spain

As the church grows in influence, other issues develop and grow too. Education is a key issue within the Inquisition. This terrible institution began in Europe. A less severe and cruel version reached New Spain—not because of the Inquisitors' sudden benevolence but because only Catholicism was allowed in New Spain.

The court of the Inquisition has its start in the south of France. Spain and other European monarchies support the initiative. The Dominicans have the distinction of operating these courts.

Let's go to Paris in those years. A woman who does not profess the Catholic religion secretly follows rites of her own faith, rites that she has practiced throughout her life. A neighbor is shocked by this aberration and denounces her to the court. Shortly after, there is a knock on the door. Men enter without saying a word and begin ransacking her home. The woman is arrested and brought to trial, while her informer enjoys the satisfaction of having done a good deed for God and the world. Inside a dungeon, the woman does not know what she is being accused of, what she did wrong. A rat watches her curiously from a corner. Screams can be heard coming from the torture chambers. The woman will soon find out that she is about to be sentenced for the most atrocious crimes according to the Holy Inquisition: heresy and witchcraft. The punishment for these crimes is death.

The term *heresy* comes from a Latin word originally meaning a philosophy, posture, or interpretation. The church appropriates this definition to assume that erroneous interpretations of religion are considered heresy. Later on, a *heretic* is defined as one whose position is different from that of the Catholic Church or who denies the established dogmas of any religion.

The matter becomes more complex when we consider that Catholic theologians were the first to begin to question the abuses and privileges of the church. So the Holy Inquisition proceeds to refine its position: those who understand Catholicism and negate or offend the religion are considered heretics. In the case of the American Indians, their ignorance of the religion saves them from punishment. They are classified as *neophytes*.

This distinction is important. The Inquisition courts do not operate the same way everywhere. The courts in Spain differ from those of Germany and even those of New Spain. The Spanish courts from that time record three thousand persons sentenced between 1478 and 1834. The guilty could be pardoned or, possibly, their sentence could be changed.

The records from New Spain are less harsh and have nothing to do with the history of blood that stains Europe. From 1571 to 1700, two thousand cases were documented, an average of fifteen per year. Of this number, the majority are natives, exempt from sentencing because they were considered neophytes.

The inquisitors assigned to New Spain graduated from the best universities in Spain. They leverage their assignments to enhance their curriculums and garner greater recognition and prestige within the viceroyalty. The Inquisition stripped the hero-priest Miguel Hidalgo y Costilla of his clerical orders, just before his execution by royalists in 1811. The end of the Inquisition, in 1820, both in Spain and in its colonies, is considered an attempt to appease insurgents who were already proclaiming independence.

The Separation of Church and State

Two important periods for Mexico are the War of Independence and the Revolution of 1910. Spanish oppression and the dictatorship of Porfirio Diaz both fall, but the Catholic Church does not lose power or influence in the country. After the conquest, the church is present in every important event. Friar Bartolome de las Casas sets an example for other friars to follow to earn the affection and respect of the indigenous population. This relationship transcends time.

The power that the church accumulates and flaunts strikes a discordant note, at odds with the religious creed. Schools, hospitals, and landed estates are added to its enormous accumulation of wealth. These economic and patrimonial resources strengthen their own political interests. We can see that church and politics are practically the same.

We observe a Mexican Liberal taking office in the middle of the nineteenth century. This man wants to raise his voice against a system that seems unjust to him. The church foresees an armed uprising. It sides with the Conservatives and creates an alliance with the army. This period in which Mexico is already paying a price for an internal crisis should be a time for solidarity, but the church shows otherwise. The church plays its cards and makes moves to maintain its interests and power, to the detriment of national stability. For this Liberal rebel, the church must return to its essential mission: watching over souls and forgiving sinners instead of meddling in the affairs of the country.

The plan to separate the affairs of the church from those of the state is under way. The restriction of military and ecclesiastical privileges is ordered. The church protests. Meanwhile, in the chamber of deputies, there is talk of a new constitution. The result is the publication of three fundamental laws that underpin the definitive separation between church and state.

It is Benito Juarez's turn to add to the presidential decree. In 1855, the ecclesiastical courts were prohibited from participating in civil matters related to individuals. Prior to these new laws, if any member of the clergy committed a crime, they would be judged by the church's courts, outside the jurisdiction of civil authorities.

The new provisions remove the clergy's immunity for criminal acts, and from now on, they would be treated as civil matters. At the same time, it deprives the ecclesiastical institution of legal authority, e.g., law and justice are left in the hands of the state. This is a significant change in the law and modernizes the concept of the rights of citizens.

This is the beginning. A year later, a law that confiscates rural and urban estates owned by civil and ecclesiastical corporations was promulgate, known as the Lerdo Law. This law benefits the church to a great extent since it is not an expropriation. The Iglesias Law, however, aimed to restrict other parish rights and benefits.

We return with our Liberal and anonymous character. He has a baby who is about to turn one and wants to baptize him under the Catholic faith. The church charges him for this service an amount that he is not able to pay. Why do the favors of heaven have to cost so much money on earth? Two of his friends find themselves in the same predicament. One wants to get married, and the other must bury his grandmother. Since the Catholic Church controls the civil registry and the cemeteries, all three are warned that if they do not pay a tithe, they could be arrested. With the Iglesias Law, this type of abuse from the Catholic Church is stopped.

The three proclamations mentioned above are pre-Reform laws. They are rejected by the clergy and the military, triggering the War of the Reform that took place from 1858 to 1861.

Benito Juarez awaits us in this next story. We observe him as he assumes the provisional presidency in 1858. Religious and military leaders, who oppose him, are conspicuously absent from his inauguration. Not only that, they bitterly resent that a person of indigenous origin is president of Mexico for the first time. The Conservative Party also opposes him. Armed conflict breaks out. Juarez will be forced to leave the country's capital in search of support.

We travel with Juarez to Veracruz, where he issues the Reform Laws. Unlike the previous three laws, these finally put an end to the church's political participation. In 1859, the Law of Nationalization of Ecclesiastical Assets was issued, expropriating properties of the Catholic Church. The church's privileges are revoked. Furthermore, when the War of Reform ended with the triumph of the Liberals, freedom of worship was enacted in 1860.

Another statute that completely weakens the church is the Organic Law of Civil Registry. Under this law, our Liberal protagonist and his friends can finally complete their civil procedures—with the state's support. Similarly, the Mexican state regains control of hospitals and cemeteries. As a result of these events and the Reform Laws, Mexico establishes itself as a secular country.

Religions on Both Sides of the Border

Religion, with its ethical values, has a bipartisan history in Mexico and the United States. The contrasts are evident and fundamental to each nation.

While the English settlers seek an opportunity to live a life without persecution because of their faith, the Spanish settlers have their sights set on conquering and plundering the New World. Religion follows both the Puritan pilgrim who flees persecution and the Spaniard who arrives with the mission of evangelizing and converting the natives to Catholicism. For the thirteen colonies of Protestant Anglo-Saxons, what is Catholic is Spanish or French and, therefore, an enemy.

With the expansion of the colonies and the establishment of the viceroyalty, internal wars occur in which religion plays a part.

During the uprising of independence, Mexico appropriates religion as a weapon and shield to justify armed conflicts. Likewise, the governors of the thirteen colonies, mostly Puritans, are the greatest proponents and leaders of the United States War of Independence.

The United States declares itself a Christian nation and goes through a period of development. Schools teach this religion, and most politicians profess their faith. There is no restriction on other religions; no sanctions are imposed if someone practices a religion other than Christianity. The King James Version of the Bible is bedtime reading for the average citizen.

On the other side of the coin is Mexico. During the viceroyalty and even after independence, the church watches over its own interests. In conflicts in which its support is required, such as in the war against the United States, it does not extend its hand to the Mexican state. On the contrary, the church will collaborate with the invaders. This explains why, later, Mexico declared itself a secular country.

Today, the United States is distant from the religious profile that defined it as a nation. As for Mexico, its current politicians are careful to stay away from religion.

Before closing this chapter, we still have unfinished business in our historical report. The presence of Catholics is growing in America, driven by migration from other European communities, such as Ireland. By contrast, the Jesuits were expelled from Spain twice in a row. In 1650, a Sephardic Jewish community, fleeing from the Holy Inquisition that threatens them in Europe, arrives in the land of opportunity where freedom of religious belief is proclaimed.

At this point, the historical background of the Jewish community merits another recap. Sephardic Jews live in the regions dominated by the Crowns of Aragon and Castile, where the official religion is Catholic. Their kings impose the Catholic faith and expel those who do not follow it. Consequently, the Sephardic community emigrates to other kingdoms. They settled in France, also under Catholicism, although more tolerant than Spain. Over time, their need for freedom and independence leads them to make the ocean crossing.

The point is that in imperial Spain and its viceroyalties, the Holy Inquisition is inflexible toward anyone who does not convert to Catholicism. Many families sought refuge in the heart of New Spain during the sixteenth century, but they were not really welcomed or accepted. When French migrants begin living in the northern border region of the viceroyalty, the Spanish Crown decides to start colonizing that area too. Families of converted and persecuted Jews, such as Diego de Montemayor, Luis Carvajal, and Alberto del Canto—who profess Catholicism in order to survive in the colonial territory—respond to the call to settle. Like the Franciscans, who will also suffer the stigma of expulsion, the exodus of Jews will end up inhabiting an area that later becomes part of US territory.

In this bipartisan narrative, the legacy of the Jews in Mexico is exceptional. In the city of Monterrey, for example, we have the settlement of Sephardic Jews. Among families that reach the highest economic status are the Garzas, Sadas, and Treviños. These families are of Sephardic origin and have charted an exemplary business course in Mexico based on values of solidarity, family integration, and forward-thinking vocation through work. There is also a Protestant presence, exemplified by Benjamin Salinas Westrup, founder of Grupo Salinas.

The contribution of the Jews in America, be it Mexico or the United States, teaches us that the full development of any nation is possible when freedom of religious belief is allowed. Let's focus on a more recent time, when President Carlos Salinas de Gortari establishes legal reforms around the church and the state. Through the Reform Laws, education becomes secular and free. The 1920 Constitution prevents a church or religious association from expressing its beliefs in a middle school or high school classroom. The Salinas Reform, which modifies the third paragraph of the Constitution, allows religious education to be taught in private schools. The Law on Religious Association and Public Worship is also created, which regulates all religious associations. Other amendments to the Constitution favor the church, but without undermining the rights of third parties. With these measures, Salinas de Gortari, who studied abroad, favors a balance of freedom of belief that is more compatible with the United States model.

From paradise to hell, Ricardo Sheffield, 2022.

Chapter 3

The Colonies and the Viceroyalty

Europeans in America

The colonization of America dates back to the end of the fifteenth century. Starting with the arrival of Christopher Columbus in 1492, lands were explored and settled continuously and zealously over the following centuries. Led by the era's maritime powers (Spain, France, England, Portugal, and Holland), the period of colonization lasted until the independence movements of the eighteenth and nineteenth centuries.

America represents an opportunity for these empires for whom sociopolitical order and religion come first. Each Crown occupies specific regions, with Spain and England having greater territorial dominance. Although both have a monarchical system of government and are master navigators, there are marked differences between them apart from language, rules of civility, and an inclination toward faith. This difference between Spain and England is evident in their treatment of the native peoples they colonized as well as in the social organization they imposed.

An empire in expansion must develop and unite the identity of the dominated area as well as forge alliances with peoples of a culturally diverse region. One important issue is to improve living conditions for those who are conquered.

Through the structure of the viceroyalty, Spain's approach is absolute control of its colony in spite of thousands of kilometers of distance from the seat of the empire. Spain grows steadily thanks to robust trading with other continents such as Asia. The cohesion this empire enjoys is due to its strong cultural traditions and strategic trading alliances with regions outside the Iberian Peninsula. The advantage of this approach is that it mitigates the possibility of uprisings by the occupied population.

The British Empire, on the other hand, had a poorly managed organization. It does not apply a government structure to maintain control of the newly conquered peoples. And it was not able to restrain American independence. A series of mistakes caused this vast empire, which in its heyday ruled over a quarter of the world's population, to fall at the beginning of the twentieth century.

The clergy played a decisive role in regulating the Spanish Empire. Although essential to the sociopolitical structure, its central function was cultural preservation through conversion to Catholicism. The nobility focused on defending against potential attacks and invasions by the Muslim army, which had dominated the Iberian Peninsula for some eight hundred years. Religious struggles are the order of the day in Spain, and death was considered a glorious event in the name of religion and God.

Let's enter, with his permission, into the home of a citizen of the Spanish Empire. He has a wife and children and is very religious. He zealously indoctrinates his children to Catholicism, even before they learn to speak. To stay on good terms with anyone up in heaven, the man makes the sign of the cross more than twenty times a day, no matter how banal or insignificant an occurrence may be. The family lives on what it obtains from the land it owns. The man respects the church because it applies the law and regulates relationships and coexistence. He never went to school, a misfortune that his children repeat. Education is reserved only for the nobility and the clergy. This man likes to enjoy street shows with his family and others of his same social class. He will have to be content with that. The nobility, on the other hand, can enjoy activities of great physical demand, such as hunting and jousting tournaments.

Although Spain possesses economic and military power, it is not until the marriage of Queen Isabella I of Castile to King Ferdinand II of Aragon in the fifteenth century that the country becomes an empire, with Catholicism reaching its peak and the kingdom's territories unified.

The Spanish Empire

Spanish nobility is close to the Crown, giving them a privileged position in terms of ownership of land and assets in the newly conquered territories. This will be possible thanks to a legal system. The nobles view the colonies as an extension of the empire's capital. Though they lead a comfortable life under the protection of the Crown, they are ready to join the conquest. The reason: their desire to control large tracts of land. If they succeed, they will earn the status of great lords. But this undertaking is not easy. They face an arduous journey, a lack of resources, and the danger of an inhospitable place. In addition, there is always the risk that the Crown may reclaim possession over any conquered territory. Why break your back exploring new lands if at any moment a royal emissary could waltz in and claim your land in the glorious name of the king? As the saying goes, if you are too greedy, you could end up with nothing. Still, this does not dampen the ambition of countless adventurers.

The arrival of Christopher Columbus on the American continent signals the start of the Spanish Crown's appropriation of natural and human resources. It was the beginning of an era of travel and migration from Europe to what was then called the New World. The travelers who made these expeditions did so for various reasons, from religious persecution to the simple desire for adventure. With everything to gain, they set out to see for themselves if the rumors about the wonders of that new continent were true.

Once the conquest is finished, and to deal with multiple claims of ownership of the territories, a viceroy is appointed as the representative of the Crown in the colonies. The viceroy is the highest authority together with the *Audiencia*, the main court of New Spain. As for outlying areas, power fell to magistrates, mayors, and even town councils and indigenous peoples.

The imposition of language and the Catholic faith is crucial to restructuring the Americas' identity, to the extent that Spanish was the most widely spoken language on the continent at that time. This coincides with a period of crisis for the Iberian Peninsula due to epidemics and crop failures. Earnings for Europeans in the New World, however, are undiminished. By applying new agricultural techniques to revitalize their own plots of land as well as extracting gold, silver, spices, and other goods, economic activity expands, and they grow richer than ever before. The rudder of this ship is the Catholic faith.

Catholicism, interpreted as evangelization and conversion of the natives, is fundamental for the Spanish empire's new territories to properly function. When the native peoples renounce their beliefs and deities—by imposition or by their own free will—the possibility of them rebelling against colonial rule diminishes. This is how the Spanish Empire reached its apogee. Economic activities continue to increase—provided by mining as well as new trade routes—as Spain advances its stranglehold across the continent.

Cuba is the epicenter of the Spanish compass in America. From here, they expand until holding close to six million square kilometers across the Caribbean, Central America, and North America. This expansion stops at California and Oregon when Gaspar de Portola reports strong earthquakes and active volcanoes in Oregon and Idaho in 1769.

Portola's warning would become a catastrophic reality centuries later when Mount St. Helens volcano—called "Mountain of Smoking Fire" by the native people—erupts on the morning of May 18, 1980. Located along the Pacific Ring of Fire, this colossus unleashed the energy equivalent of twenty-seven thousand atomic bombs in a matter of thirty seconds. In comparison, Hiroshima was hit by only one bomb and look what happened to them. In addition to the loss of countless species of flora and fauna, the area suffered heavy economic damage. Fortunately, the loss of human life was less than expected.

With its territory defined and limited by Portola's reports, the Spanish empire achieved stability, then prosperity and later, decline. Around the eighteenth century, Spain's administration of its territories in the New World worsened drastically; the economy deteriorated markedly. The Spanish monarchy will not recover from this blow. Many years later, in the town of Dolores, a restless priest from Guanajuato takes up arms one morning against Spanish rule in Mexico. But we'll get to that a little later.

The British Empire

Now let's turn to the British Empire, with a population that reached 450 million at the beginning of the twentieth century. Its territory, located in northeastern Europe, is today made up of Great Britain, Ireland, and a few small surrounding islands.

The United Kingdom is considered a sovereign and independent country, and it was established as Great Britain in 1707. Great Britain includes the territories of England, Scotland, Wales, but of these, England has the most decisive influence on culture. Not for nothing were the Beatles, for example, from England. Invasions and consequent plundering of the African continent are attributed, for the most part, to the British Empire.

Stepping back in the history of this empire, we recall the arrival of the Roman Empire on the island. The Romans conquered the British, although they never managed to dominate the Scots. They implemented and spread Christianity, but their dominance faded with the advent of the Middle Ages.

The British Empire was characterized by its ability to control and exercise power over the nobility, although Parliament was often accused of being weak or incapable of fulfilling its duties. Only empty promises from the British parliamentarians of the time. And let's remember, the British are mainly organized by counties. Under this structure, the church is an important pillar and operates with the same pattern of wheeling and dealing as in the Spanish Empire. Royalty shares power, and the church acts as a great social benefactor while promoting and maintaining culture. The empire grows, but problems come along too.

In 1321, citizens living in the English capital fell victim to epidemics that ferociously decimated their livestock, leading to famine. The empire manages this crisis and implements a series of economic strategies to avoid any repetition. With this vision in mind, they favor opening new trade routes and diversifying their revenue.

Later, in 1348, the Black Death caused millions of deaths throughout Europe and parts of Asia. Today, it is considered the most devastating epidemic in history, though there have been many, many others in the world. It is believed that fleas from rats caused the Black Death, although there is no consensus as to that theory. What is certain is that no one was safe. Rich, poor, nobles, bakers, and peasants—anyone could suffer from the plague. Death from the disease was immediate; someone could be infected in the morning, show symptoms within a few hours, and die in the evening of the same day.

Seeing the ravages of the plague—dead bodies in the streets, burning corpses, people sick and dying, closed ports, empty fields, and cathedrals crowded with the faithful seeking a cure for the disease—many thought that the epidemic was another punishment from God, another divine attempt to wipe out humanity and make it pay for its sins. The rats will succeed where the Great Flood failed, fearful people said while covering their heads with masks in the shape of birds' beaks, so as not to catch the plague. This spread of death leads to a rebellion in the British Empire. The Crown deploys its army, which eventually opens the way for the British monarchy to start incorporating satellite areas into the empire.

Centuries later, the Crown is strengthened when it explores and establishes its colonies in what is now the United States. Its stronghold is Parliament, made up of the bourgeoisie, landowners, and other upper or wealthy classes. The nobility of the time enjoyed the benefits of trade routes with the New World. But their good fortune is transitory. Competition is unleashed when other powers that want a piece of the action muscle in on trade routes (this is the case of France and Spain). The competitors also undermine the British and colonize the most desirable lands, regardless of whether this leads to war. The catalyst for the British is Puritanism, a doctrine with radical principles that emerged in the seventeenth century. The

Puritans found their settlements in America on principles of morality and order.

Over a period of more than two centuries, the Puritans evolved a system of government under the statute of freedom of faith. Meanwhile, the British Empire begins to recharge its batteries in order to expel the Spanish and French in an open territorial struggle.

The Seven Years' War between France and England lasted from 1756 until 1763. Unlike other armed conflicts named for the number of years it lasted, this war did actually last the seven years it claims. It involved several nations, and it primarily benefited the British Empire and its established colonies in the Americas. The objective of the British was always to create and exploit trade routes in America.

They also tried to exploit the colonies' success, often with a heavy hand. In the end, the original thirteen colonies gained their independence on September 3, 1783, and eventually the United States consolidated as a powerful and imposing country. Apart from the loss of its most important territory, the British Empire achieved exponential growth during the nineteenth century and maintained its colonial respite until the middle of the twentieth century. Its fall began after the First World War. Although the British won the war, the country was weakened. The empire that was master of the seas and a dominant presence on five continents suffered a collapse just like the empires that came before it and those that will come after. The flag of the cross lost its hegemonic power. The old imperial glory now lives only in the English Crown's nostalgia.

The Viceroy of New Spain

Antonio de Mendoza y Pacheco was the first viceroy in New Spain; his mandate was to represent the monarchy in the conquered territories. His government lasted fifteen years, from 1535 until 1550. In 1535, he also became president of the Royal Court. Antonio de Mendoza's difficult assignment is to govern under imprecise rules that regulate his position as the viceroy. This forces the king to exert control over the viceroy not by administrative means, but by personal means. The viceroy owes loyalty, dedication, and obedience to the monarch, but he operates without restrictions.

In spite of his allegiance to the Spanish Crown, Antonio de Mendoza y Pacheco had to govern a vast territory much larger than the country on the other side of the ocean to which he owed obedience.

Spanish rule was not limited exclusively to present-day Mexico. After the fall of Tenochtitlan, Spain expanded northward. Eventually, its territory encompassed half of what is now the United States. The present-day states of California, Nevada, Colorado, Utah, New Mexico, Arizona, Texas, Oregon, Washington, and Florida belonged to the viceroyalty. New Spain also controlled what is now Guatemala, Belize, Costa Rica, El Salvador, Honduras, Nicaragua, Cuba, Dominican Republic, Puerto Rico, Trinidad and Tobago, and Guadeloupe. But the extension of New Spain went beyond the American continent. The Philippine Islands, located in the Pacific Ocean and conquered by the navigator Ferdinand Magellan, were also part of this huge viceroyalty. With the capital of the viceroyalty located in Mexico City, imagine how long it took the viceroy to find out about an event that occurred in the upper reaches of Louisiana, for example. No one had better forget part of the message when they were halfway to the capital. In the sixteenth century, all these diverse territories formed a single entity. If it had remained united, it would today be a world power, perhaps the largest on Earth.

New Spain entered into a series of conflicts, such as the failed Conspiracy of the Machetes, a rebellion in 1799 that sought to defeat Spain using only fifty machetes, two pistols, and a lot of bravery (or ingenuity). That was all the weaponry the rebels had. Naturally, they did not get very far.

The situation in Spain did not help the governability of its viceroyalty either. In 1808, Spain endured a war against Napoleon Bonaparte, who wanted his brother, Joseph Bonaparte, to occupy the Spanish throne. This war was very costly for Spain; many of its villages were pillaged and destroyed by the French. Although, in the end, Spain won the war against Napoleon and stopped the imposition of a foreign king, it was left quite weakened. The Spanish Empire's colonies took advantage of this weakness to start their own wars of independence.

Despite the failure of the Conspiracy of the Machetes, a seed was sown for future armed struggles. Eleven years later, the priest Miguel Hidalgo leads the Conspiracy of Queretaro to remove a corrupt government from power. When the conspiracy is discovered, the priest has no choice but to call on the people of Dolores to fight against the Spaniards under the banner of the Virgin of Guadalupe.

This uprising would become the War of Independence. After eleven years of fighting, the call to arms by Miguel Hidalgo culminates in triumph for the army and independence for Mexico. Neither Miguel Hidalgo nor other conspirators such as Ignacio Allende, however, live to see the end of the armed struggle they started. Agustin de Iturbide and Vicente Guerrero, who were fierce rivals in battle, form an alliance to achieve independence. Their army triumphantly enters Mexico City, thus ending dependence on the Spanish Crown. As for the Catholic religion, the people reject the Spaniards but respect the religion the Spaniards brought and instilled in them. In the political sphere, however, power favors the aristocrats.

But let's go back a bit before all this turmoil and look at a time when the viceroyalty still oversees New Spain. The insurgent army had already removed Viceroy Juan Ruiz de Apodaca from his post. A few months later, Juan O`Donoju (O'Donohue) arrives to replace him. It is the year 1821. Meanwhile, the insurgents announced the Plan of Iguala.

Making progress, the insurgent Agustin de Iturbide signs the famous Treaty of Cordoba, which cedes independence to New Spain. New Spain, which later becomes Mexico, is now free and independent from any Spanish interference. Loyalty and obedience to the Spanish monarchy ends, something that did not go down too well in Europe. The era of the viceroyalty, and of the viceroys, is over.

The Governors of the Colonies

Until the seventeenth century, England played an important role in European politics, where monarchies reign. It is a period in which power can only be inherited by members of a family, exclusively through blood ties. The first lucky one on the list is Charles VII.

Then, a series of changes took place. Around 1820, Europeans began to question the benefits and exclusive rights of monarchs to continue inheriting power. This is a period of transition for monarchies in Europe, and most monarchies in Western Europe were disappearing. And in times of turmoil, anything goes.

The situation in the thirteen colonies is different. Although there are a few similarities, they do not operate a monarchical system. Instead, they develop a composite monarchy made up of domains or states under the mandate of a single ruler. Each domain has an individual identity. This system of government is also replicated in Europe with the Kalmar Union of Scandinavia, the Polish-Lithuanian Commonwealth, the British monarchy, and the Spanish monarchy.

By the eighteenth century, the monarchy in England had adopted a limited approach. This means that the monarch remains active, although subject to laws, regulations, and the Constitution as well as to political practices. This system that maintains the monarchical figurehead is still in place today.

As for the history of Great Britain, it is uniquely tied to the monarchy. The monarchy is its oldest institution, though its continuity has been recently broken. The political system in the thirteen colonies comprises a governor, a council, and a legislature. The only exceptions were Rhode Island and Connecticut, where the Royal Crown elected the legislature and appointed the governor.

The British colonies carry out elections of their representatives by a majority vote. We need to keep in mind that the English representative system differs from the viceroyalty that Spain has implemented to control its new territories.

A representative is a free man and a Puritan. This is an emerging democracy, given that the community he is a part of believes that they will be more productive and effective if they are united through an assembly. They assert their individual needs through their representatives.

This model began in Massachusetts, which has a largely puritanical citizenry. Under this scheme, neither Parliament nor the king have voice or vote. This system gives the New England region limited autonomy, although their independence from Parliament and the monarch does not exempt them from complying with any ordinances issued by the English Crown.

John Winthrop is a notable player in this type of government. An independent colonist with strong values, his vision still influences many politicians today (positively, we hope). He achieved success as the first governor of Massachusetts. His administration acts as a catalyst for rapid community growth, and he will be rewarded with multiple consecutive reelections—eighteen in all—between 1631 and 1648. John Winthrop is also admired and respected in other colonies. His son, John Winthrop the Younger, will become governor of the Connecticut colony years later.

Puritanism is the predominant religion in Massachusetts, later the breeding ground of the best universities in the world. With the king's consent, the rest of the colonies are inspired to emulate the political success of this colony. The legacy of this political order forms the basis of the representative government model implemented by the United States and other countries.

But let's continue with the history of the colonies in the Americas: the thirteen colonies and New Spain. We have clearly defined their differences in terms of their governance. The Spanish Empire is focused on exploiting the land and extracting resources for a trading network that prioritizes Europe. The English, on the other hand, have in mind to establish a community with freedom of religion that profits from local resources, above and beyond the economic interest outside its borders.

For the thirteen colonies, independence from the king and all that he represents, including Parliament, by means of a representative government, is fundamental. The viceroyalty system in New Spain and subordination to the interests of the king are the other side of the coin.

The French and Dutch Empires in America

While the colonization of America is centered on Spain and England, we should not forget that the promise of new lands and resources piques the interest of other empires. The French and the Dutch, having heard so many tales from the Spaniards, launch their own expeditions to find out if the stories are true.

The distinguished explorer Jacques Cartier (1491–1557) made a remarkable voyage aboard a 120-ton French vessel named *La Grande Hermine*. Cartier had a very different goal from his compatriots who were eager to raid Spanish ships laden with treasure and resources. He wanted to explore the wilderness. He had the good fortune to make three voyages to the Gulf of St. Lawrence, in present-day eastern Canada, in the space of eight years. His intention was to open a safe route to the East.

His fate takes an unexpected turn when he interacts with the inhabitants of Mont Real, between the St. Lawrence and the Rivière des Prairies. It is the last of his trips. Cartier listened to the natives, naively trusting their stories about a place teeming with gold and silver in the Saguenay backcountry.

Cartier, with no qualms, travels there and extracts a shiny gold ore and some crystals. Satisfied, he sets off on his return trip, thinking of all the things he will buy with this treasure. It takes him a while to realize that his cargo is not worth anything. It turns out that the shiny mineral he was boasting about is actually iron pyrite and not gold. Worse, what he assumes to be diamonds turn out to be simple quartz crystals. Oh well … we all make mistakes, even the French explorers. To Cartier's credit, however, his travels open an easy route through the American continent. So he will go down in history as the Christopher Columbus of France, regardless of the fact that a few simple stones had fooled him.

Samuel de Champlain (?–1635) is another French navigator worthy of mention, on par with Hernan Cortes. Less susceptible to the lure of false gold, he explored and founded the Quebec region. He is known as the father of New France, a territory in North

America that stretches from the Gulf of St. Lawrence through the Rocky Mountains and then south to the Gulf of Mexico. The French also made incursions into the southern part of the continent, but they were only able to establish a colony in what is now French Guiana. Their settlements in the north were in what is now Canada. Although they did try to dispute areas under English and Spanish rule, they did not succeed.

The French settled in the current state of Florida, which at the time was known as French Florida or *Floride française* to sound more elegant. There, they build a fort and, given the location, engage in trading. The Spanish claim the territory as their own; in fact, a group of Spaniards founded a settlement called St. Augustine near the French fort. The French, fearful of an attack on their settlement, plan to migrate to avoid conflict. However, the Spaniards overran and appropriated their territory.

The disputes between the various empires established in North America—France, England, and Spain—incited the famous Seven Years' War that wanted to resolve, once and for all, who dominates the New World. At the end of the conflict, Louisiana passes to the Spanish in exchange for Florida.

The immense Louisiana Territory has not been explored much and borders the Mississippi River, which looks to be an excellent trade route.

When US independence was achieved in 1783, Louisiana became the border between the territory of present-day Mexico and the United States. Spain regained control of Florida, reaching its furthest geographical extension and becoming the largest empire on the American continent at that time.

The Americans realize the strategic importance of the Mississippi River and the state of Louisiana. Once they had their eye on this territory, they would not let it slip out of sight. Meanwhile, the Spanish Empire exploits the land and opens up trade channels.

By 1801, Spain had decided to cede Louisiana back to the French. This leads to negotiations between France and the United States for its purchase. Two years later, Napoleon sells it for gold to the third

US president, Thomas Jefferson, who opens his wallet and buys all of Louisiana. Once they had their money, the French washed their hands of the transaction and disregarded the territorial problem between Spain and the United States.

Now let's witness the signing of the Adams-Onis Treaty. Representing King Ferdinand VII of Spain is the diplomat Luis de Onis. On the US side, John Quincy Adams, then Secretary of State and a future president carries out the negotiations. The United States claims that the Louisiana Territory extends to the Pacific Ocean. The Spanish claim that it ends at the banks of the Mississippi River.

After some back-and-forth, the boundary was finally defined in 1819, with the apparent consensus of all parties. The territory of Texas is recognized as belonging to New Spain; however, Florida becomes part of the United States.

With the acquisition of more territories, the United States, already an independent country, creates new states, in particular Louisiana. The vast territory acquired will be divided into thirteen different entities: Louisiana, Arkansas, Oklahoma, Kansas, Missouri, Nebraska, Iowa, Wyoming, Montana, Colorado, Minnesota, and the two Dakotas, North and South.

Other rather peculiar conflicts cannot escape our historical memory, such as the one that arose over beavers. No, this is no joke. This adorable and friendly rodent gave its name to the so-called Beaver War, probably the bloodiest armed conflict in North America, lasting more than fifty years. It took place between Canada and the United States, starting in 1640. In the name of the furry rodent with big teeth and a stubby tail, the tribes native to the territories dominated by France as well as a small area occupied by the Dutch (Manhattan) raise their voices in protest. Known as the Iroquois Confederacy, this group is made up of five tribes.

The conflict originates because of an insatiable demand for beaver fur. Europeans coveted the fur, and the historical context is necessary to understand why. By the seventeenth century, beavers were close to extermination on the European continent due to use of their fur for clothing. Whoever owned one of these garments is seen as a respectable, high-society individual. As beaver fur became scarcer, demand for it skyrocketed. Understandably, European ambition overflows when they find an abundance of native beavers in America. The French immediately apply themselves to their exploitation, although they will not be the only ones.

The Dutch, already settled in what is now Manhattan, quickly see an opportunity to trade beaver pelts. These settlers decide to trade with the natives, who become suppliers. In exchange for beaver skins, the natives were paid with firearms. So far, we can say that both parties are satisfied.

This voracity for pelts nearly wiped out the beavers' presence in what is now upstate New York, where they were once as plentiful as trees. In order to continue trading with the settlers, the Iroquois follow the beaver trail northward until they reach New France, present-day Canada. Their traverse through these lands will not be friendly. They massacre the native populations in order to obtain beaver pelts.

It is an unequal fight: the Iroquois attack with the firearms negotiated with the Europeans, while the opposing tribes defend themselves with arrows, spears, and tomahawks.

Once the Iroquois reach the territory of New France, there is no stopping them. They exterminate anyone who stands between them and the beavers. At first, the attacks were focused on tribes that inhabit the border with New France. When they advanced on Quebec and Montreal, the French finally decided to do something about it.

The Iroquois' handling of gunpowder, courtesy of the Dutch Empire, surprised the French. When the conflict begins to claim European lives, the French react. The conflict drags on with sporadic battles as the Iroquois retreat from the region to regroup and attack later.

While the French Empire keeps busy fighting for the beavers, the English take the opportunity to settle in the rest of the territories, although they remain outside of French-dominated areas in North America. After thousands of deaths, the powerful French army prevails over the Iroquois, who choose to concentrate on the territory of Canada. The English stayed between Canada and the United States; the Dutch settled for the area north of New York.

The Dutch had arrived in America in 1613 at the height of the Dutch maritime empire. The seventeenth century is considered Holland's golden age when it achieved important scientific and cultural advances. Like other empires, the revolutionary wars in Europe had severe consequences for the Dutch, with the loss of many of its colonies to the English army. Worse still, as if so much misfortune were not enough, France attacked and occupied its capital for twenty years.

The arrival of the Dutch in America is fortuitous. The ship carrying these immigrants loses its way and ends up running aground on the island of Manhattan. A year later, they cross Long Island to reach the bay. In 1614, they established the first Dutch colony, which they christened New Amsterdam. The island of Manhattan fades into anonymity, and they focus on exploring the forests and trading along the Hudson River.

Years later, around 1623, the island of Manhattan was once again of interest to them. It could be said that the Dutch forgot that wise saying that dictates something once lost can never return. A ship carrying families is sent to establish settlements for the Dutch empire, hoping to stop the expansion of other European empires in the area. In 1625, another ship was sent to the island with a group of families and animals.

The official founding of the colony of New Amsterdam is in 1626, when the island of Manhattan is purchased from the native peoples. The payment was paltry and could even be considered robbery. For only twenty-four dollars, the Dutch became owners of a piece of land that today is priceless. With the money they save, the Dutch Empire is able to finance a series of expeditions to the new continent. The beaver pelt is the currency that fuels their economy.

However, when England grows stronger, the Dutch will be ousted from their territory in both the old and the new continent. The English renamed New Amsterdam as New York, in honor of the Duke of York. In 1667, the Treaty of Breda officially made the Dutch surrender to the English empire. The brief dominion of the Dutch Empire in the American continent concludes.

Taxes in the Colonies and the Viceroyalty

The independence of the thirteen English colonies can be seen as a rebellion of the middle and upper classes in communities that were not accustomed to paying taxes. It should be noted that taxes were low during the first period of colonization. They were administered by each locality; these governments can be described as weak and without services. This system lasted from 1620 to 1634, when colonization was privately financed. Tax laws appeared later.

The colonists prosper and use their profits to support their own standard of living and progressive views. The Crown was not pleased and introduced a series of taxes: the Massachusetts Bay Act of 1634, the Sugar Act of 1764, the Stamp Act of 1765, the Townshend Acts of 1767, and the Tea Act of 1773. The colonies chafe under such an escalating tax burden and began to cherish ideas of independence. At first, the colonists were aware that their resources would be used for military spending since the English Crown needed to defend its territories in conflict with France and England. However, they believe in reaping the rewards of their own labor for themselves before all else—even the monarchy of England.

Finally, we turn to the tax system in New Spain. Before the conquest, the Mexica operated a well-organized tribute system. In fact, when they gained access to the lake area of the Anahuac Valley and decided to settle there, they had to pay taxes to the Azcapotzalco lordship that controlled the area. Once they dominated the region and extended their empire, they applied this tributary system to those they conquered.

During the viceroyalty of New Spain, tax administration was centralized. Taxes are high, given that the Spanish Crown is the financier of the invasion, and even the church joins in. On top of this, a series of prohibitions are imposed on certain activities and professions, and lucrative monopolies that benefit the Crown and the church are allowed. The church even goes so far as to decree that if an individual accepts the Catholic faith and wishes to be baptized along with his children, he will have to pay a tax or tithe to do so. As if life was already expensive enough, under this system, it was almost impossible to survive if one had few resources. As in the case of the thirteen colonies, such a tax system will eventually incentivize independence.

MAP OF THE EUROPEAN COLONIES IN NORTH AMERICA
IN THE XVII CENTURY

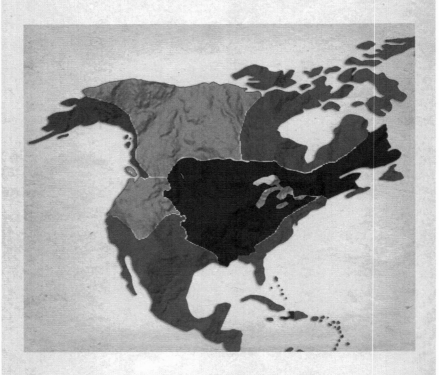

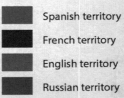

Spanish territory

French territory

English territory

Russian territory

Chapter 4

A Country Is Born

Fourth of July: Independence of the Thirteen Colonies

The birth of both countries, Mexico and the United States of America, occurred under very different political, social, and economic circumstances. In this chapter, we'll take an important historical journey through these two sister countries. We will begin with the independence of the thirteen colonies. Since much has already been told about Mexico and how it obtained its independence, I would rather begin with the United States and then make a comparison between the two countries at the end of this chapter.

Remember, the American colonies originated from England and, therefore, were governed by the laws of the British Crown. The English in America invested a lot of resources in soldiers and their ships since they always had to be prepared for war—so much so that they ended up dislodging the French from American territory. The colonies had an almost independent government, which did not please the king very much. In 1763, both the king and Parliament gained control over matters related to the military and maritime trade as well as foreign affairs.

With the appropriation of territory left by the French, plus the costs of maintaining military and civilian troops in the American colonies, England's expenses increased exponentially. As a result, they decided to start levying taxes on the colonies.

In April 1764, the Revenue Act, better known as the Sugar Act, was aimed at increasing revenues through taxes while ending the smuggling trade in sugar. This law was simply a test launched by Parliament—a sort of legislative "throw it against the wall and see if it sticks." Then, in March 1765, Parliament unveiled a new law called the "Stamp Act," so named because a tax had to be paid for stamps on papers and documents. This became the first law that directly taxed the American colonies. All proceeds were to be spent in those colonies that were under parliamentary government. The thirteen colonies quickly expressed their displeasure with this law and formed a political group called the "Sons of Liberty," who led acts of aggression in protest.

In 1766, Parliament annulled the law due to its hostile reception by the American colonies. However, it passed another law called the Declaratory Act, confirming the right of Parliament to pass laws taxing the American colonies.

Shortly after, the Townshend Acts were passed. These aimed to reduce the British tax burden and raise revenue from the American colonies. This obviously upset the American colonists, and they immediately looked for a way to revoke Parliament's right to issue these laws.

As if previous laws did not upset the Americans enough, new legislation called the Quebec Act would be the last straw. It appeared that now the expansion of the North American colonies was restricted.

Members of the Virginia assembly decided to create the Continental Congress of North America. This congress represented the majority of Britain's North American colonies; almost all the colonies belonged, with the exception of Georgia.

This same congress introduced a declaration of rights and complaints addressed to the English. The session adjourned in October 1774, and its members planned to meet again in May, as long as there were no grievances from the American colonies.

Before continuing with the battles of the War of Independence, I want to briefly touch on George Washington's background and how he influenced the history of the United States. Washington is *the* symbol of American independence and the first president of this great nation.

The Washingtons were a well-to-do family from Virginia. Thanks to this, George Washington had access to education and land that belonged to his family (land that was worked by slaves, by the way). As might be expected of a young man of his social status,

George joined the Virginia Masonic Lodge in Fredericksburg. This is very relevant since Freemasonry influenced the independence of the United States. Eighteen of the fifty-six signers of the Declaration of Independence belonged to Masonic lodges, including Samuel Adams, John Adams, Benjamin Franklin, Thomas Jefferson, and John Hancock.

George Washington married a wealthy widow. We would like to believe that it was for love, but thanks to this marriage, he was able to increase his fortune considerably, entering even more keenly into politics. It is worth noting that by this time in his life, he had already been appointed lieutenant colonel, so it can be assumed that he had military experience and training. Given his relationship with politics and the military, George Washington was appointed major general of the Continental Army of the United States.

A promise made is a debt unpaid. Having explained about Washington, we can now move on to the most important battles of the War of Independence. Bearing in mind that there were several battles, we will concentrate on just three of them, though still mention other important events within this epic journey.

Before the Continental Congress reconvened, the struggle for independence had already begun. On April 19, 1775, the first clashes, known as the battles of Lexington and Concord, took place. The gunfire on that day marked a path of no return. Congress had to make quick decisions, and George Washington was chosen as the leader of the American army, as mentioned above.

British assaults continued. On June 17, 1775, they attacked another American colony, triggering the famous Battle of Bunker Hill in Boston. Congress had to respond to the attacks and sent an expedition to Quebec to propose an alliance against the English. By the end of the same year, American troop strength had grown considerably—to the point of even having a fleet of warships.

The Declaration of Independence was drafted by Thomas Jefferson and approved on July 4, 1776. The union of the thirteen colonies against the English was announced. Unlike other wars of independence, this one is different for the ease with which the

North American colonies triumphed. The only thing they had to do was fight for what already belonged to them. In most other wars of independence, people need to fight for what they have been denied and do not yet have.

Because they had to send troops from Europe to the American continent to fight, the English government had a hard time sustaining the war. Many English soldiers were probably still feeling seasick from spending so many days at sea when it was their turn to go into battle. In addition to the complicated crossings, shipments of arms and clothing for the British soldiers also took several weeks to arrive, which worked in favor of the Americans.

One of the most famous battles of this war was the battle of Long Island, where Washington suffered his worst defeat. The British Army outnumbered the American army in personnel, resources, and firepower. However, Washington was convinced that this battle could be won. Doing so would ensure the Americans' dominance by reclaiming the strategic territory of Long Island and ending the war ahead of schedule. However, as often happens in life, things did not go according to plan. Washington lost more than two thousand men in this battle, and the British Army suffered fewer than five hundred casualties in its ranks. Although Washington lost the battle, he managed to evacuate his entire army to Manhattan Island. There, they prepared for the next blow against the British Army—one of the best in the world—who had made the terrible mistake of underestimating its enemy.

Confident in their execution and military strategies, the British decided to attack the American troops from the north at the Battle of Saratoga. This battle was a crucial one. In the meantime, while Washington was leading the army, Benjamin Franklin was sent to France to request financing for the war as well as military aid. Meanwhile, the British Army decided to march with seven thousand soldiers to face twelve thousand American fighters who were awaiting their arrival. Washington managed to win an astonishing victory, capturing more than six thousand British soldiers during the eighteen-day battle.

Once the news of this victory reached France, the French agreed to support the American government economically and by providing ships and military personnel to tip the balance in favor of the Americans.

The army commanded by George Washington managed to raise about twenty thousand more soldiers. Something that Congress had not considered, however, was how to sustain such a large army. By 1780, there was a shortage of funds. A year later, Congress made one of its best possible strategic decisions: appointing a director of finance to organize and restructure all expenditures. Unfortunately, this was not enough.

In 1781, the battle of Yorktown took place. By this time, Washington and his men knew it was only a matter of time before the commander of the British Army would give up. The British Army had expected to receive reinforcements for the war campaign, but—to their surprise—the French had intercepted the British Army's ships and succeeded in blocking this much-desired support. At the same time, the American army, commanded by Washington, and part of the French Army attacked the British soldiers and prevented them from fleeing by land.

For almost a month, Americans and French fought side by side. Little by little, the British Army weakened and began to realize that winning this war would be impossible. Aware of his imminent defeat, the commander of the British Army, W. Wallace, announced his surrender. Washington accepted without delay. However, even though the war had already ended between these two armies, this did not mean that independence was a fact. Tensions between both sides were still present.

Without a treaty to ratify what had happened, another war could break out at any moment. No one wanted that.

In 1783, the US government signed an agreement that put an end to the War of Independence. The Peace of Paris was the name given to the agreement signed on September 3. The thirteen colonies now became a federation.

For Mexico, It's September 16—Not Cinco de Mayo

Now on to Mexico. We will begin with an analysis of the battle of Cinco de Mayo. It is a well-known fact that every war has its price to pay, whether economic or social. So we will mention the prices that both Mexico and the United States had to pay to achieve their freedom. There is a big difference between the two.

Cinco de Mayo is a date on which Mexicans celebrate the victory in the Battle of Puebla against the invading French army. To be honest, most Mexicans do not give much importance to this date. The celebration of independence, the Mexican Revolution, or even the day of the Virgin of Guadalupe is more significant. Our neighbors to the north, however, seem to enjoy and look forward to this date to celebrate "all things Mexican" in a big way with margaritas, burritos, guacamole, big sombreros, and fake mustaches. The question arises: Why do Americans celebrate this date more than Mexicans? This question cannot be answered flippantly. Given that every piece of information provided throughout this book brings with it months of research and reliable sources, I will give an opinion. The main reason why Americans celebrate this date with more zeal is out of habit fueled by misinformation.

As already mentioned, Cinco de Mayo commemorates the victory obtained by the Mexican Army against the most powerful army in the world at that time. No one bet a cent that the Mexicans would triumph in battle against France. And yet, they were victorious. Americans generally think that Mexico's independence is celebrated on this date. This might sound reasonable since, in this battle, Mexico fought against a foreign army that tried to disrespect a sovereign country. The problem is that Mexico did not gain its independence from France, but from Spain. If you remember that the language spoken in Mexico is precisely Spanish—not French—it makes sense.

In addition, this celebration also became popular due to a play on words. Cinco de Mayo pronounced in English sounds like "Sink of the Mayo" or sinking of the mayonnaise. This play on words refers to the sinking of cargo carried by a large ocean liner that sank without reaching the coast of Veracruz where it was supposed to unload twelve thousand jars of mayonnaise.

This theory of why the celebration of Cinco de Mayo has become so popular is the more recent of the two. The ship believed to be carrying the shipment of mayonnaise is none other than the *Titanic*. And although its sinking was not on the celebrated date, it is simply thanks to the play on words that the goods supposedly transported by the *Titanic*, the jars of mayonnaise, are related to Cinco de Mayo.

In the United States, this date is celebrated with parades and typical Mexican costumes, with tricolor flags everywhere, and you can't miss the food. In fact, to confirm the mayonnaise theory, tacos are dipped in this dressing, in allusion to "sink of the mayo."

Although we have mentioned the erroneous reasons of why this date is celebrated, and also what should be commemorated and celebrated on this date, we should also explain why the date is important as well as what events preceded it and what took place after the Mexican Army's victory. Once this has been explained, it will be up to each one's discretion to celebrate this date. To understand what is commemorated on Cinco de Mayo, let's look at the historical events that took place in the country during the nineteenth century.

There are aspects of Mexico's independence that can be highlighted and compared with the independence of its neighbor, the United States.

One of the most important factors in a war always revolves around the resources that a state possesses to sustain its military campaign. The United States, or the North American colonies, had already been governed for several years under a democratic regime independent of the English Crown, which allowed them to afford an armed movement more easily. The case of Mexico was quite the opposite. Remember: Mexico had been subjugated by the Spanish for approximately three hundred years and did not have the economic resources to start a war so easily.

Another aspect is the time that both wars lasted. It took the Mexicans eleven years to complete their independence. The war took the lives of hundreds of thousands of people, causing enormous political instability that took years to recover from. In addition, during these eleven years, Mexico's struggle for independence was so violent that many of the movement's leaders were assassinated without seeing their cause triumph.

If we make a comparison with the American struggle for independence, we know that its leaders mentioned in their letters that the people were apathetic. They even had to be offered an economic incentive to join the armed movement. It could be said that the war waged by the Americans and the English was somewhat more civilized, which allowed them to reach an agreement in less time.

Something that is also worth mentioning is that, in the United States, the colonies were united, while in Mexico, the territories were divided. If this is analyzed, it can be concluded that each country's struggle was to end their dependence and to unveil a new political order.

The United States had to unite its colonies to give rise to a country that was independent from England. Although they had previously enjoyed independence from the English Crown, they now had to confirm that independence by showing a united front. Mexico tried to do the same. After ending its war of independence against Spain, it showed the world that it would now be its own country, independent from any other. It established a new geographical order that became the furthest extension of its territory; those states would answer to a Mexican emperor.

Clearly, the social and economic costs to the two countries were not at all similar. The United States was able to pay off its debts in a few years. Mexico continued to incur more and more debt because of other subsequent wars. Those debts created more wars. This vicious cycle was almost impossible to break.

Finally, the wars for independence that Mexico and the United States fought really are in no way comparable. We must remember that the United States began with colonies formed by Englishmen who were looking for a second chance to practice their faith. Their form of government enabled their freedom. These colonists already had rights that would have been taken away from them if they had not fought for independence. In contrast, Mexico had been subjugated for three hundred years. The Mexican people, unlike the American people, had to fight for rights they did not even know about.

To end this chapter, we must talk about the famous cry of independence, which is celebrated every year on the night of September 15. This is a tradition that Mexicans commemorate with pride since it marks such an important date for the nation.

The cry of independence was made by one of the key characters in this armed movement, the priest Miguel Hidalgo y Costilla, considered the father of Mexican independence by many historians.

Miguel Hidalgo initiated Mexican independence after giving the call to arms at Dolores Hidalgo, Guanajuato. But prior to this important event, there are also several historic incidents that I will try to summarize—without discarding the most relevant aspects—for the purposes of this book.

Miguel Hidalgo, who was a priest by profession, had the privilege of being born into a middle-class family. This gave him access to education, and he became the headmaster of the school where he studied. He had previously been appointed priest and was in charge of instructing and teaching the parishioners. At the same time, he tried to improve the living conditions of the indigenous people. His ideals led him to join a kind of secret society where he met with the future independence leaders who would write the nation's history in blood.

The insurgents of Queretaro, which was another secret group that met to discuss politics and culture, planned to take up arms during the last month of 1810. However, they were discovered and arrested in September. Josefa Ortiz de Dominguez courageously sent a messenger to alert groups in San Miguel and Dolores Hidalgo—to which the Aldama brothers and Ignacio Allende belonged—about the Queretaro arrests. After evaluating what was happening, Miguel Hidalgo summoned his parishioners, the townspeople, and gave the famous cry of Dolores in the early morning of September 16, thus initiating Mexico's independence from the Spanish Crown. The cry of Dolores is so called because it took place in the town of Dolores Hidalgo, known today as the cradle of national independence.

The flame had been lit, and it would be impossible to extinguish it. Miguel Hidalgo knew this very well, as did Ignacio Allende, who commanded this first stage of independence. Together, they led several important battles and captured territory and cities. These battles were bloody and left a great number of casualties for both ranks, both for the independence fighters and the government. Despite this and thanks to their excellent leadership, the independence fighters seized important cities. Just when they were about to reach Mexico City, Miguel Hidalgo ordered them to stop, something that Allende did not understand since taking Mexico City would have ended the armed movement sooner and without so much bloodshed. Instead, the Mexican war for independence lasted eleven long years. In the end, Mexico suffered many casualties, and the country slid into tremendous instability.

After ordering the controversial and inexplicable withdrawal of troops, Miguel Hidalgo and Ignacio Allende continued the fight. In March 1811, they were defeated in the battle of Puente de Calderón. After retreating to the north of the country in search of reinforcements, they were captured by the enemy army and taken to Chihuahua, where they were sentenced to death for the crimes committed and executed a few days later.

Even though these key independence leaders had been shot, the flame they lit turned into a fire in the hearts of many other Mexicans. New leaders emerged, including Jose Maria Morelos y Pavon, Nicolas Bravo, Vicente Guerrero, Leona Vicario, Guadalupe Victoria, and Agustin de Iturbide.

Despite so many deaths and so many years of confrontation and blood, thanks to the cry of Dolores, Mexico was able to free itself from the stranglehold of servitude it had suffered for more than three hundred years.

This Land Is My Land

This subtopic will underscore an important point touched on previously: how one country focused on expanding its territory while the other country tried to keep the territory it already had. This will help us to better appreciate upcoming chapters, particularly because we will be touching on the Monroe Doctrine and how it directly or indirectly helped Mexico during its military conflicts.

The information introduced in the third chapter will guide us in this part of the book. The United States, even before its birth as an independent country, had sought to acquire more land. Since their main source of income came from land, they looked for ways to acquire new territories in order to expand their economic activities.

This clearly contrasts with Mexico. Although its economy was also based on agriculture as well as mining—activities that needed large tracts of land—the viceroyalty's poor management, and even worse management after gaining its independence, resulted in Mexico losing territory. Later, Mexico had to make great efforts to maintain the territory they already possessed and negotiate with individual states that sought independence. It should be added that the United States took full advantage of this situation to acquire more territory for itself.

An example of the above is the acquisition by the United States of territory belonging to Spain, such as Florida and Oregon. In addition, remember the territory they bought from France and that which they took from the Dutch. There was also territory acquired from Mexico, such as Texas and other states. This land was supposedly bought—for an absurd price—after the US invaded Mexico. All this tells us how the United States grew as a country. It was always aiming for more territory and organizing different territories into states while profiting at the same time, as was the case with Texas.

After the acquisition of Texas, the United States annexed more territory, and once again, it was Mexican territory. I am referring to what happened after the US invasion of Mexico (a subject that we will discuss in more detail in another chapter of the book), which concluded with the signing of the Treaty of Guadalupe Hidalgo. This treaty was signed in February 1848 and ratified in May of the same year. The end result was that the United States added land to its territory that yielded the states of California, Nevada, Utah, New

Mexico, Texas, Colorado, and Arizona—and parts of Wyoming, Kansas, and Oklahoma. And as if this were not enough, the treaty forced Mexico to renounce all claims to the territory of Texas. To close the deal and accept Mexico's surrender, the United States paid Mexico the paltry sum of $15 million as compensation for damages caused during their invasion.

With this, a sad chapter in the history of both countries was closed. They set aside their differences and tried to move forward regarding other relevant issues as nations and neighbors. From this point forward, Mexico and the United States tried to get along, each going their own way. To avoid conflicts, they would first resort to diplomacy.

Before closing this subtopic, we should mention the Monroe Doctrine to honor the title "This Land Is My Land." The Monroe Doctrine is basically summarized in the following phrase: "America for Americans."

The Monroe Doctrine was inspired by James Monroe, the fifth president of the United States, and published by John Q. Adams. This doctrine alluded to the fact that America belonged to the Americans, and any intervention by European states would be seen as an act of war in which the United States would be forced to intervene.

This doctrine highlights three important points:

1) Neither the American continent nor any of its states should be considered for future colonization by Europeans or any other power.
2) Taking into account the great difference between the political models of European countries and the US, any attempt to introduce another political model to any American state will be considered a threat to US peace and security.
3) The United States will not take part in European wars; US policy is to not take sides in such conflicts.

These are the most significant points in this document. We could argue that the United States did not stand firm to this doctrine.

When the French invaded Mexico, the question could arise: Why did the United States not intervene against the Europeans to defend Mexico? Clearly, the French were considered a power—and they were invading a neighboring country with which by this time all differences had been set aside.

Although it is true that the United States and Mexico managed to resolve all their differences—and even President Juarez had a very good relationship with the US—the United States did not intervene even when the French occupied the Mexican capital. This would perhaps lead us to ponder US hypocrisy or perhaps a double standard. The US probably calculated that the French invasion might benefit them—and they could acquire even more Mexican territory. Based on the Monroe Doctrine, an invasion of America (the Americas) was cause for immediate action since it was a threat to Americans. And yet, that did not happen. The reason, actually, has no hidden agenda or any motive to benefit the United States. What was happening was the United States was fighting its own Civil War, which lasted from 1861 to 1865. This fact made it impossible for the Americans to take action against the European threat since they were too busy fighting among themselves.

It should be explained that the Monroe Doctrine did have an effect later on, benefiting the US more than any other country in the Americas. Let's remember that the United States intervened in Latin American countries multiple times through the twentieth century, and for this reason, the saying that Latin America had become the gringos' backyard became popular. For example, the Panama Canal. The Panama Canal was taken over by the Americans under the premise of maintaining control over any interoceanic corridor to avoid any meddling by European imperialists. Alluding to the Monroe Doctrine, the Panama Canal was left in the hands of the Americans, although its benefits were only seen by the United States.

This is how America has tried to remain in the hands of the Americans. It never hurts to have free competition and an open market, although that is not exactly what this doctrine talks about.

In the following topics, we will look at the economic engines of both the colonies and the viceroyalty and the reasons for this doctrine.

What Made the Bulk of the Economy for the Thirteen Colonies?

The economy of the thirteen colonies was based on two main pillars: first, the timber forests that could be adapted for construction and also as fuel; second, an extensive maritime space that allowed for the development of overseas trade through fishing. These types of resources contributed to New England's strategy for sugar production through the Caribbean colonies, an industry that focused on trade with Europe.

However, after having used up the area's forest resources (use is good, but not abuse), they had to depend exclusively on wood imported from New England to build the barrels used to pack sugar. Wood was also used to repair mills as well as wood presses, and of course, it was used for fuel.

Prefabricated houses were imported, ready to be assembled, and 70 percent of sugar—highly valued in British society in the seventeenth and eighteenth centuries—came from the West Indies and met demand.

Between 1771 and 1773, an average of 240,000 trees were cut down. In that period, New England was in full development. This wood supplied colonies that belonged to the British Crown in the West Indies. Wood sold by Yankee traders fetched an average of three million gallons of rum; the rum was then sent to Africa as currency in the slave trade. Wood was also exchanged for brushwood, which was then used at distilleries in Boston.

Trading in the region was unlimited and dynamic. There was a high level of trade between Europe and the Caribbean, and they did not hold back when it came to trading their products or goods as well as slaves and timber. This helps us understand the economic development of North America based on a particular religious stance in relation to trade, as well as moral and ethical restrictions.

Trade relations were also established with Portugal and Spain, and many English and New England merchants sold lumber to Portuguese and Spanish traders and sold them ships. This trade was done through manufactured goods shipped from England to the colony. These were sold at high prices, and with the proceeds, wood was bought to build ships. Both the wood and the ships were sent to the Iberian region and sold at the same time. Later, this business dynamic would be replicated in England.

During the seventeenth century, from 1667 until 1731, more than five hundred ships were built. Raw materials came from other parts of the world, such as oak and fir, and from shipyards that were established outside of Boston. This boosted an industry building lighter merchant ships, usually not exceeding 140 tons. So much money was raised that the first foundling hospital in England was built. The low cost of lumber allowed New England shipyards to produce ships at bargain prices for Europeans and reduced the cost of freight and goods being transported, helping Yankee merchants become the masters of trade in the West Indies and North America, exclusively under the English monopoly.

The New England fishing industry, supplied with ships from local shipyards, exploded. The fishing and whaling industry, which consisted of 160 vessels, supplied an average of four hundred thousand pounds of whale oil to the world per year. Likewise, tuna, mackerel, salmon, swordfish, sturgeon, and other marine species were also fished. The best production was sent to southern Europe, and the low-quality varieties were used to feed the slaves in the West Indies.

The economic value of the wood attracted immigrants and settlers for its quality and abundance. It also served as raw material for homes and firewood to produce heat against the area's fierce frigid climate. Visitors from England in 1630 commented that if a servant lived in New England and had fifty acres or so, he could have more wood for heating than any nobleman in Britain.

For the immigrants, such developments were an opportunity for economic advancement. Sawmills were established—boosting the economy and becoming part of the international economic stream.

The profit margin became very high when the danger from indigenous tribes faded. Settlers in Maine built ramshackle housing and sawmills, where they could process an average of fourteen pine trees per day. A negative ecological impact soon hit the region, threatening the eradication of forest resources. Massive deforestation caused tensions between Native Americans and the Crown. For the indigenous people, wood had a religious purpose due to their respect for nature. For the Crown, wood served for the masts of the royal fleet.

Moving to the central region of the colonies, we find agricultural and forestry activity. Forestry was also important in the northern wooded areas of New Jersey and Pennsylvania, where sawmills were established. In addition, Quaker settlers from Europe had migrated to Pennsylvania. Their main activity was cultivating wheat and raising milk-producing animals to serve the market of German, Dutch, Swedish, and Welsh immigrants.

We should also remember that although coal and iron ore were known to exist in Pennsylvania, England did not develop the metallurgical industry. The investment costs were high compared to wood, making it somewhat difficult to compete. England had to import iron from Sweden. In 1716, the Baltic War interrupted iron supplies, forcing the Crown to make a heavy capital investment and build furnaces. However, British investors found it profitable to pay for iron imports from the American colonies. By 1769, approximately 40 percent of the raw iron that England imported was supplied by its colonies established in North America. This expansion of the iron industry stimulated the colonies' emergence as a power since it was one of the best ways to produce weapons.

The British Crown did not achieve the same level of development—in economic, educational, and social terms—in the southern region, specifically in Virginia. Activity in the southern region was in forestry and agriculture. Due to the size of plantations, slave labor was used to a great extent to plant and process tobacco and cotton. Fully 100 percent of the production was exported to England. Eventually, the area suffered a shortage of rural unskilled labor. The only solution was to import labor from West Africa to perform this work under extreme summer temperatures. Goods from the South were important for the English, who depended on cotton from North America for textile manufacturing and imported tobacco as well.

A huge demand for raw materials drove English-European relations. Likewise, the migration of groups that were in disagreement with religious and economic policies that the British Crown imposed on several European countries. It is noteworthy that some 90 percent of the labor force in the nineteenth century was related directly or indirectly to the South. Horses, cattle, and pigs were raised in this area. Wheat was grown mostly in Pennsylvania, tobacco was grown mostly in Virginia and Maryland, and sheep were raised mostly in the New England region. Rice was grown in South Carolina. This agricultural activity allowed for moderate income but not the accumulation of great wealth. Many entrepreneurs in the South did not own large tracts of land or slaves. Comparing the North with the South, slave labor was not profitable in the North because farmers could not systematically accumulate wealth using third-party labor, meaning slaves.

It is somewhat evident that England did not look favorably on how economic activity was developing in its colonies, so it established certain restrictions to hinder trade. When the War of Independence began, commerce was developing at an equal pace in the different colonial regions, but due to conflicting commercial interests, things collapsed. After peace was achieved, trade reactivated. Using locally manufactured ships, trade expanded to the East and to Africa, bringing good financial returns.

What Made the Bulk of the Economy for the Viceroyalty?

The discovery of mining sites in the center and north of Mexico aided the economy of the viceroyalty (also known as New Spain) to gradually occupy a privileged position, although not specifically in silver mining. However, the development of mining led to complementary activities that turned the Valley of Mexico and Puebla into flourishing agricultural regions. In the sixteenth century, 75 percent of the viceroyalty's resources—in this case precious metals— was exported to Europe. These resources increased the Crown's wealth and were used to underwrite expenses, subsidize wars, and mint coins.

In the 1550s, a transition in the economy began with the development of silver production. Technological management evolved, and an indigenous labor force was used for mining. The discovery of silver deposits was coupled with the widespread application of a mercury amalgamation method for recovering silver from ore. This drove the exploration and exploitation of minerals with silver content. In addition, a 1549 decree prohibited the *encomenderos* (holders of estates granted to Spanish colonists, who were given the labor of particular groups of conquered non-Christian people) from requiring indigenous laborers to provide free labor and tribute. In this way, the distribution of labor was established. During the first period of New Spain, between 1559 and 1627, there was large-scale silver production with an annual growth rate of 2.5 percent.

The framework on which New Spain's economic production was built resulted in a solid monetary infrastructure as well as iron tools and livestock products. As mining activities grew, a demand for agriculture did too. And some of the large haciendas, in addition to agriculture, supported the mining industry by turning into centers where ore was crushed and metals refined. The mining sector involved indigenous people as well as businessmen, travelers, and officials.

But it was not all smooth sailing. There were many problems in mining in New Spain, such as the scarcity of labor due to a decline in the indigenous population and the ravages of sixteenth-century epidemics. This shortage was solved in an apparently simple way, which was to bring in more slaves.

In addition, there was a shortage of mercury. In 1563, mercury from the Huancavelica mines in Peru began to be imported. Mining also wreaked havoc through diseases caused by the harshness of the work, such as arthritis and rheumatism that killed the miners. Help was only given occasionally, and the workers, fed up with this injustice, organized disturbances and rebellions.

It was legal for private individuals to buy land, but the resources or minerals found in the subsoil belonged to the Crown. Any Spaniard or indigenous person could exploit a mine, but they had to pay the equivalent to 20 percent of what was found—known as the *quinto real*—an amount that was later reduced to 10 percent. However, the Crown's direct participation in mining operations was not very common, with the exception of mercury production, an essential element for extracting silver. This allowed the state to control silver mining through payment of a fee that went to the royal treasury.

Silver production helped stimulate substantial development, particularly because silver served as a commodity, a medium of exchange, and currency in New Spain's economy. It is estimated that at the end of the sixteenth century and the beginning of the seventeenth century, an average of between 1.5 and 3 million pesos were minted annually. Half corresponded to the payment of external goods and government transfers, and the other half circulated as part of the viceroyalty's economy. Even cocoa beans were used as a substitute for money.

Exports from the viceroyalty had high profit margins due to low prices in Asia and relatively quick profits. The route used was the perfect addition to the navigation system. Trade was carried out via Mexico as well as Panama and Guatemala. The ships traveled north carrying olives, raisins, salt, cocoa, and mercury, and they returned with merchandise from Asia.

Cocoa, a local product, was soon in high demand. This was reflected in demand from Mexico, which stimulated imports from Guatemala. Later, trade that came from Lima was affected when cocoa from Guayaquil, which had no competition due to its price and excellent quality, was brought to Central America. New Spain's restrictive trade policy, far from being a problem, favored the shippers from Lima. They controlled the flow coming from China at that time and smuggled the cocoa by hiding it in shipments to Guatemala and Panama.

In 1565, the Crown established rules on the cultivation of European plants in Latin America. Wheat was one of the main crops that boomed in the Atlixco-Puebla area. The indigenous people did not have agricultural contracts, but they could make use of their land and planted corn, beans, maguey, cocoa, chili, and agave. The crop most protected by the Crown was sugar. Unlike other products, sugar production was not limited to a certain social group. Owners of the fields as well as sugarcane growers, indigenous people, and sugar mills could all benefit.

In 1645, one of the rules established by the Crown was to regulate wine, a decision that affected business in Guatemala and anyone who enjoyed the good life. Spanish wine producers imagined a disastrous future for their market that was being flooded with wine from the Americas. They pressured the king to prohibit the establishment of new vineyards and to remove those that already existed.

Only the vineyards owned by the church survived. The church was granted special permission to continue producing wine, demonstrating that in the eyes of the law, there are some beverages that are more sacred than others.

By law, the Spanish colonies could only establish trade relations with Spanish ports. The port of Seville controlled this monopoly until 1717, when trading was transferred to the city of Cadiz. The monopoly continued, despite attempts by England, Holland, and France to break it. Those countries tried unsuccessfully for more than two centuries to enter the New Spain market. Their failure left no possibility for any commercial relationship between the different colonies.

These monopolistic practices exposed disparities between the different economic players. Faced with these developments, trade was liberalized through the decree of 1765, which authorized internal trade for five islands: Santo Domingo, Cuba, Trinidad, Margarita, and Puerto Rico, excluding Mexican ports.

However, within the new regulations for the Caribbean, guidelines were established in 1768 that were extended to Louisiana—and to Yucatán and Campeche in 1770. Subsequently, free trade was opened in 1778 for Peru, Río de la Plata, Chile, and other cities in Spain, thus contributing to increased trade on a larger scale.

Mexico: Two Emperors and Sixty-Three Presidents

Mexico, unlike its northern neighbor, has suffered from significant political and democratic instability. Turmoil was even greater between 1829 and 1855; during the same period, the United States grew stronger. In twenty-one years, Mexico had twenty-nine presidents, from Vicente Guerrero to Ignacio Comonfort. In 1855 alone, it had four presidents, and during this period, Antonio Lopez de Santa Anna was president six times. Many years later, in 1913, Mexico suffered a coup d'état known as the Ten Tragic Days. The result was the assassination of President Francisco I. Madero by General Victoriano Huerta, giving way to Pedro Lascurain becoming provisional president of Mexico for only forty-five minutes, enough time to appoint Victoriano Huerta as successor to the coup leader.

In this part of the book, we will analyze two Mexican emperors and sixty-three presidents and then continue with the political and democratic lives of the presidents of the United States of America.

The first emperor of independent Mexico, and with whom we will open the thread of the country's democratic history, is Agustin de Iturbide. Starting in December 1822, Antonio Lopez de Santa Anna and Guadalupe Victoria led an armed uprising against him, overthrowing the emperor and sending him into exile. A year later, he returned to the country, believing that the people would receive him with open arms. After landing at Soto la Marina, Tamaulipas, he was apprehended and shot—a somewhat different ending than that of the first president of the United States, who was acclaimed and loved as a representative of the interests of American society.

The first president of Mexico (Agustin de Iturbide is not considered president, but emperor) was Guadalupe Victoria, whose real name was Jose Miguel Ramon Adaucto Fernandez Felix. He faced three crucial problems: the precarious economic situation, the intentions of the United States to renegotiate a new border and acquire Texas, and the ambitions of various *caudillos* (a type of personalist leader wielding military and political power). Next up was Vicente Guerrero, who during an absence from the capital was declared mentally incapable of governing by Congress. This left him without any support, and he fled to the south of Mexico, taking refuge in the mountains. Following the custom of the time, at the beginning of February 1831, he was betrayed and shot.

The period of President Jose Maria Bocanegra was so fleeting that, as historians, we need to rescue his contributions in order to better understand the first half of the nineteenth century in Mexico. Pedro Velez De Zuñiga did not make a mark on politics and retired to private life following his presidency, never to participate in government again. Anastasio Bustamante fought against the US intervention. Later, he actively participated in the pacification of Guanajuato, Aguascalientes, and the Sierra Gorda.

President Melchor Muzquiz was the victim of betrayals by Bustamante, Santa Anna, and Manuel Gomez Pedraza, who agreed that the latter would become the new president, displacing Muzquiz.

It is important to mention President Valentin Gomez Farias. He tried unsuccessfully to carry out some reforms in the country, but he was hindered by a centralist and partisan system that existed at that time in Mexico. In 1848, Gomez Farias was among those who opposed the peace treaties with the United States. An honest and austere president, Miguel Barragan, was in charge of leading the country from federalism to centralism. In February 1836, while attending to the affairs of the Texas war, a typhus infection led to his death a few days after contracting the disease. Jose Justo Corro was an excessively religious president, very weak decision maker, and oblivious to military matters that were important during a time of war. It is important to mention that at the end of his term, he devoted himself to religious practices with such zeal that he was nicknamed El Santo (the Saint).

In 1842, President Nicolas Bravo had the audacity to dissolve the Congress, which had intended to discuss a new Constitution, contrary to his interests. In 1847, he occupied the position of commander in chief of the country's capital. This position allowed him to organize a fierce defense of Chapultepec Castle against the American forces that invaded Mexico City. President Francisco Javier Echeverria saved the San Carlos Academy of Fine Arts from ruin and also pushed for a House of Correction for Youth. Valentin Canalizo, faced with constant armed uprisings occurring in the country, appointed Santa Anna as commander in chief. This decision caused much commotion among the people since it was not legal for an interim president (President Canalizo) to give orders to a constitutional president on leave.

President Mariano Paredes y Arrillaga was a fervent patriot who protested against the peace treaties signed with the United States. He took the city of Guanajuato and was a fugitive in the Sierra Gorda until he contracted a disease that caused his death. Jose Mariano Salas assumed the interim presidency. Since his presidency was provisional and brief, he was unsuccessful in getting enough resources for the war that was taking place in the north and also failed in attempts to put the country in order due to the war.

During the US intervention in Mexico, General Pedro Maria Anaya presided over Congress. His conduct at the beginning of the war was unsure and indecisive until he was named interim president of Mexico in substitution of Antonio Lopez de Santa Anna. When the US intervention began, Manuel De La Peña y Peña presided over the Supreme Court of Justice. During the invasion, northern Mexico and the country's main ports fell into US hands—and even the capital of the country was besieged by General Scott. When Lopez de Santa Anna fled, Peña y Peña assumed the office as interim president. This new government was headquartered in Toluca and tasked with achieving peace with the United States.

President Jose Joaquin De Herrera is notable because he was able to hand over power in a peaceful and constitutional manner. This might seem normal and commonplace in other nations, but in Mexico of that time, it was the exception. So much so that such a display of civility had not been seen since 1829. President Mariano Arista was faced with a terrible financial situation that unleashed an uprising to bring Santa Anna back to power. This difficult situation forced his resignation. The next president, Juan Bautista Ceballos, also resigned due to the same events. President Manuel Maria Lombardini also had a transitory government and did not form a cabinet, instead focusing his efforts on undoing the causes of the civil war.

At the beginning of Mexico's independence, several events helped Santa Anna's rise to power. However, what reinforced his ambition were the uprisings of 1827 that unexpectedly placed him in government. President Martin Carrera was only in the government provisionally and had few political ambitions. One of his contributions was to separate political and military commands. He also allowed freedom of the press. Romulo Diaz De La Vega was a president who was part of the *junta of notables* (a group of Conservatives) that adopted the monarchy and invited Maximilian of Habsburg to be emperor of Mexico. After the triumph of the republic, he was sentenced to two years in prison.

The last emperor of Mexico was Maximilian of Habsburg. He arrived from Austria with good intentions and even asked for democracy to be respected (or else he would not rule a nation that did not want him as leader). These good intentions, however, were not enough to set things right in a country that was in chaos thanks to previous governments and the multiple struggles and battles unleashed in recent years. His reign is known as the Second Mexican Empire, and he ruled the country alongside the Republican government of Benito Juarez. His reign is mostly remembered for its brevity and tragic end. Abandoned by his foreign allies, Maximilian was left without support to prevail over Benito Juarez. After losing his last forces at Cerro de las Campanas, Queretaro, Maximillian was captured, brought to trial by the Republicans, and condemned to death. Important figures in world literature, including Victor Hugo and Charles Dickens, implored President Juarez to pardon Maximilian. Queen Victoria and Isabel II of Spain also did the same. Nothing worked. Juarez, responding that the law and the sentence were inexorable, maintained his position. At three o'clock on the afternoon of June 19, 1867, Maximilian of Habsburg was shot at Cerro de las Campanas along with his generals Miguel Miramon and Tomas Mejia. His last words were: "Long live Mexico, long live Independence."

Jose de la Cruz Porfirio Diaz Mori, known as Porfirio Diaz, is considered a hero by some and a villain by others. He ruled Mexico for thirty years. Clearly both his achievements and his failures have to be discussed. I promise that we will talk more in depth about this character in the following chapters of the book. It is important not to make the mistake of calling his time in office a dictatorship, as his presidency is marked by great successes for the nation's history.

Another man we cannot fail to mention in the country's history is President Lazaro Cardenas del Río, whose military career helped him reach the presidency. Cardenas is notable because of a very important historical event. I am referring to oil expropriation, which will be covered in another chapter. This has elevated him as one of the country's modern heroes. As part of his agrarian land reform, he created *ejidos* (an area of communal land mainly used for agriculture, on which community members farm designated plots and collectively maintain communal holdings), and during the Spanish Civil War, he provided political asylum to Spanish exiles.

The government of Adolfo Ruiz Cortines laid the foundations for stabilizing development. His discreet and austere approach allowed for economic growth without inflation. The next president, Adolfo Lopez Mateos, faced social unrest such as the railroad workers' strike of 1959 and an armed revolt against the government led by the campesino leader Ruben Jaramillo.

Gustavo Diaz Ordaz was a president highly questioned for his oppression of social groups, specifically the protesting students who felt his heavy hand the most. Seeking to end a student strike that had been going on for several months and that risked the viability of the first Olympic games held in Mexico, Diaz Ordaz gave the final order that culminated in the implementation of a military operation called Operation Galeana. Its fateful outcome was a massacre in the Plaza de las Tres Culturas in Mexico City on October 2, 1968. This event haunted him throughout his life, and he was never able to shake off being considered the worst authoritarian in the country's history.

Luis Echeverria became president in a political climate dominated by student mobilizations and protests. Both the PRI and President Echeverria made several efforts to neutralize the extremely politicized youth. However, social discontent was high in most of the country's major cities. During his term, a violent repression of demonstrators occurred, known as El Halconazo, or the Thursday of Corpus Christi massacre. On his orders, Mexico opened its arms to hundreds of exiles fleeing the military dictatorships of South America. At the same time, he was hard on the Mexican youth and the Mexican left. He died at the age of 100. His wake was modest, without the vainglory of the immense power he once held.

Jose Lopez Portillo was next. This president found a polarized country, and, to a great extent, a chaotic public administration apparatus inherited from his predecessor. However, his first speech in 1976 gained Lopez Portillo support and trust due to his great interest in conciliation. During his administration, important oil wells were found that brought a tremendous amount of money to the Mexican state. In the face of these discoveries of black gold, Lopez Portillo himself declared that Mexico was now ready to manage the abundance. Unfortunately, the party was over too soon. From one moment to the next, oil prices plummeted, causing a terrible economic crisis and capital flight.

Then came Miguel de la Madrid's turn. His government was marked by several major events, such as the devastating earthquake that occurred on September 19, 1985, in Mexico City. The apparent absence of the government during the catastrophe united Mexican civil society, which did not wait for help or permission from the government to start rescuing injured people from the rubble.

Carlos Salinas De Gortari assumed the presidency of Mexico after highly controversial elections under the suspicion of electoral fraud. During his administration, the economic changes initiated by his predecessor, Miguel de la Madrid, were deepened. These changes included the signing of the North American Free Trade Agreement, the privatization of state-owned companies, and the implementation of the National Solidarity Program, a crusade to combat extreme poverty. In addition, relations between church and state were restored, and diplomatic relations were established with the Holy See. Apparently, everything was going great during the Salinas administration. Just when he felt he was the king of the world, the wind of misfortune caught up with him. The Zapatista Army of National Liberation (EZLN, for the acronym in Spanish) took up arms in Chiapas on the first day of 1994. This political crisis as well as assassinations that scandalized the country—notably the assassination of presidential candidate Luis Donaldo Colosio—threw away forever his colossal dreams of greatness.

Ernesto Zedillo Ponce De Leon arrived to clean up the previous government's mess, as was also customary in Mexico's history. During his presidency, he faced one of the worst economic crises ever, which began a few weeks after taking office. What a welcome gift the new president received. He distanced himself from his predecessor, Carlos Salinas de Gortari, blaming him for the crisis and all the ills of the world. His administration was also marked, among other things, by new confrontations with the EZLN and the Popular Revolutionary Army. He fully supported competitive elections in the year 2000, which allowed the presidency to be won for the first time in seventy years by a candidate from outside the PRI.

Dissatisfaction with the kind of participatory democracy that the PRI represented allowed Mexico to break the hegemony of a single political party. The elections were won by the PAN (National Action Party) and Vicente Fox Quesada. Fox assumed the presidency with one of the highest popularity ratings in recent Mexican history. However, the honeymoon gradually ended, mostly due to disagreements about the administration of the executive branch. Fox did not dare to break with the old political system. The mandate for change was too big for him. The once-great candidate ended up becoming a disappointing president.

In spite of disappointment with Vicente Fox, support for the PAN continued for another term. Felipe Calderon Hinojosa assumed the presidency after a controversial election that was won by a very narrow margin. The election was so controversial that Felipe Calderon was inaugurated in the Congress accompanied by a strong military and police presence, not in a republican ceremony as the Constitution dictates. It would seem that the disaster of the inauguration was an omen for the future. Added to this was a devastating policy against organized crime that led the country into a war against criminal groups, which left many families suffering and numerous lawsuits for violation of human rights. The consequences of this war against drug trafficking are still being felt in Mexico even today.

The next president of Mexico was Enrique Peña Nieto. He represented the return of the PRI to power after twelve years. He promised important constitutional reforms, progress, order, and prosperity. But his mandate was plagued by numerous corruption scandals, demonstrating that the PRI had not changed, no matter how much it swore it had.

And so, we come to the current democratically elected president. Andres Manuel Lopez Obrador assumed the government of Mexico after eighteen years of struggles and sacrifices. More than once, he was denied and robbed of the possibility of reaching the presidency. However, he never gave up, and as the saying goes: "Victory belongs to those who persevere." President Lopez Obrador, who has a very high approval rating, is leading the Fourth Transformation of Mexico. To this end, he is implementing a policy of austerity at the highest levels to address the acts of corruption and waste that characterized previous governments. Lopez Obrador is convinced that the fight against corruption must be like a stairway that is cleaned from the top down. One of the measures worth highlighting is the appointment, for the first time in Mexico's history, of a woman as head of the Ministry of the Interior.

Olga Sanchez Cordero held the office until August 16, 2021, when she returned to the Senate. Another achievement of President Lopez Obrador is putting the less fortunate—those who have been ignored by power all their lives—at the center of the national debate. Lopez Obrador's triumph was not solitary; the common people—who were unjustly always used to losing—won too.

I believe that the political instability under which Mexico was born has been improving. Today, we have a head of state who represents social interests more than partisan ones. We have gone from bipartisanship to a single idea of a country. Although it is not enough, we can be sure that it is the beginning of a change in the political and democratic history of the nation.

Joe Biden: Forty-Sixth President of the United States of America

The political stability of the United States contrasts with the conflictive Mexican reality. This is evident by looking at the number of presidents that both countries have had throughout their histories. While it is true that the birth of both countries is different due to their internal wars, the democratic trajectory in both countries is also different. To illustrate this, we will take a brief look at each president of the United States in contrast to what took place in Mexico.

George Washington (1789–1797), also known as the father of the country, was its first president as well as a prosperous farmer and slaveholder. Despite this stain, he is remembered as a man who was committed to his country in the fight for its independence.

Following Washington was John Adams (1797–1801). He belonged to the Federalist Party and was in charge during the Boston Massacre. After making the decision to remain in Washington's cabinet, he lost credibility with the people. Thomas Jefferson (1801–1809) was recognized for his liberal ideas and always moved in important political circles. He was also a pioneer in the defense of Native Americans, which benefited the United States.

James Madison (1809–1817), known as the father of the Constitution, reduced the country's debt and taxes. He had also participated in the movement for US independence. James Monroe (1817–1825), formerly Secretary of State, was president when an economic crisis hit the country, and unemployment grew as a result. John Quincy Adams (1825–1829) had a background as a public servant working in different political parties. He was the son of one of the founding fathers, John Adams. Andrew Jackson (1829–1837) was the seventh president of the United States. A victim of the War of Independence due to his English background, he was the first president to have been a prisoner of war.

Martin Van Buren (1837–1841) is infamous for being in office during an economic crisis that destabilized some important sectors of the economy. A well-known Democrat, he came to power with Jackson's help. William Henry Harrison (1841–1841) was in power one month before his death. He died thirty-one days after taking office as a result of a bad cold he contracted after giving a long inaugural speech in the rain. However, he is remembered for his great work as secretary of the Northwest Territory. John Tyler (1841–1845) was president during the acquisition of Texas. Among his contributions were construction of the Center for Meteorological Studies and ending the war with the Seminole Indians in Florida. James Knox Polk (1845–1849) was at the forefront of the war in which Mexico ceded Arizona, New Mexico, California, and Nevada, expanding the US border to the Rio Grande and the Pacific Ocean.

Under Zachary Taylor (1849–1850), who was known for his military strategies, partisan tensions (over slavery) accelerated. Due to the annexation of Texas, tense relations with Mexico also continued. Millard Fillmore (1850–1853) became president upon Taylor's death. Unfortunately, he is recognized for being one of the least effective presidents in all of US history. Franklin Pierce (1853–1857) alienated antislavery groups, signed trade treaties with Great Britain and Japan, and failed in an attempt to acquire Cuba.

James Buchanan (1857–1861) is considered the worst president the United States has ever had. He was impassive in the face of growing divisions over the slavery issue, which in the long run ended up unleashing the Civil War. In other words, Buchanan watched the monster grow without daring to confront it.

There is no doubt that Abraham Lincoln (1861–1865) is one of the most highly regarded presidents in history. He set the United States on the road to becoming the great power it is today and led the country through the Civil War. Sadly, Lincoln was shot by an actor sympathetic to the Southern cause at a theater in Washington, DC, joining the short list of American presidents assassinated in office.

After Abraham Lincoln's assassination, Andrew Johnson (1865–1869), assumed the presidency and had the challenge of having to fill very big shoes. He is remembered for being the first president to be impeached, primarily because he advocated for reconciliation with the South.

Ulysses S. Grant (1869–1877) was a man of the people and, following Lincoln's example, favored reunification and reconstruction. He was able to remove the last vestiges of slavery and worked to protect the African American communities in the country. During the presidency of Rutherford B. Hayes (1877–1881), people began to trust in politics again, and he kept up the work of his predecessors. James A. Garfield (1881–1881) was only in office a short time, just six months and fifteen days. He was the target of an attempted assassination. He did not die from the shots that hit him but from an infection caused by doctors who treated his wounds. It could be said that the cure was worse than the disease.

After Garfield's death, Chester A. Arthur (1881–1885) took office as president and removed the cabinet members of the previous administration. Grover Cleveland (1885–1889) was a president who, due to his honesty, was extremely popular. However, during his term, the US underwent an economic crisis, and he lost control of his party.

Next was Benjamin Harrison (1889–1893). During his term, Republicans came into power in both the Senate and the House of Representatives. He came from a political family and had been active in politics since he was a young man. William McKinley (1897–1901) increased commercial activity and was recognized for supporting the independence of Cuba. He was reelected to the presidency in 1900.

Theodore Roosevelt (1901–1909) is one of the most popular presidents in the country's history. He managed to regulate economic activity in the United States. William Howard Taft's (1909–1913) term in office was ineffective due to a series of policy decisions that affected tariffs and transportation rates.

Woodrow Wilson (1913–1921) had to face no less than the onset of the First World War. He also had a fractious relationship with Mexico because of occasional skirmishes and gunfire across the border areas during the Mexican Revolution. Warren G. Harding (1921–1923) implemented social programs for medical assistance and federal subsidies as well as labor reforms and the eight-hour workday. However, pressure made him give up some of his presidential responsibilities. Calvin Coolidge (1923–1929) came to power in the midst of political, economic, and social problems. He also won passage of three major tax cuts, making him highly popular. Herbert Hoover (1929–1933) guided the United States through the economic and political crisis of the stock market crash and Great Depression of 1929. Despite this, he failed to achieve economic recovery. Franklin Delano Roosevelt (1933–1945) overcame the crisis of 1929 through the New Deal. He also led his country during World War II, joining the conflict after the infamous Japanese bombing of Pearl Harbor.

Harry S. Truman (1945–1953) had in his hands one of the most difficult and controversial decisions in world history. To end World War II, he used nuclear weapons against Japan, something that fortunately has never been repeated. He also refused to participate in the war in China and made an air link to Berlin a reality.

Dwight D. Eisenhower (1953–1961) initiated the space race against the Soviet Union, built infrastructure, and sent American troops to defend South Vietnam from the Vietcong. President John F. Kennedy (1961–1963) was the first Catholic president of the United States. His charismatic personality opened many doors for him in the political arena. He faced the Cuban missile crisis and sought ways to remove Fidel Castro, which led to a CIA fiasco known as the

Bay of Pigs invasion. He was assassinated by Lee Harvey Oswald on November 22, 1963, while touring Dallas in a convertible car with his wife, Jackie Kennedy.

Lyndon B. Johnson (1963–1969) took office after Kennedy's assassination. He focused on fighting racial segregation. There were many protests against his administration due to the Vietnam War and labor discrimination.

Richard Nixon (1969–1974) improved relations with China and the Soviet Union. To counteract demonstrations against the Vietnam War and the youth counterculture, his campaign targeted what he called the "silent majority." He resigned from office after the Watergate scandal, where it was discovered that President Nixon had ordered illegal spying on political rivals. Gerald Ford's objective (1974–1977) was the economic stability of the nation, though he was unable to achieve this. During his presidency, he had to address the energy crisis. The Vietnam War finally ended while Ford was president, but it was considered a defeat since the United States was never able to control all the territory it invaded and bombed.

The next president was Jimmy Carter (1977–1981). The country went through economic weakness and high inflation, and the Iran hostage crisis contributed to his loss of the presidency. Ronald Reagan (1981–1989) is considered an advocate of economic liberalism as a school of thought. He favored aggressive tax cuts and the reduction of the state apparatus. He was also a fierce proponent of the war on drugs.

George H. W. Bush (1989–1993) was an oil businessman with ambitions of becoming president of the United States. He witnessed the fall of the Berlin Wall and the dissolution of the Soviet Union. Because he broke several campaign promises, including the promise not to create new tax rates, he lost his reelection bid to a young but astute politician named Clinton.

Bill Clinton (1993–2001), the youngest president to be elected, thwarted Bush's reelection. He was criticized for some of the indiscretions he committed while in office, such as his infidelity with Monica Lewinsky, a White House intern. This scandal led to his impeachment for having lied to the American people when he denied his relationship with Lewinsky.

George W. Bush (2001–2009), son of the former Republican president, was a Texas businessman who focused on the war on terror. The world changed forever after the terrible terrorist attacks that destroyed the Twin Towers and damaged the Pentagon. Bush started a military campaign in Afghanistan and Iraq, which ultimately ended up costing the United States a lot of resources and blood.

Barack Obama (2009–2018) made history by becoming the first African American president of the United States. He took charge of solving the economic crisis of 2008 and also helped to strengthen US security. Considered highly efficient, he managed to eliminate Osama Bin Laden, enemy number one of the United States.

Donald Trump (2017–2020) is undoubtedly one of the most controversial presidents in recent years—if not in all of history. Hailing from the world of television and entertainment, Trump promised to end government corruption by "draining the swamp" in Washington. His immigration policies were harshly criticized since he favored the deportation of millions of Mexicans living illegally in the United States. But if anything characterized this president, it was his plan to build a border wall with Mexico, which was one of his main campaign promises. It should be remembered that on August 27, 2017, Trump assured Americans that Mexico would pay for the construction of the wall through reimbursements or other means. However, Mexico responded that this would not be the case and that this was not under negotiation as foreign policy.

Joe Biden, forty-sixth president of the United States, was sworn in amid record numbers of infections due to the COVID-19 pandemic, one of the world's greatest health catastrophes. His administration implemented unprecedented health measures. In addition, President Biden's inauguration was marked by a huge security deployment due to threats from Donald Trump's supporters. It was undoubtedly the tensest presidential inauguration in recent US history.

After this brief overview of the democratic history of both countries, it becomes clear that the two are very distant, especially in political and social terms. While the United States has had forty-six presidents since its independence as a nation, Mexico has had almost twenty more presidents with fewer years of independence. And, yes, the circumstances have been completely different, as already established. However, it is something to acknowledge when comparing the two nations and that will be expanded upon in other sections of this book.

Counting votes in Times Square. Photo by
Mariano Moreno, November 2016.

Chapter 5

Patchwork or Amendments

We the People in 1787

The constitution of a country makes clear the historical background and the reality of its people who, in the spirit of community, accept certain rules of governance. Both Mexico and the United States established their identities as independent nations based on their constitutions. If we think about how these laws and principles—so essential for democracy—came about, we find a marked historical difference between the two countries. The United States has preserved the same Constitution since it was adopted. Mexico's Constitution, conversely, has been subject to constant partial modifications. Changes that depend, in part, on the policy agenda of the president in office.

Mexico has had several constitutions throughout its history, each different from the others. Their drafting and enactment have been a consequence of rebellion and dissent when people took up arms against whoever was in office. Each constitution has also contributed something to the next one, until finally transforming into the *magna carta* that governs Mexico today. Like someone who tries on different shoe styles until finding the one that fits best, Mexico has gone from constitution to constitution due to political instability and frequent armed conflicts.

In contrast, the United States Constitution has been the same since it was signed on September 17, 1787. Just like the Americans say: If ain't broke, don't fix it. Although twenty-seven amendments have subsequently been made to the US constitution, this is a very small number of changes considering the almost two and a half centuries since its enactment in Philadelphia.

The United States' use of amendments, without modifying the original text of the constitution, is notable. In Mexico, the custom has been to reform the constitution all the time, as if the problem were the lack of more laws and not that the existing ones are ignored in most cases. This constant alteration distances modern laws from the spirit that contributed to the birth of the Mexican nation.

Although their beginnings have different contexts and reasons, something unites the constitutional texts of Mexico and the United States. What motivates the signing of the US Constitution in Philadelphia and the signing of the Mexican constitution in Queretaro are revolutionary movements that sought to achieve peace and governability by creating a project of nationhood.

Regarding the Mexican constitution, it is worth pointing out that its signing in Queretaro is based on a series of changes to previous constitutions—those of 1824 and 1857. The latter is considered the foundation, without losing sight of the fact that it is based on a political dispute among elites. It is a project with a vision of a republic, federative and liberal at its core, which reaffirms the abolition of slavery, stops the excesses of the church and advocates individual guarantees and freedom of expression. This document was an attempt to achieve a long period of peace—without achieving it, of course. The virtues of the 1857 constitution were not recognized by the Conservative Party, unleashing the Reform War, which we will come to later.

As for the United States, the times forced a change to the Articles of Confederation. As a result, the US has its first and only Constitution. To understand a constitution's content and how it works, one needs to get a better, more detailed, and far-reaching view of each country's beginnings.

Let's go back to the end of 1777, when the North American colonies fought the War of Independence against England, and the Congress approved the Articles of Confederation. These articles become a document to unite the thirteen colonies and serve as the first frame of an independent government.

The document is made up of sixteen articles and a brief conclusion. Although this is the first official document that accredits the colonies as the "United States of America," such designation would come years later when they become free and sovereign states following the war against the English. In addition, it is also worth noting that some of the colonies distrusted the Congress.

Let's look in on a colonist who victoriously claims the triumph of the thirteen colonies over the English. After fighting so many battles, inhaling gunpowder from countless rifles, and coming close to death many times, this colonist declares himself free. But from experience, he knows that he should be wary. Like his companions in the struggle, he agrees on the need for a document that will serve as a foundation and guide to self-governance. The last thing they want is to be subject to a central government, given the experience with the English Crown that led them to war.

The year is 1786. This freedom fighter lives by selling goods to other countries. He is worried because the colonies, now renamed states, do significant business through foreign trade. But business with England hangs by a thread since the English refuse to negotiate unless there is a treaty with each and every one of the thirteen colonies; they want a direct and separate deal with each colony.

Faced with such a dilemma, our protagonist is in favor of reaching consensus among all the states. The task does not sound easy. A constitutional convention is called to take place in the city of Annapolis. Only five states participate: Delaware, New Jersey, New York, Pennsylvania, and Virginia.

During a four-day session, the participants draft a report and send it to the congress. This document requests the presence of all the states through delegates authorized to express opinions and make proposals on a future federal constitution.

The congress listens to the presentations, evaluates the report, and approves it. On February 21, 1787, they extended an invitation to all the states to attend a convention scheduled for May in Philadelphia.

The purpose is urgent: to review and evaluate the Articles of Confederation in order to subsequently create a federal constitution.

The response is favorable, and twelve states out of thirteen attend. Only Rhode Island plays hard to get by refusing to participate and does not send any representative. A total of fifty-five delegates ends up attending the event.

Our protagonist, who participated in the War of Independence, has the honor of being chosen as his state's delegate. He is young, not more than thirty years old, as are four other delegates; the average age is between thirty and forty. All of them have the support of some of the founding fathers, such as Thomas Jefferson and John Adams.

This is a generation with well-defined goals and a clear vision of what they want for their state and the federation. Consequently, their position is based on empirical, rather than theoretical, knowledge.

The main focus of the convention was to deal with issues related to modifying the Articles of Confederation, but a group of nationalists proposed additions to the agenda. One of them is Edmund Randolph, who introduces the Virginia Plan, which contains a government structure for the republic. The proposal lacks robustness and does not address the root of the core problem. Randolph's plan is fervently discussed for two weeks.

William Paterson presents a counter proposal called the New Jersey Plan. It is quite similar to the Articles of Confederation—with one difference that serves as a precedent for the supreme law. Treaties approved by Congress, and any other law endorsed by Congress, will be considered supreme law. In other words, in the event that one of the laws (or treaties) of any of the thirteen states should conflict with the one endorsed by Congress, the one approved by Congress will prevail. The judiciary of each state would have to abide by the provisions of Congress.

The motion is not to the liking of the larger states, which were not convinced of the idea of a supreme law, so they supported the Virginia Plan. The discussion stretches on until finally they accept the New Jersey Plan proposed by William Paterson. The conclusion is that a complete and perfect Constitution would take longer than expected—and that the creation of a new government was urgent.

In exchange, they resort to a more straightforward charter that the American people can accept.

Commercial, and now political, interests would have to be included in this legislative project. The Federal Convention spent months listening to proposals, complaints, claims, problems, solutions, and problems with the solutions to problems. Although there were many disagreements among the states, the desire to strengthen trade relations kept them united and involved in this constitutional project. When all the states reached agreement as to what the Constitution should contain, it was approved and signed on September 17, 1787.

The painting by Howard Chandler Christy, *Scene of the Signing of the Constitution of the United States*, shows the setting. Hanging from the ceiling, a gilded chandelier bears witness to the bustle below. The men assembled there, dressed in striking clothing with white hair, are ready to sign the Constitution of the United States of America. These men are about to create a nation. Light coming through the windows illuminates the sacred document that is about to be signed. Benjamin Franklin, seated with a cane in his hand, listens attentively as Alexander Hamilton whispers in his ear.

Secretary William Jackson keeps his arm raised, as if politely asking to speak to an unheeding audience. Only one of these men looks at us, the spectators of that historic scene. He is Robert Morris, better known as the financier of the revolution of the thirteen colonies. Sitting beside an open book, his hands clasped, Morris looks at us as if posing seriously for a photograph. Standing out from the others, at the highest point of the room, George Washington puffs out his chest. Next to him, Richard Dobbs Spaight signs the document on behalf of North Carolina. But Washington's gaze is not directed at any other member of the Philadelphia Convention; he is focused on something more distant that cannot be seen in the oil painting. No one else is looking at what he sees. While most of the convention looks at Washington, he looks upward, triumphant. What is he looking at? What is it that triggers his proud stance? An ambition, a project, an idea for a country? Washington is looking at the outcome of the signing before it even exists, hence his satisfaction. He does not need to live more years to witness how far the dominance and power of the United States will reach. He already knows. Away from the noise of the great hall, George Washington's gaze lingers gloriously as he envisions the future that will someday come.

All members of the convention are satisfied with the results obtained, and the course is set for the nation. Still pending is the approval of the document, which requires at least nine of thirteen states. So the process continues, and in the struggle for the ratification of the Constitution, the country is divided into two large groups: the Federalists who want the Constitution to be ratified and the Anti-Federalists, open opponents to ratification.

Our protagonist takes the side of the Federalists. This group is made up of a majority of young people with intelligence and vision, just like him. For their part, the Anti-Federalists appeal to the voice of the people and argue that to accept a constitution as proposed by the Federalists would be to follow the fateful path of Rome in its time of empire. Federalists believe that old or conservative ideas are unhelpful, that states do not need division or independent government but rather require a general union that will enable them to influence the world. Like our anonymous protagonist, they consider trade a transcendent issue that should be regulated by a central government and not individually by each state.

With such conflicting positions, the ratification of the Constitution is not easy. Meanwhile, the Federalists argue that the Constitution should also define citizens' rights. For this reason, on February 6, 1788, the Massachusetts Convention ratified the amendments to the Constitution, which became known as the Bill of Rights.

It was not until 1789 that the Congress of the Confederation declared the Constitution ratified and legal in what would become known as the Union. Each signatory state now obeyed under the umbrella of the Constitution, with the exception of Rhode Island—the only state to reject it in its convention of 1788. It would not be until May 29, 1790, when Rhode Island would stop its tantrum and decide to ratify the constitutional document. Its recapitulation was due to the subtle warning that, as a foreign government, it would be excluded from trade with the union of states. No longer feeling so self-important, Rhode Island finally joined. The US Constitution with its twenty-seven amendments came into being. After so many negotiations, assemblies, and debates, a constitution with seven articles and 7,591 words makes history.

The Twenty-Seven Amendments to the Constitution of the United States

The first ten amendments to the US Constitution are known as the Bill of Rights. In fact, there are thirty-three amendments in all, but only twenty-seven are currently in effect. We should note that some amendments to the Constitution have already expired or have not been ratified. To understand the nature and purpose of the amendments, it is necessary to delve into their historical context.

The First Amendment refers to the freedoms of worship and expression. As stated in this amendment, Congress exempts the establishment of religion or the prohibition of the free exercise thereof. It does not impose obstacles to the freedoms of speech or press, and it does not abridge the right of the people to peaceably assemble or to petition for the redress of grievances.

Remember: the first Puritan settlers fled their land because of religious persecution, and their community foundations are based on biblical principles and the free exercise of their faith. The First Amendment is of transcendent value to both the founding fathers and American citizens.

The Second and Third Amendments emerge from the same historical background. The Second Amendment refers to the controversial right to bear arms. It reads: "A well regulated Militia being necessary to the security of a free State, the right of the people to keep and bear Arms shall not be infringed." In other words, neither federal, state, nor municipal governments may prevent any citizen from carrying firearms within its territory. Several critics of this amendment claim that violence in the streets or massacres in schools would be prevented by banning, or even regulating, the sale of guns. On the other hand, proponents of this amendment believe that a population with access to firearms is more effective against crime than the police, and that gun ownership prevents the eventual arrival of a tyrannical government. In their logic, if an authoritarian, despotic, and cruel government comes to power, citizens should have an arsenal to overthrow it. The truth is that the American love of guns is a complex issue, a strange world, which at times has found defenders in both the Democratic and Republican Parties. This is partly due to the enormous power of gun manufacturers and the National Rifle Association, better known as the NRA, which have been able to profit from leeway in the Second Amendment's text. As for the Third Amendment, it prohibits the housing of military personnel in private homes in times of peace without the consent of the owner.

The US Constitution is the consequence of the War of Independence. During that time, our anonymous protagonist, his family, and his friends had to be alert in case of an enemy counterattack. Therefore, he openly applauds the Second Amendment, feeling safe living in a house with access to rifles and pistols. He also feels secure in the Third Amendment, which provides that no soldier can be lodged in or enter any citizen's home if not permitted to do so, even in time of war, except in the manner described by law.

The Fourth to the Eighth Amendments were created based on the experience of the legislators and what they observed during the years under English rule. Consequently, they chose a series of rights that had been unknown until then. The Fourth Amendment protects unreasonable searches and seizures and sets out requirements for search warrants based on probable cause. The Fifth Amendment achieves a significance that will end up as a favorite theme, decades later, in Hollywood cop shows and movies. The provision warns that if someone is a suspect and is being questioned about a crime, that person has the right to not incriminate himself. That's why when we see police officers arresting a suspect the first thing they tell them is:

"You have the right to remain silent, anything you say can and will be used against you."

The Sixth Amendment also covers part of judicial procedure. This amendment says that the accused must be informed of the crime they are accused of, how the trial will be conducted, and other guarantees as well as advised of their right to a defense attorney. The Seventh Amendment states that the defendant must have a jury present at the trial. The Eighth Amendment states that fines or bail shall not be excessive at any time and also prohibits cruel and unusual punishment.

The Ninth Amendment deserves a separate mention since it refers to implied rights that are not written in the Constitution but are still inherent to individuals. This amendment prevents states, authorities, or courts from riding roughshod over the rights of the people on the grounds that they are not described in the supreme law.

The Tenth Amendment is the last of the Bills of Rights. It alludes to the reserved powers that rest in the people as well as in each of the states that make up the Union. In sum, the amendments described above are the most important for the citizens of the United States since they name individual guarantees. Let's continue with the rest of the amendments.

The Eleventh Amendment makes states immune from foreign lawsuits; that is, out-of-state citizens or foreigners not living within the state borders may not use the US judiciary as a resource to initiate litigation against one of the states. It is worth remembering that following the creation of the Constitution to bind the colonies together, any entity reluctant to sign the charter is considered a foreign state.

The Twelfth Amendment outlines the process to be followed in presidential elections and also the manner in which a vice president is to be elected. The provision includes all possible scenarios in the event that a majority of votes for a president is not achieved or if the person elected does not qualify for the office. The amendment covers all scenarios to avoid any possible future dissatisfaction on the part of the citizens as well as to avoid mismanagement by the Senate.

Sixty-three years after the Twelfth Amendment—in 1865, just after the Civil War—the Thirteenth Amendment was enacted. It decrees the abolition of slavery. Again, the historical context is fundamental; the Civil War laid the groundwork for abolishing slavery in the United States.

The Fourteenth Amendment is one of the most extensive. It has five sections and addresses issues of citizenship as well as the equal protection and due process that every citizen deserves.

The Fifteenth Amendment says that no state shall abridge the right of any person to vote on account of race or ancestry. It further states that Congress has full power to enforce this article by law. Federal taxes are included in the Sixteenth Amendment while the Seventeenth Amendment indicates the manner in which elections for the US Senate shall be conducted. The Eighteenth Amendment, which establishes a dry law prohibiting the sale, distribution, and production of alcohol, will be examined in a separate section of this chapter.

The Nineteenth Amendment establishes the right of women to vote. This fundamental right was achieved after many marches, hunger strikes, and protests. Prior to this amendment, whether women were allowed to vote or not depended on the laws of their respective states. In California, there was full suffrage for women, but in Texas, women could only vote in municipal elections—and in other places like Alabama and Pennsylvania, this right was completely denied. Every time women organized to claim their right to vote, Congress rejected them. It was thanks to the patriotic role of American women during World War I that public opinion demanded that women be compensated with the right to vote. This pressured President Woodrow Wilson to support this amendment in 1918, which was approved on May 21, 1919.

The Twentieth Amendment defines when the president assumes office as well as Congress. It also establishes the protocol to be followed in case of absence of both the president and the vice president, so that no one panics—and everyone knows what to do in such a scenario.

The Twenty-First Amendment officially repealed the Eighteenth Amendment that imposed dry laws and prohibited the sale of alcohol.

This amendment was published and became effective thirteen years after the ban. The limitation to serve more than two presidential terms is included in the Twenty-Second Amendment; its validity applies as long as it is ratified by three-fourths of the states.

The Twenty-Third Amendment grants electors in the Electoral College to the District of Columbia. Failure to pay taxes, as provided for in the Twenty-Fourth Amendment, does not constitute grounds for restricting the right to vote for any citizen.

In the event that something happens to the president while in office, such as an assassination attempt, accident, kidnapping, or natural death, the Twenty-Fifth Amendment establishes the actions to be taken. It also underscores the role to be played by the vice president in such time of crisis.

The penultimate amendment establishes the minimum voting age for US citizens (eighteen) and mandates that their right to vote must be respected in all states.

The last amendment, the Twenty-Seventh Amendment, includes the issue of compensation for members of Congress. In the event that a law is presented that increases or decreases the salary of members of Congress, it will not take effect until the next elections of the House of Representatives have occurred.

As mentioned at the beginning, in addition to these amendments, there were six others: four were never enacted or ratified, and the other two expired in 1882 and 1885.

The Eighteenth Amendment: Prohibition

The Eighteenth Amendment, which was later repealed by the Twenty-First Amendment, gave rise to hundreds of stories in novels and movies about gangsters and families made wealthy by flouting the provision. In essence, the amendment bans the purchase, sale, manufacture, and distribution of intoxicating liquor within the United States as well as in any other territory under its jurisdiction. It also prohibits the import or export of alcohol.

The law took effect in the first month of 1920, with noncompliance subject to fines or imprisonment. The amendment was intended to reduce alcohol consumption and return to the teetotal principles on which the United States was founded.

During this era, the nation is growing at a dizzying pace. Large cities are expanding, increasing demand for the construction industry and manual labor. To meet this demand, migrants arrive from different parts of the world. But the integration of foreigners with dissimilar social spheres and customs, who sometimes mix and often clash with the local workers, is a challenge. With the advent and accelerated popularity of dance halls and taverns, the culture of alcohol is a point of connection, laughter, hugs, kisses, and fights.

This emotionally charged and bohemian scene provokes the discontent of conservatives, who oppose such social interactions and lobby for restrictions on the sale and consumption of liquor. Prohibition becomes law, but few comply with it at first. People think that it is just a bunch of hogwash from the authorities. Consequently, sanctions are imposed as a warning to offenders. The legislators bet that this would be enough to quell the effects of alcohol on society and its values. Reality proved otherwise. Worse still, clandestine trade springs up.

Human predilection for the forbidden is well-known. The times when any prohibition quenches desire are rare in history. And even so, there will always be someone in the shadows ready to satisfy demand. The Mafia emerges, and their profits soar through bootlegging as well as their control of distribution channels, outlets, and lounges. In a short time, the Mafia owns the illegal liquor market.

As the saying goes, the cure was worse than the disease. Things went from bad to worse. The dry law was counterproductive in every way. It was intended to eliminate alcohol consumption, but it generated a much bigger problem. Alcohol consumption does not stop despite the fact that it is illegal. The Mafia bribes public officials to avoid the closure of clandestine saloons and the liquor trade.

This scenario is compounded by a wave of violence, chaos, and social instability that floods the nation for more than a decade. In 1933, under President Franklin D. Roosevelt, the Eighteenth Amendment was repealed; each state was empowered to choose how to manage the liquor trade. However, the repeal of Prohibition did not annihilate the Mafia, which quickly found other illegal businesses to survive the blow that the legalization of alcohol consumption represented.

The Mexican Constitutions of 1824, 1857, and 1917

A nation's free will and independent nature is defined and strengthened through its *magna carta*—a document constituting a fundamental guarantee of rights and privileges and that cements an identity and profile beyond the act of signing. The Constitution of the United States has added few amendments throughout its history, although one of these is the controversial Prohibition. The Mexican Constitution, on the other hand, has a more complex trajectory in every sense. To begin with, it contains 136 articles and nineteen transitional provisions. In addition, it is constantly being amended.

The United States has only one constitution. Mexico, on the other hand, has several constitutions to its credit, the result of a society under constant transformation and conflicts that have undermined its process of reconciliation and prosperity.

Something important to highlight is that prior to each constitution, there was an armed movement, and the enactment of each constitution was a consequence of the previous armed conflict. The Constitution of Apatzingan was preceded by the War of Independence and the document "Los Sentimientos de la Nación" ("The Sentiments of the Nation," a document setting out Jose Maria Morelos's vision of the future nation of Mexico). The Constitution of 1824 emerged when Guadalupe Victoria was the first president of Mexico, after he convened a constituent assembly. The constitutional laws of 1836, better known as the Seven Laws, appeared as a consequence of confrontation between Federalist and Centralist forces that opposed the Constitution of 1824. The 1857 Constitution was enacted after the Ayutla rebellion against the dictatorship of Antonio Lopez de

Santa Anna. The Conservatives did not like some precepts of this *magna carta*, such as the expropriation of church property and the fact that the Catholic religion was no longer official or obligatory, and this led to the Reform War. Finally, the 1917 Constitution is a consequence of the Mexican Revolution. It was particularly influenced by Venustiano Carranza's Plan de Guadalupe, a political manifesto proclaimed on March 26, 1913, to reject the usurper government of Victoriano Huerta. In summary, the history of Mexico is reflected in the history of its constitutions.

We will focus on the three most important constitutions that Mexico has had in its history. All of them, in some way, promised the moon and the stars. Let's follow an anonymous citizen, participant in the construction and modification of these important documents.

We go back to 1810, and the first constitution we have evidence of is the Political Constitution of the Spanish Monarchy. This comes about when the French Empire of Napoleon Bonaparte invaded the lands of the Spanish Empire in the Americas. It was critical to show solidarity among the Spanish territories as they faced the French invaders.

Our anonymous citizen is one of the delegates from the Spanish Empire's territories that meet in the Supreme Central Governing Board of the kingdom. Those assembled accepted the text as the supreme law. In addition, and for the first time, the Spanish colonial territories were recognized as part of the Spanish monarchy.

The meeting of the representatives took place in the port of Cadiz in 1810, which is why it is also known as the Constitution of Cadiz. The sessions that ratified the constitutional text concluded on March 19, 1812. This constitution harbors both liberal and democratic principles and will accelerate the process for the disappearance of the old political regime.

It is the year 1813. Our anonymous character reads with elation and surprise "Los Sentimientos de la Nación," the document written by General Jose Maria Morelos y Pavon, one of the leaders of the War of Independence. Our character sympathizes with the writing that claims that America is free and independent from Spain and any other nation. He is particularly moved when he reads the following line: "That as religious law is superior to all men, those dictated by our Congress must be like those, so that they force constancy and patriotism, moderate opulence and indigence; and in such a way that the wages of the poor are increased, that they improve their customs, keeping away ignorance, robbery and theft." The anonymous character finishes reading, moved to tears. How could he not agree with what is dictated by Jose Maria Morelos y Pavon?

This writing inspires the Constitution of Apatzingan, which takes up some of the principles of the Constitution of Cadiz. It also incorporates the French model that recognizes a series of rights related to labor and human rights. The Constitution of Apatzingan remains in effect until 1821, when the War of Independence ends, and the Spanish army signs the Plan of Iguala and, later, the Treaties of Cordoba.

The Constitution of 1824 is first on the list following Mexico's independence. Our character, now starting to turn gray, joins the group that brings this document to life. He has the privilege of forming part of the First Constituent Congress, which will later be called the National Institutional Junta. The people make their voice heard so that Congress is reinstated. The latter brings about the Constitution of 1824, with 171 articles that indicate the form of government the country should follow. It remained valid until 1853. It stipulates the separation of the executive, legislative, and judicial powers, specifies that the offices of president and vice president must last four years, and declares the Catholic religion the only official religion, prohibiting any other creed.

During its period of validity, there were clashes between Federalists and Centralists, and several states tried to gain independence from Mexico. Before continuing, we must keep in mind that although this constitution lasted from 1824 to 1853, it was briefly suspended. In 1836, Antonio López de Santa Anna, who still served as the power behind the throne, promoted the highly conservative Seven Laws (a series of changes intended to centralize the federal government). Once the Republicans regained power, the Constitution of 1824 was reestablished with modifications that did not affect its integrity.

During this period of change, civil wars are on the rise, as Mexican custom dictates. And as if Mexico did not have enough problems with its internal war, it then had to face an invasion from the United States, with the resulting loss of more than half of its territory and a new crisis, as if it needed another one.

In 1856, once Santa Anna was completely out of power, elections for a new congress were held. Our anonymous protagonist, now using a cane, lives like all citizens, caught in the midst of a complete social and economic disaster. The Reform War, whose main hero is Benito Juarez, is about to break out. A year later, in 1857, new laws were issued that signified a hard blow to the church. The president in office, Ignacio Comonfort, announces a new constitution composed of 128 articles. The laws enacted upset the clergy because they affect their interests—and end up unleashing the Reform War.

Antagonism ensues between Liberals and Conservatives, and the church leads the Conservatives who completely reject this new constitution. Benito Juarez is appointed as interim president, and he is faithful to liberal principles and the Reform Laws. The Liberal side wins the war, and its constitution is imposed. It is not until 1917 that dictatorships in Mexico came to an end. In fact, Porfirio Diaz is the last dictator of Mexico. Following his exile to France and the first stage of the Mexican Revolution, the Constitution of 1917 was produced. By this time, the reasons for the struggle had changed, and the first ones were forgotten, the enemies were different, the ideals were different, and all the revolutionaries were apparently tired of killing each other. The Constitution of 1917 is the one that is currently in force, although this does not exempt it from having undergone more changes and modifications than a variant of the coronavirus.

The Many Modifications of the 1917 Constitution

After the beginning of the Mexican Revolution of 1910, Francisco I. Madero led an anti-reelectionist movement against the dictator Porfirio Diaz, who had been in power for more than thirty years and wanted to remain there for years to come. Madero achieved his goal thanks to popular support, but his mandate as president of the republic was brief due to treason and an assassination perpetrated by the army of Victoriano Huerta, one of his closest generals. Once in office, there were several armed rebellions from movements that did not recognize Huerta as a legitimate president. Among the revolutionary heroes were Pancho Villa, Emiliano Zapata, and Venustiano Carranza. They had markedly different interests, but they had a common enemy after Madero's assassination: Victoriano Huerta. After defeating Huerta's army, these revolutionary leaders began to fight among themselves to obtain power. Venustiano Carranza had political experience, unlike Villa and Zapata, which he applied to defeat them. His first move was to create an army called the Constitutionalist Army, with himself as its general.

Together, the rebels overthrew President Huerta, sending him straight into the dustbin of history. Disagreement among the revolutionary leaders led to the continuation of armed movements. Carranza again applied his political experience, and his wiles, and began to act using the power of the law. With his triumph consolidated, Carranza focused on refining his constitutional project.

After so many years of armed struggle, the 1857 Constitution was already obsolete. On December 1, 1916, the Constituent Congress met in the city of Queretaro to draft a new document that would be more in tune with the realities, injustices, and complexities of the country. The discussions took place while the world was enduring World War I and the Bolshevik Revolution, something that did not go unnoticed in the essence of the constitution that was about to be written. Finally, the Venustiano Carranza government enacted the constitution on February 5, 1917, with a corpus of twenty-two thousand words.

The current Constitution has 136 articles, 111,000 words, and 229 decrees. Since it was enacted in 1917, there have been 699 changes.

Consider that due to the magnitude of these modifications, the text has increased to five times its original size. According to research carried out by the Belisario Dominguez Institute, the articles with the most modifications are 27, 73, 89 and 123, with an average of 144 modifications in the more than one hundred years that this constitution has been in effect.

In order to understand the scale of so many changes, let's consider that each democratically elected president has modified the constitution during his term in office. Presidents Emilio Portes Gil and Adolfo Ruiz Cortines made the fewest changes to the Constitution, only two articles in a one-year period. The figure grew to excess with Enrique Peña Nieto, with 155 changes. He is followed by Felipe Calderon, with 110 changes, and Ernesto Zedillo, with seventy-seven.

So many adjustments have changed the original spirit of the Mexican Constitution of 1917. The elected leaders in the presidential succession have applied modifications to fit their own agendas and not the agendas of the public.

Influence of the Colonies

The processes of independence from a colonial empire and designing a constitutional identity are not isolated. It is important to recognize that events in Great Britain, from the seventeenth century to the time the American colonies won their independence, had an influence. Our benchmark is the so-called Glorious Revolution of 1668 against absolutism, from which the Bill of Rights of 1689—the basis for public law—evolved. This was a complex period in which the formal constitutional model (doctrine with a constitutional monarchy) and the material constitutional model (with a parliamentary monarchy vision) were debated.

Add to this the French Revolution of 1789 and the end of its empire in America with the Cortes of Cadiz. These events in Europe, plus transformations in the Americas, gave way to a plurality of independent and republican nations.

For Mexico, influenced by Spain and its political constitution with a monarchical spirit, the triumph of liberalism sought to put an end to an old and absolutist regime. In exchange, a constitutional monarchy was established. Later, due to the territorial dispute between Spain and France over America, the Spanish Crown tried to consolidate its political control over the colony, without success.

Meanwhile, the approach of the United States of America is influenced by the experience of the United Kingdom, using innovative ideas that differentiate it from the rest of the European countries. What is new is a mixed government structure. We should bear in mind that this model of governance, plus its constitutional organization, is strongly influenced by ideas from continental Europe. The philosopher Montesquieu, for example, stresses that there must be mutually balanced powers to avoid tyranny.

Likewise, the due process clause of the US Constitution is partially based on common law with a strong reference to the Magna Carta of John I of England in 1215, the first constitution in the history of humanity.

Consequently, we have two independent nations whose influences cannot be overlooked. Even so, there is some degree of connection between the two countries' constitutions. US influence on constitutionalism in Mexico cannot be denied, although the legal cultural practice comes from Spain at the end of the twentieth century.

A couple of other points can be touched upon. The co-called Common Law defines natural law in England. It has its origins in the Middle Ages and is a precursor to the US Constitution. As for Mexico's sovereignty and its relationship with the Constitution of Cadiz, the latter lacks a declaration of rights. This detail is not unintentional and will support freedom under *habeas corpus*, which permeated the liberal radicalism of independent Mexico.

As for the Mexican Constitution, it aligns with the presidentialist tradition that already differentiates European nations with a federalist vision, as is evident in the Constitution of 1917, with mechanisms of parliamentary control over the executive. The objective is to build up the government's stability and avoid what occurred during the Third French Republic.

Breaking with the Past

The year 1917 is emblematic for Mexico. We have already mentioned that this was the year that the constitution that still governs Mexico was enacted. After the fall of the dictatorial regime of Porfirio Diaz in 1911, the war continued, first against the traitor Victoriano Huerta, and then among the revolutionary leaders themselves. What is at stake is reshaping the Constitution of 1857 with its liberal ideology.

This was an extremely convulsive period, even with the revolutionary triumph. General Venustiano Carranza, at that time head of the Constitutionalist Army, proposed the project of nation to be debated in Queretaro. Meanwhile, in the north of the country, US troops under the command of General John J. Pershing pursue Francisco Villa, looking to make him pay for an attack on the small town of Columbus, New Mexico. The incursion of Villa's men into Columbus is considered one of the few enemy invasions of US territory, and General Pershing plans to return the favor. Villa, hiding in the hills of Chihuahua and hearing the American troops' footsteps, does not dare to leave his safe house.

Villa's knowledge of the terrain gives him an advantage over the foreign soldiers looking for his head. General Pershing will have to return to the United States empty-handed. The south of Mexico is dominated by the rebellious and revolutionary presence of Emiliano Zapata, whose most famous demand and motto is "Tierra y Libertad" (Land and Liberty).

In Queretaro, in the midst of this social disorder, efforts were made to restore a large part of the 1857 Constitution, in particular, the sections on rights and guarantees. Modifications were focused on how to grant more controls to the current president, and he was given authority that was not found in previous constitutions. As a result of this restructuring, the president of the republic was endowed with immense power. This was due to the need for a single commander in charge of cleaning up the disaster left by so many years of struggles, destruction, and death. It is one of the Constitution's most striking components, as well as the integration of the social and democratic ideologies distinctive of the revolutionary movement. At the time, it was the world's first social constitution. It favors labor rights; workers have the power to freely unionize. It also applies progressive ideology to the agrarian sector and guarantees the nation's control of natural resources, especially hydrocarbons (oil, for example). In short, it is a *magna carta* with the vision of a popular democracy.

In the world order at that time, the production of hydrocarbons and their derivatives was a very lucrative and strategic catalyst. Ships that used to run on coal now operate on oil-based combustion. Just as the 1917 Constitution rightly prioritizes oil, it also gives back subsoil rights, canceling previously granted concessions that were probably granted in collusion with corrupt interests. As for the United States, its Constitution of 1787 manages to eliminate the Articles of Confederation, thereby completely detaching itself from the English Crown. However, we should note that the articles of the independent Constitution of the United States do not meet expectations; they bring about an imperfect system that gives way to restructuring.

In their effort to revise the Articles of Confederation, representatives from each state, independent of each other, participated. At that time, there was no executive branch, much less the notion of the United States. In other words, governance to regulate the forms of commerce among the states was lacking a clearly defined head. Then, when the constituent body met in Philadelphia in May 1787, they decided to design a new system that invalidated the legal system in place. When the government's functions disappeared, uncertainty put the union among the states at risk.

The situation becomes more complicated when a coup d'état is incited. Naturally, you can't please everybody—and differences arise among some constituents. A rebellion takes place that, in the end, will become a factor in the confirmation of the nation's constitution.

There are differences between the US and the Mexican constitutions, such as the length of working hours, the way of electing representatives for Congress, and the degree of representation for each section of national territory. There are also differences in the manner in which each constitution is born.

In Mexico, this birth takes place in Queretaro. A session is held over a two-month period; there are a few meetings held beforehand with a lot of scheming and wheeling and dealing. Those gathered in Queretaro approved the Constitution on November 20, 1916. They also take on responsibility for its enactment as formal law, which happened on February 5, 1917.

Meanwhile, in the United States, the process began on May 14, 1787, with a quorum of twenty-five delegates and no time limit. The sessions concluded on September 17. In the US, the delegates were chosen by each state's congress, and in Mexico, they were elected directly by the people. Political parties did not yet exist constitutionally in Mexico, which explains the fact that 216 representatives had to be elected from all over the country.

With differences and similarities, and even though to some degree the US Constitution influenced Mexico's, each *magna carta* has its own political and constitutional spirit.

Constitutional Contributions and the Federation of Nations

The Constitution of the United States of America establishes a model for republican government, eliminating the monarchical structure. It creates a representative democracy that will end up encouraging Mexico's struggle and that of other Latin American nations in search of their independence.

Mexico followed the path traced by the United States and decided that the people must choose their representatives by popular vote. Monarchic power and aristocratic privileges of any kind were rejected in both federal and state governments.

The defense of human rights is a pivotal issue that each country handles differently. While the US Constitution omitted this in its original body of work, it is corrected through amendments. In the case of Mexico, individual rights are established as a constitutional guarantee in the first twenty-nine articles of chapter I.

Apart from the issue of human rights, the number of amendments between the two documents marks a notable difference. The Mexican Constitution has more than seven hundred changes that proceed according to the agenda—and sometimes the mood, good or bad— of whoever was president, aligned with their political interests. In contrast, in the United States, amendments are more complicated because they require ratification by at least three-fourths of the states in order to take effect.

At this point, it is worth noting that federalism is a constitutional model for both Mexico and the United States, with the same focus but different spirit. These documents were endorsed at different times: 1787 and 1917. The former blazed a trail, and Mexico carries forward this legacy, which will be followed by other nations like Brazil and Canada.

The Constitution as the Foundation of the Presidency

Both the constitutions of the United States, from 1787, and that of Cadiz, Spain, from 1812, provide clear benchmarks for presidential rule in Mexico. After 1917, Mexico's political life invoked institutional well-being and domestic development in terms of political stability and a strong executive figure.

In contrast, in the United States, a specific process takes place. Since the eighteenth century, presidential decisions have been subject to the Supreme Court's intervention. As for Mexico, the Supreme Court of Justice is in charge of ensuring that the president does not overstep his bounds and assume powers that contravene the Constitution.

As we can see, an executive branch is in both constitutional systems, with a president who is responsible for all the states as well as the federal government. The people confer this power: indirectly in the United States and directly in Mexico. With this power, the president has the ability to appoint his Secretaries of State, although with some measure of accountability to the legislative branch and Congress. As for the legislature, the Mexican state has a long way to go and is paying attention to the successes of the United States in this area.

The differences between how the two constitutions developed are striking, as well as the number of modifications made to the original documents by each. What is important to consider now is the spirit of the two constitutions. The United States created its Constitution for the purpose of uniting thirteen independent states to form a powerful union. Mexico, on the other hand, signs its constitution and divides its states, which at the time were nineteen, plus five territories.

As the years have passed, the United States added states, increasing its territorial area. Alaska and Hawaii were the latest states to become part of the Union in 1959. Since 1917, when it became a territory of the United States, Puerto Rico has sought to become a state but has not yet been successful. Mexico divided its unified territory from the viceroyalty into several states. Some of them, as is the case of Yucatán, sought independence from the republic to form a country of their own. Each country has written the history of its own democratic path in its own way.

The signing of the American Constitution.
Painted by Howard Chandler Christy in 1940.

Chapter 6

Black Lives Matter

History of Slavery in North America

Slavery is a thorny issue from any perspective. Without restraints or restrictions, it enables one person to oppress another. Why it happens throughout history, and how it is justified, is complex. Today, the suppression of an individual's dignity and basic rights, regardless of sex, race, or creed, raises international indignation. But in the past, societies used the blood and sweat of slaves as inputs of production.

When the Europeans arrived in the Americas, they had a profitable and formally accepted slave system, with significant participation by monarchies, such as Portugal. The system of slavery in the United States dates back to British colonization and was based on the concept of economic usufruct.

In the sixteenth century, Spain and Portugal, the major powers of that time, invaded the territory south of the Rio Grande where gold was presumed to be plentiful. This is precisely the area chosen by the English Crown in its colonization plan. England's strategy was to obtain raw materials at minimum prices for export to Europe. The plan contemplates converting those raw materials into manufactured products that were returned to America with tax added to the price. The rivalry for this kind of territorial bulwark strained relationships among the European Crowns. And in order to exploit this desired wealth, slave labor was used. The population that the English and the Spaniards brought to the new world came mostly from the African continent. Not surprisingly, Black citizens in the United States are called African Americans. Entire families were abducted from their homes and forced to give up their freedom and their status as human beings. On the boat trips to America, those slaves who did not have the physical strength to work were mercilessly thrown overboard.

126

Crammed in the hold of the ship, tied by the hands and neck, very few could defend themselves. Could they imagine what was in store for them when the voyage was over? They finally arrived in an unknown and cruel land. Having done nothing to deserve it, they—and their descendants to come—were condemned to submission and forced labor.

In Mexico there are also Afro descendants, though in smaller numbers. This does not mean that slavery was unknown in the region. Pre-Hispanic civilizations, such as the Mexica, made use of slaves, most of whom had been prisoners of war. One of the proclamations from Miguel Hidalgo and Jose Maria Morelos during the War of Independence was precisely the abolition of slavery. In fact, the Revolution of 1910 arose in part due to opposition to the slave system used by haciendas that worked henequen under the protection of the Porfirio Diaz government. Many Yaqui Indians from Sonora were driven from their land and brought to haciendas in Yucatán to work under subhuman conditions. One practice of the time was the use of company stores located in campesino workplaces.

Workers were forced to buy their basic products from company stores and nowhere else. The trick was that the workers, most of whom were illiterate, would sooner or later end up indebted to the store, which was also owned by their employer. In this way, the employer recovered money intended for salaries, and the worker acquired an unpayable debt that could even be transferred to his entire family, forcing his children and grandchildren to pay off a debt that had nothing to do with them. American journalist John Kenneth Turner wrote a heartbreaking book about enslavement in the haciendas of Yucatán called *Barbarous Mexico*, where he reveals the misery, cruelty, starvation, and extermination suffered by slaves during the government of Porfirio Diaz. The author recounts that if someone murdered a slave, the authorities did not intervene. Many times, it was cheaper for the landowners to let their laborer die than to treat them with dignity and fairness. The book is also a harsh denunciation of Porfirio Diaz and Mexican tycoons of that time—the so-called Divine Caste—whose wealth came from slave labor on the haciendas even though slavery had been officially abolished in Mexico a century earlier. Such was the hypocrisy of the regime that slaves were not called slaves; they were known as laborers. The injustices witnessed by John Kenneth Turner made him realize that it would not be long before a revolution would begin in Mexico, and his denunciation clearly angered Porfirio Diaz.

In the United States, the Civil War divided the country along ideals for and against the practice of slavery. The Southern states defended the right to buy, sell, and own slaves while the Northern states demanded the complete abolition of slavery. It was this straightforward disagreement that led a country like the United States to engage in a bloody civil war.

When we talk about the abolition of slavery, we remember those who gave their lives to end this infamous practice.

A review of the data helps measure slavery under the European Crowns. From the arrival of the Spaniards on American shores in the sixteenth century to when the last slave landing was recorded in the first half of the eighteenth century, it is estimated that nearly three hundred thousand African slaves were brought, with Portugal acting as a commercial intermediary. This figure is a bit less than 2 percent of the total population of the viceroyalty. The percentage is intermingled exponentially, both with other Africans and with natives of New Spain. It is estimated that just prior to the War of Independence, approximately 10 percent of the viceroyalty's population was of African descent. According to the classifications of the time, this included Blacks, mulattos, *pardos* (triracial—European, Native American, and African—descendants) and *moriscos* (former Muslims and their descendants).

It is also known that African Americans taken from the Atlantic coast of Central Africa were enslaved in America through the Portuguese. The recorded human flow gives us the following figures: 241,000 slaves arrived alive in New Spain between 1619 and 1810 and 307,000 in the thirteen colonies from 1619 to 1808. The importation of slaves was prohibited as a consequence of independence. In the United States, this happened in 1808. In Mexico, slavery was abolished *de facto* in 1810 and formally in 1824. However, as we saw with John Kenneth Turner and his *Barbarous Mexico*, the ending of slavery was not completely fulfilled.

Father Hidalgo and the Abolition of Slavery in Mexico

Now we'll accompany a slave in New Spain who meets the priest Miguel Gregorio Antonio Ignacio Hidalgo y Costilla Gallaga Mandarte y Villaseñor—for simplicity's sake, we will call him Father Hidalgo. The slave has just learned that this priest, who already had a reputation for crazy and outlandish ideas about freedom, has just declared slavery abolished. As mentioned before, the characteristics of slaves in the viceroyalty are diverse. This slave has known no other life than that of forced labor and mistreatment. His parents and grandparents were also slaves, and he believed that it was normal for his children to follow the same path. But Father Hidalgo has taken up arms under the banner of the Virgin of Guadalupe. The slave listens to diatribes against Spanish suppression and, fearfully, applauds. Later, Miguel Hidalgo decrees the unthinkable: every slave in New Spain must be freed, and whoever opposes this measure will be condemned to death.

The newly freed slave, to whom emancipation and free will are anathema, approaches the priest to thank him. At that moment, he makes a decision: "How can I help you, Don Miguel?" he says as he grabs Hidalgo's hand. Then he goes back to his humble abode to grab his machete and say goodbye to his family. Our anonymous protagonist has decided that he will fight alongside the priest who made him a free man.

Hidalgo's antislavery declaration is the first to be proclaimed in the entire American continent. Although he made it as a side note to the War of Independence, many slaves—like our anonymous protagonist—joined the fight, excited by the dream of freedom. It is often thought that Hidalgo's proclamation was aimed at liberating the native peoples of New Spain. It is therefore important to clarify that the then-king of Spain, Carlos V, had already prohibited their enslavement, with certain exceptions.

Years after the conquest, wars continued in the new continent to the detriment of the native population. Since the colonists could not make them slaves, they annihilated them in battle. Missionaries, who were charged with converting the natives to Christianity and watching over them, quickly informed the Royal Council of this. Consequently, the prohibition of slavery was modified.

Now those who were taken prisoner because of the war could be enslaved, but they could not be traded.

As for women and minors under fourteen years of age, they could not be enslaved; however, they were made to serve as domestic workers.

Carlos V's decree only applied to the native peoples. Black slaves continued as slaves and were considered merchandise. Remember: New Spain was a center for the slave trade, and most of the ships that transported slaves arrived headed to New Spain.

Facing this scenario, Father Miguel Hidalgo urges that slaves be freed and that the native peoples be exempted from paying taxes.

On December 6, 1810, as head of the insurgent army, Hidalgo abolishes slavery. He announces that slaveowners have ten days to set their slaves free or face the death penalty. Consequently, they were freed for fear of the punishment. Not until the Constitution of 1824 was this proclamation by Hidalgo formalized.

So now our anonymous protagonist—whose ancestors arrived by ship to New Spain to be sold as merchandise—is free. And once freed, he did not hesitate to accompany Hidalgo in search of an independent Mexico.

Memin Pinguin and "Negrito Sandia": Racism Mexican Style

Thanks to figures such as Father Miguel Hidalgo, slavery was eradicated in America, although, it must be said, this does not excuse controversial symbols in popular culture. One example is the comic strip character Memin Pinguin. He is a Black child with exaggerated and stereotyped features, meant to be humorous. The name Memin is a diminutive of Memo (similar to Bill), while Pinguin refers to mischievous. This cartoon was created by Yolanda Vargas Dulche and was sold at newsstands in Mexico starting in 1940.

Controversy did not arise until 2005, when a White House spokesperson discovered the Mexican comic strip and condemned it as having no place in today's world with its daily struggle against racial stereotypes. This protest was immediately echoed by President George W. Bush, who ordered the removal of the Memin Pinguin cartoon from US supermarkets.

Another episode with this character occurred when the Mexican Postal Service decided to use it on one of its postage stamps. This time, anger and protest came from the African American community.

The White House intervened and requested the removal of the stamp. Mexico's response was negative. The diplomatic corps of President Vicente Fox argued that it was a tribute to a cartoon emblematic of Mexican culture but not intended to be offensive. They also noted that Mexico had never complained to the United States about Looney Tunes's creation of the character Speedy Gonzales, the famous and fast little mouse dressed as a Mexican campesino.

Ironically, President Vicente Fox was also involved in a controversy with the African American community when he stated at a meeting with US businessmen that in the United States, Mexican migrants do jobs "that not even Blacks want to do." As was usual for the Fox government, many tried to explain what the president meant, affirming that the president's statement had no racial motivation.

However, several voices from the African American community demanded an apology from the Mexican president for his offensive comments.

Back to Memin Pinguin. Ultimately, Mexico's appeal wins on the grounds that Memin Pinguin is a hero. Like Charlie Chaplin's character created to make his audience laugh, Memin Pinguin's cartoons also portray complicated issues such as divorce, racism, crime, and parental neglect. It was also argued that the character possessed remarkable inner beauty above and beyond the physical, a symbol of

Mexican culture. And as is often the case when trying to ban certain objects, Memin Pinguin postage stamps fetched very high prices as people from countries around the world wanted to have their own.

With the advent of globalization, these types of controversies are more visible. Something similar happened with the image of Aunt Jemima, a US product for making hotcakes. Aunt Jemima was depicted as a Black servant, a slave, but happy to serve her white masters. The term "aunt" was a pejorative term; an aunt was someone who was considered insignificant. Even during the 1980s, Aunt Jemima became known in Mexico as "La Negrita" (little Black woman). It was not until after George Floyd's murder that the company decided to change its image and name, claiming that they were seeking to make progress toward racial equality.

These classic characters do not cause controversy at their creation or at their moment of success. They are judged over time, when the context is different, as in the following case.

"Negrito Sandía" is a song by Francisco Gabilondo Soler, an artist and singer-songwriter from Veracruz who wrote children's songs in the middle of the twentieth century. Gabilondo Soler is better known for the Cri-Cri character, the little singing cricket. A young historian from Rice University who was researching songs of the 1950s pointed out that, although seemingly harmless, the song's lyrics encourage discrimination against both African Americans and people of African descent. The song talks about a Black boy, cute and "with an angelic face," but prone to swearing. Cri-Cri claims the child has turned out "more foulmouthed than a parrot from a poor neighborhood," which will cause him problems as an adult; he will grow up to be rude and impolite if he does not correct his vulgar language. The song also implies that the only way to educate the child is by hitting him.

A fragment of the song goes:

Negrito Sandia
Don't say naughty things anymore
Negrito Sandia
Or I'll tell your aunt

And while she's grabbing you
I'll look for
A notebook to write down
The whacks she's going to give you
With the stick she uses
You're shocked by the punishment
And after the beating
I'm going to die laughing
Negrito Sandia
Don't say naughty things anymore
Or you'll see
Or you'll see

In addition to "Negrito Sandia," other censored Cri-Cri songs are "El Negrito Bailarín" (the little Black dancer) and "La Negrita Cucurumbé" (Cucurumbe, the little Black woman). The use of the diminutive to refer to someone Black can demonstrate discrimination and condescension. The song "El Negrito Bailarín" denotes the laziness of a toy in the shape of a small Black man with a cane and a bowler hat who does not feel like dancing, even though he has been bought for that purpose. The lyrics are: "Little Brown Man, let's see if you finally get up the courage and dance some tap for us." The song "La Negrita Cucurumbé" shows that the protagonist is not happy with her skin color. She bathes in the sea, hoping the water will whiten her face, even feeling envious of the shells for their pale color. She looks at the moon and the foam of the waves, wishing her skin had the same tone. In the end, the song has a message of acceptance and self-love. A fish in a hat comes up to the girl on the beach and says, "But oh my God, don't you see. You look pretty being Black like that, little Cucurumbe." And "El Negrito Sandía," as already mentioned, scolds a Black boy who does not know how to behave and who gets beaten up for being very foulmouthed.

The point is that the author on trial, Gabilondo Soler, was a humanist. His songs, following the tradition of Aesop's fables, use animals and living objects to reveal the complexity of the human condition. The poetry of the singing cricket's lyrics has touched entire generations of children and adults. Gabilondo Soler gave up songwriting and dedicated the rest of his life to astronomical observation. As a fan of the pirate novels of Jules Verne and Emilio Salgari, he joined the Astronomical Society of Mexico because—like the pirates—he wanted to understand the sky, the stars, and the constellations. Moreover, his musical catalog goes beyond three controversial songs. He was also the composer of true classics of Mexican music, such as "Di por qué," "La muñeca fea" and "El comal y la olla." In "La Patita," Cri-Cri talks about the difficulties that single and working mothers have raising their children when fathers neglect their responsibility. It is a sad song loaded with strong social criticism. It seems unreasonable, therefore, to accuse Francisco Gabilondo Soler—who wrote his songs in a time very different from our own—of racism. Viewed in the historical context of each era, we can see there was a different understanding back then of certain actions, customs, and characters. Just as we now consider those reprehensible, who is to say that in twenty or fifty years, someone from the future will not be scandalized by the things we see as normal today?

Electoral Quota for Afro-Mexicans in Mexico during the Twenty-First Century

The visibility of Mexicans of African origin has been a long process. They are a mostly forgotten people whose customs, traditions, history, and origins are unknown. Many may think that there is nothing in common between Mexico and Africa. However, that statement is wrong. Let's remember that the first Africans to arrive in Mexico were kidnapped from their homeland and brought as slaves by Spain and Portugal. Once they arrived in New Spain, they formed communities and put down roots, likely because they had no other choice and could not board a ship and return to Africa. But they also became involved in the culture and contributed to creating the Mexican identity.

Mexico's history has had important Afro-descendant protagonists. Gaspar Yanga, for example, led a slave rebellion and sought freedom during the era of the Spanish colony. Vicente Guerrero was a hero of the independence movement and a former president of Mexico, and Alvaro Carrillo was a Oaxacan composer of beautiful boleros. There was Antonia del Carmen Peregrino—better known as Toña La Negra—considered by Agustin Lara as the greatest songstress of all time.

Sadly, the Afro-Mexican population has not been spared from racism, discrimination, prejudice, lack of opportunities, and invisibility. Even the terms Afro-Mexican and Afro-descendant are relatively new. Coined by researcher Odile Hoffman, these terms came about after reaching consensus among various institutions, intellectuals, and social organizations on a name for Mexicans originating from Africa in a way that is neither offensive nor folkloric.

As Odile Hoffman rightly points out: "In today's Mexico, the idea of 'Black' does not exist in the registry of multiple identities that represent the nation. It is not part of the collective national imaginary and only refers to decontextualized stereotypes (the Memin Pinguin cartoon) or foreigners (a Black person is a Cuban, a gringo, or an African)."

The truth is that the Afro-Mexican population cannot be regarded as marginal or small. Nothing of the sort. Afro-Mexicans are mainly located in the state of Guerrero, particularly in the Costa Chica area, and are also present in the states of Oaxaca, Veracruz, Chiapas, Jalisco, and the state of Mexico. According to a 2020 survey conducted by the National Institute of Geography and History (INEGI, for the acronym in Spanish), Afro-Mexicans represent 2 percent of the total population, i.e., there are approximately 2,576,213 Afro-descendants living in Mexico. This is a significant number that for a long time has had no political representation, were not taken into consideration for important public policies, and were not nominated for elected office or named to government positions.

A reform that could give voice and representation to the Afro-descendant population in Mexico was urgently needed. Like native peoples, Afro-Mexicans have suffered domination, exploitation, plunder, and oppression since colonial times. An electoral reform that would include them in the political life of Mexico was fair and necessary, considering that the chances of an Afro-descendant reaching Congress were almost null. As mentioned at the end of chapter 1, on August 9, 2019, a fifth reform was made to article 2 of the Mexican Constitution. This reform contemplates Afro-Mexicans as part of the multiple cultures existing within Mexican territory. It also mandates that they enjoy the same rights as any other Mexican because they are Mexicans and deserve to live without discrimination or obscurity. Likewise, the National Electoral Institute (INE) determined that at least 1 percent of candidates for office must be Afro-descendants; probably now more than one candidate will begin to identify themselves as such, without being so. Let's hope that this recent reform is not a reform in name only and rightly helps to correct the unequal and historical conditions of the Afro-Mexican population.

Honest Abe and the End of Slavery

Before becoming president, Abraham Lincoln had limited military and political experience. Through self-education, he was able to become a lawyer and leader of the Whig Party. After law school, he was elected to the Illinois House of Representatives. Almost twenty years later, a more mature Lincoln joined a new political party with which he agreed on ideals and values, including an antislavery stance. He found it unacceptable for the United States to have slavery as part of its daily life, without remorse or conscience; he considered slavery a moral, social, and political evil. In 1858, he was chosen to represent his party and contended for its nomination as US senator for Illinois. When he accepted the Republican Party's nomination, Lincoln delivered a speech that read as follows: "A house divided against itself cannot stand. I believe that this government cannot endure, permanently half slave and half free." The audience must have listened in shock.

Thanks to his eloquent speeches, Lincoln begins to gain popularity; however, he loses the election to the Democratic Party candidate. Lincoln stands firm. Now the whole country is aware of his antislavery stance, and perseverance is the key to success. He runs in the presidential election. To his good fortune, the Democratic Party is divided internally; Lincoln wins the election and is declared the sixteenth president of the United States.

Now let's look in on a slave in the Southern United States, who works from sunrise to sunset harvesting crops. Let's remember that the North is more industrialized area, but in the South, slave labor is indispensable. The owners of this slave did not like Lincoln's thinking and stance on slavery.

They felt that at any moment they could lose their most valuable asset: their slaves. Disagreements between the Northern and Southern states erupted, and the country became embroiled in a war that Lincoln sought to avoid at all costs. This anonymous slave joins the Civil War to fight for his freedom and that of his race. In early 1863, President Lincoln declared freedom for all slaves in the rebellious states. The Southern states opposed such a decision. Who else but slaves would work on the cotton plantations?

Up until that time, the Constitution had protected the practice of slavery. Although the importation of slaves was banned in 1808, the practice never ceased. If a slave escaped, the legislation prescribed his return. This is the misfortune of our protagonist. The first chance he gets, he manages to escape to a Northern territory where slavery is not practiced. Under the protection of the law, his owner locates him and demands he be returned, like someone who demands the return of a lost dog. A forced return would imply punishment, humiliation, and beatings. The slave is not recognized as a citizen and is deprived of the right to vote.

During the Civil War, thousands of slaves from the South migrated to the North to support the antislavery struggle. With Lincoln's decree and the amendments to the Constitution, the abolition of slavery became a reality. Lincoln achieved an unprecedented historic feat for the Black population of the United States. We can see how divisive the issue was, given Lincoln's assassination in a theater at the hands of a Confederate sympathizer, a failed actor named John Wilkes Booth.

Like almost everything in life, Lincoln's story has its share of legends. It is said that he owned slaves himself and that he supported a relocation program to move them to Central America. There are also those who claim that he had several children with his slaves. These are ideas about which there is no certainty, falling more into the much-talked category of conspiracy theories. What is not in doubt is his fight for freedom. As such, he is considered one of the best presidents the United States has ever had. The Civil War ended on April 9, 1865, with the triumph of the Northern states. Slavery was abolished, and more than four million slaves were freed and granted civil rights. Unfortunately, at the first opportunity they had, the Southern states implemented segregationist measures against which a courageous reverend named Martin Luther King Jr. would later fight.

Martin Luther King Jr.

"I have a dream" is one of the most famous phrases in American history. Those four words have inspired thousands of people to dream of a better world, without injustice and cruelty. We now look in on a descendant of our previous protagonist, the slave freed by Abraham Lincoln. Just as his grandfather was thrilled by Lincoln's ideas, this young man is thrilled by Martin Luther King. He will never forget King's speech on equality.

African Americans were already considered free; the Thirteenth Amendment to the US Constitution prohibits slavery and forced servitude. Nevertheless, hatred and unequal treatment of Blacks prevailed. The distinction between Black and white people is clearly seen in the Southern states. Even after the Civil War and the Thirteenth Amendment to the US Constitution, the South refused to treat Blacks as equals, relying on segregationist laws known as Jim Crow laws.

The Jim Crow laws were of a local nature and applied racial segregation under the motto "separate but equal." Under these legal provisions, the Black population was marginalized. The laws established a sharp distinction between the races. African Americans were denied the right to vote and had restricted access to various jobs and positions. They were also educationally marginalized and even restricted to designated spaces in public places and on public transportation. Blacks had to use different public bathrooms from those used by whites, and they could not sit in the front seats of a bus.

Our young Black protagonist lives in the South, the land where his grandfather fought bravely. He knows he is risking his life if he violates Jim Crow laws or protests against their injustice.

And as if that were not enough, a white supremacist hate group makes his existence even more difficult. The Ku Klux Klan's (KKK) primary targets are homosexuals, Jews, Muslims, foreigners, and above all, Black people. Although the KKK was disbanded and banned by President Ulysses S. Grant in 1871, the organization remains a secret and clandestine society. It was declared a terrorist organization by a judge as early as 1868. Its ideology is the most rancid and intolerant extremism.

Our protagonist has heard about Blacks who have been murdered without the police being interested in solving the crimes. Someone comments to him, fearfully, that those responsible are men covered in white blankets, dressed as a bad imitation of ghosts. These men carry torches and intimidate Blacks with violence. Days later, he begins to hear stories of beatings committed by the KKK against lone, defenseless Blacks. Some confrontations between KKK members and Blacks have even ended in gunfire. Our protagonist is afraid to walk the streets of his city at night. In his nightmares, white ghosts surround him, humiliate him, and beat him until they leave him almost dead, naked, hanging from a lamppost. Then he wakes up, breathing heavily. He wipes the sweat from his face, and a glare catches his attention. He looks out of the window. In front of his house, a cross on fire will burn all night long.

Martin Luther King grew up with a father figure who fought for the rights of African American citizens and was head of the National Association for the Advancement of Colored People (NAACP). King recounts his first experience of racial segregation at the age of six when two white boys told him that their parents forbade them to play with him. King grows up in a home with Christian principles and values. His mother's wisdom strengthens his character; she advises him, "Don't let anyone who puts you down make you feel inferior to them."

King's career as an activist and advocate for African American rights began at an early age. He became a minister, a platform he used to preach against mistreatment of his race, mistreatment that made no sense, according to God's command.

King is known for his vocation and dedication to nonviolent struggle. He declares himself a follower of the peaceful ideals of Mahatma Gandhi. He admires what Gandhi achieved without taking up arms, without spilling a drop of blood, and without confronting the authorities with violence. His protest is based on love and forgiveness.

Apart from being a minister of worship, Martin Luther King had a broad academic background. Like his father, he was also a member of the NAACP. King was convinced that *Satyagraha*—nonviolent civil disobedience—is the ideal way to win a struggle, as Gandhi did to gain India's independence from British rule.

A boycott catapulted him to fame. It happened that an African American woman, fed up with unequal treatment, refused to give up her seat to a white woman and move to the back of the bus, as was the law at the time. As a result, she is stopped by the police. This woman's name is Rosa Parks, and she made history by performing a peaceful but powerful act of protest. Rosa Parks's mother posts bail to free her daughter and contacts an activist, who in turn calls King. A meeting is held between civil rights activists and religious leaders. They decide to boycott the buses in the town of Montgomery, Alabama, the city where the altercation with Rosa Parks took place.

The movement gained the attention of the authorities, which King describes as a true miracle. This boycott causes significant economic losses for the transportation sector, with consequent discontent from the authorities and radical white groups. In response, Martin Luther King's house is burned down.

In addition, he becomes the victim of attacks and threats, just like the other members of the boycott. The response of the authorities is to arrest the leaders of the movement as a clear-cut solution to the conflict. Instead of arresting the whites who threaten the integrity and lives of the Black activists, it is easier for the police to imprison the latter. True to his principles, King decides not to pay his bail and to remain in prison as long as necessary. He argues that if activism means a crime, he is proud of it, surrendering freedom as an offering to the cause.

The Montgomery boycott culminated with the Supreme Court ruling that Alabama's race laws were unconstitutional. The lawsuit lasted a little more than a year and was an important achievement for the African American community. After the verdict, Blacks could now enjoy their right to ride freely in any seat on a bus. However, this is just the beginning. Extremist whites will continue to lash out against King and the other leaders.

With his fame and popularity on the rise, King decided to lead a peaceful march in Washington D.C., where he delivered his famous speech in front of the George Washington Monument. More than 250,000 people witnessed this event. Before the statue of Lincoln, who a hundred years earlier was instrumental in abolishing slavery in the United States, King addresses the huge cheering crowd.

The words of that memorable speech will go down in history:

> I have a dream that one day this nation will rise up and live out the true meaning of its creed: We hold these truths to be self-evident: that all men are created equal.
>
> I have a dream that one day on the red hills of Georgia, the sons of former slaves and the sons of former slave owners will be able to sit down together at the table of brotherhood.

I have a dream that one day even the state of Mississippi, a state sweltering with the heat of injustice, sweltering with the heat of oppression, will be transformed into an oasis of freedom and justice.

I have a dream that my four little children will one day live in a nation where they will not be judged by the color of their skin but by the content of their character. I have a dream today.

Fate does not allow him to see his dream realized. Martin Luther King died on April 4, 1968, shot in the head by a sniper. But his persona and actions influence an entire generation and transcend history. Hidalgo, Lincoln, and King are examples to follow for those who seek a world without racial and social discrimination. King's invitation will remain open for us to follow the nonviolent rebellion of *Satyagraha* as the best way to fight against an unjust and egregious system.

Black Panthers

The Black Panther Party is a political organization that emerged in the 1960s. A couple of Black students, Bobby Seale and Huey P. Newton, founded the Panthers to fulfill the dream of equality within the United States. In the beginning, their purpose was equality for all races and to stop the continual abuses against Blacks by police.

This organization differs from the Black Lives Matter movement mainly because of its ideology regarding the use of violence. The Black Panther Party is characterized by the use of force to defend itself, just as a black panther does in the jungle, only attacking when attacked. Consequently, the Black Panthers are committed to watching that the police do not trample on the rights of Black citizens, which did not please either the police or other authorities.

In addition to their action on the use of force, the Black Panthers were also outspoken against the use of drugs and the Vietnam

War. At the same time, they carried out charitable actions in every community where they appeared.

As more members joined the party, the US government began to view it as a threat. The Black Panthers became the radical left in the United States, to the extent that the FBI, led by long-term director J. Edgar Hoover, called them the greatest internal threat to the nation. Such a position only made the group of well-organized, well-informed, motivated African Americans stronger and more willing to defend their rights with firearms if necessary.

Their membership grows—as does their social approval. By the 1970s, the Black Panther Party reached its highest numbers, having a presence in sixty-eight US cities. But this success led to persecution by the US government. At first, the press took it upon itself to tarnish the image of the party and its leaders. At the same time, several Black Panthers had violent confrontations with the police and were blamed for the deaths of several officers.

Police harassment increased day by day. The jails were filled with young Black men who had committed no crime, imprisoned without due process. Little by little, the number of Black Panther members decreased. In the 1980s, there were a little more than twenty active members.

Some researchers and historians point to the party as a criminal organization that took pleasure in defying authorities and inciting hatred. On the other hand, some say that the Black Panthers have been the most influential organization in recent years, pursuing fundamental issues such as protection of Black communities, job opportunities, decent housing, and an end to police brutality and the murder of Black people.

Black Lives Matter Movement

A grassroots social movement called Black Lives Matter, or BLM, has gained traction in current US history. It is a movement that must be understood in light of the players and events that preceded it.

Its cause follows the same tenor pursued by Martin Luther King and Nelson Mandela, the demand for the same rights pursued by John Lewis and thousands of other African Americans. Although this is a new movement, it is part of an ongoing struggle for freedom and equality.

Black Lives Matter is harnessing the power of social media, and herein lies its innovation and capacity for social projection. If we ask ourselves the reason for this initiative that makes use of current technology, the answer is that discrimination against the African American and native populations continues to exist in the United States.

In a 2014 report from the Anti-Defamation League, the United States ranks as the most racist country, surpassing by far the rest of the world. In Latin America, discrimination is exercised against native peoples, and in the United States, it is centered against the African American population.

The BLM movement arose after the death of a young seventeen-year-old African American named Trayvon Martin. George Zimmerman is the name of his murderer—let us never forget that. Martin was visiting a residential area where his father lived. Zimmerman was part of the neighborhood watch team in the area. It all started when Zimmerman made an emergency call to the police, alerting them to a possible suspect roaming the streets.

Zimmerman claimed his concern stemmed from a string of recent burglaries in the area. A boy with a hoodie pulled over his head, walking in the rain and looking at houses, seems to him to be worthy of suspicion. In the same call with the police, Zimmerman mentioned that Martin took off running; he signaled him to stop, but the young man ignored him. A chase began that led to a struggle. Ultimately, the incident ended Martin's life as a result of a shot from Zimmerman's gun. Martin died a few feet from the residence where he was staying. When police arrived at the scene, Zimmerman was arrested. The murder investigation and the judge's ruling will follow later.

The investigation concludes, and the judge rules the following year. Against all odds, Zimmerman is acquitted of all charges. This unleashed a wave of commentaries, protests, and outrage on social media.

The historical context is vital for us to appreciate all that happened. In a nation with important milestones in favor of equal rights for the African American population, the incident occurs precisely during the term of the first Black president, Barack Obama, who soon comments on the case.

During a White House press conference, President Obama warned that he himself, or any other young African American, could have been Martin thirty-five years ago and shared his tragic end. He also states that despite achievements on equal rights, there is still a long way to go—and he invites all citizens to reflect on the issue.

After this pronouncement, the majority of social networks expressed open support for Martin's family and the president's words. Some, however, alleged that the president's message is one of vindication and hate. The case monopolized the national press. The whole country was talking about it; everyone had an opinion on the subject. Civil organizations began to get involved in the issue, revealing a long-pending agenda for Black citizens in the United States.

In order to evaluate the role of Black Lives Matter, it is useful to trace its origin. Although the United States is ranked as the country with the highest degree of racism, it is also the country with the largest number of civil rights and antidiscrimination associations and organizations. The movement's creators and leaders are three African American women: Opal Tometi, Alicia Garza, and Patrisse Cullors.

Alicia Garza published the following about the murder of Trayvon Martin: "I continue to be surprised at how little Black lives matter. ... Our lives matter." Patrisse Cullors shared this post with the hashtag "Black Lives Matter." This is how the movement went viral.

The words of these young women reach more people than they ever imagined. Not content with this, they decide to act to bring about change. Black Lives Matter is born as a sociopolitical movement that will gradually increase its followers.

As if the situation was not tense enough following Martin's murder, on August 9, 2014, on the outskirts of St. Louis, Missouri, another death of a young African American man at the hands of a police officer occurs. This crime, unlike Martin's, has an eyewitness to the events, who also had the good sense to video record the aftermath. The police officer's statements are contradictory. What happened?

An eighteen-year-old, Michael Brown, was shot and killed. The official version of what happened is that Brown was walking alongside his friend, Dorian Johnson, when they were intercepted by a patrol car with officer Darren Wilson at the wheel. The young men are asked to stop and sit on the sidewalk because their appearance matches the physical description of a report just received about shoplifting.

Brown lunges at Officer Wilson and allegedly punches him to keep him from exiting the vehicle. The officer and Brown struggle. Wilson, fearful of Brown's violent attitude, opens fire and repeatedly shoots Michael Brown in self-defense, killing him.

The eyewitness differs from this account. Indeed, the patrol car driven by Officer Wilson intercepted the two young men walking down the street. But the trouble began when the officer attempted to pull Brown into the vehicle. A struggle ensued, and Brown attempted to escape. The officer fired his weapon, and the bullets impacted Brown's arm. Officer Wilson then punched him several times in the face and discharged the remaining rounds from his gun into Brown's body.

The forensic team confirmed the above. President Obama condemned the incident and publicly offered his condolences to Michael Brown's family. He stated that a full investigation would be conducted into the case. The BLM movement arrived in the city of Ferguson, where the events occurred, and the first nationwide protest was held.

Dozens of groups committed to the rights of African Americans are present. Banners with the initials BLM appear on the streets. Angry shouts rattle the windows of closed stores. Thousands protest peacefully for justice. In response, the governor of Missouri declares a state of emergency and imposes a curfew. The National Guard intervenes and represses the Black Lives Matter movement.

Images of the conflict went viral on social networks. Even the then-UN Secretary General, Ban Ki-moon, warned that US authorities must look after and protect the rights of their population. Consequently, a committee of observers was sent to the conflict zone. This is a precedent never seen before: a warning and action against US authorities.

Within a year of its emergence, the Black Lives Matter movement demonstrated strong organization, with minor but promising results. Over the years, the group has grown from a small cluster organizing marches and protests to an organization with an international presence. Year after year, it gains strength; every day, more and more people become aware of the banner of equality it pursues. In Missouri, for example, BLM held several protests at universities. At the same time, it grew closer to activist groups in other countries.

Marches continue to take place to raise awareness and protest against police brutality of the African American population. BLM beats all unfavorable predictions and succeeds in gaining the support of countless US citizens. It positions itself on the national agenda; social media platforms are flooded with conversations about racial justice, and the movement garners backing from the art world to national political parties. At first, some BLM activists were viewed as radical, and there was speculation that their protests were a strategy from partisan interests. Gradually, the movement's political stance becomes more nuanced, and positions are defined: the Democratic Party stands in solidarity with the victims, listens to their demands, and promises to do something to change things. The Republican Party is mostly critical of BLM, claiming that this movement only incites violence and police hatred. Any resemblance to the attacks and condemnation against the Black Panther Party?

Unfortunately, another incident in 2020 fuels the fire as yet another case of police brutality against an African American person occurs. The victim is George Floyd, whose death at the hands of Minneapolis police officers was recorded on video, with dozens of onlookers at the scene. The incident caused an uproar on social media due to the horror and helplessness conveyed in the video of Floyd's death. Hundreds of thousands once again took to the streets to demonstrate. Large demonstrations and marches were organized across the nation. Public pressure and outrage as well as compelling evidence of the facts led to the firing of four officers linked to the crime.

Let's take a look at the facts as verified by video cameras and disseminated on the internet. George Floyd was inside a vehicle with a friend. A police car parked nearby, and four officers arrived on the scene. They forcibly removed both people, based on a report of an attempt to purchase something from a neighborhood store with a counterfeit bill. The policemen claimed that the description matched Floyd; they handcuffed him and proceeded to complete the arrest. George Floyd protests. He begs not to be shot. He is then thrown to the ground and subdued by an officer who places his knee against Floyd's neck. Floyd's breathing becomes difficult. He tries to free himself, but cannot, and he screams for help. The knee that suffocates him is stronger than his cries. His head feels the hardness of the pavement. "I can't breathe," Floyd says in a pained, agonized voice. As the scene is captured on a cell phone camera, bystanders ask Floyd to stop resisting because he has no way to stop the police.

Floyd pleads, again and again, that he can't breathe, to let him stand up. The officers yell at him to relax, Officer Derek Chauvin's knee still pressing on Floyd's neck. More people begin to gather around and ask the officers to listen to Floyd, who is no longer showing resistance. Officer Chauvin's knee was on Floyd's neck for eight minutes and forty-six seconds, causing his death. The video is a compelling testimony to police brutality in the United States.

With the release of the various videos that captured the murder of George Floyd, the nation erupts. The public awaits the trial of the police officers. The BLM movement returns to lead marches and peaceful protests in several states. However, with the deployment of police to restrain the demonstrators, a violent clash between the two sides ensues.

Claims of police abuse of the African American population continue. And just in case the fire needs more gasoline, a new incident occurs in Wisconsin, where an African American was shot and killed while walking to his vehicle. The videos show a struggle prior to the shooting, then the victim—Jacob Blake—prepares to get into his vehicle without complying with police. This prompts an officer to shoot him in the back. Three of Blake's children were in the back of the vehicle at the time, witnessing their father being shot by the police. Miraculously, Jacob Blake survived to tell the tale. Luck allowed him to live, even though he was paralyzed from the waist down as a result of being shot in the back. Everything was recorded and broadcast on social networks.

This new aggression adds to the outrage in the aftermath of Floyd's death. Once again, the BLM hashtag floods social networks. A massive anti-racist protest is planned to take place in Wisconsin. It is a violent demonstration, and protesters set fires and looted businesses. The governor declares a state of emergency and curfew, but the violence continues.

Given this state of affairs, it is important to remember the principles of the Black Lives Matter movement, which does not encourage or support the use of violence. These recent events only make clear the degree to which African Americans are fed up, that their struggle to overcome racism has not ended, and that they still fight for the right to fair and equal treatment, the same rights for which Abraham Lincoln and Martin Luther King fought.

One thing to note is that the police officers who have been involved in these police brutality scandals have all been white, and very few have gone to prison for their crimes. And if it were not for the fact that someone videotaped the police abusing their power, these murders would probably have gone unpunished.

In light of this, it is worth remembering the words of former President Barack Obama. He himself, or any young African American man walking down the street, could have been Martin or Brown or Floyd or Blake when a police car pulled up beside him.

Yes, We Can, Yes, We Did: The First Black President

The trajectory of former President Barack Obama is unparalleled in US history. Obama worked for community organizations and prestigious law firms. In 1996, he held public office for the first time as an Illinois state senator and was subsequently reelected twice. In 2000, he lost the election that would have taken him to the US House of Representatives. But one thing that victories and defeats share is that neither is final. In 2005, Obama won a seat in the US Senate, becoming the fourth African American senator in the history of the country. With this impeccable trajectory, he seeks the presidency. He is a role model for African Americans, who had not had such a leader since Martin Luther King Jr.

There is an air of hope in the country that translates into an electoral campaign like no other. His campaign slogan—"Yes we can"—thrilled voters who wanted to be part of a historic event. Obama won the candidacy for the Democratic Party and then the 2008 presidential election, defeating the Republican candidate, John McCain. Barack Obama is the first African American president in the history of the United States and also becomes the candidate with the most votes.

During his mandate, women played an unprecedented role. His wife, Michelle Obama, is a key player in this process and dignifies a movement of femininity and strength. Obama does not direct his speeches and promises to the oppressed; he shifts the focus in favor of equal treatment, appealing to peace and hope. This message is especially dedicated to the most vulnerable groups in the country: African Americans, Latinos, and migrants.

Obama's campaign also marks a before and after in the country's political history. Thanks to excellent political marketing and use of social networks, "Obamamania" swept the presidential elections. He won reelection four years after his first triumph. Barack Obama's arrival on the national scene created a wave of excitement in a nation where the majority of African Americans have no voice or vote.

Few US presidents have failed to win reelection. Trump joins this list by losing to Democrat Joe Biden in the 2020 presidential election. In that election, the majority of African American votes supported Biden; just 12 percent supported Trump. In this election, Latinos surprisingly leaned more toward Trump, who has been a proponent of harsh anti-immigrant measures.

To recap, when talking about US history—events, deeds, achievements, and goals— the participation of Blacks is often omitted no matter the historical period, be it the struggle for independence, the Battle of the Alamo, or World War I. This is why the voter turnout in the recent US elections is so significant. A record was set, and the participation of African Americans grew by 8 percent. That figure speaks of a population that demands historical presence and wants to be a protagonist—and not a servant.

An Aunt Jemima advertisement, 1940.

Memin Pinguin is a Mexican comic created
by Yolanda Vargas Dulche in 1943.

Chapter 7

Remember the Álamo, but Do Not Forget Veracruz

A Friendship under Fire

The man is awakened by the heavy noise of cannons that someone is positioning along the walls of the fort. In the distance, he hears the sea and the crashing of the waves against the rocks. He is reassured that no one has sounded the alarm bells yet. The man sees brave soldiers, some poorly dressed, poorly equipped, preparing to defend the port of Veracruz. For days, they have been hearing that enemy ships are about to arrive.

The man turns to look at the sea. It looks just as calm as the day before; seagulls hover over the fortress of San Juan de Ulua. Shirtless boys help load cannonballs; others arrange rifles on the walls or clean weapons while drinking coffee. A dog rests in the shade. Both the troops and the country still feel the sting of having lost Texas and its subsequent annexation to the United States. Could it be that now they are coming for all of Mexico? The occupation of California and New Mexico has been humiliating enough. The troops have heard stories about battles against the Americans up north, and they know that Veracruz is the last bastion of defense against them. Otherwise, the invaders will take the capital, flying their flag from every rooftop and balcony in the country.

An old man approaches our protagonist and asks, "Do you know if we are winning the war?"

He apologizes; he has no answer. The only thing he has heard is that they asked Mexico City for reinforcements, but their plea fell on deaf ears because the *Polkos* (regiments who revolted against the government in protest over legislation that would seize money and

153

property from the Catholic Church) had paralyzed the capital due to their rebellion. As if the nation was not being invaded by a foreign country! *Those Polkos would probably be happy if all of Mexico were part of the United States,* the man thought. *They can imagine themselves speaking English and celebrating the Fourth of July.*

The sea continues to show an almost suspicious calm, and the brave defenders of the port wait for support that will never come. The humid weather makes their patience wear thin.

A sound interrupts the thoughts of our protagonist. Frantically ringing bells mobilize the troops, chasing away birds that were dozing in the church towers. The man looks out to sea, and in the distance, he can see the arrival of the American ships. People take their positions, preparing to receive the enemy. The cannons are aimed at the ships heading for the beach. It is the morning of March 9, 1847. Someone hands a rifle to our protagonist. Now, with the gun in his hands, he is certain that no gringo will ever call a Mexican a coward again.

The first time the United States invaded a foreign country was when it declared war on Mexico, seeking to take over a large part of its territory. But before delving into the separation of Texas and the battle of the Alamo, we need to put into context the confusing state of affairs in Mexico.

As we have already seen in this book, for almost three hundred years, the Spanish monarchy dominated Mexico. Finally, the people had enough. In 1810, the struggle for independence began, a struggle that would last for eleven long years. Thousands of Mexicans gave their lives to the cause of freedom, and several were immortalized as heroes of the homeland. Thanks to these efforts, Mexico achieved independence after three centuries of subjugation.

After reaching the much-dreamed-of independence on September 27, 1821, the *Trigarante* army (the army of the "Three Guarantees," referring to the three guarantees that it was meant to defend: religion, independence, and unity) made a triumphal parade through the streets of Mexico City, led by Agustin de Iturbide. He was the man of the moment, the same one who had pulled off the Plan of Iguala that proclaimed the country's independence. A day after the parade and the celebration, still feeling the hangover of victory, the act of Mexican independence was signed.

Although the country was now free, it would have to organize itself and look for an emperor; they were not yet convinced about having a presidential regime. In 1821, Mexico was a territory of 4.4 million kilometers with a population of approximately six million inhabitants. The people only knew the monarchical form of government and expected that daily life would be unchanged. Agustin de Iturbide, Mexico's first emperor, often said, "Now that you know how to be free, it is up to you to learn how to be happy." This phrase undeniably conveyed security and confidence in the future of the nation, but the reality was different. After eleven years of war, the country had no public resources and a lot of inexperience when it came to the new political regime. Difficult years lay ahead.

As if that were not enough, Spain refused to recognize Mexico's independence. So, the new country could forget about any kind of Spanish aid. It took fifteen years for Spain to finally recognize Mexico as an independent country, but that would be the only good news that year. Imagine what the other news must have been like.

By 1836, the United States already had an appetite for expanding its territory. After nearly a century of independence, it seemed to have clear plans, which included taking over Texas and other northern Mexican states, by hook or by crook.

Within the history of the breakaway of Texas and its annexation to the United States, there are characters that are not often mentioned in history books. It would even seem they are purposely omitted. However, in this book, that will not be the case. Throughout this chapter, we will mention men who have been underrated by history and who greatly influenced its course.

One such person, Joel Roberts Poinsett, served as US ambassador to Mexico. In 1822, Poinsett arrived at the port of Veracruz apparently with only one purpose: to inform his government about the current situation of the new Mexican Empire. However, his real task was to propose the purchase of the country's northern territories.

While Poinsett was establishing himself in Mexico and building relationships with people close to the country's internal politics, the government, under the command of Agustin de Iturbide, was collapsing.

Knowing no limits, the great liberator of Mexico began to squander the little money that remained in the public coffers, handing out titles of nobility left and right. This began to generate doubts about his ability to govern. Congress was divided between those who still trusted their emperor and those who deliberated the creation of a republic similar to that of its neighbor to the north. The Mexican emperor imprisoned his congressional opponents, and then, to save himself further embarrassment, he decided to dissolve Congress outright. By December 1822, the country seemed to have returned to an absolute monarchy.

It was during this time of uncertainty that the US plan, entrusted to Poinsett, began to surface. As mentioned earlier, Poinsett had formed good friendships with Mexican politicians. Among his friendships were men imprisoned by the Mexican emperor. Poinsett visited his friends in the Santo Domingo prison, and upon learning of the situation Mexico was going through, with public coffers emptier than a student's refrigerator, he decided to share with Iturbide the expansion plan the United States wanted to carry out. However, the emperor left this matter in the hands of his friend, the lawyer and politician Juan Francisco Azcarate y Ledezma.

Poinsett declared that the United States was willing to buy Texas. After hearing the proposal, Azcarate asked him to get accredited diplomatically in order to continue with talks and possible negotiations. Poinsett responded that he was in the country as a visitor, not as an official representative of the United States, and the offer was left up in the air.

With the disbandment of Congress, Mexico's Masonic lodges were the equivalent of today's political parties. These were divided into two great lodges: the Scottish Lodge and the York Lodge. The former was in charge of representing and supporting the interests of Spain during the War of Independence, and the latter favored the American government.

After the War of Independence, both lodges continued to gain strength in Mexico, to the point of becoming representatives of the nation's political interests. After the dissolution of Congress by Iturbide, the lodges confronted each other, each supporting the candidate that best represented their interests.

That same year, with unrest all around the country and an uprising looming—led by Santa Anna who was then governor of Veracruz—Iturbide reinstated Congress. Seeing how the country was falling apart and the numerous rebellions against him, Iturbide decided to resign his position and leave Mexico with his family. Agustin de Iturbide was condemned to exile, an order that was issued by Congress, warning him that if he ever set foot on Mexican soil again, it would cost him his life. He and anyone who dared to help him return were declared traitors. Unfortunately, no one warned Iturbide about this. After some time in Europe, he returned to Mexico, saying that he wanted to help and warn the government about plans to reconquer the country. His captors did not believe him and, remarkably, decided to apply the law. The former Mexican emperor was shot on May 4, 1824.

The country was in need of someone to take the reins of government, and the lodges were aware of this. In the meantime, Congress published the supreme law under which the country was governed. With this, the Mexican people could have a little breathing space, and surprisingly, for the first presidential elections, there were no problems at all. Guadalupe Victoria was recognized as the legitimate president, and for a moment, it seemed that stability was coming to a people tired of wars and misfortune.

However, at the end of Guadalupe Victoria's presidential term, during the 1828 elections, Manuel Gómez Pedraza emerged victorious over Vicente Guerrero (supported by the York Lodge and Poinsett). As was the Mexican tradition, Guerrero—not satisfied with the results and with the support of Poinsett, now the American ambassador—decided to challenge the election results.

After the electoral defeat, a group of soldiers loyal to Vicente Guerrero organized a riot in La Acordada prison, a fearsome prison known to be rife with weapons and ammunition. The riot extended to the famous El Parian Market, which was reduced to ashes by the mayhem. This act achieved its goal, which was the acceptance of Vicente Guerrero as the legitimate president of Mexico. His political rival, Gómez Pedraza, fled the country's capital to seek refuge in France.

During his government, Vicente Guerrero was advised at all times by US Ambassador Poinsett and York Lodge. But Guerrero's time in office was brief. At the end of 1829, he was deposed in a rebellion led by Vice President Bustamante. Vicente Guerrero fled the capital, leaving Congress in charge of the country, which branded him unfit to govern and named Bustamante as president.

After the fall of Vicente Guerrero, Poinsett's political influence would come to an end. He was accused of being one of the intellectual authors of the riot that had caused so much havoc in the capital. The secretary of foreign affairs, Jose Maria Bocanegra, requested that the US government remove Poinsett as ambassador to Mexico. After Poinsett returned to the United States, he wrote down everything he had learned about Mexico and its internal politics and was adamant about the idea of purchasing the Texas territory. Though Poinsett was no longer in Mexico, the York Lodge continued to strongly influence the country's internal politics. Poinsett continued to be involved in politics in the United States—and later was an enthusiastic supporter of Texas joining the American Union.

With no respite for the nation, Spanish troops were now rushing to retake their lost territory. Against this background, Antonio Lopez de Santa Anna will emerge.

When Spanish troops tried to retake Mexico's territory, the Mexican army led by Santa Anna repelled the aggression and negated once and for all Spain's pathetic attempt to recover its colony. As a result of this victory, Santa Anna was thrust into the public spotlight. Such was his recognition and approval that in 1833 he was elected as president of Mexico.

Much has been said about Santa Anna. He is accused of being a traitor and favoring and cooperating with invading forces. However, this could not be further from reality. Historical characters are complex, full of nuances. Throughout this chapter, you will be able to appreciate the real Santa Anna and the great love he had for his country.

Something worth noting is that Santa Anna loved to take breaks due to the difficult task of governing a country. When he felt exhausted, he would retire to his hacienda and delegate a vice president or the Congress to take charge. He was in and out of power many times, partly because of the affection and admiration the Mexican people felt for him. Santa Anna was never a stable president. Over the course of twenty-three years, he held power eleven times. During that period, the country fought several wars, and under his watch, the territory of Texas gained its independence and became part of the United States.

While Santa Anna was enjoying one of his breaks, Vice President Gomez Farias tried to implement new policies, among them the separation of church and state and the proposal to pay the country's public debt using the church's substantial assets. When public opinion turned against these measures, Santa Anna took control again. The centralist Republic was reinstated, and everything seemed to return to normal.

But Texas took advantage of this disorder, arguing their opposition to the restoration of a centralist republic and seizing the opportunity to take up arms against the Mexican government.

The Mexican-American War or Invasion

In the aftermath of the War of Independence, it was apparent that Mexico was wounded. Even though the longed-for freedom had been achieved, after eleven years of war, the country was devastated. Most of the country's northern states were pretty much neglected, including Texas. The Americans, who dreamed of expanding their territory, sought after Texas. The people of Texas themselves felt left out and forgotten by the new government.

With the passage of time, US citizens began to settle and put down roots in Texas, which would strongly influence plans for independence. In 1830, Mexico began to prohibit immigration from the US due to the large number of Americans already living in Texan territory. Over the following years, the Mexican government began to incentivize its citizens to migrate to the northern states so that the North American immigrants would not outnumber the Mexican population. However, in 1835, Texas rose up in opposition to the centralist government in Mexico and, in 1836, declared its independence.

History as told by the Mexicans omits certain battles, perhaps because of their irrelevance to the independence of Texas. In US history, almost all the battles fought by the Texan army are recounted—no matter how insignificant they may be.

For US history, Texas independence began with the battle of Gonzalez. This first battle took place in 1835 when a group of Texans, commanded by Henry Moore, attacked a group of soldiers from the Mexican army. In this first encounter, the Mexican troops had to withdraw from Texas territory.

The commander of the Mexican soldiers, Francisco de Castañeda, immediately wrote to General Antonio Lopez de Santa Anna about the situation in the north. The Mexican army began to gather under the command of Santa Anna. The Texans established a provisional government and formed their own army under the command of Samuel Houston.

While the Texas territory was engaged in this struggle, on March 1, 1836, a group of individuals—the overwhelming majority of Americans living in Texas—signed a Declaration of Independence. On March 2 of the same year, the constitution of the Republic of Texas was adopted and published. This constitution was based entirely on that of the United States. It authorized slavery, which was prohibited in Mexico, and denied recognition and citizenship to African Americans and Native Americans.

This was a reversal for Texas. One of the main reasons Mexico fought so hard for independence was freedom, and once Mexicans gained their freedom, the first thing they did was abolish slavery.

At the end of the day, most of the inhabitants of the Texan territory, or at least those who had a say, were Americans, so it was easy for them to declare Texas's independence.

Among the battles that led to the consolidation of the Republic of Texas, it is accurate to say that the Alamo was not crucial to this goal. However, over the years, history has been altered for many reasons, one of them being that there were no Texan survivors who could correctly narrate the events that took place there. Those who told the story were children, women, or individuals who were far away and who had not seen what happened in detail. Another factor that contributed to misrepresentations and half-truths is the Hollywood factor: the movie industry has managed to distort reality.

In order to tell the story of the Alamo, and therefore, the independence of Texas, it is necessary to rewind a little and understand some of the history of this place.

The Alamo dates back to the time of New Spain. This compound was a shelter for Native Americans and Franciscans. The largest number of people it ever housed was 328 Native Americans. In 1803, it was converted to a mission, becoming a fortress where dungeons, barracks, and even a small and rudimentary hospital were built.

During the Texan War of Independence, the Alamo mission remained abandoned and neglected. As tensions grew, Mexican General Martin Perfecto de Cos gave instructions to fortify the Alamo. While the Alamo mission was a makeshift fortress, partly because there was only a short amount of time to make improvements, it was designed to withstand attacks.

As the war broke out, Santa Anna traveled through Mexico, gathering an army to fight the Texan rebels. This task was not easy, as one of the main obstacles for the Mexicans was the lack of funds to finance a real army. However, Santa Anna managed to gather a good number of soldiers and set out for Texas.

While he was recruiting men and looking for funds to finance his army—since the public coffers of the Mexican state were, naturally, empty—he sent part of the army to join General Cos, who was already in Texas.

On his march toward the Texan territory, Santa Anna managed to add new men to his troops, approximately 1,500. However, upon arriving in Saltillo, he received the news that General Cos had surrendered in San Antonio.

By January 1836, Santa Anna had two thousand soldiers ready for battle. Positioned in Saltillo, they were waiting for the right moment to attack.

On the other side, General Sam Houston gave instructions to James Bowie for the rebels to withdraw from the Alamo and take all the ammunition and weapons and barricade themselves in Gonzales. Bowie's response was negative, claiming that mules would be needed to move the heavy artillery. Samuel Houston leaves them to their fate while he sets up in San Felipe.

Although Santa Anna's army grew in numbers, they lacked food and still had a long road ahead. Despite not having sufficient supplies, General Santa Anna does not turn back. He leaves for Monclova to reach the troops who were waiting for him there under the command of General Sesma.

The days pass, and good news reaches the Alamo. William B. Travis would join Bowie's and Neill's troops. By adding Travis' men, the defenders at the Alamo would now number 130.

In February, rumors began to spread regarding Santa Anna's troops. Some said he would not reach the Alamo or that he would not even make it to Texas, and others said he was very close. The rumors were also flying around the Mexican army's camp. A rather gossipy priest lets General Santa Anna know that there are no more than 250 men in San Antonio, and he also mentions that they are having a party.

On February 23, Santa Anna's troops arrived at a nearby hill, and residents began fleeing.

The Mexican army was greeted by cannon fire once they reached San Antonio. General Santa Anna quickly took San Antonio and advanced toward the Alamo. The mission was surrounded by Mexican troops. Santa Anna had personally scouted the limits of the Alamo and organized his artillery. Travis was on his own since

Bowie had suddenly fallen ill, leaving Travis in command. Desperate, Travis sent messages left and right, pleading for support to no avail.

The attacks continued. One of Travis's frantic messages finally got a favorable response. On February 27, 1836, reinforcements left from Gonzales, while a group of mercenaries headed for the Alamo from Washington.

News came quickly, both for those besieged at the Alamo and for the Mexican army. Travis sent more letters requesting as much support as possible, and Santa Anna sent men to cut off Travis's reinforcements and communications.

One point that deserves to be addressed is the number of men who were in the Alamo; this has been the subject of debate for years. According to the numbers in Travis's letters, there were 150 men, plus another thirty-two who joined the call for help, for a total of 182 soldiers. However, this number does not take into account Black slaves or the wounded; if these were counted, the number would rise to approximately 250.

On March 6, the inevitable happened—and the Alamo was captured. Mexican troops advanced rapidly toward the mission walls, there were a few casualties, but in less than an hour, it was all over. It was not a battle; it was a massacre. The soldiers who tried to escape from the Alamo were killed by troops waiting outside the mission. Not a single soldier was left alive inside the small fortress. Later, the American version of history claimed that the battle lasted four to five hours, and other versions even said that the battle lasted a whole day. Mexican history tells another version. However, one thing can be said without fear of being wrong: this victory did not mean much to the Mexican army or deter Texas's independence.

Texas Becomes One More Star of the United States of America

After their quick victory at the Alamo, General Santa Anna and his troops expected the Texas fighters to surrender. After advancing on enemy troops, the Mexican army arrived at San Jacinto. The general, confident and relaxed, still savoring the victory, established his camp eight hundred meters away from the rebel troops.

General Houston ordered his men to be discreet and began to plan his counterattack against the Mexican army, which was resting peacefully.

April 21, 1836. All seems calm in both camps. With everything quiet, the Mexican soldiers let their guard down. Santa Anna is confident, perhaps imagining the acclamation he would receive when he returned to the capital. Suddenly, the rebel cannons thunder. General Houston had set his plan in motion, surprising the Mexican army.

Santa Anna, bewildered, began to give orders to his soldiers, but they had no idea where the attacks were coming from. The soldiers themselves, not knowing what to do, succumbed to enemy fire. Chaos erupts in the Mexican camp, and survivors flee the battlefield. General Santa Anna began to retreat, but he was soon captured by Houston's men.

Santa Anna was a prisoner of war for seven months. During that time, he suffered the worst humiliations; he was chained and deprived of food and mocked by anyone who saw him. During those months in captivity, he was forced to sign the Treaties of Velasco, which recognized Texas's independence. The wars would cease immediately, and the Mexican army would withdraw from the Texan territory. Texas also requested that the Black slaves and livestock that had crossed into Mexico be returned as well.

Texan independence was achieved—with the leader and greatest figure of the Mexican army and people as a prisoner. Despite casualties on both sides, Texas was now a republic.

Texan independence could not have been achieved without support from the Americans, who were crucial to the events, even financing the Texan rebels. Once independence was achieved, there was no obstacle to annexing Texas to the United States. Suspiciously, everything seemed to go according to the plan the US government had from the beginning.

After the independence of the Texas territory, Santa Anna's government still had hopes that Texas would come to its senses and return to Mexico. Unfortunately, they were left whistling in the wind because the Texans had never felt Mexican. Washington fully supported the actions of the new Texas government, welcoming them with open arms.

It took a long time for diplomatic relations between Mexico and the United States to improve. Texas was trying to establish itself, Mexico was having internal political and financial problems, and the United States was happy with its future acquisition. But would they be satisfied with Texas—or would they seek more territory? As the saying goes, leopards don't change their spots.

In 1843, Jose Maria Bocanegra was in charge of diplomatic relations on behalf of Mexico, when US Secretary of State Abel P. Upshur publicly stated that he advocated the annexation of Texas. After learning of this, Bocanegra sent a letter to the US official, informing him that if negotiations between Texas and the United States persisted, Mexico would take this gesture as a declaration of war.

Upshur did not heed the warnings about Texas, and in late 1843, Bocanegra was informed that the US Congress would accept the annexation of Texas. Secretary of State Upshur lets the Mexicans know that President John Tyler has full confidence in the wisdom of Congress to resolve the Texas question. To appease the feelings of distrust, Upshur proposes to resolve the conflicts related to the Texas territory in an amicable manner.

However, nothing could come to fruition due to Upshur's sudden death in 1844. The Secretary of State died on a steamboat on the Potomac River during a demonstration of cannon fire that clearly went wrong. Negotiations between the two countries were suspended. The new US Secretary of State, John C. Calhoun, was determined that Congress should go forward with the annexation of Texas and summoned Texas representatives to convince Congress to vote in favor. He also requested a meeting with Juan Nepomuceno Almonte to renew the negotiations that had been interrupted after Upshur's death.

Calhoun did not care about what Almonte had previously expressed. Ignoring Almonte's response, he sent word to Bocanegra that if the United States signed the accession of Texas, it would only be to protect their interests since they felt threatened by the British.

After winning the presidential election of 1844, James K. Polk promised to annex the Texas territory to the United States. Meanwhile, the outgoing president, John Tyler, anxious for recognition and to leave some noteworthy event for his administration, decided to sign the treaty of annexation with Texas. Congress approved it on February 26, 1845, just days before the new president took office.

Likewise, the Texan congress approved the resolution in July of the same year. James Polk would sign the bill to admit Texas to the United States in December 1845.

This is how the Texas territory became part of the United States, with the US taking into very little consideration diplomatic relations with Mexico and ignoring warnings made by Minister Bocanegra about Mexico's rejection of such a decision. On the Mexican border, there were still hundreds of thousands of square kilometers that were still in the sights of the United States. Texas was the beginning of an onslaught that looked to be much greater, and more painful, for the Mexicans.

The American Intervention in Mexico, the Heroic Children, and the Treaty of Guadalupe Hidalgo

The US invasion of Mexican territory, which would end with the signing of the Treaty of Guadalupe Hidalgo, began with the annexation of Texas by the United States.

Although Mexico made its position on Texas clear from the beginning, in January 1846, President James Polk instructed General Taylor to occupy a disputed territory. Mexican soldiers marched toward this territory, met the Americans, and a confrontation ensued. It was not a massacre or a battle; it was simply a few exchanges of bullets between sides, with some casualties and wounded, but that was enough to arouse the anger of the United States.

President Polk falsely accused Mexico of having spilled American blood on American soil. It should be noted that the US president still had expansion plans in mind. And luckily for him, there were groups in the coveted territories that were opposed to the centralist republic that had been imposed by the Mexican government in 1836 under the *Siete Leyes* (the Seven Laws, a series of constitutional changes that fundamentally altered the organizational structure of Mexico to create the centralist republic).

Meanwhile, Mexico was again experiencing instability. The public treasury was still bankrupt, some states were trying to become independent, and there was war between natives and whites. But above all, there was indifference on the part of the many Mexican states. The nation lacked unity, the unity it once had when it fought against the Spaniards, but that was already in the past.

With the events on the border between Texas and Tamaulipas, President Polk saw a clear opportunity to implement his expansionist plans. Supported by the US Congress, he declared war on Mexico in May 1846. In the US Congress itself, there was some—though not much—opposition to the invasion, partly because any land taken from Mexico would add more slave territory to the United States.

Before this declaration of war was made official, the Americans already had their plans ready to attack and invade Mexican territory. Their first action was to mobilize their fleets and blockade the main ports of Mexico, both in the Gulf and the Pacific.

Once the ports were blockaded by US ships, General Taylor made his way into the interior of Mexico, making clear that the United States was not only trying to defend the Texas border, but to expand it.

The United States allocated $10 million to finance the war and added more than fifty thousand men, most of them volunteers, to its troops. It was the first time in history that US soldiers would fight in a foreign country. In addition to this, US ships were blockading Mexican ports, and more ships were added with military weapons.

General Taylor crossed the Rio Grande and took Matamoros easily. This made the American troops think the military campaign would not last long; however, the Mexican people proved them wrong. The government alerted the population about the foreign invasion in the north and called upon them to take up arms against the invaders. September 21 marked the beginning of one of the toughest battles the US Army faced: the Battle of Monterrey. For the first time in a long time, Mexicans were united in putting up resistance. It was one of the bloodiest and longest encounters of the war.

The first day, there were considerable casualties for the Mexican army, who defended their city with fury and glory under the command of General Pedro de Ampudia. On September 23, the battle reached its climax. The heaviest piece of American artillery opened fire against Mexican troops who were defending the city. There was fierce street fighting, the sound of muskets and cannons, and the screams of men slashed by bayonets. Every rooftop and every window were taken advantage of by the Mexicans to open fire. Both armies fought throughout the day.

At nightfall, General Ampudia sent a letter to the US general, requesting a truce to evacuate the city; his soldiers were exhausted, and the civilian population was shattered. On the morning of September 24, General Taylor asked for the unconditional surrender of the city, recognizing that Mexican troops had defended their territory with honor. On September 25, the truce was signed—and Monterrey surrendered.

This agreement, carried out by the leaders of both armies, continues to generate great controversy to this day. The Mexican army troops not only resisted but also severely damaged the invading forces. Casualties reduced the American forces; the Mexican army held them at bay for four days, yet despite this, the Mexican general opted for an agreement that surprised even Taylor, who was about to withdraw from Monterrey, disconcerted by the Mexican soldiers' bravery.

The Battle of Monterrey was the first in which the famous St. Patrick's Battalion participated. It was made up of immigrant soldiers, mostly Irish, who decided to abandon the US Army and join the Mexican forces. Why did they change sides? Were they suddenly seduced by the power of tequila and mariachis? There was another reason. The members of the St. Patrick's Battalion were Catholics, and because of their religion, they felt more affinity with Mexicans than with Americans.

At the same time that the invasion was advancing, Mexico was sinking deeper and deeper into its own political instability. Taking advantage of the situation, the US government sought to place General Antonio Lopez de Santa Anna as president of Mexico once again, who at the time had retired to Havana, Cuba. The United States wanted to bring back Santa Anna in order to negotiate the border territories and end the war.

Polk sent Mackenzie as representative of US interests to negotiate with Santa Anna over his return to Mexico. Santa Anna, who was nobody's fool, accepted Mackenzie's proposal. Now the general could cross any port or beach without being stopped by any of the US ships blockading Mexican ports.

In August 1846, a passenger disembarked from a British ship that arrived at the port of Veracruz. Locals' uneasiness turned to delight when they found out that their former general had returned.

Santa Anna, now back in Mexican territory, began to plan his political and military future. From Santa Anna's perspective, what he negotiated in his meeting with Mackenzie in Havana had been so vague that he preferred to forget it.

Santa Anna met with military officers and politicians in Puebla, among them Valentin Gomez Farias, who supported the return of General Santa Anna and represented the interests of the Liberals. Following this meeting, the people of Mexico were called to take up arms and defend their homeland from the invaders.

Santa Anna marched to Mexico City and was received with a parade and cheers. Once installed in the capital, Santa Anna announced his decision to march north, and he took command of the Mexican army, ready to defend national sovereignty. This news raised the spirits of the generals and their troops, rekindling the flame of patriotism among Mexicans.

General Santa Anna consulted with Juan Nepomuceno Almonte about the military situation and with Gomez Farias about the financial situation of the country. Both answers were not encouraging. On one hand, the national army had twenty thousand men, less than half that of the invading army. On the other hand, the public coffers were as empty as they were twenty years ago. The Mexican army's weapons were obsolete, and despite their unquestionable bravery, its soldiers did not have the professionalism of the invaders. Once again, General Santa Anna encountered difficulties.

Santa Anna began his plan to recruit troops, but this time, he could not afford to wait for people to volunteer because the American army was quickly moving into the country. He asked the governors of various states to draft as many men as possible.

For his defense plan, Santa Anna consulted with Generals Ignacio Mora and Gabriel Valencia, his most trusted men. Mora thought it convenient to march toward the north of the country, where the attacks had already begun. Valencia proposed protecting the port of Veracruz, where there was a possibility that the American ships would disembark. Santa Anna decided to confront the invading army in the north, to later return quickly and head off an invasion in Veracruz.

Santa Anna left the city with an army of three thousand men, ready to defend the country with their lives. On his way through Queretaro, a group of brave individuals (approximately three hundred) joined its ranks. Once the troops arrived in San Luis, they were greeted with bitter news: the capitulation of Monterrey. Overcome by a feeling of patriotism and courage, Santa Anna ordered the arrest of General Ampudia so that he could be brought before a court-martial.

While Santa Anna was gathering men and making his battle plans in San Luis, General Taylor sent letters to the United States with his strategies, among which he proposed invading the port of Veracruz. He also requested more men and supplies to continue his passage into the interior of Mexico. However, the news from Washington did not go as expected. He was informed that he should hand over his best men to General Winfield Scott, who would take care of the rest. Taylor would be limited to maintaining his position on the northern border.

Thanks to the interception of a letter from General Taylor, Santa Anna accelerated his plans and encouraged his army to continue on. In the intercepted letter, General Taylor had requested reinforcements on the border, so Santa Anna decided to begin a two-hundred-kilometer march northward through the desert.

On February 21, 1847, he arrived in Coahuila, where the battle of Angostura would be fought.

Although the Mexican soldiers were outnumbered and outgunned, their courage and bravery pushed them to defend their land. After several hours of intense fighting, the Mexican army managed to gain ground. On February 23, the Mexican troops were exhausted and without provisions due to the difficult desert crossing. So, even though the Mexican army seemed to be winning the battle, General Santa Anna ordered a retreat to reorganize his forces.

At the same time, the presidency was being disputed in the Mexican capital. Santa Anna had left Vice President Gomez Farias in charge of the country while he assumed command of the national army. Gomez Farias wanted to use the church's assets, which were very large, to finance the war against the United States. This seriously displeased the clergy, and they organized a movement headed by the *Polkos*; their intention was to disavow the authority of Gomez Farias and rebel against the government.

The rebellion of the Polkos, made up mostly of the elite, led to riots and confrontations in Mexico City. They were called Polkos for two reasons. The first is that the polka was the favorite dance of the wealthy, and the second is that it was rumored that they secretly had sympathies for President Polk's invasion. Because of this uprising, Santa Anna abandoned his troops and immediately returned to the capital to bring order.

At the same time, Taylor's troops had gained more ground in the north of the country. Among the occupied territories were

Chihuahua, New Mexico, and California. And the invasion of Veracruz under General Scott was imminent.

At the beginning of March, the United States naval force approached the beaches and ports of Veracruz with more than 150 ships and a little more than twelve thousand soldiers. The plan was to occupy the capital of Mexico from Veracruz, just as Hernan Cortes had done three centuries before.

On March 9, 1847, the American ships arrived at the Veracruz port, and General Scott sent men to scout the area. His only concern was the old fort of San Juan de Ulua. The walled city of Veracruz and its fort were considered the most protected in North America, almost as impenetrable as Troy.

Crafty as an old fox, General Scott sends some ships close to the port to test the range of the enemy cannons. The Mexicans take the bait and fire with everything they have; however, the cannonballs do not even graze the American ships. The invading troops easily disembark in Veracruz since almost the entire Mexican army was in Mexico City, trying to put down the rebellion of the Polkos.

The residents of the port did not have the necessary artillery to face such an army. They only had two hundred cannons, not the four hundred the Americans had estimated, and their forts were old and not prepared for war. The general commander of Veracruz, Juan Morales, urgently requested reinforcements from Mexico City, but it was all in vain.

Despite these weaknesses, the *Veracruzanos* (as people from Veracruz are known) were not going to surrender their city. Aware that no reinforcements would arrive to help them, they set out to defend the port. The US soldiers heavily bombarded the walled city, overcoming the defenders of the port, without mercy or regard for the city's inhabitants. Scott asked General Morales to surrender his army; however, Morales responded that they were willing to die defending Veracruz.

The bombardment lasted day and night, causing fires and destroying buildings. People ran without knowing where the next cannonball would fall. General Scott received a letter from the foreign consuls in the city, asking him to allow citizens of neutral countries to leave Veracruz with their women and children. Scott replied that he would not agree to deal with anyone other than General Morales—and only if the latter surrendered and gave up Veracruz.

The city was engulfed in flames. Some 6,700 cannon shots were fired on the port. On March 26, General Scott proposed negotiations; however, he would only accept surrender. Morales refused to surrender and dishonor his country. He was replaced by General Juan Landeros, who signed the capitulation on March 27. The following day, after so much heroism and sorrow, the surrender was complete.

The US army continued to add crushing victories, mercilessly destroying anyone who crossed their path. The Mexicans suffered a number of military defeats, undoubtedly lowering the country's morale. The generals of the Mexican army met in the capital, awaiting instructions from their leader, General Santa Anna.

Santa Anna was trying to decide on his last offensive. The rebellion of the Polkos was resolved when the general promised the church to protect it from its enemies in the government. But ... you scratch my back, and I'll scratch yours. In exchange for this favor, Santa Anna asked the church for a loan to continue financing the war. The Mexican soldiers, guided by their general's patriotism, began to organize the defense of Mexico City on August 19, 1847.

Battle after battle, the Mexican army became weaker and weaker. It was vastly outnumbered by the Americans' military armament. The advance of the invaders was imminent. After almost a month of relentless combat, on September 13, the invading forces reached Chapultepec Castle, a former military college that was protected by a few soldiers and young cadets.

The battle of Chapultepec Castle has been filled with myths over the years. It has been said that six cadets, just young boys, heroically defended the military college. It has been said that the boy heroes were the last to die in the defense of Chapultepec, and that when they ran out of ammunition, they killed enemy soldiers with bayonets. The most famous myth corresponds to Juan

Escutia. The story goes that when the enemy forces overran his position, Juan Escutia wrapped himself in the Mexican flag and threw himself off the hill to the ravine below, preferring suicide before the Americans took possession of the flag. These facts, as epic as they may seem, have no historical basis. Even so, these exploits are taught in schools as an unquestionable truth. The first point to clarify is that Chapultepec was not only defended by the boy heroes, but that more than nine hundred Mexicans died in defense of the hill. The only children who fought were Francisco Marquez and Vicente Suarez, who were approximately fourteen years old. What is not in doubt is the bravery and heroism displayed by these "children" in the defense of Mexican soil.

One day after the fall of Chapultepec, on September 14, the invading army occupied Mexico City, raising the American flag at the National Palace. And while the American flag was being raised at Chapultepec Castle, the captured survivors of St. Patrick's Battalion were being executed by hanging in retaliation for their treason.

Days before this event, the federal government had changed its headquarters and settled in Queretaro, where negotiations began to put an end to this painful war once and for all. Antonio Lopez de Santa Anna resigned as president of Mexico, and Manuel de la Peña, president of the Supreme Court of Justice, took his place. The new president ordered that Santa Anna be tried in a court-martial.

As US soldiers were also pursuing him, Santa Anna fled to Jamaica. From that exile he wrote the following farewell:

> Compatriots, misfortune has deprived me of the incomparable satisfaction of presenting you with a splendid victory, but I have never committed a crime against my country. I have desired everything great and glorious for Mexico, and to obtain it I have not spared even my own blood. You know this, and you will do me justice.

Finally, on February 2, 1848, the Treaty of Guadalupe Hidalgo was signed, putting an end to the war between Mexico and the United States. The treaty established Texas as the new boundary; the Texas border would be fixed at the Rio Grande. The US government would lift its blockade of Mexican ports and commit to repatriate prisoners of war. Finally, Mexico would sell the territories of New Mexico and Alta California to the United States. These territories were later divided into the current states of California, Nevada, Arizona, New Mexico, and Utah, as well as part of Colorado and Wyoming. With this, Mexico ceded more than half of its territory for the paltry amount of $15 million, which was not even paid immediately, instead deposited to the national coffers a few months later. The Mexicans who remained in the seized territory were given the option of keeping their land and becoming US citizens.

With this infamous dispossession, one of the grayest and saddest eras between the two nations came to an end, after years of war and thousands of lives lost. The two eagles, Mexican and American, finally stopped fighting.

Second Attempt To Invade Veracruz

If there is one thing the port of Veracruz has, it is the misfortune of being the favorite spot when someone wants to invade Mexico. This new invasion is different in that it was not for political or territorial purposes; it is for money. As is well-known, money makes the world go 'round, and in this case, it brought the Americans back to the shores of Veracruz.

Mexico was, once more, going through political and social instability. The cause was the Mexican Revolution, which lasted ten long years and during which the country went through many different crises. While Mexico's neighbors to the north were growing as a country and on their way to becoming a world power, in Mexico, they were still taking up arms and shooting at each other.

The state of Veracruz was also home to most of the country's oil wells at that time. Let's remember that those wells belonged to foreign companies. President Cardenas's oil expropriation of 1938 was still in the future, so almost all the oil companies belonged to foreigners. When the revolution broke out, foreigners felt unsafe, fearful of losing their companies, properties, and interests, and with good reason, taking into account the ideals represented by Francisco I. Madero and the other revolutionary leaders.

The US government urged the Mexican government to stop all this revolutionary agitation and secure their interests. The Americans installed a type of battalion on their southern border in case they had to intervene to defend their citizens (and businesses) in Mexico. The Americans were not the only oil companies in Mexico; the British dominated the industry, and companies of other nationalities were also in Mexico. If the United States intervened in this conflict, it would benefit other foreigners who had particular interests in Mexico.

Diplomatic relations between Mexico and the United States were again broken due to many factors. The main reason was that the United States did not recognize the government of President Victoriano Huerta, who led a coup d'état against Madero. The US decided to immediately withdraw its ambassador to Mexico, firmly displaying its position. Clearly this benefited the Mexican revolutionary leaders who sought to overthrow Huerta. But the pretext that allowed the United States to invade the country and support its interests was the Tampico Affair, in addition to rumors about the purchase of weapons from the Germans and the sale of land to the English in Veracruz. Remember: in those years, the First World War was being fought in Europe. These reasons provided the perfect excuse for President Woodrow Wilson to order the military to intervene in Mexican territory. With this new invasion, the United States once again demonstrated that a leopard cannot change its spots.

I will address the reasons mentioned above, and then I will explain the invasion of the port of Veracruz and what could have ended very badly for Mexico. Starting with the Tampico Affair, we can see that this was not really that serious. On April 9, 1914, US sailors crossed Mexican waters and once ashore, they set out to buy fuel for their ship. Mexican forces detained the sailors and took them to a military barracks to clear up the matter. Once the misunderstanding was settled, they were released with the classic "sorry about that." When this reached the ears of the US high command, they were more enraged than a fighting bull. The naval commander demanded that the Mexican officers salute the American flag as an apology, a request that Mexico refused.

As if the above were not enough, rumors spread about an alleged sale of land in Veracruz by the Huerta government to the British, which would give British oil companies an advantage, to the detriment of the Americans. There were also rumors of an arms purchase by the Mexican government from the Germans. The United States discussed these absurdities with its southern neighbor and came to the conclusion that they had to intervene again.

The United States sent its warships to the port of Veracruz. On April 21, 1914, three warships were ready to take the historic port, which was mostly defended by young cadets, who, as in the 1847 invasion, were outgunned and outnumbered. Later, more American troops came to occupy important buildings and strategic locations. The Mexican government troops were ordered to withdraw from the area, and the Americans were able to take the port of Veracruz easily.

Once the Veracruz customs office was taken, the United States would make sure that the Huerta government could not receive any military cargo. Seven months later, in November 1914, the US troops abandoned the port, leaving it in the hands of Venustiano Carranza's army.

Since these comings and goings were taking place during World War I, the interests of England and the United States were at stake. These countries were concerned that Germany, a rival in the war, would offer Mexico help against the United States. There was even a rather tempting proposal. On January 16, 1917, a telegram from Germany was detected that discussed offering support to Mexico in exchange for fighting against the United States. If the war were won, Mexico would recover the lost territories of Texas, Arizona, and New Mexico. Despite its appeal, President Venustiano Carranza declined the proposal. Later, the United States entered World War I, to Germany's misfortune.

Finally, it should be made clear that the United States could easily have taken advantage of the chaos in Mexico to invade and do what it wanted. However, World War I stopped it from intervening further. Thanks to this, Mexico did not suffer another invasion. Although it did suffer one, on a smaller scale, when US troops crossed the border to hunt Pancho Villa.

The One-Day Invasion of Pancho Villa

It was hot that day in the town of Columbus. Some dry clouds were visible in the distance, and the hills were full of weeds. The hot air immediately made anyone who breathed it thirsty. The villagers knew that a few miles away, in Mexico, a civil war had been raging for several years, but they considered that conflict as distant as the few clouds that provided shade. Better to focus on the daily needs of a small town. No one in Columbus imagined that Pancho Villa, a bandit turned revolutionary leader, needed the United States to declare war on Mexico and on his enemy, Venustiano Carranza.

Some of the people of Columbus have heard stories about Villa. They know that he is called the Centaur of the North, the Mexican Napoleon. They also know that their government forbids selling arms to Villa's forces. When night fell, the people of Columbus went to sleep with the peace of mind that the war was far away. While they slept, hundreds of men loyal to Villa illegally crossed the border into the United States. Under the cover of darkness, they evaded the Palomas checkpoint. At four o'clock in the morning, before the sun came out to spread its heat, Villa's forces began attacking the sleeping town.

Gunfire awakens the inhabitants of Columbus. The American garrison tries to repel the attack. Anyone with a weapon defends themselves against the Mexicans, who outnumber them. Destroying everything in their path, Villa's men reach the center of the town. They spray a hotel with kerosene, and fire spreads to the surrounding houses. But thanks to the fire, the invaders can now be seen in these early-morning hours. Civilians join the American troops to defend Columbus, and to Villa's surprise, his men are falling rapidly. They take what little they can plunder and their wounded comrades, leaving behind a town in flames. No one would have imagined that a Mexican could have ordered an invasion of the United States.

This was the first invasion that any country dared to carry out against the United States. Although it is considered minuscule, history still considers it an intrusion.

Some argue that Villa's attack was because of US support for the Mexican constitutionalists. Others allege that he did it to take revenge on an arms dealer, a property owner in Columbus, who had sold him weapons in poor condition.

The town of Columbus, New Mexico, at that time, was basically a military camp. On March 9, 1916, Villa arrived at the border between the United States and Mexico. His small army consisted of 589 men.

A curious fact is that no author has bothered to give an exact number of invaders led by Villa. Some authors mention around four hundred men, others say between four hundred and five hundred, and some say more than five hundred. American authors who narrate this battle exaggerate the numbers, declaring that Villa's army had a thousand men.

The US press confirmed this stratospheric figure one day after the attack. Even General Hopkins, in order not to make himself look bad, claimed that the invading army numbered three thousand men.

The attack on Columbus lasted only three hours; however, it devastated the small town. The Villa army left the place at sunrise, taking with them a booty that included horses, ammunition, and military artillery.

Undoubtedly, this attack was one of the revolutionary leader's worst executed and most poorly planned. Despite this, the fiasco was overshadowed by the abysmal response of the US Army that was stationed there.

For the United States, this could not stand; nobody was going to give them a taste of their own medicine. The next day, President Woodrow Wilson announced that the enemy Pancho Villa would be pursued, putting a price on his head. He sent a military team, led by General John J. Pershing, to capture Pancho Villa, dead or alive. This mission is known as the "Punitive Expedition," and according to President Wilson, it would be carried out respecting Mexican sovereignty. In Mexico, Venustiano Carranza also ordered the commander of his Constitutionalist forces to pursue and capture General Villa. At the same time, he ordered his other generals to prevent the entry of US troops into Mexican territory.

But Carranza's efforts were not enough to assuage the Americans intent on revenge. On March 15, an army of more than five thousand soldiers led by General Pershing invaded Mexican territory, entering through Chihuahua. The Punitive Expedition lasted ten months, but they never had any contact with Villa's troops. The only thing they found in the mountains of Chihuahua was silence. On only two occasions did the Americans clash with Mexican soldiers, leaving casualties for both sides. They never captured Pancho Villa or were able to make him pay for his crimes in Columbus.

In 1917, with the United States about to enter World War I and President Wilson fearful that Mexico might decide to ally with Germany against the United States, the US decided to withdraw its troops and fully recognize Carranza's presidency, restoring diplomatic relations between the two countries.

In this way, the US army was defeated, not by a nation, but by a simple man and his faithful followers, who invaded the territory of a superpower. Villa's fame and legend continued to grow through word of mouth. The revolutionary became a hero, a national legend who is still admired today by many Mexicans.

Mexico and the United States share a lot of history, many memories, most of them bitter and sad, but I like to think it's the good memories that endure. Therefore, to end this chapter, I leave this quote from Jose C. Valdes:

> Bitter, very bitter, must always be the times in which the homelands are defeated by aggressive and superior enemies, and in which they lose lands that are part of their heritage and lineage; but happy, very happy, are those peoples that after falling victim to degrading and disloyal desires, know how to forgive the offender to restore their happiness not in territorial surfaces, but in the values of reason, which are eternal.

Ruins of Columbus, New Mexico, after
being raided by Pancho Villa, 1916.

Chapter 8

Civil Wars: The Rebellion against Iturbide

In Mexico, we have hidden the pain of internal wars. We suffer their ravages, but we know not where they come from. Our history bears the weight of civil wars that have shaped modern Mexico, although a large part of Mexican society is unaware of the impact internal wars have had on the country. Although these conflicts broke out more than a century ago, the scars persist.

If we were to randomly ask people on the street how many people died in the Cristero War, chances are they would not know that this conflict claimed 250,000 lives. Much less would they know that a few years later, a Second Cristero War broke out because the religious rebels disagreed with the government's education program, which they considered "socialist." The *Cristiada*, as it is also known, is not commemorated with an official day, a day of rest, or an ephemeris. In place of official or even religious discourse, this conflict has instead survived in art, as in the novel *Recuerdos del Porvenir* by Elena Garro, in the stories of Juan Rulfo, and in the history books of Jean Meyer.

Civil wars are more painful than other types of wars because they involve people who share families, traditions, cities, language, and a national identity. It is sad when people who coexist in the same territory are unable to find a better alternative to reconcile their differences than to take up arms and kill their own countrymen. Mexicans against Mexicans, Americans against Americans, Catholics against Catholics, brothers against brothers. Civil wars represent the failure of politics.

It can be said that there is a correlation between the backwardness of a country and the number of civil wars it has undergone. When a civil war occurs, everything in the country stops. If one nation invades another, when it triumphs, it keeps its resources; there is an incentive to fight a war and win. In a civil war, there is usually no

183

gain; the scenario is one of pure loss. In addition to the disastrous impact on industry, the civil wars in Mexico affected tax collection. The few resources the state had were not destined for the welfare of the people but to continue financing the fight. And the alternative to tax collection was to request loans from abroad so that the country would not end up falling apart, causing Mexico to drown in debt or be invaded for failing to meet its payments.

For example, New Spain, which was the richest colony in the Spanish Empire and had significant mining, textiles, and sugar industries, became a poor and ruined territory after the War of Independence, forced to focus on activities such as agriculture and cattle ranching. This is not to say that Mexico's first transformation was not necessary, only that the price for freedom from Spain in human and economic terms was very high. Worse yet, after the War of Independence, Mexico followed a path of conflict and political instability that would take a century to end.

The United States only had one civil war—the Civil War between the Union and Confederate states, which broke out because the former sought to abolish slavery and the latter wanted to maintain it. Mexico, on the other hand, was immersed in several internal wars (and a few foreign invasions) that gave the country no breathing room to grow on a par with its northern neighbor.

In this chapter, we will see how Mexico was a country fond of the *pasito tun tun*, the dance in which for every two steps forward, it's one step back.

Once Mexico achieved its independence from the Spanish Crown, wars continued unabated. The country had to grapple with foreign invasions and bloody civil wars, as if its destiny were perpetual violence.

As for the United States, its fierceness and massive military strength are widely acknowledged on the world stage. Any country would think twice before directly entering into war with the United States. Perhaps that is why, in some science fiction movies, the US can even fight extraterrestrial armies. Not even Martians can beat Uncle Sam's bald eagle. The United States has had few armed conflicts within its territory. Instead, the United States has tirelessly invaded other nations (Mexico had the misfortune of being the first) or has financed or joined wars all over the world. It is like that person who, in order not to dirty his own house, prefers that the party be held in someone else's.

This is a fundamental difference between the two nations. While one country concentrates on defending itself from invaders, the other invades and declares wars beyond its borders. One seeks to live in peace—even if its citizens are engaged in endless internal wars—and the other does not allow others to live in peace.

If we tally up the most famous wars on the Mexican side, we have the War of Independence, the Reform War between Republicans and Liberals, Texas Independence, the Pastry War, the US invasion of 1846, the Caste War, the French intervention, the 1910 Revolution, the Cristero War, and in a very minor role, the Second World War.

Meanwhile, the United States collects armed conflicts as if its entertainment depended on it. They had the internal wars of the colonies, the War of Independence, the Civil War, the Indian Wars, the Banana Wars, World War I, World War II, the Cold War, the War on Drugs, Star Wars, the Vietnam War, the Korean War, the Gulf War, and the invasion of Afghanistan and Iraq, just to mention a few.

The contrast is obvious. Mexico has a long history of internal struggles and invasions, although its only intervention in an external conflict occurred during World War II. The government decided to send a group of Mexican pilots—Squadron 201—to war as a consequence of German submarines sinking a Mexican oil tanker, the *Potrero del Llano*, thinking that Mexican ships were supplying fuel to the United States, which was true. The role of Squadron 201 was more symbolic than practical; Mexico's participation did not factor into the Allies' victory. Unfortunately, we cannot confirm whether the Germans quaked in their boots when Mexico declared war on the Axis countries. Squadron 201 barely made it to Asia to fight the Japanese, who were not the ones who had sunk the Mexican oil tankers. As a result of this declaration of war, military service became mandatory in Mexico. In comparison, since its independence, the United States has carried out countless military campaigns against various countries. After its intervention in World War I, it established itself as a world power. Following World War II, it became a superpower, and when it entered the war after the Japanese attack on Pearl Harbor in 1941, it tipped the scales to stop Hitler's advance and guarantee the Allied victory.

Now let's follow Agustin de Iturbide, a Creole (person of Spanish descent born in the colonies of New Spain) whose family enjoyed a comfortable socioeconomic status and whose father was Spanish and mother was Creole. His first-rate education enabled him to rise in the army. At first, Iturbide did not completely agree with the ideals of the insurgents, led by Father Miguel Hidalgo from the town of Dolores. However, both men wanted Mexico's independence from Spain and the abolition of slavery, although in the pursuit of these ideals, they had different visions.

Hidalgo was executed during the first phase of the armed uprising. Iturbide then became a hero of the victorious independence movement and crowned himself as the first emperor of independent Mexico. He took control of a territory with divided interests and deplorable economic conditions. In addition, both he and the Congress lacked experience running such a large empire. Iturbide's enemies and some members of Congress did not like the idea of Mexico being an empire. They wanted a republic. Instead of achieving conciliation with Congress, Iturbide found it easier to dissolve it. This authoritarian act would leave its mark as a betrayal of the ideals of independence.

The emperor's enemies conspired to create the *Plan of Casa Mata*, with Antonio Lopez de Santa Anna leading the rebellion. This plan was signed by Bourbonists and Republicans to put an end to Iturbide's empire. Let's recap the following: Mexico's independence was achieved on September 27, 1821. Agustin de Iturbide was proclaimed emperor on May 18, 1822, In December of the same year, Santa Anna took up arms against him with the *Plan of Veracruz*. In other words, after a war against Spain that lasted a decade and left behind great human and material losses, Mexico could not maintain the calm for even two years before shooting started up again.

Santa Anna was a malcontent who was constantly announcing armed rebellions against the governments in power. He was also a man of very broad convictions, given that sometimes he fought in favor of the monarchy, other times against it, and he was on both the conservative and liberal sides. Political bipolarity, one could call it. In the face of Santa Anna's uprising, Iturbide decided to restore the Congress in 1823. After several confrontations, Iturbide was forced from the position of emperor, going into exile in Spain.

Once the new Republican Congress was installed, a decree was published that declared Agustin de Iturbide a traitor and enemy of Mexico, and he was condemned to death if he ever set foot on Mexican soil again. A year later, unaware of this sentence, Iturbide returned to Mexico with courage born of ignorance. The government of Tamaulipas arrested him, and the sentence was carried out. Without a trial, Iturbide was shot the same afternoon of his tragic arrival. His last wish was to not be remembered as a traitor to his country or as an enemy of Mexico, a country he loved so much and helped to liberate from the repression of the old regime.

Coup: Liberals against Conservatives

Essentially, liberalism was triggered by the Industrial Revolution. Liberals were in favor of a progressive society and certain freedoms. Political parties did not exist in the eighteenth century, but the Masonic lodges played a decisive role in public policy decisions. Conservatives sought a centralized monarchy with the bourgeoisie as its axis. Oblivious to the pressing reality of other social strata, they favored colonialism. In this vein, the party was divided into the liberal York Lodge against the conservative Scottish Lodge. Both lodges ended up confronting one another, which occurred during the Veracruz rebellion of 1827.

Once the first Mexican empire fell with the execution of Agustin de Iturbide, the Conservatives favored a centralized government, while the Liberals favored the model of the US government, which was centered on a republic.

In the new and convulsive Mexico of the nineteenth century, the norm was that elections were held—and the loser disagreed with the results. This led to the loser gathering his backers, getting some rifles, and rebelling. These acts were so recurrent that it became a cyclical process with predictable results. In newly independent Mexico, each election brought with it a post-electoral conflict. No sooner were Mexico's second presidential elections held in 1828—whose candidates were Manuel Gomez Pedraza and Vicente Guerrero— than a brawl broke out. Even though the results favored Gomez Pedraza, Vicente Guerrero and his sympathizers ignored them like a mad dog, regardless of the fact that President Guadalupe Victoria recognized Gomez Pedraza's victory.

Antonio Lopez de Santa Anna, who sympathized with Vicente Guerrero, took up arms and captured the fort in Perote, Veracruz, with his men. From there, he rejected the elected government of Gomez Pedraza and sent word that he would not suspend his rebellion until Vicente Guerrero was named the new president of Mexico.

Meanwhile, in Mexico City, Guerrero's sympathizers incited riots at the Acordada prison, which apart from prisoners also housed a considerable amount of ammunition and weapons. The riots reached other major areas of the city, such as El Parian market, where people looted as many luxury goods as they could find. To Gomez Pedraza's misfortune, Guadalupe Victoria's government was lukewarm and did not fight the rebels very hard. This emboldened the rebels even more, and Gomez Pedraza was forced to flee the city for exile in France. And since the person who was to be named president of Mexico was no longer around, in his place, Congress proclaimed Vicente Guerrero as president.

They say that history often repeats itself. Just as Vicente Guerrero snatched the presidency from Gomez Pedraza by force, his vice president, Anastasio Bustamante, paid him back with the same coin, rebelling against the government. Protected by the *Plan of Xalapa*, he pursued Guerrero until he was betrayed, captured, and executed. And just as Anastasio Bustamante rose to power after Guerrero's death, he lost it due to protests against his ordering that assassination, led by Antonio Lopez de Santa Anna. Bustamante had to cede the presidency to Manuel Gomez Pedraza, who returned from exile to reclaim what had been his since the 1828 presidential election. However, he was only in power for three months as he was retaking his original term that, unfortunately, was about to conclude. Poor Gomez Pedraza got his candy back after everyone else had tasted it. And just as Santa Anna had taken up arms several times, years later, others took up arms against Santa Anna when he was finally in power, as happened with the *Plan of Ayutla* in 1854.

Another notable coup is the Tuxtepec Rebellion of 1876, proclaimed by General Porfirio Diaz who was upset (ironically) that President Sebastian Lerdo de Tejada wanted to be reelected, something allowed by the Constitution at the time. Previously, General Diaz had already rebelled against the reelection of President Benito Juarez in what is known as the *Plan de la Noria*, which ended when Juarez died of natural causes. Following in the footsteps of other national heroes, Porfirio Diaz took up arms against the government of Sebastian Lerdo de Tejada and gained strong popular support, given that Diaz was a war hero while President Lerdo de Tejada was the son of Spaniards. After several confrontations, Diaz triumphed, forcing Sebastian Lerdo de Tejada to flee to the United States. With nothing standing in his way, Porfirio Diaz quickly assumed the presidency of Mexico, initiating the era of the *Porfiriato*. After thirty-five years in power, having completely forgotten his old slogan of "effective suffrage, no reelection," Porfirio Diaz would not be overthrown in a coup but by an armed uprising led by a man from the north of Mexico, Francisco I. Madero. That would be the beginning of the Mexican Revolution.

It should be remembered that the United States has never suffered a coup, although there are those who claim that the assault on the Capitol in 2021 was very similar. The US has financed many coups in other countries, but it never had one in its own territory. In contrast, just in the period from 1824 to 1855, Mexico had an endless number of rebellions and coups. One of the most significant, due to imprudence and miscalculation, was the one instigated by the *Polkos*, members of the upper class who rose up against the government of Valentin Gomez Farias because he wanted the church, with its considerable resources, to help the Mexican state finance its war against the United States. Apparently, this proposal was more terrible than the worst of blasphemies, causing the Mexican government, in the middle of a war with the United States, to be distracted by an internal conflict and to have to deal with the Polkos and the American invaders at the same time.

The Independence of Yucatan

The sovereignty of the Republic of Yucatan was brief, lasting about as long as an ice cube under the sun. Before independence, Yucatan enjoyed certain benefits and autonomy, without being a fully independent state, and its judicial matters had to be resolved in the capital of the country.

As a result of the armed movements unleashed by the War of Independence, Yucatan decided to jump on the bandwagon and seek its own emancipation. Consequently, once Mexico declared its independence from Spain in 1821, Yucatan did the same and split from Mexico. Two years later, with the fall of Iturbide's regime, Yucatan decided to return to the open arms of Mexico, which was already a federated republic; that is, Yucatan recognized Mexico's authority but retained its sovereignty.

When Antonio Lopez de Santa Anna assumed command of the country, he repealed the Constitution of 1824 and enacted a new one. The document was published as the *Seven Laws of 1836*. Among its statutes, it empowered the president to appoint the governors of each state and make any important decisions for the country. Yucatan was on the payroll, without any differentiation whatsoever.

At that time, Yucatan was made up of the current states of Quintana Roo, Campeche, and Tabasco. Once they became aware of the statutes of the new centralist government of Mexico, the Yucatan Chamber of Deputies broke off relations with the rest of the country. In short order, they approved the "Act of Independence of the Peninsula." They proclaimed themselves a republic, proceeding to enact their own legislative constitution. Tabasco rejected joining the new republic after negotiating with the centralist government of Santa Anna.

Mexico responded militarily. This led Yucatan to agree to rejoin Mexico in 1843, as long as the sovereignty of the state and the free election of its governors were guaranteed. In 1844, Congress denied this request, and in 1845, Yucatán again declared itself an independent republic.

True to pattern, conflicts in Mexico increased in intensity. The so-called Seven Laws of Santa Anna were repealed, and the Constitution of 1824 came back into law, enabling Yucatan to join the country. A year later, in 1847, the so-called Caste War began in Yucatan, which started as a Maya rebellion.

The conflict was so brutal that the Republic of Yucatan requested military aid from the United States, and their support would be compensated by Yucatan joining the American Union. President Polk, inclined to annex Mexican territory to the United States, liked the idea, but the US Congress rejected the offer. Those who did support the Maya rebellion, out of purely commercial interests, were the British, who wanted to conquer the Maya territories. Meanwhile, Mexico waited day and night for Yucatan to accept its support. Mexico sent military troops and money to quell the uprising and decimate the Maya rebels. The governor decreed the accession of Yucatan to the republic on August 17, 1848. Although Yucatan resigned itself to becoming part of Mexico, this did not end the Caste War, which lasted for almost fifty years and cruelly repressed the Maya people. In 2021, the Mexican state asked for forgiveness for having participated in that war of extermination.

The Reform War

After the War of Independence, and even after the Revolution of 1910, the Catholic Church did not lose an ounce of power or influence in the country. The symbol of the Virgin of Guadalupe on the libertarian banner speaks for itself regarding the weight of religion in spite of the ups and downs of war.

Since the conquest, the church has been involved in every important event, not missing out on any of the armed conflicts in Mexico.

The church and politics were inseparable. When the Liberals protested, the church allied with the Conservatives to prevent an insurgency. In addition, the church established alliances with the military.

With the country suffering the consequences of war and its collateral damage, Liberals increased their criticism of the Catholic Church. They accused the church of not caring about the interests of the nation or its faithful. The church's attention was focused on money. It had a fortune that could well help defray the nation's expenses, but the church washed its hands of matter, claiming that it was not their problem. There was a backlash against a church that counted schools, hospitals, and estates among its assets, yet it did not distribute the wealth it extracted from its faithful. Such economic resources only supported its political interests without any benefit for the nation.

Liberal groups were determined to return the church to its original mission: to watch over souls without interfering in the affairs of the country. The plan to separate the church from the state was set in motion. The church did not accept the clampdown on military and ecclesiastical jurisdiction. Meanwhile, in the Chamber of Deputies, there was talk of a new constitution, and three laws were passed for the purpose of definitively separating church and state.

Benito Juarez expanded the presidential decree. In 1855, ecclesiastical courts were forbidden from participating in individuals' civil affairs. This was followed by the Lerdo Law, named after its author, Miguel Lerdo de Tejada, who was minister of finance when the law was enacted, which still did not strip the church of any of its property. Then came the Iglesias Law, which prohibited the church from charging for any religious service, such as baptisms or marriages. Prior to this law, the Catholic Church had the power to use public force to collect tithes, regardless of whether the person in question had resources or wanted to pay or not. Thanks to this law, no citizen could be forced to make a contribution to the church.

These series of laws are known as pre-reformist laws. Both the military and the church ignored them, of course, since the laws affected their interests, taking away their political and economic power. Consequently, the Reform War broke out.

Benito Juarez assumed the presidency in 1858 without support from religious or military leaders in addition to facing strong opposition from the Conservative Party. In Veracruz, he published the Reform Laws, which nullified political participation by the church. In 1859, the Law of Nationalization of Ecclesiastical Property was issued, dictating the expropriation of the Catholic Church's vast properties in favor of the nation.

In 1860, at the conclusion of the Reform War, freedom of worship was decreed. In addition, the Civil Registry Law was enacted, which exempted citizens from making any payment to the church. The state assumed responsibility for these types of services, free of charge to citizens. Likewise, hospitals and cemeteries became property of the nation. Mexico assumed a secular identity, detaching itself from the control that the Catholic Church had over the country's political life.

The Mexican Revolution

The main objective of the 1910 Mexican Revolution was to put an end to the everlasting government of Porfirio Diaz. A controversial figure, history usually gives Diaz all negative marks. Nonetheless, just like Benito Juarez, he risked his life for an ideal of nationhood and defended the country against the French army.

He assumed the presidency under the banner of non-reelection and remained there for thirty-five years. His period of government included large infrastructure projects as well as the construction of railroads to modernize the country. During the Porfiriato (the era of his presidency), the transition to electricity took place, and when the centennial of independence was celebrated, Diaz pulled out all the stops to show the world that Mexico was also progressing—even though millions of Mexicans were not part of that progress.

His favorite motto was "little of politics and plenty of administration." Thanks to his unbeatable iron fist, the country experienced a kind of political stability, unfamiliar to a population used to unrest and constant armed uprisings. On the other side of the coin, Diaz tolerated a system of large estates that ended up becoming a kind of fiefdom where employees lived in miserable conditions. Remember the chronicles of journalist John Kenneth Turner about the mistreatment of the Yaqui and Maya Indians in the haciendas of Yucatan or in Valle Nacional. The Diaz government was also stained by electoral fraud. Period after period, Porfirio Diaz claimed that he would allow free elections, that Mexico was ready to be governed by someone else, but that was all just a lot of hot air. Diaz would end up being the winner, using all sorts of tricks to win every election in which he participated.

It was not until 1908 that Diaz declared that he was tired of leading the people after so many years—and it would be best to look for a replacement. Let's look in on Francisco I. Madero when he heard this news. Madero, a businessman from Coahuila, had made a significant fortune thanks to his businesses. It was even said that Madero was fond of talking to spirits, and that in some mystical ritual, he understood that he had to change the injustices of his country from the seat of government. At that time, it was not only the working class who wanted a regime change; most of the population was fed up with the situation. Madero seized the opportunity, took the old president at his word, and began his political campaign under the slogan "Effective suffrage, no reelection"—the same phrase that Porfirio Diaz had used to oppose the reelection of Sebastian Lerdo de Tejada. His impact was such that two years later, the phrase was repeated in all corners of the country. Prior to that, he had written a controversial book— *The Presidential Succession of 1910*—widely read at the time, which earned him the disdain of Porfirio Diaz. Madero believed that it was time for change and was chosen as a candidate to compete in the 1910 presidential election. But the inevitable is yet to come.

As Madero prepares for his campaign, however, he is taken prisoner in San Luis Potosí. He is accused of attempted insurrection and insulting the authorities. After naively believing that, in Mexico, power could be gained through democratic means, he was disappointed that things had not changed. In the solitude of his cell, he thinks about his uncertain future and the next political move, when he learns that Porfirio Diaz has proclaimed himself, once again, president of the republic.

Four months later, Francisco I. Madero is released and flees the country. In the city of San Antonio, Texas, Francisco I. Madero is sitting at his desk with pen in hand. He has just drafted an important document. He takes a deep breath. In his hands, he holds the *Plan of San Luis Potosi*, which calls on the people to rise up against Porfirio Diaz, declaring the last presidential election fraudulent and illegal. The document demands free elections and the creation of laws for the defense and benefit of the workers. The people were asked to rise up against a stale and aging dictatorship that continued to deny democracy in Mexico.

After the publication of the Plan of San Luis, on November 20, 1910, armed uprisings break out in different parts of the country. Madero had added fuel to the fire. Figures such as Emiliano Zapata, Pancho Villa, and Pascual Orozco enter the fray in opposition to the Porfiriato. In the wake of his plan's success, Madero decides to return to the country and lead the revolution. President Diaz tries to defend his government, but defeat is imminent; the federal forces lose ground in short order. With no other alternative, Diaz decides to reach an agreement with Madero by signing the *Treaties of Ciudad Juarez* on May 11, 1911. On May 25, Diaz leaves office for exile in France. The old dictator would never return to Mexico. He dies a few years later, in Paris, longing for his homeland. Before boarding the *Ypiranga*, the ship that took him from Veracruz to Europe, Porfirio Diaz had an epiphany and issued a last warning to the new president: "Madero has released the tiger, now we will see if he is capable of taming it." The old general knew a lot about releasing tigers.

Madero triumphantly enters the capital in June 1911. He announces that free presidential elections will proceed, as promised. Madero himself campaigns as a candidate and wins the presidency on November 6 of that same year. The result of Madero in power is dramatic. He fails to fulfill several commitments made during his campaign and makes the mistake of dissolving the revolutionary army in anticipation of a coup, while keeping a good part of the former Porfirian army in their posts. This earns him the disdain of revolutionary leaders Emiliano Zapata and Pancho Villa.

They say that forewarned is forearmed. Zapata announces the *Plan of Ayala*, a manifesto whose points included agrarian reform, the removal of President Madero from office, and proposals for social equality. Freedom of speech, a novelty in Mexico, allows Madero to be attacked day in and day out. The press is cruel to the new president, branding him as weak.

More and more voices clamor for him to abandon the presidency and conspire for this to happen. This results in the *Decena Tragica* (the Ten Tragic Days). As described by historian Paco Ignacio Taibo II, it is a time of vultures, abundant in betrayals, pettiness, and scavenging directed against Madero. Remnants of the old regime take up arms to overthrow the president. Clashes take place during ten days in Mexico City. Madero, entrenched in the National Palace, makes the terrible mistake of blindly trusting Victoriano Huerta, the general who would end up betraying him. On February 19, 1913, Madero is arrested and forced to resign his presidential post. The opposition, with the help of US Ambassador Henry Lance Wilson, elects Victoriano Huerta as leader—but not before assassinating Madero and his vice president, Jose Maria Pino Suarez, outside the Lecumberri prison.

In Paris, Porfirio Diaz listens to the news reporting the assassination of Francisco I. Madero with sadness. We can imagine the old general thinking that Madero underestimated the tiger without taming it; that's not the way to do things. For months, Diaz has been following the war in Mexico through the newspapers. Could it be that the people miss him? Could they think it was a mistake to banish the only man who could guarantee order and progress in the country? If only he had the strength and youth of before, he would return to reclaim the lost power, just like Iturbide and Santa Anna and so many others. Probably the people, upon seeing him, would cheer the return of the old hero as they had during his years of greatest glory. But the country has already changed, and Porfirio Diaz knows it. In spite of having been rivals, of owing his overthrow and his exile in France with no possibility of returning to Mexico to Madero, he feels genuine sorrow over his death. No one deserves to die a treacherous death. At least Diaz was given the opportunity to leave Mexico, never to return. Which of the two fared worse? The frail, bony hand covers his closed eyes. Who would have thought that death would take the apostle of democracy first—before an octogenarian general?

Cursed for his treachery, Huerta does not manage to remain in power for long either. Venustiano Carranza, governor of Coahuila, calls for a mobilization against him. The constitutional army rises up with Carranza at its head; he soon takes over the troops commanded by Pancho Villa and Emiliano Zapata, who sought to avenge the death of Madero. All revolutionary leaders join forces against the usurper. Clashes break out in different parts of the country. Soon after, the constitutionalists obtain Huerta's resignation. In 1915, Venustiano Carranza installs his own government, with headquarters in the port of Veracruz.

Meanwhile, in the country's capital, Pancho Villa and Emiliano Zapata debate the type of regime that should govern the nation. Now the contest is between the revolutionary leaders themselves: Villa and Zapata against Carranza and Alvaro Obregon. The battle of Celaya, which was actually fought in Leon, ended with the defeat of Pancho Villa's army, tipping the balance in favor of Carranza's regime.

The consolidation of the ideals of the revolution was still pending. After the defeat of the armies of Pancho Villa and Emiliano Zapata, the constitutionalists of Venustiano Carranza triumphed. In 1917, the new Mexican Constitution was declared, which enshrined the rights of the people and in essence governs Mexico to this day. It also prohibited the exploitation of labor that had happened during the Porfiriato and granted the expropriation of land that would give shape to agrarian reform.

More than one million people died during the Mexican Revolution. When the US-made carbines fell silent, the atmosphere was somber. The country was plagued with ruined cities, destroyed trains, erased roads, wasted crops, shootings, summary executions, rapes never reported, corpses that no one claimed, and thousands of orphans who had to find some way to make a living. The work of reconstruction would be immense—and so would the work of reconciliation among all Mexicans.

President Alvaro Obregon, aware of the need for a Mexican renaissance, would bet on a return to its roots. The greatness of Mexico, captured on public walls by Mexico's best painters, would be found in its past. After so much death, art would emerge in that field of crisis that was the revolution and would help build a new national identity.

The Catholic War

This war took place during the administration of President Plutarco Elias Calles and is considered the last civil war in Mexican territory.

The church, once again, played a leading role. Remember, its influence was eroded following the Reform War. Nevertheless, indirectly the church always kept an eye on the important events taking place in the nation. After the Revolution of 1910, the church once again took an active role in politics.

Pope Leo XIII led the church's initiative, inviting Catholics to actively participate in the country's politics, become aware of the social aspects of the human person, and return to everyday life described in the book of Acts. His intention was to match interests with a socialist movement that was growing stronger and stronger in Mexico. The church in Mexico alleged that unions were de-Christianizing the country.

Following this call, with the church's support, numerous workers began to get involved in unions. Then, a union of Catholic workers emerged. This is the start of a larger plan to return to power. The National Catholic Party, with a presence throughout the country, was born. Its motto was "God, Homeland, and Liberty."

This group looked after the needs and demands of the working class, which was compatible with revolutionary politics of the time. Catholics collaborated with Francisco I. Madero and later with Victoriano Huerta—and opposed Venustiano Carranza.

With the Constitution of 1917, Carranza retaliated and settled the score with the enactment of anticlerical measures. The Catholic Church assumed that these articles only restricted religious freedom.

After President Plutarco Elias Calles assumed power, he put into place certain restrictions on the activities of the Catholic Church. He had in mind ending the political power the church still retained. Calles modified the articles of the Constitution that safeguarded the free exercise of religion and education, amid a flood of protests from the clergy.

Then, the Catholic Church used its own strike team—the National League for Religious Freedom, created by clerics in 1925—to take on the task of leading protest movements against the government. Calles was unable to quell the fire, and the Cristero War broke out in 1926. The government's blunder of wanting to control the people's consciences ended up clashing with the mostly Catholic population's freedom to worship.

Although lacking a clear leader, the church started an armed conflict based on their displeasure with the Calles Law. What did this law stipulate? The registration of churches, limitations on the number of priests, prohibiting priests giving their opinion on political issues, requiring priests to have a license issued by Congress, and the expulsion of foreign clergy from the country. If these norms were not complied with, priests were subject to harsh prison sentences.

The people were enraged when the government of Plutarco Elias Calles closed some churches and expelled foreign clergy from Mexico. In response to this outrage, the Mexican Episcopate ordered the suspension of all Masses in all churches, which made the people even angrier. It was the first time in four hundred years that no Mass had been celebrated in Mexico. The clergy had the support of the campesinos who were dissatisfied with the lack of agrarian reform promised by the former revolutionary leaders. Workers also joined the struggle, shouting, "Long live Christ the King!" and opened fire against the Mexican armed forces.

During the rebellion's first year, the church gained followers. By 1927, they began winning some major victories—but they were unable to conduct a more forceful campaign due to scarce resources.

In 1928, after so much blood had been shed, top religious leaders began to secretly negotiate with the Mexican government. Meanwhile, the Cristero army adopted the old Constitution of 1857 for their movement, disregarding any changes brought about by the reform laws. They also disregarded the previously established power held by each state, emphasizing the agrarian issue, which brought them the campesinos' support.

The movement continued to gain followers until the assassination of President-elect Alvaro Obregon, on July 17, 1928, by a sketch artist, Jose de Leon Toral, who sympathized with the Cristero cause. Obregon was eating with his entourage in a restaurant known as La Bombilla. Like Porfirio Diaz and so many others, Obregon could not overcome the temptation to stay longer in the presidential chair, forgetting that one of the proclamations of the Mexican Revolution had been non-reelection. Obregon was chatting happily with his people. Perhaps he imagined the opportunities that would come with his second presidential term. Most of his opponents had been shot, but how could he suspect that the boy who drew portraits at La Bombilla was hiding a pistol? Leon Toral approached General Obregon. It is said that prior to Toral drawing his gun and shooting him six times, Obregon was impatiently waiting for an order of *frijolitos*.

Both Plutarco Elias Calles and the church blamed each other for Obregon's assassination. After this event, the Mexican government decided to put an end to the conflict to avoid further assassinations. The interim president, Emilio Portes Gil, took the step of negotiating with the Catholic Church. By 1929, and following the failed Escobar rebellion, the Cristero movement began to crumble. Against this backdrop, the church and the Mexican state reached an agreement on June 21, 1929.

President Portes Gil granted amnesty to the Cristeros and ordered the immediate return of churches and religious buildings that had been taken by the government. The movement collapsed, and its military groups began to dissolve.

In a civil war, cruelty, like the devil, is unleashed everywhere. The humanity of the combatants is blurred, committing atrocities against their countrymen. In the Cristiada, both the federal soldiers and the Cristeros committed what we know today are war crimes. Caught in the middle was the civilian population, the poor, rural and religious believers, who were also targeted for executions and plunder because of unfounded suspicions of supporting the enemy.

The Cristero War left 250,000 Mexicans dead. It also showed the extent of the Catholic religion in Mexico, a deeply religious country willing to take up arms and fight and die against the government in order to defend its faith. In contrast, the revolutionary presidents were proud to declare themselves anti–religious, as if believing in dogma was a sign of weakness. Obregon was a believer, but of education, and he was convinced that religion kept the Mexican people ignorant. He boasted of his anticlerical spirit. Plutarco Elias Calles considered that the best thing for Mexico was the closing of churches, the expulsion of foreign priests, and restrictions on Mexican priests. His persecution of the church shed blood and pitted Mexicans against Mexicans and Catholic campesinos against soldiers who probably professed the same religion. My grandfather, Don Taurino, who belonged to the Catholic Association of Mexican Youth of Leon and sympathized with the Cristeros, had to flee to the United States because if he had stayed in Mexico, he would have ended up being shot by federal soldiers.

Diplomatic relations between Mexico and the Vatican would resume almost a century later, during the government of Carlos Salinas de Gortari, perhaps because the president was anxious for absolution.

The Zapatistas and Their Mediatic Rebellion

The Zapatista Army of National Liberation (EZLN, for the acronym in Spanish) began a rebellion in the northern part of the state of Chiapas. It gained national attention during Carlos Salinas de Gortari's term in office.

On January 1, 1994, an armed group formed by indigenous people detained a journalist in Chiapas. They asked him to disseminate a declaration of war. Although social media did not yet exist, their messages soon became public. San Cristobal de las Casas is the headquarters of the so-called Zapatistas, as the rebels are popularly known.

In response to the declaration of war, President Salinas sent the Mexican army to the conflict zone to put down the uprising. The Zapatistas made a pact with religious authorities in San Cristobal to intercede on their behalf in order to avert fighting in the city. Before the army arrived, the EZLN abandoned the place.

Although this rebellious movement took Mexico and the world by surprise, we must understand that it happened in reaction to the extreme poverty and social deprivation of the region's native peoples. Even today, there are still communities that remain under the Zapatistas, living in the same conditions of abandonment and oblivion.

In 1994, President Salinas de Gortari had a clear interest in the North American Free Trade Agreement, envisioning Mexico becoming a first world economy. An internal rebellion did not help this expectation. The dream of entering the first world was at odds with televised images of soldiers fighting ill-prepared and poorly armed indigenous rebels.

The confrontations between the army and the Zapatistas were sporadic, resulting in two hundred rebel casualties. In March, the Zapatistas and the Mexican government began negotiations to put an end to the rebellion. That same year, presidential elections were held that made the previous agreements conditional, and Ernesto Zedillo Ponce de Leon emerged victorious. The government appointed Manuel Camacho Solis as a mediator for the negotiations in Chiapas. The bishop of San Cristobal de las Casas, Samuel Ruiz, also served as a mediator between the EZLN and the government, always putting the rights, respect, and dignity of the indigenous people of Chiapas first.

The Zapatista movement made extensive use of the media in what could be considered a mediatic rebellion, very much in line with the political events of the country. Its charismatic main spokesman, Subcomandante Marcos, was a hooded, anonymous Zapatista who loaded his speeches and communiqués with poetry. Behind that hood, from the same mysterious mouth that smoked a pipe, there was a powerful and calm voice that said phrases such as: "They want to take the land from us so that we have no ground to walk on." Or this one: "Freedom is like the morning. There are those who wait, asleep, for it to arrive. But there are those who stay awake and walk the night to reach it." Subcomandante Marcos claimed that the Zapatistas covered their faces so that they could be seen—and that they denied their names so that they could be named. By betting on the present, they would have a future.

Despite agreements with the government, the Zapatistas never surrendered their weapons or the territories under their control. In fact, some areas of the state of Chiapas still declare themselves to be autonomous entities under the command of the EZLN, where the same laws do not apply as in the rest of the country. They say that the smell of oblivion is still in the air surrounding their struggle.

The Only War among Brothers in the United States

The American Civil War was triggered by slavery. While the northern states of the American Union sought to eradicate it, the southern region, which included the states that joined after the war with Mexico, valued slavery as normal and necessary. Their labor force was based on this unjust practice.

During the presidential elections of 1860 the issue intensified, dividing the country. The Republican Party's candidate for president, Abraham Lincoln, held an iron-willed and unwavering stance against slavery. The opposition from the South let to the inevitable happening. In order to continue taking advantage of slavery, seven states in the South seceded from the United States, calling themselves the Confederate States. With the first battle at Fort Sumter in Charleston Bay, the Civil War began.

The country was divided between North and South, with marked economic, social, cultural, and political differences. The northern region was more developed, moving toward industrialization and modern capitalism. Most Northerners sympathized with the Republican Party, which favored imposing tariffs to protect the US market. In contrast, the South's economy was based on agriculture; the implementation of import taxes was detrimental to them. On their side was the Democratic Party, which declared itself against tariffs and in favor of free trade and slavery.

By 1861, the Civil War was in full swing. The Confederate States deployed their army, and the offensive succeeded in seizing a number of forts. It should be noted that in the beginning, some states sympathetic to the Union remained on the sidelines of the conflict, but they later ended up joining the Confederates. This is the case of Virginia, which was divided into those both for and against the rebellion.

The Union had everything in its favor to win the conflict. It had an experienced army and navy. Moreover, its population was larger than that of the South. However, they squandered this magnificent advantage. The Confederates began to win victory after victory.

Rather than luck, the Northern states were more industrialized and had better technology than the Southern states. The Northern economy was large because of its industry; the Southern economy was sustained mostly by slave labor in the cotton and sugar fields. The North was capitalist, labor was remunerated, and no one was forced to work; in the agricultural South, slaves and their offspring were condemned to forced labor or death.

The triumph of the Northern states goes hand in hand with Abraham Lincoln, who met the challenge and led the nation. Lincoln knew that his abolitionist cause was on the right side of history, and he worked hard to make the American people understand that America's dream of greatness was incompatible with slavery. Even Mexico had beaten the United States to the issue, abolishing slavery half a century earlier, thanks to the struggle waged by Catholic priests Miguel Hidalgo and José Maria Morelos. Lincoln won the presidency, but his conflict with the Confederates did not end with that victory. On April 14, 1865, he fell victim to a Southern sympathizer; John Wilkes Booth assassinated the president while he was enjoying an evening at the theater in Washington, DC.

The Confederate army surrendered its arms, slavery was abolished, slaves became free citizens with some rights, and the reconstruction of the country began. From that point on, America's ideal was to become an indivisible nation, united by the myths of the American dream, the land of opportunity, and by its desire for world dominance. The United States was to truly live up to its name, and that was its essence. It exerted its power on the continent, and the French, who had already envisioned themselves conquering Mexico, had to hurry back to Europe as soon as the United States recovered from the Civil War. Unlike other nations that have suffered through civil wars, which can take centuries to recover from, the US economy grew rapidly despite the decline in cotton production due to the abolition of slavery and the northern states imposing protectionist measures and high tariffs on all of the nation's trade. It took the South a long time to recover economically from the ravages of war, and other countries, such as Egypt and India, filled the gap left in cotton exports. The issue of rights for African Americans would continue to cause controversy in a country that boasted of being modern. The southern states, although they lost the war, would not give up so easily, and although they could no longer be independent or re-implement slavery, they exercised racial segregation and the infamous Jim Crow laws in their territories for decades.

Unlike Mexico, the United States only needed one civil war within its territory. If you do the math, in no other US war did as many Americans die as on the battlefields of the Civil War. What is certain is that at the end of this bad spell came the splendor. Peace was restored, the economy improved, and wages rose higher than in other European countries, causing thousands of immigrants to arrive in the United States.

After the war and the assassination of Lincoln, Americans continued to hold elections, and no losing candidate failed to recognize his defeat, calling his supporters to take up arms against the government under the Plan of New York, for example, or the Plan of Wichita, the Plan of Palm Springs, or the Plan of McDonald's. It would take 150 years for a peculiar president of the United States, who had lost his reelection, to claim he was the victim of electoral fraud and incite a multitude of sympathizers to rise up in what could have been called "The White House Twitter Plan."

The Trump Mob That Stormed the Capitol

Nothing like this had ever happened before. A president who did not recognize the results of an election and put up obstacles to handing over power, and a crowd, furious with institutions and democracy, believing that they were stolen by a system that excludes and marginalizes them. Before the eyes of the world, President Donald Trump ended his term in office in a spectacular and infamous manner. Yet in Washington, DC, his supporters blindly believed their leader's speech. "When you ain't got nothing, you got nothing to lose," goes a famous Bob Dylan song. Reluctant to surrender the power he considered his alone, Trump incited the masses to demonstrate their indignation and destroy everything. And since the masses do not think on their own but collectively, they did not hesitate to listen.

Initially, Trump demonstrated full confidence in winning reelection. His opponent, Joe Biden, had the political experience of having served as Barack Obama's vice president and offered the electorate a certain return to sanity and to the old but prudent way of doing politics. Trump guaranteed a repeat of his surprise 2016 triumph, when a silent majority, who never revealed their voting intentions, gave him their support to drain the Washington swamp. The electorate decided to give him the benefit of the doubt, but four years later, few of Trump's promises were kept.

That 2020 election took place with the highest voter turnout in the nation's history. Such a large turnout occurred in the midst of the pandemic caused by COVID-19, which at the time had the world in crisis. The elections began on November 3, and four days later, there was already a clear winner: Joe Biden.

For twenty-eight consecutive years, no US president had lost a reelection. Joe Biden's victory was overwhelming—with more than 51 percent of the vote—and Trump barely exceeded 45 percent.

The next step was for the Senate to ratify the election through a symbolic vote count. There was no doubt that Biden was the legitimate winner of the election, despite Trump's discontent and fury. The Senate recount was scheduled for January 6, 2021. During this period of time, Donald Trump alleged that the election had been stolen from him. Through his social media and televised speeches, the US president claimed to have been the victim of massive voter fraud. Consistent with his claim, he refused to recognize the new president of the United States. He urged citizens not to fall for the deception of the system and to defend "true" democracy, i.e. his own.

President Trump's speech incites his supporters, throwing gasoline on the fire. Marches and protests against the incoming government take place in several states. The largest turnout was in Washington, DC, outside the Capitol, where the final vote count by the Senate, with the subsequent ratification of the new president, was taking place.

On the morning of January 6, Donald Trump gave another speech of open disagreement with the electoral result. What few expected was the violent reaction of the screaming mob outside the Capitol. Trump's supporters had briefly hoped that Vice President Mike Pence would overturn the election, and they were even more surprised, and disappointed, when they saw that Pence had chosen to go the institutional route. Trump supporters called him a coward and a traitor and called for his hanging.

The protests escalate, and the police force that is guarding the building intervenes. Suddenly, the mob tries to enter by force, amid shouting and fighting. The police are unable to stop the crowd. Desperate, they call for reinforcements. The session inside the Senate is suspended, given the imminent risk of protesters taking over the Capitol.

Finally, the mob enters the building, seeking the return of their lost power. Inside the House of Representatives, armed guards protect the entrances, blocking them with wooden furniture to stop the crowd from entering. Some demonstrators enter the offices of several legislators. One photograph that becomes famous is of a Trump supporter sitting gleefully at Nancy Pelosi's desk, placing his feet on top. Others run through the halls, causing havoc while Capitol staff hid in locked rooms, as if seeking shelter from a firefight. The seizure of the Capitol left four demonstrators and a police officer dead in addition to several wounded. As if this were not enough, security guards discovered an explosive device in the vicinity of the building.

Joe Biden called on Donald Trump to make his supporters see reason and end their protest, which was already bordering on terrorism and sedition. He urged Trump to accept the election results. Hours later, Donald Trump released a video maintaining his position as a victim of electoral fraud while inviting his supporters to leave the Capitol and go home.

Due to Donald Trump's incendiary actions, his social media accounts, which were powerful tools for his communications, were restricted. After the seizure of the Capitol, which is described as a failed insurrection, Democrats called for the immediate impeachment of the president. And there was no shortage of those who asked Vice President Mike Pence to invoke the Twenty-fifth Amendment, which would strip Trump of the powers of the presidency under the argument he was unable to discharge the rights and duties of his office.

An FBI investigation has led to the arrest of more than 950 rioters who caused mayhem. It remains to be seen whether that investigation will hold accountable the person who decided to throw gasoline on the fire. This scandal continues to further crack the rift that keeps the US population polarized. It would have been good for Donald Trump to learn from the sit-in that occupied Paseo de la Reforma in 2006. That massive encampment lasted forty-seven days and occupied Mexico's most important avenue, asking the Electoral Tribunal to order a recount of all the votes of a controversial election. Instead of an attempted rebellion in the Capitol that ended badly, Trump could have been inspired by the peaceful demonstration organized by Andres Manuel Lopez Obrador and his thousands of followers who protested a real electoral fraud, a demonstration, unlike the riots in the Capitol, that did not cost human lives, where no glass was ever broken, no wallet was stolen, no police intervened, and that served to show the discontent of the people in the face of an injustice.

It is an exaggeration to say that the assault on the Capitol can be considered the beginning of a civil war in the United States, an insurrection that came close to breaking the institutions of the most powerful country on the planet. Some television commentators have exaggerated the real scope of these riots, which in reality never endangered the transition of government, much less resulted in a coup provoked by the outgoing president. Despite its participation and influence in almost all the war conflicts that occur in the world, the United States does not like wars to occur within its territory, and the idea of a new civil war, despite the political polarization, is unthinkable. One was more than enough! Part of the success the United States has had throughout its history is precisely because they are smart enough to realize that civil wars are bad business, unlike military interventions abroad.

Let's compare how many civil wars Mexico had with the one the United States had. Mexicans spent the nineteenth and early twentieth centuries fighting among themselves to see who would stay in power. The United States only had the Civil War, which pursued the noble goal of abolishing slavery. Four years of fighting and 750,000 deaths were enough to avoid repeating the same mistake. And while the US economy was growing after its civil war, in Mexico, they were busy taking up arms, destroying what little was left after the previous civil war.

Although there is always a victorious group left in power after a civil war, the country really gains nothing. What remains behind is the destruction of cities, poverty, the pain of the population, the exodus of people seeking refuge from bullets, families broken by the death of one or all of their members, paralyzed industries, institutions and the economy in ruins, political instability, the rule of law forgotten, and infrastructure that took decades to build turned into rubble to constantly remind us of the futility of internecine wars. There is always slow reconstruction. There are no benefits for a nation in which its citizens kill each other. Nor can there be investment when a country is on fire.

Mexico took decades to learn that lesson, but the United States learned it quickly. Civil wars mean death, pain, destruction, debacle, and backwardness. If Mexico stagnated in its growth during the nineteenth century, it was largely due to the fact that the country was immersed in constant internal wars, where it had just come out of one to immediately enter another. And curiously, the one who ended up benefiting from the civil wars in Mexico was the United States, who watched as its neighbor destroyed its house, broke its windows and doors, set fire to its roof, and inexplicably hammered its foundations, while they remodeled their mansion, bought a new car, kept their garden green, and enlarged it to become the envy of the entire neighborhood.

Photograph of young soldiers during the Civil War, 1865

Photograph of soldiers during the
Mexican Revolution, 1916.

Chapter 9

Between Wars and Conquests

The Calvo Doctrine: A Pan-American Vision

Throughout its history, Mexico has been a pacifist country on the outside and violent on the inside. That internal violence is reflected in its multiple civil wars, but Mexico has never invaded another nation, nor has it started wars abroad. When it has fought wars against other countries it has been in its own territory, and this due to the invasion of powers such as the United States and France. In that sense, Mexico is a country that prefers to avoid conflicts with the rest of the world. The famous phrase of the hero Benito Juarez, which has been a beacon and guide in Mexico's international relations, stands out: *"Among individuals, as among nations, respect for the rights of others is peace"*.

Let's go back to the time when the Argentine jurist Carlos Calvo (1824–1906) applied his knowledge of international law to develop a thesis to prevent the abuse of weak nations by more powerful nations. With a focus on legal nationalism, Calvo affirms that foreign investors are not entitled to a higher degree of protection by the state than its own citizens.

This position, which is called the Calvo Doctrine, stresses that a foreigner must use local courts rather than their home country courts to make any claim, demand, or complaint, not the recourse of diplomatic pressure or military intervention. In other words, it establishes that any conflict with a foreigner must be adjudicated in the country where the conflict occurs, in accordance with equality between nationals and foreigners. Basically, foreigners should bring their claims in the local courts, so that they do not go crying to their own governments to bail them out. Calvo, in developing this doctrine, was thinking mainly of the vulnerability of Latin American nations.

Carlos Calvo lived through the gunboat diplomacy of the nineteenth century. In the face of any conflict, especially of a commercial nature, force was used to resolve it, as if there were no other peaceful alternatives. European powers, in particular, used their maritime fleets to demand their rights against the emerging nations of the Americas. To give us an idea, the British Empire used this approach at least forty times in the Americas alone.

Clearly, this doctrine was unacceptable to countries accustomed to exploiting their military might. Around 1902, gunboat diplomacy was used when a group of ships from different European countries laid siege to several Venezuelan ports. The blockade was the work of Great Britain, Germany, and Italy, which demanded the payment of debts that the Venezuelan government had contracted with companies in their countries. In the end, the United States had to come in to mediate the matter, and Venezuela had to pay off its debts with a large percentage of its customs revenue. But let's continue this narrative with Mexico and, specifically, let's go back to 1873.

At that time, Jose Maria Lafragua, Mexico's minister of foreign relations, sent a message to John Watson Foster, the US ambassador to Mexico from 1873 to 1880. The letter stated that Mexico would not be held responsible for damages caused to foreign-owned properties under the Calvo Doctrine.

The immediate response to Mexico's letter is that the Calvo Doctrine, which was pretty much dedicated to United States interventionism, is not officially recognized in international law. This is one of the first positions of the United States on this Pan-American doctrine.

Other Latin American nations joined in defending the doctrine's validity. Let's look in on the Pan-American Conference, or the International Conference of American States, taking place in Washington between 1889 and 1890. Latin American nations are attending, with the exception of Santo Domingo.

On the agenda for the conference is promotion of the Calvo Doctrine's principles. An expert commission in international law proposes that equal rights should prevail between foreigners and national citizens, according to their equal opportunities to deploy judicial remedies. Haiti refrains from joining this recommendation. The US is wary, but the rest of the participants reach a consensus on this legal and diplomatic position.

At the second conference, held in Mexico City between October 22, 1901, and January 31, 1902, fifteen participating states approved the Calvo Doctrine. The premise is that foreigners have the right to enjoy all civil rights just like nationals; therefore, they must submit to the same rules that govern nationals. Regarding foreigners, countries do not recognize any other type of rights or obligations, more favorable or different from those established in their respective national constitutions.

In summary, the Calvo Doctrine was created from the standpoint of protecting the sovereignty of states when dealing with foreign investors. It says that the legal jurisdiction of each nation takes precedence in international investment disputes whenever national rights are violated and constitutional rights are affected. It is a doctrine that supports political, economic, social, and commercial stability in Latin America.

World War I

The First World War was a turning point in the history of the United States since the country managed to excel in several areas after participating in the conflict. Mexico followed its tradition and remained neutral, as it was in the final phase of the revolutionary period. Therefore, and fortunately for the Central Powers, it was complicated for Mexico to participate in an international war when it had its own fight going on.

Prior to the conflict, the United States was already enjoying enviable economic growth thanks to oil deposits in its territory. In addition, it controlled most of the oil coming from Mexico.

The Great War began with the assassination of Archduke Franz Ferdinand of Austria in Sarajevo on June 28, 1914. It was not long before things reached a boiling point, and several European countries went to war with each other. At the beginning of the hostilities, the United States claimed neutrality—even though it provided resources to the European countries in conflict. We should keep in mind that both airplanes and warships run on oil derivatives, and the availability of supply benefited US production. For the same reason, the US greatly increased the number of bonds issued because of WWI. The war in Europe was a lucrative business. Private investment bankers joined in the bonanza.

In the event of conflict with the warring countries, the US government could dissociate itself on the grounds that it was the bankers' responsibility. As an added plus, the economy rebounded on increased demand for arms destined for the British and their allies.

The European press at the time was quick to label the neutral and pacifist stance of the United States hypocritical, who had no qualms about becoming the main arms supplier during the war. The United States would have continued to do so until the end of the conflict, lining its pockets while the soldiers of other nations fought in the trenches of a distant continent. But man proposes, God disposes, and then the devil comes along and messes everything up. A series of events turn history upside down, and this has to do with Mexico.

In 1916, Pancho Villa and his entourage had crossed the border between Mexico and the United States to attack the small town of Columbus. Because of this affront, the United States decided to support the government of Venustiano Carranza, Villa's enemy. At the same time, it sent a punitive expedition under the command of General Pershing to capture Villa, dead or alive. For a year, Villa managed to evade his pursuers. Nobody's perfect, and the US army was never able to find Villa, who sought protection in the mazelike sierra of Chihuahua. This was a serious blow to the US military. Although they returned to their country empty-handed, at least they had the opportunity to test, in Mexican territory, the state-of-the-art weaponry they themselves had manufactured.

About this time, the US Secret Service intercepted a highly confidential message: the Zimmerman telegram. The Germans were confident of winning the war thanks to their submarines, although their situation was not entirely favorable. Victory depended on the United States remaining neutral.

Germany fought against European powers that received indirect support from the United States. As a strategy to defeat this bloc, at the beginning of 1917, Germany sent the Zimmerman telegram, offering aid to Mexico in exchange for the latter attacking the United States. If they could keep the United States distracted in a conflict with Mexico, Germany would have a clear path to victory in the Great War. With Venustiano Carranza still in the presidency, this unseemly proposal meant the possibility of recovering territories lost to the United States in the Guadalupe Hidalgo treaty. It was a checkmate that did not materialize.

Think of the repercussions that a bad decision in this dilemma could have brought. Allying with Germany represented a high risk, even though at the time the recovery of New Mexico, Texas and Arizona sounded attractive to the Mexican people. In addition, a feeling of resentment towards the United States was still fresh because of the second intervention in Veracruz in 1914. Perhaps the people would have welcomed the offer of the Zimmerman telegram, but the truth was that the Carranza government was barely in control of the country as it had to fight its own war against Emiliano Zapata and Pancho Villa. As a result of its constant internecine wars, Mexico was not prepared to face the United States again, not even with the support of Germany. Most likely, Mexico would have been left on the mound, eternally waiting for the arms and money offered by the German Empire, and one day, after losing another war against the United States, Mexico would have fared worse than in 1848.

The Zimmerman telegram was intercepted by British intelligence services, and it was they who brought the gossip to the United States, which was instantly enraged. The President of the United States, Woodrow Wilson, shared the telegram with the population to obtain popular support in his fight against the German Empire. Venustiano

Carranza, in a fit of sanity, declined the German offer and devoted himself to settle the internal conflicts in Mexico, and a few days later the United States declared war on Germany, sending an army of 127,500 soldiers to Europe.

After four years of conflict, Europe and its cities were devastated, with thousands dead and a harsh social and economic recession in many nations, including Germany, Austria, France, Hungary, England, and Russia. In the particular case of Germany, the big loser of the war, by 1918, internal conflicts had weakened it, forcing it to request an armistice.

During the last summer of the war, the United States played an active role in tipping the balance against Germany. Germany was forced to sign the Treaty of Versailles in 1919, not realizing that this would pave the way for the rise of fascism. This treaty stipulated that Germany had to assume responsibility for having caused the war, thus obliging it to pay huge economic indemnities to the victors to cover losses and damages.

World War I left a toll of ten million soldiers dead and seven million civilian casualties. During this war, war weapons were modernized, and armies went from fighting with horses and bayonets to using machine guns, airplanes, armored vehicles, and telephones. Despite its prohibition, the war also saw the massive use of toxic gases, which were then blown by the wind to villages inhabited by women and children, causing them great harm.

On the side of the victors, there was a victor superior to the rest. And that victor established its hegemony over the rest of the world. In addition to the fact that the conflict endorsed the war policy of the United States, the European disaster turned in its favor with unparalleled economic growth, while other nations suffered terrible economic crises. During the disaster, Europe lost its crown as king of the world, which the United States, a young and ambitious country, quickly took over. The defeated nations were clearly unable to meet their war reparations, and countries as prosperous as the United Kingdom had to go into debt to the United States to recover from the debacle. But it was not only the United Kingdom. Because of

America's new role as the world's creditor, almost everyone turned to it as if it were the millionaire in the family. From now on, the international economy was bound to be driven by American interests. When peace returned to the trenches in Europe, the name of the United States was inscribed in history as a world superpower, as a nascent empire that did not like to think of itself as such.

After the Treaty of Versailles, the League of Nations, precursor of the United Nations, was created to establish peace among countries and prevent a recurrence of armed conflict on a global scale. Perhaps after the League of Nations was created, its members went to sleep peacefully that very night, wrapped in the certainty that the world had had enough of wars. Would a similar conflict never happen again? Just twenty years after the Treaty of Versailles, an even worse catastrophe would be unleashed.

World War II

Sooner or later, the world would again take up arms with the intention of destroying each other. Adolf Hitler, resentful of Germany's humiliating defeat in World War I, took the reins of the country to restore its greatness. While the United States had established itself as the world's sole superpower, Germany was suffering from economic crises, hyperinflation, dispossession of its territory, foreign control over its military, and a dangerous sense of humiliation, of feeling that the victors of World War I had gone way overboard with them. Somehow, such humiliations hatched the Nazi snake egg. And from that egg hatched a man who, despite his Austrian origins, promised Germany its stolen glory. Both Fascism and National Socialism rose because the German people were dissatisfied with the indignities after the Great War. They did not even accept that they had started the conflict, therefore they denied their responsibility, considering war reparations as unjust and excessive. A good part of the population began to believe that those responsible for the defeat were not the high commanders of the empire, but the leftists and the Jews, and against these groups the generalized hatred was felt. Adolf Hitler repeatedly violated the Treaty of Versailles, and once the German nation felt empowered again, he ordered the invasion of Poland on September 1, 1939. France and the United Kingdom declared war on Germany but could do little in the face of Hitler's sudden expansion throughout Europe.

At first, the US position was similar to that of the beginning of the Great War. The Franklin D. Roosevelt administration proclaimed neutrality and characterized the European conflagration as a foreign conflict.

At that time, Coca-Cola was already being bottled in the European market and experiencing exponential growth. Consequently, the United States did not wish to enter into conflict with European customers who were already consuming its "black gold."

Speaking of black gold, this brings us to the subject of oil, the other great bastion of the US economy. The US was dealt a hard blow in 1938 when President Lazaro Cardenas issued a decree expropriating petroleum production, aimed at foreign oil companies.

During the first quarter of the twentieth century, control of Mexico's oil industry was in the hands of England and the United States. Prior to expropriation, British petroleum companies clashed with the Americans. The end result was that the English left Mexico, which gave the United States total control of the oil industry.

The United States, with the ideal pretext of defending the interests of its oil companies, had the option of invading Mexico again, but a bell saved Mexico: the beginning of World War II. It was a fact that sooner or later the United States would enter the war, and an invasion of Mexico over oil issues would take up effort, time, and resources that it could well dedicate to its fight against Germany. So, the United States limited itself to demanding just compensation for the expropriated companies. It preferred to keep Mexico as an ally, in case it intervened in the war, or in case Germany repeated the Zimmerman telegram strategy.

It would not be until December 7, 1941, that the US government entered the war following the Japanese attack on Pearl Harbor, a military base in Hawaii. Japan had decided to attack in revenge for an oil embargo imposed by the United States. The bombing awakened a sleeping giant. One day after the attack, the United States declared war on Japan. In retaliation, the German government quickly shut down all Coca-Cola factories in its territory, unaware that they were actually contributing to improving the public health of all Germans.

The United States joined the Allies, along with the United Kingdom and the Soviet Union, at the height of the conflict, when France was already occupied by German forces. The superpower did not skimp on resources and troops. Mexico also changed its neutral and pacifist stance once Germany sank the Mexican oil tankers "Potrero del Llano" and "Faja de Oro". To Hitler's nightmare, Mexico declared war on the Axis countries and sent Squadron 201, a group of Mexican pilots, also known as Aztec Eagles, to the fight. This happened in 1944. The participation of Squadron 201 has the following numerals: a total of 59 missions, with 1,966 flight hours, in combat; although the official number of casualties performed by the Squadron was never published, it is said to be around 30,000. On the other hand, the casualties that the Squadron had are counted in two pilots who died during their training and six pilots who did not pass the medical exams, saving them from going to war. The 201st Squadron was sent to fight in the Philippines against Japan, to the relief of Hitler, who was busy fighting the Americans on one side and the Soviets on the other. Imagine if they still got the Mexicans on top of him! Five other members of the Squadron died in battle: one fell in combat, another crashed and the remaining three fell into the sea after running out of fuel. Despite this string of misfortunes, Mexico's participation in World War II was dignified and fundamental to recovering Philippine territory.

Mexico was very important for the United States during the war since it collaborated with the manufacture of clothing and footwear that the American Union could not produce at that time due to lack of labor. This boosted the Mexican economy, which, by filling a gap in American industry, experienced unusual growth. The U.S. labor force, upon leaving for the war, was legally replaced by Mexican migrant workers known as braseros. This program killed two birds with one stone: it took care of the U.S. countryside and industry and reduced unemployment in Mexico. If before the war Mexico had had differences with the United States and the United Kingdom over the expropriation of oil, these dissipated with Mexico's involvement in the war and its integration to the Allied side. Nor did it have any repercussions that in 1942 General Lázaro Cárdenas, promoter of the oil expropriation when he was president in 1938, was appointed nothing less than Secretary of National Defense by Manuel Ávila Camacho. Paradoxically, some of the countries that continued to buy Mexican oil in spite of the commercial blockade sponsored by the United States and United Kingdom companies, after the nationalization, were precisely Italy, Japan and Germany. As they say, nobody knows who they work for.

The Nazi extermination camps are one of the many dark spots in human history. Jews, Gypsies, homosexuals, the disabled and members of other minorities were transferred to these camps for forced labor. In other camps, these groups were mass executed, whether by gas chambers, firing squads, starvation, or any other available method. In some European cities, the Nazis interned Jews in overcrowded and unsanitary ghettos, where they could execute anyone for any reason. But concentration camps were not unique to Europe. In the United States, camps were set up to confine thousands of Japanese American citizens, treating them as criminals or traitors whose allegiance was to the Japanese empire and not to the American Union. These American citizens lost property, patrimony and several years of their lives in internment because of a war for which they were not responsible. It would not be until 1988 that President Ronald Reagan would recognize that this racist measure was a mistake, apologizing for it.

Something that is not often mentioned is that during wartime, the Mexican government confined German and Japanese citizens living in the country to certain neighborhoods. In the municipality of Perote, Veracruz, a detention center was created where more than five hundred German, Italian, and Japanese citizens ended up, accused of being spies or of violating Mexican laws. This could never be proven, however, and the inmates had to wait until the end of the war in 1945 to be released.

During World War II, historic events took place that left a mark on humanity. Among these were the evacuation of Dunkirk, the fall of Paris, the Allied landing in Normandy, the bombing of Dresden, and the battle of Stalingrad between German and Soviet forces, the bloodiest of all time. There is the Holocaust, the most infamous extermination ever seen, resulting in millions of deaths made possible by an efficient system that perfected murder. Berlin, the imposing capital of the country that stirred up the hornet's nest, was reduced to rubble by the unilateral invasion of Allied forces. Gone were the glorious dreams of the German people. The country that once had been a reference for philosophers and thinkers and the birthplace of brilliant musicians was turned into a country of murderers, thanks to Hitler's delirium.

Let's accompany the last few citizens defending what little is left of Berlin. The Soviet bombs are coming closer and closer. In the absence of soldiers, it is the people themselves, including children and the elderly, who have to take up arms. It is hard for them to recognize the obvious. If anyone points out that the war is lost, they are immediately accused of being a coward and a traitor. Many do not know if the Führer is still alive or dead—or if he has fled to some distant place to regroup his forces and raise the Reich from the ashes. In the meantime, there are buildings in flames, buildings destroyed, and buildings blown up.

The people of Berlin make sandbag barricades. A boy, no older than ten years old, lays mines in the streets to destroy Russian tanks. A few days ago, the boy received an award from the Führer in a brief ceremony amid the rubble. The boy recalls the praise: "I wish my generals had had your courage." That was the last sighting of the great leader, the man who promised a glorious future. "What happened?" the Germans ask themselves, walking through the ruins of their city. "At what point was victory stolen from us again? Now all is lost."

News spreads among the last resisters: The Führer is dead. He has committed suicide in his bunker, along with his partner, Eva Braun.

"That's a lie!" shouts someone, incredulous at the death of a person who portrayed himself as immortal. What little hope they had left vanishes. The suicides of officers of the once-powerful regime are numerous. None of them, not even the Führer, wanted to fall into Soviet hands and then be tried for war crimes and crimes against humanity.

"What next?" the children ask themselves, now bereft of parents, leaders, and homeland. Hungry, dirty, and sad, the children raise their hands in surrender to the Soviet troops who capture the German capital and burn the swastika flags, replacing them with those of the Red Army.

After much fighting, the end of the war was decided when the United States dropped a pair of nuclear bombs that devastated the Japanese cities of Hiroshima and Nagasaki. Faced with this unprecedented attack, with no strength to continue the fight, both Germany and Japan admitted unconditional defeat and agreed to the terms of surrender.

The world was restructured geopolitically, and Germany was divided by the Allied forces. The United States is cataloged as a world superpower due to its use of nuclear technology. This is the first time this term has been used. The United States was instrumental in the reconstruction of Europe, which it helped through the Marshall Plan. Uncle Sam returned from the war stronger than ever and proved that winning a war abroad can bring great benefits, such as enviable economic growth, a strong and aspirational middle class, better wages, and prosperity. The United States consolidated its role as the sole superpower, and expanded its hegemony, its culture, its values, its idea of a unique, exceptional, and invincible country throughout the world.

The next major conflict was the Cold War, which pitted the United States and the Soviet Union, former allies against the Nazis, against each other to see which of the two blocs could impose its ideology and political system on the rest of the world.

The Attack on the World Trade Center and the War on Terrorism

Those who predicted the end of history after the fall of the Berlin Wall could not foresee what would happen on the morning of September 11, 2001, or the consequences that fateful day would bring to the rest of the world. Those who saw the planes crash into the Twin Towers could not understand that the destruction and horror they witnessed was within the realm of the probable and the possible.

During the Cold War, the superpowers were in dispute, although they never directly confronted each other. During that same period, wars were fought in Korea, Vietnam, and Lebanon; the first two are also known as the Indochina War. The world was divided into two blocs: the Western Bloc, formed by the United States and its allies, whose economic system is capitalism, and the Eastern Bloc, formed by the Soviet Union, whose ideology is communist. In the case of the Korean conflict, the United States had no justification for participating; however, it intervened with troops on the South Korean side.

The Vietnam War, the worst defeat of the US military to date, deserves special mention. America supported South Vietnam, and North Vietnam had communist backing. The United States decided to intervene to prevent communism from spreading in Asia. During the conflict, other nations allied themselves with the United States, and the fighting went on for three years, during which time the image of US government aggression was widely circulated, thanks to television. In the end, the perception of the United States was tarnished, with many casualties on both sides. The metaphor for US involvement in Vietnam can be depicted as a mighty elephant being attacked by a tiger it can neither see nor control. It did little good to spray the Asian jungles with napalm. The United States withdrew from Vietnam humiliated and wounded, without accomplishing its main objectives.

As for the Persian Gulf War, or simply the Gulf War, the US participated for a strategic reason. Kuwait was among the major oil producers, and it was not in America's interest to allow another country to invade. They must have decided in Washington, DC, that if someone were to invade Kuwait, it would be better for it to be the United States. Another compelling reason is that in this area of conflict lies an important trade route. During the war, the UN backed US claims. The operation to liberate Kuwait began—with the not-so-hidden interests already mentioned.

Then we come to the morning of September 11, 2001. Very few people knew that on that day the world would change completely. For most, it would be an ordinary Tuesday. In New York, people were heading to work, some in a hurry, others were on the subway calmly reading newspapers that predicted other news for that day. On the radio, they were talking about the weather. Tourists were walking with their eyes fixed on the tall buildings of Manhattan. Office workers at the World Trade Center entered the buildings without noticing how clear the sky was. Panic broke out when the first plane hit the North Tower of the World Trade Center. A few were able to capture that terrible moment on video. The vast majority of New Yorkers thought it was an accident until minutes later, when a second plane hit the remaining tower. There was no longer any doubt that the nation was under attack. While thousands of people watched in horror as the Twin Towers burned, thousands more were trapped inside amid the fire, chaos, fear, panic, and smoke that quickly littered the blue New York sky.

With extensive media coverage worldwide, the attack served as an excuse for the United States to intervene militarily in Iraq even though there was no evidence that Saddam Hussein's regime was behind the attack on the Twin Towers. At the time, the US claimed that Iraq had weapons of mass destruction, which were never found. In principle, its involvement is self-justified as being against terrorism, but there are other factors that should be emphasized. If we look at the big picture, prior to the attack on the Twin Towers, the US government was already disputing oil reserves in Iraq and other Middle East territories. It is useful to broaden the picture in order to understand the US position in this conflict.

We cautiously accompany someone demonized in an intense media campaign: Osama bin Laden. He is the founder of the terrorist organization Al Qaeda, and he planned the September 11 attacks against the United States. However, it turns out that, behind his vilified profile, is a family close to Saudi royalty. The bin Ladens are well positioned socially and economically, and they have investments in energy and weapons. In some ways, the U.S. had helped create the monster that would provoke the biggest attack in its history when, during the Cold War, it funded Afghan insurgent guerrillas to fight against Russian invaders. Out of those leftovers would come Al Qaeda.

After the September 11 attacks, President Bush declared war on terrorism. This favored the United States, which became the largest producer and exporter of weapons in the world. With its invasion of Iraq, it entered the dispute over one of the largest oil reserves on the planet.

In the aftermath of the September 11 attacks, the Department of Homeland Security was created in 2002 with the mission of protecting the United States from any terrorist attack. This was reflected in stricter inspections of flights and airports, as well as increased government surveillance of every citizen's private life. The Patriot Act limited freedoms while offering a sense of security from terrorist danger, and much of the U.S. population agreed to give up certain constitutional rights in exchange for protection.

It should be noted that George W. Bush visited his counterpart, Vicente Fox, in Mexico. The two discussed immigration and other issues in what was reported in the press as a very cordial visit. There was optimism that the US Congress would approve "the whole enchilada," an ambitious immigration plan proposed by then Foreign Minister Jorge Castañeda Gutman. This plan sought to legalize millions of Mexicans in the United States, increase the number of work visas, and grant some sort of amnesty. But as it has been said before: Man proposes, God disposes, and then the devil comes along and messes everything up. The "whole enchilada" collapsed just like the Twin Towers; it was unthinkable that the United States would pass an immigration plan after suffering a terrorist attack. In addition, Vicente Fox officially stated his rejection of the war in Iraq before the UN

Security Council, and this annoyed Washington, who were looking for support from their allies to legitimize the Iraq invasion. Fox also did not express diplomatic condolences in honor of the victims of September 11, which was questioned by the international press.

In his memoirs, published in Spanish as *Amarres Perros,* former Foreign Minister Jorge Castañeda narrates what went through his mind when he saw the planes crashing into the Twin Towers on television:

> I understood, once we knew who the perpetrators of the atrocity were, that there also crashed my hope of achieving an immigration agreement, good, bad or regular, with the Bush administration, at least during his first term ... Washington would be engaged for a while in discovering and destroying those guilty of the death of thousands of Americans, and another while in making sure that nothing similar would happen again.

As they say, only he who carries the coffin knows what the dead man weighs.

There were two positions within the Fox administration: that of Secretary of the Interior Santiago Creel, who argued that support for the United States after September 11 could not be unconditional, and that of Foreign Minister Jorge Castañeda, who stated that support for the neighbor to the north could not be haggled over, and that the only possible alignment with the United States should be complete. At that time, Mexico was a member of the UN Security Council, and its vote was essential to support the U.S. invasion of Iraq. Apart from Mexico, other countries such as France, Russia and China were opposed to the invasion, but they did not want to directly confront George W. Bush and appear to be accomplices of Saddam Hussein's regime. Basically, they did not want to give the United States a blank check that would legalize a clearly controversial and unsubstantiated invasion. With time, we now know that Bush, his Vice President

Dick Cheney, Donald Rumsfeld and Colin Powell lied about the existence of weapons of mass destruction on Iraqi soil. Mexico did not support military intervention in Iraq, and President Bush decided to invade anyway, even though he didn't have the international legitimacy to do so.

Many years later, Osama bin Laden was killed in Pakistan by US Special Forces. That achievement belonged to George W. Bush's successor, President Barack Obama. The US participation in Middle East conflicts finally concludes with President Joe Biden's decision to withdraw troops from Afghanistan in 2021 after twenty years of fighting. This is the longest war that the United States has ever fought, leaving without a clear victory, as in Vietnam.

Two Hundred Years of Diplomatic Relations between the United States and Mexico

Diplomatic relations between Mexico and the United States began in 1822. A year after its independence from Spain, Mexico was recognized by the also young United States. Two hundred years ago, the golden eagle and the bald eagle greeted each other and decided to work together for the benefit of their territories. Their joint history is one of many vicissitudes, with its successes and mistakes, highs and lows, moments of friendship and cooperation as well as tension and complaints; just as good marriages that have been together for several years tend to be. Or as Jorge Ibargüengoitia sums it up very well: "They admired and loved each other as people who do not know each other well usually do".

But after so much idyll, Mexico and the United States know each other well. The relationship between the two countries is indispensable. The United States and Mexico share 3,000 kilometers of border, as well as interests, culture, problems, and histories of their citizens. It is known that the United States is the country that hosts the most Mexicans after Mexico, although it is unknown that out of 9 million Americans living outside the United States, 1.5 million reside in Mexico.

This bilateral relationship is based on two requirements. Mexico needs an autonomous government free from interventionism. The United States needs Mexico's stability and the security it provides in the southern border area. The benefit expected by both nations is economic influence and growth.

Before the 1930s, a conflict arose during the government of Plutarco Elias Calles, and not exactly due to an issue of border security. President Calles, who served from 1924 to 1928, was intent on seeing that 1917 Constitution enforced. But his US counterpart, Calvin Coolidge, did not agree with the retroactive application of Mexican laws regarding restitution for properties that the Americans acquired before May 1, 1917, when the Constitution went into effect.

Consequently, the Coolidge government appealed to the international law, claiming that infringements befall on those rights that were already obtained by foreigners. The 1923 Bucareli Treaty (an agreement regarding the expropriation of US landholdings in Mexico as well as the ways of calculating compensation and forms of payment) established the prerogatives on those infringements at the time of legislating on the rights that had been obtained by foreigners. Consequently, Mexican legislation must regulate issues of an internal nature and without affecting the rights of foreigners.

President Coolidge named James R. Sheffield as US ambassador to Mexico on August 26, 1924, shortly before Plutarco Elias Calles took office. A Republican, at sixty years of age, Ambassador Sheffield had a record of service with his party and maintained a close relationship with national and state leaders, especially with Secretary of State Charles Evans Hughes. The press viewed his knowledge of law and finance favorably; journalists in Mexico shared the same perception.

In October 1924, Sheffield met with President Alvaro Obregon, who was nearing the end of his term, and stated, "We do not dispute any right or privilege or power for ourselves that we would not freely grant to you, we do not seek territory, we do not desire exclusive privileges."

At first, Sheffield was well-received by the Mexican bureaucracy, given his Hollywood-worthy diplomatic profile. What leads to public censure is his sense of humor full of social and racial prejudice. With little sensitivity to Mexican culture and philosophy, Ambassador Sheffield would make offensive jokes in private. He was terrified that chickens and turkeys would mill around in front of the US embassy, for example, among many other such stories told about him.

After his first meeting with the new President Plutarco Elias Calles, in February 1925, Sheffield took rigorous note of the fact that this president had set his sights on nationalizing land, mining, forests, and oil without taking into account that this could lead to the expropriation of US property.

Elias Calles does not refute this. In his government's agenda, he stresses that foreign capital in Mexican territory is exploitative. He calls for raising taxes and increasing salaries to strengthen unions in Mexico. Sheffield counters that such measures will delay progress in a material way, given that investments boost foreign trade. He also noted that the United States wanted to support Mexico in all the indicated areas, on the condition that properties that belonged to US companies would be respected. President Elías Calles concludes that these properties will only have the protection stipulated by Mexican law.

Later, at a public event outside of Mexico, Sheffield stated that when a country is a member of an international agreement between nations, it has to adapt to the rules that define diplomatic relations in accordance with international law and with complete protection of the rights of foreigners. He insists that every US citizen is guaranteed that their rights will be respected and preserved.

Due to health issues, Sheffield was absent from Mexico for some time. When he resumed his duties as ambassador in October 1925, President Elías Calles had already put his plan in motion under Article 27 of the Mexican Constitution. Months earlier, on June 12, 1925, the US Secretary of State, Frank B. Kellogg, had declared that Mexico was on trial before the world.

Sheffield's presence in Mexico became complicated when he began to act on his own to reprimand the government, which was supporting the revolutionary movement of Augusto Cesar Sandino in Nicaragua. President Coolidge's administration decided to replace Sheffield with Dwight Morrow in order to maintain a nonconfrontational policy with Mexico. Morrow succeeded in improving the relationship with President Plutarco Elias Calles.

For Mexico, being a friend of the United States does not mean dancing to their tune whenever they want. Mexico has even acted against U.S. wishes on several occasions. The Mexican government supported Guatemala's right to self-determination through the Organization of American States (OAS). However, at the behest of the CIA, it stayed out of the coup against President Jacobo Arbenz in 1954. This drew strong criticism of Mexico at the time. Mexico offered political support to Cuba, but as with Guatemala, held back during the crisis of Soviet missiles aimed at the United States from Cuban territory, although the Americans rightly claimed that this endangered their security.

Another area that deserves our special attention is effective and democratic suffrage. Despite episodes of questionable results, as in the controversial 1988 elections, the United States has remained on the sidelines and respectful of Mexico's internal politics. After Carlos Salinas de Gortari ceded the presidency to Ernesto Zedillo at the end of 1994, economic change took place through negotiations that included the signing of the North American Free Trade Agreement, better known as NAFTA, which incorporated Canada, the United States, and Mexico. This treaty resulted in significant growth in trade and finance through the expansion of institutional relationships.

The signing and enactment of NAFTA is consistent with the profile of other global policies, including the financial integration of the European Union. The latter is made up of twenty-seven European states and came into effect through the Maastricht Treaty on November 1, 1993.

Despite institutional inequality, NAFTA has a binding legal framework for its member states. The benefits of NAFTA are not exclusive to any one country, given that its normative structure establishes a process of unification regardless of the positions or conditions of inequality among its members. On this platform, NAFTA offers a lower or higher profitability to its members, according to internal regulations.

The implementation of NAFTA brought winners and losers. In the case of Mexico, it was undoubtedly beneficial for its economy, although unfortunately many Mexican products could not compete against U.S. products. The ejido, the legacy of the Mexican Revolution, was also unable to compete against U.S. transnationals. The peasants were among the most affected, being forced to emigrate to the United States in search of work. The Mexican Constitution also had to adapt to the clauses established in NAFTA, since you can't look a gift horse in the mouth.

One of the fiercest critics of NAFTA was President Donald Trump. Interestingly, he claimed that Mexico had "screwed" the U.S. on NAFTA, causing it to lose jobs and billions of dollars. Trump called it the worst trade deal in history, claiming that the decline of the U.S. Manufacturing Beltway was precisely due to NAFTA. So, it was no surprise that Trump wanted to replace the treaty as soon as he became president. NAFTA gave way to the USMCA with the participation of Canada, the United States and Mexico as a competitive platform for the 21st century economy, under the slogan of certainty and correct regulation of free trade.

The USMCA becomes effective on July 1, 2020, providing assurance to investors, consumers, producers, and service providers. At the same time, it consolidates the trade benefits acquired during NAFTA. For a nation like Mexico, it allows a greater competitiveness of the domestic economy, with more active participation of SMEs. The domino effect is that more employment opportunities are generated with a new labor model, especially in those regions located in the south of Mexico.

It should be noted that not everything in the USMCA has been smooth sailing. This is normal in international treaties. When disputes arise, they are settled in panels, and it is there where it is seen who is right. Currently, different interpretations of the USMCA on energy issues have generated disputes between Mexico and the

United States and Canada. The problem is technical and complex. They claim that Mexico gives preferential treatment to Mexican state-owned companies, such as Pemex and CFE, over U.S. and Canadian companies and investors in energy matters; they claim that these policies are contrary to what is stipulated in the treaty, while for Mexico this is a defense of energy sovereignty. Mexico is nobody's colony; the Mexican President has reiterated several times.

The signing of the USMCA took place during a period of political change in Mexico and following criticism from Donald Trump's government about Mexican exports, alleging that NAFTA had been disadvantageous for the United States. After the historic results of Mexico's presidential elections of July 1, 2018, a new important protagonist emerges: Andres Manuel Lopez Obrador (AMLO), who wins the presidency as the representative of the leftist National Regeneration Movement (MORENA).

We accompany Lopez Obrador as he is declared the winner with more than 53 percent of votes cast. This is the first time that a leftist candidate has won in Mexico. On his third attempt to win the presidency, AMLO's movement obtains a decisive majority in the two congressional chambers, as well as in governorships, municipalities, and local legislatures.

We are now with the president-elect, and his transition team, in an intense work session behind closed doors. They review the discredited administration of his predecessor, Enrique Peña Nieto, and take the reins of the Mexican government between the months of July and December 2018. In other words, before the official end of Enrique Peña Nieto's term of office, Lopez Obrador was already making decisions, such as the cancellation of the new Mexico City airport project.

The international community approves of AMLO's undisputed triumph. Less than forty-eight hours after his electoral victory was announced, Lopez Obrador spoke by telephone with Donald Trump, then president of the United States. This was an obvious endorsement prior to Lopez Obrador formally taking over the administration of the country.

Apart from the call's distinctly cordial tone, Donald Trump touched on the possibility of carrying out bilateral trade negotiations between both nations, with the implicit inclusion of Canada. Lopez Obrador proposed reducing the migration of Mexican nationals to the United States through a comprehensive program to promote security and employment.

Donald Trump's administration reaffirmed its confidence in Lopez Obrador's social commitment plan. A few weeks passed before a delegation from the United States visited Mexico, headed by Secretary of State Mike Pompeo. In addition to meeting with then-Foreign Minister Luis Videgaray Caso, one of the priorities on the agenda was a meeting with the new president-elect.

During the meeting with Lopez Obrador, the US government expresses its interest and concern regarding the border and its impact on national security. Pompeo, the former director of the CIA, shows his extensive knowledge of the issue. They discuss the electoral triumph. Lopez Obrador delivers a document to President Donald Trump, which includes guidelines to optimize relations between Mexico and the United States. Marcelo Ebrard Casaubón, who later replaced Videgaray as minister of foreign affairs, adds that the document addresses security, migration, trade, and development. This document touches on the lack of solutions addressing migration as well as the inequity of development existing in both Mexico and Central America.

A few weeks after the document was sent, a caravan of seven thousand migrants from Honduras entered Mexico, bound for the United States. The migration debate was then prioritized once again, with worldwide attention.

The migration phenomenon impacts El Salvador, Guatemala, and Honduras, known as the Northern Triangle. Caravans of thousands of people leave from this area, inevitably crossing Mexican territory. This is an imminent challenge for the current Mexican government, and there are multiple social and humanitarian difficulties.

This human flow makes the crossing in adverse and extremely dangerous conditions. We should also point out that, since the summer of 2014, the number of children traveling alone to the United States has risen sharply. This is causing a humanitarian crisis that has been highlighted by the mass media.

Back then, President Barack Obama requested support via telephone from the Mexican government. Jointly, and with the involvement of the Ministry of the Interior, the Proyecto Frontera Sur (Southern Border Project) was created for the purpose of deporting Central American children back to their country of origin. The United States shows no interest in modifying its own migration policies, even though this is entirely within its responsibility.

During Donald Trump's administration, rumor had it that his administration asked Luis Videgaray to turn Mexico into a safe third country, similar to what Turkey provides to the European Union with refugees and migrants. The initiative would create shelters and other forms of accommodation for those who are seeking asylum in the United States. In the event that the request for asylum is rejected, Mexico is responsible for ensuring their return to their home countries. In order to obtain approval, Trump offered economic support to cover the needs of migrants throughout this process.

The initiative comes during the change of administrations in Mexico; once Lopez Obrador assumes the presidency, such a possibility is ruled out.

During the presidential transition period between July and December 2018, migration and national policy positions differ, as we have seen, which generates uncertainty for the United States. However, the signing of the USMCA affirms the political trust between these nations, although there are issues to be resolved, such as the issue of tariffs on steel and aluminum.

In addition to the delicate issue of migration, which is far from being fully resolved, there are other important problems. These include arms trafficking from the United States to criminal organizations, the development of US agencies in Mexican territory for intelligence purposes, the DEA, the CIA, and the FBI, and finally, the training of Mexican army and navy troops in the United

States, which dates back to the time of Felipe Calderon's government from 2006 to 2012.

There are key points on the bilateral agenda that have an impact on Mexico, such as the US economic and commercial dispute with China. The outcome affects Mexico since it constrains its capacity for production diversification, while its economy shrinks and is vulnerable to the United States.

On November 7, 2020, the triumph of the Democratic Party in the elections for the presidency of the United States was announced in all the world's media. President Lopez Obrador decided to wait to congratulate Joe Biden until the election was officially confirmed (by the Electoral College) on December 14.

Once in office, the new president focuses the US–Mexico agenda on arms trafficking, drug consumption, and migration. Once again, Mexico and the United States begin a new stage in their diplomatic relationship, with the challenge of resolving pending agendas on security and violence.

Relations between Mexico and the United States have not been broken, nor will they be broken, by the absence of López Obrador at the Summit of the Americas, or by U.S. complaints on energy issues. The relationship has survived 200 years. Now the situation is different. The United States has the right to complain if it believes that the USMCA is not being complied with, just as Mexico has the obligation to defend its energy sovereignty and not give in to the interests of foreign companies. Diplomatic channels have been effective in maintaining the bonds of friendship even if disputes are settled on the other side. No friendship is free of arguments and conflict. The talent lies in dealing with them intelligently. Both countries know that they are better off together than apart, especially when China and Russia lurk in the world. Such relations are stronger than a trade dispute that will eventually be resolved, and it is illustrative that one of the most frequent visitors to the National Palace has been none other than Ken Salazar, U.S. Ambassador to Mexico.

The USS *Arizona* in flames after the Japanese
attack to Pearl Harbor, December 7, 1941.

Chapter 10

Two Cities in Parallel

Why Two Cities?

Mexico and the United States of America acquired their historical identity as a result of independence from European empires. Each nation's purpose is stated in a constitution that embodies its political ideals. Each nation charts its own course, with its own leaders and transcendent events. Mexico continues developing as a nation, while the United States has strengthened its position as a world power—or a superpower.

Within Mexico and the US, there are several world-class cities. Because of the strategic political and trade alliance between the two countries plus *transculturation* (a term coined by Cuban anthropologist Fernando Ortiz to describe the phenomenon of merging and converging cultures) due to migratory flows—mainly from Mexico to the United States—we can discern similarities between cities of both countries.

Efforts by both nations' diplomatic corps makes this perspective possible, with the famous saying, "He who does not know history is doomed to repeat it." So, let's take a look at history and a look at the cities that allow us to anticipate the continuance of bilateral development.

Our list includes the capitals of both countries: Mexico City, with its solid social and economic structure and Washington, DC, whose development places it among the best cities in the world. Another important milestone for Mexico and the United States is the creation of their first universities: the Universidad Michoacana de San Nicolas de Hidalgo in 1540, in Morelia, Michoacan, and in 1636, Harvard University, in Cambridge, Massachusetts.

Among its significant ports are New York and Veracruz. Both San Francisco and Leon, Guanajuato, have a mining history and today are positioned in manufactured goods. As for Leon, whose full name is Ciudad de Leon de los Aldama, foreign investment is driving its current growth, with the expectation that the city will take on the challenges posed by sustainability.

This same scenario is shared by the cities of Monterrey and Pittsburgh. Both are recognized as the cities of steel, with strong economic growth and future potential. In the case of Monterrey, capital of the state of Nuevo Leon, located in northeastern Mexico, the city has challenges with high levels of pollution and continual water shortages. Today's world does not tolerate falling behind, and development that does not consider issues of sustainability is no longer acceptable.

The Ports of New York and Veracruz

We begin our historic journey guided by a Mexican citizen who will travel with us to the country's main cities. We arrive at the port of Veracruz, the first city on the American continent. Three years before the fall of Tenochtitlan, in 1519, Hernan Cortes founded this city by the sea, calling it Villa Rica de la Vera Cruz.

After its founding, Veracruz becomes the scene of large cargo shipments coming and going from Europe. The ships arrive at the port with animals, weapons, soldiers, and an infinite number of products that might be legal or not. In exchange, the ships leave filled with all kinds of treasures, from metals to fabrics and food. Because of this great economic activity, a customs office is set up. The constant flow of wealth quickly draws the attention of pirates, who try to steal other people's goods.

To deal with the threat, in 1535, this gateway to the continent is walled off, and the fort of San Juan de Ulua is built. Several cannons jut out from its walls to intimidate the pirates, inviting them to plunder other ports. With our guide, we tour this fort steeped in history, which is now a tourist destination. The guide reveals that San Juan de Ulua Fort, located on a small island, witnessed a bloody battle in 1568 between the Spanish Armada and a flotilla of English pirates under the command of Francis Drake, who had a reputation for stealing for the Crown. Later, Veracruz resisted the American and French invasions, and San Juan de Ulua became a prison for political detainees. This penitentiary was probably the most feared place in Mexico; conditions were deplorable. It is also said that the prison, being surrounded by the sea, was infested with sharks hungry for escaped prisoners. The most notable characters who set foot in the San Juan de Ulua prison were Brother Servando Teresa de Mier, Benito Juarez, and the bandit Chucho el Roto—a type of *jarocho* (a native of Veracruz) Robin Hood who stole from the wealthy and managed to escape from the prison several times. Another prisoner was La Mulata de Cordova (the Mulatta of Cordova), a woman who painted an enormous ship on the wall of her cell to escape the terrible punishments of the Inquisition. The drawing showed a ship sailing calmly toward the horizon as the sun began to set. The guards were slow to notice the absence of the Mulatta; her cell was empty. After searching everywhere for her, that drawing on the wall became the main suspect in her escape. We ask our guide if he believes the story.

"Of course," he replies. "Don't you?"

We are now in the port of New York, where a US citizen in charge of guiding us through this country's emblematic cities welcomes us. New York was built in 1648, some 129 years after Veracruz. It was first under the rule of the Dutch Empire, then passed into the hands of English colonists, and later to the government of the United States. Under the US, New York became the entry point for immigrants from all over the world who longed for the so-called American dream. Before setting foot in the promised land, they first had to disembark at Ellis Island, which became the largest immigration center in America. After weeks of travel at sea, vulnerable to the vagaries of uncertainty, hopeful gazes look closely at the Statue of Liberty as their ship silently slips past. A new life awaits the migrants once they are cleared at Ellis Island to enter New York. Laden with dreams and hope, they will build much of America's greatness.

Let's continue with Veracruz. By 1860, an average of two hundred ships and more than twenty-five thousand tons of merchandise passed through the port of Veracruz per year. This same port welcomed the first and last emperor of the Second Mexican Empire, imposed by the French at the request of Conservatives: Maximilian of Habsburg, who disembarked in Veracruz hand in hand with his wife, Empress Carlota, in 1864.

In 1873, the railroad line connecting Mexico City with Veracruz was inaugurated, boosting trade in the port area. Our guide informs us that the port's early history ends at this point; its journey to modernity begins in 1882, during the government of Porfirio Diaz. Going back a little further, the port witnessed the first US invasion of Mexico in 1847, when American ships bombarded Veracruz before disembarking to take the country's capital, with sad and tragic consequences.

The port of Veracruz also witnessed the departure into exile of Porfirio Diaz, the old dictator who had lost to Francisco I. Madero. It is said that before boarding the ship—called the *Ipiranga*, which took him to France, Porfirio Diaz had coffee at La Parroquia, the most famous coffee shop in Veracruz, which still exists today. It is also said that the overthrown president wept as he ate his last breakfast on Mexican soil. He knew, more than anyone, that he would never again return to his beloved Mexico. Porfirio Diaz sadly raised his hand and said goodbye to the entourage that accompanied him to the port. As the *Ipiranga* sailed away and the port of Veracruz became smaller in the distance, he hung his hat in his cabin and, in the solitude of the sea, continued weeping.

Back to New York, and our guide takes us 1900, and this US port is now iconic. After World War II, its growth exploded. Afterward, it became the busiest port in the world.

The creation of administrative entities to manage and regulate the two ports occurred at different times. New York was regulated at the beginning of the twentieth century. In Mexico, it was not until the end of the twentieth century when the Integral Port Administration (API, for the acronym in Spanish) was put into operation.

Today, the port of New York is still positioned as one of the busiest worldwide due to the arrival of merchandise and products, mainly oil. As for the port of Veracruz, it has no competition within the Mexican Republic. The government of Andres Manuel Lopez Obrador plans to make Veracruz one of top ports in the world, boosted by the new Trans-Isthmus Corridor project. This project aims to compete with the Panama Canal by connecting the ports of Coatzacoalcos, in southern Veracruz, and Salina Cruz, in Oaxaca, via a railway line. This will create an overland connection between the Gulf of Mexico and the Pacific Ocean, ideal for transporting goods.

The Capitals Also Differ: Washington, DC, and Mexico City

Washington and Mexico City are the settings for decisive events in the life of each nation. Both Washington and Mexico City are full of important landmarks and have a history forged during difficult years. In fact, there is a parallel that draws on the founding of these capitals: Mexico City was built on an islet that progressively dried up, while current political dialogue says that Washington was founded on a swamp, from which it has not been able to emerge.

Before New Spain—capital of the Spanish viceroyalty and predecessor of Mexico City—was built, the great Tenochtitlan dazzled locals and foreigners alike. This capital of the Mexica Empire was founded on an islet, which the Mexicas considered to be the site predicted by their mythology. Legend has it that when they saw an eagle devouring a snake on top of a cactus, this was the sign for where to found their empire. Later, the conquistador Hernan Cortes described the architecture, urban layout, and complex commercial system of Tenochtitlan with astonishment.

The Mexica built this city on a spot that was practically unthinkable: a swampy area, with scarcely drinkable water and vermin everywhere. However, their ingenuity and determination enabled them to build an unprecedented fortress. After the arrival of the Spaniards and the fall of Tenochtitlan, the colonizers built a new city from its ruins. But they faced a problem that the early inhabitants solved with pure hydraulic engineering talent: floods. The surrounding lake area was drained, and piping was installed. But over the years, it has remained a problem. Today, heavy rains cause flooding problems in Mexico City. This happens in certain areas and provokes traffic chaos, although people haven't had to go to the extreme of driving through the streets in the chinampas when it rains too much.

With our guide in Mexico, we tour the remains of the Templo Mayor, the sacred building of the great Tenochtitlan. He shows us that the Mexica had a system to regulate the problem of floods, and they even developed methods to divert water to the most appropriate locations. Their *tlatoanis*, or rulers, enjoyed swimming pools that were supplied with water from the best springs. Such was their affinity for water that they were able to move easily throughout the length and breadth of canals and rivers.

The great Tenochtitlan fell in 1521. According to official records, New Spain was founded 1585. Washington was founded in 1790 with a Parisian touch in its design, given that the architect responsible, Pierre Charles, was of French origin; later, Paris itself takes elements from the capital of the United States. Its name is a tribute to George Washington, hero of the independence movement and first president of the nation.

With the help of our guide in the United States, let's debunk the swamp myth. It turns out that the city of Washington was built on the banks of a river, the Potomac River to be exact. George Washington himself thought it could be an excellent option as a communications mean. However, once the layout was mapped, the proposal was rejected.

After the Civil War, the number of residents grew. Nine months prior to the signing of the Emancipation Proclamation, slaves living in Washington were freed. In subsequent years, Washington became home to many African Americans, including the abolitionist

Frederick Douglass. During the war period, a large army was formed to protect the capital, a step toward federal involvement in running certain aspects of local government.

Accompanied by our guide, we walk through the streets of Washington and note that it is a diverse and impressive city, where different cultures from all over the world are welcome. The heritage of African American culture is present in multiple expressions. Washington, DC, is a city that accepts gender and sexual diversity and was one of the first to recognize same-sex marriage. In 2015, the US Supreme Court ruled that same-sex marriage is a citizen's right.

Washington has grown as a twenty-first-century metropolis. Because of its security and political and economic power, the city serves as the headquarters for a number of international organizations, including the World Bank, the Organization of American States (OAS), and the International Monetary Fund.

We continue on this tour with the help of our guide, who shows us monuments to Washington, Lincoln, and World War II. We stroll through the famous Arlington National Cemetery, which houses the remains of veterans of all US wars, from the Revolutionary War to the conflicts in Iraq and Afghanistan. We stop in front of the Tomb of the Unknown Soldier, a large marble headstone dedicated to American soldiers who died in World War I and could not be identified. After walking the paths of the cemetery, with the silence of thousands of graves, we return to the streets of Washington and the noise of everyday life.

We bid farewell to Mexico City and Washington DC, two friendly cities, warm and generous to tourists; two metropolises that serve as the backbone for their nations' development.

The Cities That Went from Mining to Manufacturing: San Francisco and Leon

With our guide in Mexico, we go back to the era of the viceroyalty, in the middle of the eighteenth century, when mining invigorated an economic system that depended on the Spanish Crown. We are in the state of Guanajuato, and a report from 1766 and 1767 indicates that an average of forty thousand men worked in mining. Working conditions were unfavorable—and frankly exploitative. At that time, the *"raya"* system was imposed, which was a kind of piecework system for which the pay was ridiculously low and miserable. The paltry pay forced workers into debt with their employers. This practice, which lasted for a long time in Mexico, was similar to slavery. During these years, the government of New Spain had to confront several rebellions from the subjugated population.

The records that might detail these events were suppressed by the viceroyalty's authorities. What can be verified is that the Spanish government repressed the insurrections with clubs and gunpowder to maintain the pace of work in the mines.

Let's look at data that allows a reliable reconstruction of the facts. Around 1770, the participation of Spaniards in the mining sector increased, and a new division in the distribution of labor arose.

According to official royal records issued in Guanajuato in 1773, in addition to what was documented by Manuel Dominguez de la Fuentes in 1774, we see that mine administrators took steps to limit their responsibility for collecting taxes.

The labor force was divided among natives, free mulattos, mestizos, and Spaniards; the first two bore the brunt of the hard work inside the mines. The anger and irritation over forced labor in the state of Guanajuato was a precursor for what the viceroyalty of New Spain would experience. Once independence from the European Crown was achieved, which began with the armed uprising of Father Miguel Hidalgo, Mexico followed an eventful trajectory that included the Revolution of 1910. When Mexico enacted a constitution that regulated the exploitation of its natural resources and defended workers' rights, the state of Guanajuato proved to be a pillar of the national economy.

Today, Guanajuato no longer depends on mining production. In the past two decades, its economic growth has been above average. The state currently contributes 3.7 percent to Mexico's GDP. Its growth comes from manufacturing, with 28 percent of the state's production, as well as services and trade.

According to the National Institute of Statistics and Geography (INEGI, for the acronym in Spanish), Guanajuato's industrial production represented 17 percent of total domestic manufacturing in 2009. And its investment climate is favorable.

As for trade, it accounts for 16.3 percent of the state's economy. We also note that agricultural activity decreased by 4.6 percent, and the construction industry dropped by 6.5 percent at the local level (this last score is similar to the national average of 6.4 percent).

Guanajuato state's municipalities are directly involved in industrial activity, thereby diversifying the production of manufactured goods. Looking at data for the entire state, the municipality of Silao accounts for 43 percent of GDP; Leon registers 37 percent and 45 percent in terms of better salaries and higher employment, respectively; Salamanca attains 30 percent capitalization of fixed assets; and Leon accounts for 22 percent.

Let's leave the numbers and figures for a moment and continue with our guide as we tour the business district of the city of Leon. Shoes on display in shop windows are desirable for their quality and design. Our guide tells us that the manufacture of shoes here began in 1645, so the people of Leon have formidable experience in this business. All leather and hide tanning production is local; the manufacture of plastic and rubber is also profitable. Although we promised to leave the figures for a moment, this one is important: footwear production in Leon alone accounts for 87 percent of the local GDP. If you want to buy good shoes, Leon is the place!

It is a niche that supports micro and small businesses. After our tour of Leon, it's clear to us that its industry is diverse.

Back in the United States, our guide awaits us in a city that years ago was also a bastion of mining production: San Francisco. We go back to January 1848. A lucky carpenter named James Marshall, who was working at Sutter's Mill, by pure chance finds some gold nuggets in the American River, near the village of Coloma. This river today crosses the city of Sacramento, California.

At the time, the area was still part of Mexico, although the United States had been after for this territory for quite some time. In February 1848, the Treaty of Guadalupe Hidalgo was signed between Mexico and the United States, ending hostilities between both nations. After the signing of this treaty, Arizona, California, Nevada, New Mexico, Texas, Utah, and other Mexican territories were annexed by the US, which became an even stronger country than it already was.

Let's go back to Marshall, who intends to keep the existence of gold a secret. But we know that this is impossible. Fortune, like love, is difficult to hide. Marshall probably came to his most trusted friend and revealed to him, in a very low voice, the marvel of his discovery. This person, stunned by the presence of the tiny gold nuggets, swears on his life, his children, his mother-in-law, and on all the gods that he will keep the secret. And probably within a few hours, the whole town had heard that James Marshall had found gold in the river. Soon the rumor of a supposed abundance of gold spreads, attracting many Americans as well as foreigners from Latin America, Asia, Australia, and Europe. It is estimated over a period of seven years, thirty thousand people arrived in California, following the call of gold.

The harshness of the journey could cost these adventurers their lives. There was the risk of being attacked by bandits as well as by groups of Native Americans. Just as the ancient conquistadors fervently searched South America for the mythical city of El Dorado, thousands of people now traveled with the burning desire to get rich. The first immigrants, known as forty-niners, managed to reach the gold area after five months sailing around the tip of South America, and that was the fastest route! A curious fact is that the 49ers, the popular San Francisco football team, owes its name to the gold prospectors of California.

Other routes to the promised land involved crossing the Isthmus of Panama to reach San Francisco via the Pacific Ocean or crossing Mexican territory. In the end, most in pursuit of gold decided to cross US territory from one end to the other. Before the gold rush, the population of California was moderate, and that of San Francisco was very small.

What happens next is that the region prospers at an accelerated rate, and its economy soars like wildfire. New cities spring up, bringing with them the construction of schools, hospitals, and roads. Along with urban development came financial and commercial development. Gold became the currency of exchange for the American dream. You are what you own, they say.

For the first year following Marshall's discovery of gold nuggets, California had no laws governing private property or handling taxes. Essentially California was legally leaderless. In 1848, it was newly annexed by the United States and under military control, as if it were still getting used to its new owner. Without a legislative charter, the early freelance miners had an unparalleled advantage.

At first, gold extraction was simple and manual, done by a system of sampling and sifting dirt and sand in the rivers. This changed in 1855, when a hydraulic system involving dredging and other techniques was brought in—with serious consequences for the environment.

Around 1869, the transnational railroad was inaugurated, linking Omaha, Nebraska, with Sacramento. This greatly reduced travel time between the two, bringing with it a host of benefits.

The gold rush in California had another side of the coin, a darker side that contrasts with the glitter of the precious metal. Native Americans in the area were marginalized and exposed to starvation and disease. In the end, they were moved onto reservations so that they could not hinder American progress, decimating their population. Many men from other parts of the country, even the world, abandoned everything—including families, land, property, and jobs—to embark on the search for gold and find the fortune that was talked about so much. The curious thing is that very few people actually became rich during the gold rush. Ambition outweighed precious metals. As for the environmental issue, consider that the traditional practice of separating gold from stone involves the use of arsenic or mercury. Thanks to this, many rivers in the area are still polluted today.

As we walk with our guide through the streets of today's San Francisco, we admire a multicultural population that embraces civil rights, is tolerant, and is nondiscriminatory. The hippie movement in San Francisco celebrated the famous Summer of Love and the birth of the counterculture. But what strikes us most about today is the positioning of fashion design firms. The economy based on mining is long gone. From gold fever, we have moved on to fashion fever.

Over the past twenty-five years, the fashion industry has rebounded thanks to innovation. To give us an idea of the power of this sector in the US economy, here is another figure: 1.8 million people are engaged in the design, manufacture, marketing, and modeling of clothing throughout the country, whether on a small or massive scale. It should be noted that in several cases traditional textile production is outsourced to other countries, most of them developing countries; fashion labels are attracted by cheap labor, unfortunately unprotected by laws.

Added to this boom is cutting-edge technology, such as 3D printing and above all the explosion of e-commerce, benefiting both major designers and those with less experience. With high-value components, this is a global supply chain.

While much of the fashion industry's economic footprint is concentrated in New York and Los Angeles, other cities including San Francisco, San Diego, Providence, and Miami deserve respect in the market. The trend of clustering fashion retailers and designers by region promotes the exchange of ideas, increases efficiency, and generates creative and productive innovation. This development strategy is strengthened by the support of the best design schools, which prepare their students to be competitive in this sector. This is how the United States has achieved innovative leadership in the fashion industry.

In the case of the San Francisco area, there is an average of four hundred designers: 190 in Oakland and 160 in San Francisco. Their salaries average around $80,000 per year, on par with what is earned in New York. San Francisco is home to Gap Inc. (which owns the

Gap, Banana Republic, Old Navy, Athleta, and Intermix brands), Levi Strauss & Co., and the North Face, to name a few.

The city also hosts San Francisco Fashion Week, which focuses on new technologies and the future of fashion. The California College of the Arts and the Academy of Art University are also located in San Francisco. The wide range of opportunities, prosperity, and wealth that San Francisco offers continues to attract people from all over the world who want to live in the city but who are well aware that all that glitters is not gold. The rush is not over.

The Steelmaker Cities of Pittsburgh and Monterrey

For a city to grow, it has to have the capacity to generate jobs. Pittsburgh and Monterrey are perfect examples of what an industrialized city offers for the economic growth of its nation. This pair of metropolises achieved their development thanks to the steel industry. Monterrey is known as the Steel Giant, and Pittsburgh is known as Steel City. Not for nothing is the city's football team called the Pittsburgh Steelers. Although these two cities owe most of their growth to the metal industry, a diversity of activities maintains their competitiveness in the market today. Their economic evolution is a broad history of changes and transformations.

We shift to the city of Monterrey, where our guide, a native of Monterrey, is already waiting for us. Thanks to the information he shares, we know that Spaniards and their descendants founded Monterrey. Prior to that, there were a couple of unsuccessful attempts to colonize the region. In 1596, Diego de Montemayor, along with twelve other families, founded the city of Monterrey in honor of Viceroy Gaspar de Zuñiga Acevedo y Velasco, the fifth Count of Monterrey of the Province of Orense—among other noble titles of endless surnames. The native peoples that inhabited the region put up no resistance when the Spanish arrived.

The story in Pittsburgh is different. Before the arrival of the Europeans, Native Americans took advantage of the rivers that supplied the region. Years later, both the French and the English successively settled and disputed these lands until the region came under English rule. Pittsburgh became its own city in 1758, named in honor of William Pitt the Elder, British Secretary of State and prime minister during the reign of George III. Pitt the Elder should not be confused with his son, William Pitt the Younger, who also served as prime minister of Great Britain. Thanks to Pittsburgh's natural resources, the settlement gradually grew once US independence was achieved.

In the case of Monterrey, after its founding, the settlers faced various challenges that could not be alleviated by the joy of a *carnita asada* (the equivalent of a social barbecue, an event especially popular in northern Mexico). Among these problems was the first great flood of Monterrey, which occurred in 1611 and motivated the relocation of houses to a higher area. Over the years, the city's population density increased, with a significant number of inhabitants by the beginning of the nineteenth century.

Monterrey is among the few cities in Mexico that have a record of its founding. By the 1880s, the city experienced real growth thanks to industrialization and its proximity to the United States. Water continued to be a challenge. A flood control channel was built to prevent flooding, but it is not always infallible. In this same decade, due to its rapid urban and population growth, the city was provided with streetcars. In 1882, the railroad connects Monterrey with the border zone of Laredo, bringing exponential growth to the city's industry. During this period, textiles were the most profitable, and mining was not far behind. Later, the beer industry also occupied a privileged place in Monterrey. The most emblematic company, founded in 1890, is the Cuauhtemoc Moctezuma brewery, which has long been responsible for ensuring that the people of Monterrey—and the rest of Mexico—never lack beer.

Now we turn to our guide in Pittsburgh, who explains that in the beginning, the city's mainstay was based on the cargo and passenger boat trade, although years later, alcohol became a vital source of income. This product became a currency of exchange among its inhabitants. Whiskey grew in value in the last decades of the seventeenth century. But at the beginning of the next century, the steel industry became important due to the War of Independence against England. Such was the growth of this industry that the first steamboats were built in Pittsburgh.

During this same period, the English blocked certain commercial activities in the colonies, and the merchants of Pittsburgh took advantage of this. It was recognized as a city in 1816; its strength is the steel industry, although the production of manufactured goods is already gaining ground. Coal is the fuel that makes everything work.

The United States has large reserves of coal, which allows it to feed its growing industries. This is a point of difference between Pittsburgh and the rest of the world's industrialized cities. Pittsburgh is fueled by its homegrown energy source, which other countries struggle to obtain.

Large coal reserves are key to the commercialization of Pittsburgh's steamships and those of North America as a whole. With luck working in its favor, 1840 is an important year for Pittsburgh. To complement the river, which gives it an advantage over neighboring cities, it starts building a network of bridges and roads. That same year, the city of Monterrey, at that time with a population of twenty-six thousand inhabitants, also advances in its industrial activity.

In Pittsburgh, by 1850, there is concern about water reserves due to strong demand from a booming industry. But as the saying goes: destiny will find you. And a quick solution to the problem is found. By the end of the decade, Pittsburgh's river port is the third busiest in the nation, behind only New York and New Orleans.

In the early 1860s, steel production and sales increased. Even the Civil War generated large profits for this sector. Later, local production of steel weapons began, which were sold in the city itself to the highest bidders. At the same time, the glass industry began to take off. In a short period of time, the city was trading large quantities of steel and steel products. Large companies such as US Steel appeared, and with them also came entrepreneurs with vision.

During this period, Monterrey exploited the mining and steel industry. This earned it an invitation to participate in a trade fair in New Orleans, where industry and modernization issues were discussed. The Mexican city also participated at fairs in Texas and Paris, proudly receiving an award for being a city of technological innovation in industry.

The boom continues toward the end of the nineteenth century. Banking institutions clamor to finance Monterrey's industrial sector. The glass industry increases its productivity, and finally, the Fundidora de Fierro y Acero begins its operations in 1900. Its imposing blast furnace, which produced thousands of tons of steel per year, can still be seen in Fundidora Park as a reminder of what was once a great company, the pride of Monterrey.

Increasing costs for industries in the United States ignited success in Monterrey. American businessmen began to relocate their businesses and their capital to a city that was more profitable for them—even if it that meant in another country.

All this industrial growth requires huge amounts of water and electricity to supply businesses. Consequently, the power plant allocates 70 percent of its production to supply just this sector, and the other percentage is divided between residential and commercial use. As for water, large industries consume it thirstily and without measure. This leads to intervention by the state government to regulate its consumption; at the same time, the subsoil is drilled to find water sources. It is paradoxical that the city at times suffered terrible floods, while at other times, it suffered droughts and begged for rain and floods. Such measures fail to alleviate the problem, and the water shortage motivates the migration of the population from the residential areas, while large companies begin to extract their own water.

Monterrey keeps growing, just like Pittsburgh, the Tule tree, and the iguana that turns into Godzilla. We move ahead in time to the middle of the twentieth century, when a series of strikes paralyzes Pittsburgh's production, affecting its industry. For Monterrey, on the other hand, new technologies and processes for the steel industry are developed during the same period. Their patent is a noteworthy success.

But the pitcher went to the well once too often. The steel bonanza comes to an end when the phenomenon of deindustrialization arrives. The 1973 oil crisis caused the world's demand for steel to fall. A new course was set for the economies of Pittsburgh and Monterrey.

As demand for steel declined, Monterrey's flagship steel mill, Fundidora de Monterrey, declared bankruptcy in 1986. Pittsburgh's industries were forced to lay off tens of thousands of employees. The former Steel City had to watch with resignation and sadness the exit of its steel mills. In short, both cities have had to adjust to the demands of a new market model. The path is open toward a service-based economy. Today, the economy of these cities has adapted to change, facing the modern world.

The Student Hubs of Boston and Morelia

Education is always an important stimulus when it comes to measuring a city's progress—and, even more so, that of a country. The first university in the Americas was founded in Mexico, the Colegio de San Nicolas de Obispo, which later became the Universidad Michoacana de San Nicolas de Hidalgo.

Harvard University is the first in the United States, and it is considered among the best in the world today.

Out of respect for being the first, we'll continue our parallel history with the Universidad Michoacana de San Nicolas de Hidalgo (or the Universidad Michoacana, for short). This university opened its doors in 1540 in the city of Patzcuaro, Michoacan. Today, the National Autonomous University of Mexico is considered the foremost university in Mexico, although this does not detract from the excellence of the long-lived Universidad Michoacana.

Vasco de Quiroga, the first bishop of Michoacan, of whom we only know the date of his death in 1565, founded the university. He was respectful of the Purepechas, the original people of the region.

Remember, that once the conquest was achieved, the Spaniards treated the natives as inferior beings. Christian missionaries arrived in New Spain with the task of spreading Catholicism nonviolently. Different orders joined this effort, with some representatives learning the native languages, trying to achieve better dealings between colonists and natives. Bishop Vasco de Quiroga, who received his education from the church, was a worthy representative among this group.

In addition to the task of evangelizing the natives, Vasco de Quiroga was to direct the bishops and priests to teach various trades to the population. This included learning to read and write.

The founding of the Colegio de San Nicolas de Obispo in Patzcuaro was part of his mission. In 1580, the Colegio moved to Valladolid, which today is the city of Morelia, capital of the state of Michoacan.

Accompanied by our guide, we walk through the corridors of the Universidad Michoacana and enter one of its many classrooms. It is exciting to think that these walls received great leaders and participants in Mexico's history. Father Miguel Hidalgo is one of its most outstanding students, later becoming rector. Melchor Ocampo also attended this school; in his honor, an auditorium bears his name. Due to Mexico's different internal wars, the Colegio had to close its doors several times. It was not until 1917, when the nation was a little more peaceful, that it was designated a university. Currently it is the institution with the most traditions and houses a number of different schools on its campus.

We go back in history with our guide to the time when Mexico's independence struggle is over. After a long period of closure, the Colegio begins extensive negotiations between church and state, lasting until October 21, 1845, for permission to reopen. A few years later, on January 17, 1847, the governor of the state of Michoacan, Melchor Ocampo, allows its reopening. The institution begins a new chapter, now under the name of Primitivo y Nacional Colegio de San Nicolas de Hidalgo.

Time goes by, and we find ourselves during the victorious Revolution of 1910. A few days after Pascual Ortiz Rubio takes office as governor of Michoacan, on October 15, 1917, the Colegio becomes the Universidad Michoacana de San Nicolas de Hidalgo. Under its jurisdiction are the Industrial and Commercial Schools, Arts and Trades, the Superior School of Commerce and Administration, the Normal School for Educators (for both men and women), Medicine and Law, and the Public Library. Later, the Michoacan Museum, the Museum of Independence, and the state's Meteorological Observatory are added.

Traveling now to the United States, we find ourselves in a recreational area of the famous Harvard University. Here our guide greets us, reminding us that, like the University of Michoacan, Harvard was founded before the United States was an independent nation.

It is worth remembering this period. The English Puritans founded this university. Their relationship with Oxford University in England was excellent. Driven by the desire for religious freedom, they emigrated to North America, and they created an educational institution in accordance with their own principles. This is how the New College was born in 1636, without professors, students, or a teaching building. Three years later, it changed its name to Harvard College, in honor of one of its main benefactors, John Harvard, who donated books and money to the school.

The final name of Harvard University would come a century later. Harvard eventually becomes the best educational center and first choice for the elite of the United States. This changed after World War II, as the institution began opening its doors to other social sectors while maintaining its strict educational standards.

To give us an idea of the significance of Harvard University, eight US presidents have graduated from its classrooms. For years, it has been ranked among the top three universities in the world.

In 1869, Charles William Eliot was chosen as president of Harvard. He liked the position so much that he remained as head of the university for forty years. In 1909, he stepped down, becoming the longest-serving president in the university's history. Under Eliot's tutelage, significant changes were implemented that moved the then-college toward university ranking, with a focus on contemporary research. Eliot was also responsible for the dissemination of the *Harvard Classic*, a collection of books from different disciplines, the first publication of which dates back to 1909.

Harvard's educational system ended up positioning itself as a standard for the nation. It is worth noting that for four centuries, the institution was governed under male leadership. In 1999, Harvard completely annexed Radcliffe College, a women's college founded in 1879; when it became part of Harvard University, it changed its name to Radcliffe Institute for Advanced Study. Among its notable students are important writers such as Gertrude Stein and Margaret Atwood, famous for her dystopian novel *The Handmaid's Tale*. It was not until 2007 when Harvard accepted Drew Gilpin Faust, a professor of history and chronicler with five published books, as its first female rector. She had previously been director of the Radcliffe Institute for Advanced Study.

In its early days, Harvard had only nine students and one tutor. Today, it is home to a large enrollment with a long list of prestigious academics. Students might have taken notes at lectures by up-and-coming writers, the scientist Humberto Maturana, or the psychologist Howard Gardner. Among its students, alumni, and faculty are 161 Nobel Prizes, forty-eight Pulitzer Prizes, ten Oscar winners, and thirty heads of state. How about that!

Bill Gates, founder of Microsoft and unquestionably brilliant, failed to complete his university studies, dropping out of Harvard in 1976. Thirty years later, the university awarded him an honorary degree for his contributions to modern business. The social network Facebook was born on the university campus thanks to Mark Zuckerberg, one of the richest men in the world, who also dropped out of Harvard.

A key to Harvard University's success lies in the meticulous selection system of its candidates. Those young people who demonstrate the ability and track record to succeed in their studies are awarded scholarships and support for their development on campus.

With our guide, we tour the university and find that its infrastructure includes more than three hundred buildings. Their functions range from museums and bookstores to family housing. Among its museums are one for archeology and ethnology, three focused on natural sciences, and an equal number for art.

Before saying goodbye to Harvard University, we admire the harmony between nature and urban design, with its crimson brick buildings plus a classical touch that reminds us of the cathedrals of medieval times.

Finally, we cannot close this chapter without again recognizing both universities, Harvard and the Universidad Michoacana de San Nicolas de Hidalgo. Notwithstanding great names or trajectories, the human spirit breathes there, regardless of ideology, race, or creed. These universities assert the importance of knowledge for the free and sovereign development of a nation.

Chapter 11

Black Gold

Coke in the White House

The product is everywhere in the world, as if it were the sun or the sky from which no one can escape. Its cultural influence is equal or superior to icons like the Beatles, McDonald's, Walt Disney, and Juan Gabriel, as blasphemous as that sounds. It can be found at parties and family meals and in restaurants, bars, and movie theaters. Its omnipresence is like air. When other products are in short supply, it fills empty shelves with its unmistakable image. The one that never goes out of fashion, the last one to appear in the desert. Just as no one is denied a glass of water, no one refuses to try a sip of this black elixir—not even Santa Claus, who promotes the soft drink as if he invented it. Listening to its all-pervading jingles, one can believe that there really is world peace. Its image is on T-shirts, trucks, caps, and vending machines. Its slogans appear on billboards, blimps, and television, subtly commanding us to drink that black gold to uncover happiness.

When we think of "black gold," most likely, we think of oil. But in this chapter, we take a look at Coca-Cola, a beverage whose history is much more than that of a simple refreshing liquid. This product transcends the relationship between producer and consumer like no other. It has played a distinctive role in political rivalries, as demonstrated by the bilateral ties between the United States and Mexico.

The story begins with its controversial creator, a pharmacist named John S. Pemberton, whose credit still appears on the official website of the Coca-Cola Company. Pemberton was born in Georgia in 1831 and died in Atlanta in 1888. An obsessive person, addicted to morphine, he had been a colonel in the Confederate Army.

The consumption of Coca-Cola had nothing to do with his death. Pemberton died in poverty of stomach cancer, never imagining the vast and omnipresent empire that would emerge as a result of his invention.

We accompany him after the end of the Civil War. Laboratories and beakers have replaced trenches and guns. After a period of experimentation, Pemberton introduces his miracle drug, which is patented by Pemberton Chemical. It is not the beverage we know today; originally Coca Cola was a preparation that promised to cure a thousand and one ailments (just like Enrique Peña Nieto's energy reform, but we will get to that later). This product is the base of today's soft drink, and it comes out of the laboratory as Pemberton's French Wine Coca, alluding to its ingredients: wine and coca leaves. This is not stated on the brand's official website, as if they would like to keep the original recipe a secret. However, the Massachusetts Institute of Technology (MIT) corroborates the above.

Decades later, after Pemberton's death, when dry law was declared in Atlanta in the early 1920s, alcohol was eliminated from the original recipe. Kola nuts were added to the recipe, which led to the syrup being renamed Coca-Cola. It became phenomenally successful. Pharmacies in those years obtained Pemberton's syrup and mixed it with carbonated water. This concoction was offered at soda fountains that shared space with drugstores.

In 1888, Pemberton sold the rights to Pemberton's French Wine Coca to pharmaceutical entrepreneur Asa Griggs Candler (1852–1929), who later became mayor of Atlanta. Candler's philosophy was that everything is sellable as long as it has enough advertising. Coca-Cola's marketing began with calendars; these were given away with the idea to distribute the calendars widely and position the logo everywhere. This strategy was effective; by 1899, the beverage was already being sold in bottles.

Success brought competition, and hundreds of new brands emerged trying to get a piece of the "black gold" pie. Coke's quality stayed the same, though its image suffered a blow when it was accused of affecting the health of its consumers. A bottle was also designed to have a marketing impact. In 1916, the classic glass bottle with the Coca-Cola trademark engraved on it was launched.

Thanks to its recognizable trademark, Coca-Cola is a rousing success in the United States. The Coca-Cola Company was sold for $25 million to a group of investors, led by Ernest Woodruff. Although seemingly a large figure, nothing compares to the company's current value, which is almost as priceless as the moon. Political cartoonist Eduardo del Rio, better known as Rius, in his best seller *La Droga Que Refresca (The Drug That Refreshes;* Debolsillo, 2009) confirms that the company spends millions of dollars on advertising. The following data backs this distinguished writer's claim: around 1931, Coca-Cola decided to exploit the image of Santa Claus, portraying him with soft drink in hand while reading letters and handing out toys to children. The ad was placed in the top-ranking magazines and newspapers. For a time, it was unthinkable to have Santa Claus without his Coca-Cola in hand, drinking a cold soda in the middle of a snowfield at the North Pole to take the heat off. The famous plastic artist Andy Warhol declared that one of the good things about the United States was that in that country the rich and the poor buy practically the same things. Coca-Cola is one of them. According to Warhol: "you can see a Coke ad and you know the President drinks Coke; Liz Taylor drinks Coke and you think you can drink Coke too".

Fast-forward in time, and we find ourselves in the midst of World War II. Few remember the names Pemberton and Candler, but Coca-Cola is still around. After the attack on Pearl Harbor in 1941, the United States entered the conflict in retaliation. At that time, Robert Woodruff was the company's president (he held the position from 1923 until 1955). Woodruff had the acumen to declare, "Every man in uniform gets a bottle of Coca-Cola for five cents, wherever he is and whatever it costs the company." In response, an urgent telegram arrived from North Africa, signed by General Dwight D. Eisenhower (later president of the United States), requesting three million bottles of Coca-Cola as well as supplies to produce that same amount twice a month and the material and resources for ten bottling plants. Six months later, a plant was opened in the capital of Algeria, the first of sixty-four started during World War II. It is estimated that military personnel alone consumed more than five billion bottles of Coca-Cola. It could be said that during the war, American soldiers were never short of armaments, morphine, or Coca-Cola.

Another chapter in the company's history during World War II was the creation of Fanta, which replaced Coca-Cola in Nazi Germany. That version of Fanta has nothing to do with the orange soft drink we know today. Before the conflict, Coca-Cola was sold in Europe and was the drink of choice in Germany—even becoming the official soft drink of the 1936 Berlin Olympics. However, when the US entered the war, Germany prohibited the sale of Coca-Cola in countries under its influence, including Denmark, France, Italy, and Poland. With local producers facing an imminent disaster, factory managers decided to create a new soft drink with the ingredients at their disposal. Fanta hit the market in 1941 and sold three million bottles in its first twelve months in Germany alone.

Once the war was over, an Italian Coca-Cola factory decided to create a Fanta with citrus flavors, characteristic of that region. Consequently, Orange Fanta was born, a familiar drink to Mexicans, where it was introduced in 1956.

Despite its global expansion, there were also countries that decided to say no to Coca-Cola's charm, and not precisely for reasons of health. After the success of the Cuban Revolution, Fidel Castro's regime began to nationalize several foreign companies. Before being expropriated, the company preferred to close its factories, lock the doors, and leave the Caribbean island. Little did it matter that the mixture of Coca-Cola and rum resulted in the popular "Cuba Libre" cocktail. The Cuban government came out with its own version of the soft drink, called "tuKola." The appearance of that cola—so sovereign and revolutionary—did not stop the real Coca-Cola from continuing to be sold in Cuba, although only through the black market and at exorbitant prices, as if it were really black gold.

Another communist country that has closed its doors to Coca-Cola is North Korea. There have never been any Coca-Cola offices or bottling plants there, but they do have their North Korean imitation—only the supreme leader, Kim Jong-un, knows if its taste is the same as the original. China also gave Coca-Cola the boot, along with other foreign companies, when Mao Tse Tung proclaimed the People's Republic in 1949. However, as we will see below, this ban did not last forever. Recently, Coca-Cola and other US multinationals, such as McDonald's, announced their withdrawal from Russia in retaliation for the invasion of Ukraine ordered by Vladimir Putin. It won't be long before we see the appearance of the Russian version of Coca-Cola.

Once General Eisenhower became president of the United States, Coca-Cola was the drink of choice in the White House. A stumbling block to this preference was Vice President Richard Nixon, who was in office at the height of the Cold War. Besides his political positions, Nixon was an attorney for the Pepsi-Cola Company, a perennial competitor of Coca-Cola. Nixon attended a trade fair in Moscow, where he met with Nikita Khrushchev, leader of the Soviet Union from 1958 to 1964. When Khrushchev stopped at the booth representing an American kitchen, in the middle of a conversation with Nixon, he was presented with a glass of Pepsi. The media captured the moment, and Pepsi was quick to capitalize on the publicity. Due to the power of this image, Pepsi began to become popular in Europe and also won a contract to set up a bottling plant in the Soviet Union.

Years later, in 1972, as president of the United States, Nixon traveled to Asia to reestablish diplomatic relations with China, becoming the first sitting US president to visit the Asian giant. At a gala dinner, during his toast (not with Coca-Cola), Nixon said that it was the week that changed the world. Coca-Cola had joined the US delegation, bringing along thousands of cases of the product—bottled happiness, which must have been an amount insufficient for China's enormous population. At any rate, following the death of Mao, Coca-Cola would no longer leave the country, especially not for political reasons. It is said that Nixon introduced the beverage to the Chinese market to balance the scales and avoid favoritism among brands. The opening of China has brought success to the US multinational. Even so, China wanted to keep pace with Cuba and North Korea, and launched China Cola, which has been sold in the United States since 2001.

Coke Is King in Mexico

Coca-Cola's arrival in Mexico was imminent. By the 1920s, the concession for its production was granted to Manuel L. Barragan. In 1926, Coke occupied its own plant in the city of Monterrey. Within a short time, it reached the country's capital, and from there, its growth was unstoppable. Before the decade ended, Coca-Cola was already positioned in the country's most important and largest cities.

Coca-Cola's invasion was definitive in the 1940s. There were more than fifty bottling plants operating throughout Mexico—with an excellent distribution system. The company's strategists worked tirelessly until Mexican families accepted this product as an essential part of their meal, replacing juices and *aguas frescas* (a light, nonalcoholic drink of fruits, cereals, flowers, or seeds blended with sugar and water). Massive advertising campaigns began, and all possible means of communication were involved.

With eighty-five plants nationwide, changes to bottling the product followed. The nonreturnable bottle appeared, as well as special edition bottles—collectibles—coinciding with high-impact events such as the World Cup. The venerable Santa Claus was replaced by the polar bear that became a famous advertising icon. In the 1980s, Pepsi went through an exceptional period of publicity with Michael Jackson as brand ambassador under the slogan "the new generation." Seeing how the competition, for the first time, was starting to eat up their business, Coca-Cola's response was to launch a new product line: New Coke. In 1985, they announced that the original Coca-Cola would no longer be sold. This decision ended in failure, so the company returned its flagship product to the market.

Before he became Mexico's President, Vicente Fox worked at Coca-Cola FEMSA, a Mexican multinational beverage company headquartered in Mexico City for fourteen years, starting as a local distributor and ending as president of the Latin America Division. Thanks to Vicente Fox when he served as president of Mexico, FEMSA was unequivocally positioned in the industry nationally, including with contracts detrimental to public health. Water concessions were given away like candy. And if you don't believe me, just ask the people of San Cristobal de las Casas, Chiapas, where the presence of Coca-Cola has caused such a shortage of drinking water that its inhabitants have to consume soft drinks in order to avoid dying of thirst—as we will see later on.

Today, Coca-Cola is the best-selling soft drink both in Mexico and worldwide. Still, some nations are imposing certain health measures to combat the damaging effects of excessive consumption, partly because of high levels of sugar in the formula that cause diseases such as diabetes. Not for nothing is Mexico is one of the countries with the highest rates of diabetes and obesity in the world.

Coke versus Pozol

Pozol, a traditional drink from southeast Mexico, is being ousted by the invasion of Coca-Cola. Pozol is prepared from ground corn and cocoa beans and served with ice. It is a drink that refreshes and quenches thirst. In spite of its attributes, it is not known or sold in northern Mexico; in central Mexico, its existence is known, but it is not popular.

This preparation is characteristic of the diet of the Chontal Maya from the Tabasco region, although they also like it in Chiapas. Those who perform heavy work consume it regularly. It does not spoil easily, and it is an excellent supplement when food is scarce. Before the arrival of the Spaniards, the Mayans called it *pochotl*; the Europeans began to call it pozol, which is the name that is used today.

Before Coca-Cola cornered the Mexican market, the inhabitants of southeastern Mexico had pozol in their homes as part of their basic pantry. It was even used for energy during long trips. But "black gold" is now here, and it does not admit competition either in price or production volume. In short, it imposes itself on the indigenous communities.

In the past, pozol was much cheaper than Coca-Cola. Today, the situation is completely reversed; it is easier and cheaper to buy a Coke than to enjoy the emblematic drink of the region. With the passage of time, plus the increase in the consumption of Coke, communities began to suffer from various illnesses.

In 2015, the Proyecto Pozol (Pozol Project) was launched. This is an international campaign, led by several interested social organizations and universities. It has the support of a number of world-renowned chefs, including Jamie Oliver, a celebrated British chef and presenter on the BBC network. Both Oliver and his colleagues are amazed by pozol. Their assessment is that Mexico has everything to overcome its health deficit and the diseases that afflict the population; it is just a matter of returning to the eating habits of the past.

Although the project represents an incredible opportunity to improve the health of Mexicans, and at the same time to encourage pozol producers, unfortunately it has been slow to take off.

Coca-Cola and its refreshing taste knock on the door of Mexican homes, and the cuddly polar bear delivers diabetes. Mexico faces one of the highest rates of this disease in the world as well as of obesity; diabetes is one of the main causes of death in Mexico. According to the National Institute of Public Health:

> Diabetes is a condition in which blood glucose is at an elevated level. This is because the body does not produce or does not properly use insulin, a hormone that helps cells transform glucose (which comes from food) into energy. Without enough insulin, glucose stays in the blood and over time, this excess can lead to serious complications.

In 2018, the *New York Times* published an article entitled "In a Town with Little Water, Coca-Cola is Everywhere. So is Diabetes," which exposes a problem that involves both the Mexican government and the Coca-Cola company. The article talks about health conditions in a community in the state of Chiapas, where the soft drink is consumed due to lack of drinking water. Its inhabitants have no choice or alternative. By 2016, the mortality rate from diabetes increased 30 percent, blamed on the excessive consumption of soft drinks. Some of the town's inhabitants drink up to three liters a day. A security guard, whose parents suffer from obesity and diabetes, says, "Soft drinks have always been more available than water."

The Coca-Cola plant has the necessary permits to extract large quantities of water, up to 1.2 million liters per day. This activity is part of a sweetheart deal from during the administration of Vicente Fox. And while Coca-Cola is not the only cause of diabetes in Mexico, it is one of the main contributors.

This unhealthy scenario was complicated by the arrival of COVID-19. Although the new virus has unleashed a pandemic, let's not forget that diabetes is a worldwide epidemic. So far, the close relationship between the two diseases is unquestionable. The International Diabetes Federation (IDF) warns, "When people with diabetes develop a viral infection, it can be more difficult to treat due to fluctuations in blood glucose levels and, possibly, the presence of diabetes complications."

One of the measures implemented by the government of Andrés Manuel López Obrador to counteract this evil is the front labeling of foods with high calorie, saturated fat, sugar, and sodium content. A well-informed consumer is an empowered consumer, and labels that inform whether a product has excess fat or calories help people decide whether to buy it or not. Of course, this measure is not to the liking of several companies, including soft drink companies (some have even filed injunctions against it), but it is undoubtedly essential for consumers to know whether what they are eating is good or bad for their health. Front labeling has been a success, and has shown that thanks to this information, people opt for healthier options. It has also forced some companies, such as Coca-Cola, to reformulate their products to make them healthier. It's about time.

The scenario is complex. We cannot ignore the fact that Coca-Cola and other companies of its kind are an important source of jobs in Mexico. But the impact on public health, which is caused by extreme consumption of beverages with excess sugar, is obvious and worrying. Hopefully they will begin to assume their share of responsibility for the poor health of Mexicans and act accordingly. Stratospheric profits cannot be worth more than the lives of millions of people.

The Pepsi Challenge

No cola drink shook the Coca-Cola empire more than Pepsi. Thanks to Nixon, it was the first to open a bottling plant in the Soviet Union, in the middle of the Cold War—and just when they were trying to resist any trace of capitalist culture. What should not be overlooked is the payment mechanism. The USSR cannot afford to enrich an American company. So the solution is to exchange Pepsi for vodka, the Soviet's traditional drink. When this contract expires, and the USSR gets a new head of state, the agreement is renegotiated—and now Soviet military equipment is used to pay Pepsi.

Let's go back to the origins of this beverage. Like its rival Coke, Pepsi is the creation of a pharmaceutical chemist. Its name comes from the combination of pepsin and cola. In its first years, it did not achieve the same spectacular success as Coca-Cola. Pepsi arrived in Mexico in 1907, but it positioned itself discreetly and behind its competitor, with its first bottling plant in the state of Mexico. Following the Second World War, the company embarked on its worldwide expansion. By the 1950s, it had 118 plants in fifty-three countries. Today, thirty-nine plants operate in Mexico, one of which is for concentrated syrup.

Unlike Coca-Cola, Pepsi did change its original recipe in order to sweeten the drink more. The brand's advertising talent creates a distinctive identity for the product. At the height of its international popularity, the controversial singer Michael Jackson agreed to be its ambassador; other sports figures also signed with the company, aiming for the youth market.

The battle for the market between the two companies is known as the Cola Wars. Each brand launched its most daring campaign to make it clear who wins the consumers' taste test. Coca-Cola took a gamble with its New Coke, which resulted in a resounding failure. In 1975, Pepsi launched its global Pepsi Challenge campaign.

Pepsi was presented in the largest and most prominent shopping malls around the world; the challenge consisted of giving a consumer a couple of glasses of each soft drink. The result could not have been more satisfactory for Pepsi since most of the participants chose Pepsi's flavor over Coca-Cola. However, even with the success of this aggressive campaign, Coca-Cola remains a mainstay in the market due to the company's stronghold in most fast-food restaurants and vending machines. For the Pepsi Challenge, the popular phrase "the battle was won, but the war was lost" applies.

Coal and Petroleum

The history of petroleum is more complex than that of Coca-Cola and Pepsi combined. Although it is a source of trade and commerce between Mexico and the United States, the production, use, and distribution of oil have given rise to bilateral conflicts. But before looking at the periods of confrontation and diplomatic solutions, let's travel back in time to verify the presence of this nonrenewable resource in ancient cultures.

In Babylon, petroleum was known as *napata*, which is naphthalene. The story of Noah's Ark from the book of Genesis mentions that Noah used petroleum to caulk the ship. According to the Bible, God told Noah, "Make an ark of resinous wood and coat it with pitch inside and out." The people of the Middle East also used it for caulking; they even applied it to incendiary arrows in the catapults that launched balls of fire, known as Greek fire, toward their enemies. Around the first century, the Persians learned to distill oil, converting it into fuel for lamps. Such innovation and use spread throughout Europe.

In Mexico, the Nahua people used oil as an aromatic in their temples as well as to waterproof houses. The first settlers of Mesoamerica call crude oil *chapopote*; a word that comes from *tzaue,* meaning glue, and *popochtli*, meaning perfume. Another name given to this hydrocarbon is resin oil, or asphaltene.

Of course, many ancient civilizations used oil as long as they could obtain it close to the surface, where it is scarce. Its boom came when extraction techniques were developed, displacing coal in industrial processes.

We are now in the midst of the Industrial Revolution, which has been modernizing Europe since the eighteenth century. At that time, the world was powered by coal and wood, the main sources of energy for machinery. England had the largest coal deposits in the world. They depended on them completely since their wood reserves were exhausted, and they had no more forests to exploit. London, then the largest city in the world, consumed a thousand tons of coal a day; England's factories and foundries required this resource.

However, there was a technical problem. The deeper the coal mines are dug, the more they were flooded by water that emerged from the subsoil. When confronted with this situation, there was no other alternative but to close the mine. Some resorted to animal-drawn pumps to extract the water from the depths of the mine, but that was slow and costly.

The situation took a momentous turn when Thomas Newcomen invented and introduced his revolutionary steam engine in 1712. This took place at the Coneygree Coal Works in Staffordshire, site of the largest coalfield in England. His invention replaced the use of animals to power water pumps. In addition to its effectiveness, costs were reduced by up to 85 percent.

England was catapulted into a new era, and coal extraction increased beyond measure. By the end of the eighteenth century, the country was producing ten million tons, consolidating its position as the world's leading energy economy. The nineteenth century progressed along this path. Coal as an energy source supplied the mining, transport, and textile industries, transforming trade and influencing society. The more coal that was produced, the more coal was burned.

Steam locomotives began to transport people and cargo, including coal. Similarly, England changed its traditional sailing ships for those powered by coal. Coal was the fuel of the century and triggered the Industrial Revolution.

Following British success, Germany and France, not wanting to be left behind, set up sizeable coal industries. Later, the United States discovered coal reserves that turned out to be the largest in the world. However, in the US, they preferred to continue using firewood for fuel, given the abundance of forests in the nation. The changeover occurred around 1900, and the country began to produce more coal than the mines in England.

At this point, it would be useful to mention the degree of dependence on this nonrenewable resource. In 1701, an English citizen consumes less than half a ton of coal per year, on average. By 1850, that increases to three tons and by 1900, it increases to more than four tons. Such an increase in consumption brings with it a dark cloud—this is not rhetoric or a metaphor for bad omens. Toward the end of the nineteenth century, the atmosphere of the most industrialized cities became dark from massive combustion of coal, with negative consequences for human health and the environment. Even so, this did not stop coal production, because that meant stopping the world.

On January 10, 1901, in Beaumont, Texas, on a hill called Spindletop, the Hamill brothers found a large oil field, the largest recorded at that time. Once it is exploited, it yields one hundred thousand barrels per day; in Russia, they top out at five thousand, and the vast majority of wells only add up to fifty to one hundred barrels per day. The coal empire comes to an end, and the oil boom begins.

The First Oil Wells in America

The United States invented the oil business. The world's oil industry was born in Texas, and its second birthplace was Mexico. After the Hamill brothers' oil discovery came one by another oil protagonist in the United States, Edwin Drake (1819–1880). He found a deposit at a depth of more than twenty meters, something unheard of before then. On August 27, 1859, Drake became the owner of the deepest and richest oil field in the country, in Titusville, Pennsylvania, which produced thirty barrels per day. While not much by today's standards, at the time, it caused a sensation throughout the country, especially in Pennsylvania, where the oil rush began.

Oil is associated with economic wealth, abundance, and development, but the story of Edwin Drake is a sad one. In the United States, whoever owns land also owns the subsoil. Drake used a new technique, the percussion drilling method, to extract black gold from the earth, but he never patented the technique. After a series of bad investments and financial decisions, Drake ended up in ruin, dying in poverty.

Years later, the Hamill brothers also used a coal-fired steam engine. Unlike Drake and so many others, they employed a rotary bore that allowed them to drill limestone and, consequently, reach deeper excavation.

After the success at Spindletop, entrepreneurs from the United States decided to venture into the world of oil, eventually arriving in Mexico. Edward L. Doheny, the first to drill an oil well in Los Angeles, was one of them. In 1900, during the Porfirio Diaz era, he created the Mexican Petroleum Company of California and set his sights on exploiting the lands he owned in the state of San Luis Potosí. The well that started the oil industry in Mexico was drilled in the municipality of Ebano in 1901. Porfirio Díaz was the first president to grant oil exploitation concessions to foreign companies. Subsequently, other Mexican presidents tried to follow his example.

In 1901, Mexico passed a law that empowered the executive branch to grant permits to individuals and companies to explore and exploit federal lands. Wells began to be built after that, but it was not until 1904 when oil was finally extracted from a well 503 meters deep, discovered by a local employee of the Mexican Petroleum Company of California, Ezequiel Ordoñez. At its peak, this well produced 1,500 barrels per day. It was the beginning of the oil industry in Mexico.

Soon, more foreign companies joined in the exploration for oil in Mexican territory. By 1908, the Dos Bocas well in Veracruz produced one hundred thousand barrels per day. The English company S. Pearson & Son owned this well, and its profitability led to the creation of the Mexican company El Aguila (the Mexican Eagle Petroleum Company).

The black gold discovered in Mexico and the United States would be put to good use in a conflict that was breaking out on the other side of the ocean: the First World War. Oil was indispensable for the operation of trucks, tanks, ships, and war planes. Thanks to oil, ships could move faster than if they used coal as fuel. The technological and armament innovation brought about by the Great War cannot be explained without the arrival of gasoline. Thanks to the war, the oil industry was born in the world.

The Mexican government's own concessions allowed the legal rights of its natural resources to fall into the hands of foreigners. Decades later, the government will have to settle scores with them.

Mexico's Expropriation of the Petroleum Industry

Attempts to nationalize Mexico's oil date back to 1916, when in the Constituent Congress of Querétaro, President Venustiano Carranza proposed that all natural resources in the subsoil, including oil, should become property of the nation. Consequently, he received too much pressure, especially from the United States, to prevent this from happening. Article 27 of the Constitution established that the riches of the subsoil are nation's property, so this caused protests from the foreign companies and the United States. Despite their protests, the approval of this article took them by surprise, and they had no choice but to ask that Article 27 not be applied retroactively. In other words, they were determined that foreigners should continue to own Mexico's oil.

The foreign oil companies were almost as powerful as the Mexican government, and even had private armies, known as the white guards. Their abuses were constant. Apart from stealing the nation's treasure, they exercised their own law with total impunity. It was common that, upon locating a piece of land where there was oil, they would tell the owner to sell it to them because if he refused, they would end up buying it from the widow anyway.

The presidents who succeeded Carranza also faced pressure as soon as they showed the slightest intention of nationalizing oil. There were even threats to invade Mexico if those attempts prospered. In response, the brave Candido Aguilar warned that if the United States invaded Mexico, they would set fire to all the oil wells and the flames would be seen as far as New Orleans.

It was all windfalls and celebrations for foreign companies until the Mexican government decided to assert its sovereignty. On March 18, 1938, President Lazaro Cardenas signed an order expropriating the assets of most of the foreign oil companies operating in Mexico. As part of this move, he later created Petroleos Mexicanos (PEMEX), establishing a state oil monopoly and prohibiting the operation of any foreign oil company in the country. This courageous decision led to a period of tension in international politics for the US government; they subsequently backed Mexico's expropriation of foreign assets, as long as those affected were compensated promptly and effectively.

Let's take a step back in history to fully understand the events as well as to appreciate the protagonist of this period: General and President Lazaro Cardenas.

In the 1920s, Mexico was the world's second largest oil producer. But the foreign oil companies' economic bonanza was not viewed kindly in the forum of public opinion. Oil fuels progress in nations that control it, but Mexico's domestic economy was still based on agricultural production, with a developing market.

The economic depression of 1929 impacted the entire world. Foreign oil companies reduced their production, which decreased the Mexican government's income at a time when there was already a surplus in the world oil supply. In addition to these factors, foreigners were better paid than Mexicans for the same type of work under equal circumstances. Faced with this injustice, Mexican workers went on strike in 1937.

It is a crucial moment. President Cardenas instructs a government commission to draft a new labor agreement. The foreign companies fail to comply with the agreement and defy the Mexican Supreme Court.

Lazaro Cardenas hardens his stance and issues an expropriation decree on March 18, 1938. In a domino effect, retaliatory actions were taken, and there was an international boycott against Mexico. Countries refused to sell Mexico the materials necessary for oil refining. Even the sale of silver, fundamental for the country's revenue, was severely affected. Crude oil exports fell substantially, with collateral damage to the economy.

President Cardenas decides to break diplomatic relations with certain countries. There was a period of claims from the affected firms and a period of assessment by the Mexican government. Eventually, the US supported Mexico's right to expropriate foreign assets. The reasons were compelling: with one foot in the Second World War, the US was not in a position to exert political pressure or intervene militarily in Mexico. Standard Oil Company, perhaps exaggerating somewhat, stated the value expropriated from American companies was around $2 billion.

Two years after the expropriation decree was issued, the oil companies filed lawsuits against the Mexican state. Under the threat that Mexico would enter into an alliance with Germany, the United States pressured companies to reach a settlement in order to secure a strategic ally for its southern border. Finally, on April 18, 1942, the same day of the bombing of Tokyo in World War II, the governments of Mexico and the United States signed an agreement in which Mexico would pay roughly $29 million in compensation to US companies.

One of the most poignant moments in Mexican history occurred right after the oil expropriation. The decision to nationalize oil received strong, and unprecedented, popular support. Rarely has there been so much solidarity from the Mexican people toward a government decision. In the center of Mexico City, one hundred thousand people from different social classes gathered to show their support for President Cardenas. As a symbolic gesture, people began to collect goods to pay the heavy compensation demanded by foreign companies. Besides money, several ladies of society donated jewelry, gems, and dresses. It is even said that one old woman donated a hen to help cover the payments. Even the church itself, which was in the habit of opposing the government, supported the president's decision.

But the negotiation did not end here. Foreign companies fought for their readmission to Mexico when Cardenas concluded his presidency in 1940. Mexico considered such a possibility as long as it retained ownership of the subsoil and PEMEX, its domestic internal monopoly. The Mexican government also rejected accepting any US government loans as leverage. The US government abandoned negotiations in 1950 and subsequently focused on the Middle East and Venezuela.

The debt generated by the oil expropriation was paid thanks to the contributions of the people and the fortitude of General Lázaro Cárdenas, who did not give in to international pressures and blackmail. Thanks to nationalization, the abuses of foreign oil companies ended and PEMEX, which has proven to be a national pride, took the reins of exploration, exploitation, refining and distribution of Mexican oil. After so many years of plundering and surrender, Mexico was finally able to see the profits of the oil industry as its own.

The Petroleum Boom

Now that we have reviewed the political balancing that impacts oil production, it makes sense to look at its industrial output. In 1910, following the success at Dos Bocas, the Huasteca Petroleum

Company, a subsidiary of the Mexican Petroleum Company, discovers a large deposit with the potential to extract sixty thousand barrels per day. That same year, El Aguila reports an even larger field—with a potential of up to one hundred thousand barrels per day. These two foreign companies have no competition in Mexico.

Around 1915, when the Revolution of 1910 has given Mexico new status, the first tax on crude oil production is announced. Shortly thereafter, the government of Venustiano Carranza created a ministry for the regulation and control of the emerging oil industry. On February 5, 1917, the government, backed by Article 27 of Constitution, declares that ownership of land and water corresponds to the nation, and this includes oil. The business community creates an organization to serve its interests, and the Association of Petroleum Producers in Mexico is born.

With negligible petroleum extraction, the United States began to appreciate the benefits of oil as early as 1895, in Pennsylvania. The industry then took off at the beginning of the twentieth century with the discovery of the Hamill brothers. And what really heralds the oil monopoly is the arrival of the internal combustion engine, based on gasoline.

The manufacture of cars with this mechanism revolutionized the early twentieth century. In 1903, the Ford Motor Company presented its first gasoline-powered automobile. A decade later, more than a million cars and trucks were on the road in America and Europe. Once the era of oil and gasoline arrived, society looked with disdain or nostalgia at steam- or wood-fueled cars. Between 1901 and 1915, per capita energy consumption doubled in industrialized countries.

Companies the produced and sold oil for lamps had to adapt to the market in order to supply an increasingly demanding society. At the same time, new companies emerged, among them Royal Dutch–Shell, British Petroleum, and Standard Oil, eventually becoming the most powerful oil companies of the time.

Meanwhile, as the demand for oil increased, countries like England, which lacked natural oil reserves, began to explore remote areas. Remember: before the oil boom, this country relied solely on its large coalfields. Because of the radical shift to crude, its warships, formerly steamships, convert to oil. The British Empire hopes to gain a significant advantage over Germany's fleet. Because its sights are set on expanding oil reserves in the East, it requires a military buffer in the event of a conflict in the Mediterranean Sea. Later, the United States applied the same measure with the so-called Fifth Fleet.

British companies strike deals with oil-rich countries. British Petroleum does this with Iran in order to explore and exploit its deposits, and Royal Dutch-Shell signs an advantageous agreement with Iraq, which has even greater reserves than Iran. Royal Dutch-Shell was also negotiating with the El Aguila company in Mexico. In this way, England protects itself with respect to the demand for oil.

The United States, which has enormous oil reserves, keeps pace with England. New deposits are constantly being discovered in its territory, including in California, Louisiana, Oklahoma, and Texas. Before the expropriation by Lazaro Cardenas, US investors owned the Huasteca Petroleum Company, which dominated the oil industry in Mexico along with El Aguila.

With so many oil fields being exploited every day, and with wells being routinely opened, the price of oil fluctuates and even drops drastically. If one day there is no supply due to the number of barrels available, the reserves run out the next day. The main problem lies in the tremendous imbalance between extraction and production, plus refining and marketing. But as is often the case with great visionaries, where everyone saw a problem, John Davison Rockefeller (1839–1937) saw an opportunity.

Oil companies, even the largest, limit themselves to only one part of the petroleum chain. Rockefeller had the vision to cover all aspects—from exploration to marketing of crude oil. The idea became reality with his company, Standard Oil, which owned wells and gas stations. With everything on its side, it was positioned as the largest oil company in the world. However, the US government issued antitrust laws for the oil industry, and Standard Oil was forced to split up. Eventually the company restructured, and it currently controls a large part of the energy sector with its subsidiaries Exxon and Mobil, which recently merged.

Today, due to excessive demand for oil, Western governments, supported by international companies, dispute the control of oil reserves in developing countries such as Mexico and Venezuela. Crude oil has played a leading role in the conflicts of the twentieth century.

Mexico nationalized its oil industry, which was an important and necessary achievement. The bad thing is that after the expropriation, Mexico was left with a navel–gazing attitude. Instead of becoming a transnational company, even if the owner was the Mexican government, PEMEX was limited to being a company for internal consumption, to the delight of North American companies. Nationalization achieved energy sovereignty, but unfortunately PEMEX did not achieve the growth of other transnational oil companies, placing it at a disadvantage in the international context. It is easy to imagine PEMEX as a company of the Mexican people but with investments all over the world, putting itself on a level playing field with companies such as Chevron, Shell, and BP. That was not the vision of the past Mexican governments. It could have been.

Petroleum and Wars

The Pelaez family prospered at the beginning of the twentieth century due to their activity with foreign companies. Ignacio Pelaez was a lawyer for the English company El Aguila; the rest of his family leased their lands to this company. Ignacio Pelaez's responsibilities included negotiating with landowners on the company's behalf, an ability in which he was skilled.

At that time, most of the oil wells were located in the state of Veracruz. This explains the presence of a large number of foreigners; the state had the third largest number of foreign citizens. US oil companies established settlements whose residents worked as supervisors for the oil company; a smaller percentage was dedicated to agriculture.

When Francisco I. Madero took up arms against the dictatorship of Porfirio Diaz and called the people to join the Revolution of 1910, foreign settlements became alarmed. The US government asked Mexico to guarantee the peace; however, just in case, they placed troops along the border. The oil companies denounced this action. They sent an urgent letter to the State Department in which they requested that the US not intervene in Mexican territory since this would only favor British companies.

Nevertheless, around 1914, the United States invaded Veracruz. A series of rumors contribute to the invasion; among these was the supposed offer of the English to acquire lands in Veracruz, with the acquiescence of Victoriano Huerta as broker for the Pearson Oil Company. There was also strong speculation that the Mexican government was about to receive a shipment of arms from Germany.

Two years later, when the United States government sent a punitive expedition to Mexican territory to catch Pancho Villa, Venustiano Carranza met with German leaders, which fractured relations with the English government. England could not intervene in matters concerning the 1910 Revolution for fear that the Mexican government would decide to ally itself with Germany, under the maxim that the enemy of my enemy is my friend. England has no oil reserves and, in those years, it depended on Mexican crude oil.

In 1917, Venustiano Carranza is elected president and the United States announces its participation in WWI. President Woodrow Wilson takes a firm step toward improving relations between both countries. Although petroleum companies in England and the United States mull over the idea of overthrowing Carranza, Wilson maintains his support.

During this conflict, any possibility of an alliance between Germany and Mexico is cleared up. Once the war is over, the demand for oil continues to increase. Relations between Mexico and the United States are on the right track, and the oil wells produce large quantities day after day. There are even good diplomatic relations with the British government. Mexican crude oil is shared freely between Shell, of English origin, and Standard Oil, from the United States.

But in 1938, Mexico decides to nationalize the oil industry and expel all foreign companies. The US businessmen actively appeal to their government to intercede. But history plays against them. The United States is about to enter World War II, and it cannot afford another conflict; it limits itself to demanding fair compensation for the affected companies. The motive continues to be the possibility that Mexico, with all its oil, will go over to the German or Japanese side. Keeping Mexico on its side means for the United States the possibility of being able to count on its crude oil, under new conditions.

During World War II, oil was as necessary as ammunition, airplanes, morphine, and Coca-Cola. France and England asked the United States for help in obtaining supplies of crude oil. When the US agreed, which Germany considered a hostile gesture, German U-boats sank fifty-five US tankers.

On December 7, 1941, in the midst of the struggle for oil, Japan decided to attack the Pearl Harbor base where a large part of the US Navy was stationed. Its objective was to prevent the United States from obstructing Japanese oil tankers in Indonesia.

On the other side of the world, oil is the protagonist in Hitler's desperate and ambitious campaign to capture Soviet oil fields. They march against the Red Army, and the battle of Stalingrad turns into a resounding defeat for the Nazis that marks their downfall. World War II ends when the United States drops two atomic bombs on Hiroshima and Nagasaki, with no possibility of response from Japan, which has exhausted its crude oil reserves.

Decades later, oil consolidates its position as a bargaining chip in geopolitical power. From 1945 to 1960, while countries affected by the war were gradually recovering, the daily consumption of oil increased from six million barrels a day to twenty-one million. This goes hand in hand with the growth of the automotive industry worldwide.

After the war, the United States consumes more oil than it can produce. As extraordinary as it may seem, its next step is to become an importing country for the first time in its history. After supplying the world during two world wars, the United States turns to the reserves of Arabia and Venezuela with a political and economic strategy that maintains it as a world power.

The Botched Energy Reform

Oil becomes an energy source through industrial processing. Its value is measured in growth and wealth, but, as we have seen, it also becomes a great bone of contention.

After the expropriation carried out by President Lazaro Cardenas, US companies insist on their compensation. President Manuel Avila Camacho, who governed from 1940 to 1946, signed the (Cooke-Zeveda) agreement in an attempt to arrive at sound diplomatic relations as well as to exercise total control over the nation's petroleum without the intervention of foreign companies. Avila Camacho was succeeded by Miguel Aleman Valdes (his term covered 1946 to 1952), who focused on the search for economic resources to promote self-sufficiency of the nation's oil industry. The shadow of foreign investment in the sector still weighed heavily.

At the end of his term, his former secretary of the interior, Adolfo Ruiz Cortines, came to power and implemented a six-year plan to export significant quantities of oil. This went hand in hand with a more efficient infrastructure for its exploitation as well as an increase in production. During this six-year period, the processing of crude oil provided a collateral incentive to the electricity industry; in order for thermoelectric plants to produce the necessary output, large quantities of hydrocarbons were required. With the federal government's support, the oil sector was in third place in terms of national growth.

President Adolfo Lopez Mateos reaffirms the importance of oil as the basis of the economy and of the growing manufacturing sector.

Consequently, he develops a strategic policy that contemplates the petrochemical sector generating greater amounts of derivatives from crude oil. As the saying goes, if one does not know to which port one is sailing, no wind is favorable. At the same time, President Lopez Mateos involved the private sector so that, together, they could strengthen the national economy. Banking on the progress that preceded his presidency, Gustavo Diaz Ordaz, makes oil a priority during his six-year term from 1964 to 1970. He implements a plan to stabilize the sector following the indebtedness created during the previous administration. He continues promoting the petrochemical industry as well as the alliance with the private sector.

Greater development and more efficient organization were pursued when Luis Echeverria Alvarez came to power in 1970. The sector's indebtedness was curbed and, most importantly, there was an increase in production that positively impacted the economy. Mexico is a country that reflects stability. It is an optimal moment for the national oil industry.

When Jose Lopez Portillo assumes the presidency in 1976, he focuses his government on doubling hydrocarbon production in order to increase exports and inject capital into the economy. Lopez Portillo even declared that Mexico, thanks to oil, was ready to manage its abundance. In fact, the mega oil field of Cantarell had just been discovered in Campeche. However, diplomatic friction with the United States affects the distribution of hydrocarbons when the Mexican government rejects a US request to construct a gas pipeline to supply energy. The killing of the goose that lays the golden eggs follows the administration of abundance. Little by little, the decline of PEMEX and the Mexican oil industry began.

When Miguel de la Madrid Hurtado took office, the demand for oil continued to decline. During his six-year term, the price of crude plummeted, exports dropped dramatically, and the economy collapsed. In the midst of all this financial chaos, Carlos Salinas de Gortari becomes president in 1988. Oil prices rise during the Salinas period; the sector recovers its strength in the national economy.

Six years later, President Ernesto Zedillo Ponce de Leon takes office during a deep economic crisis and the deterioration of Mexico's oil-based energy policy. Against this backdrop, the United States applies policies for its own benefit, which end up affecting Mexico's oil industry. The blow causes a terrible economic recession in 1995.

It is important to remember the succession of Mexican presidents up to this point come from the Institutional Revolutionary Party (PRI). Some successful policies were applied, and for a period of time, policies promoted Mexico's industrial and economic growth, mindful to protect national interests over foreign interests in oil. As we have seen though, this does not ensure stable development and prosperity. And this brings about a political reorientation that triggers the so-called energy reform.

In 2000, Mexico's political baton passes to the National Action Party (PAN) and Vicente Fox Quesada, whose administration promises to move the oil sector forward with the prospect of opening up to the outside world. This remains a mere paper exercise; instead, the Mexican Petroleum Institute and the Strategic Center for Scientific and Technological Research, both linked to PEMEX, are dismantled. Energy reform only finds a field of action with natural gas.

Under the same right-wing political banner, the next president, Felipe Calderon Hinojosa, continues with the plan to modify the energy and oil policy. His administration allows contracts with US companies to extract offshore deposits in the waters of the Gulf of Mexico. Calderon institutes the privatization of the petrochemical industry that was controlled by the state. By the end of his six-year term, it is estimated that 80 percent of the oil industry and 55 percent of the electricity industry are already in private hands.

The Mexican government returns to the PRI during the six-year term of Enrique Peña Nieto. One year into his administration, on December 20, 2013, the Official Journal of the Federation publishes constitutional reforms in energy matters. The participation of public and private sectors in hydrocarbons is allowed.

This reform is carried out under the promise of an unprecedented economic change for the country. It claims future development and productive growth, with substantial impact on labor supply and quality of life for Mexicans, such as the promise that electric energy users would see their electricity rates decrease.

In essence, Peña Nieto's energy reform once again grants the exploitation of natural resources to transnational companies in Mexican territory. The arguments to do so are lack of resources to invest, high risks inherent to exploration and production activities, as well as the technical and financial difficulty of exploiting hydrocarbons in deep waters.

To support expanding the role of the private sector in the national oil industry, a multibillion-dollar strategy is created that entails the plundering of Mexico's natural resources. Its scope is not an exclusive idea of the Peña Nieto administration; it has been incubated since the Salinas de Gortari administration. In short, it is about establishing an energy monopoly under the deceitful promise of economic improvement for the nation.

At the time, it was considered a macro project aimed at consolidating a long-term sustainable hydrocarbon model with the following objectives: to increase oil production, to promote greater integration in the value chain from the extraction of hydrocarbons, and to trigger a sufficient supply of gasoline at competitive prices. According to such discourse, an increase in investment and production is presumed, with favorable repercussions on GDP growth and job creation. It also assumes that additional fiscal resources will be obtained after its implementation.

However, history tells us a different story. In principle, the approval of this reform involves corruption, not surprisingly, and underlies a deep-rooted governance problem. From the legal point of view, its implementation is inadequate, and it ends up moving away from its original principles and objectives. With the disproportionate allocation of contracts to individuals, a sector within the upper social and political sphere benefits. The various promises of abundance made to the Mexican people never materialized. By strengthening transnational companies, job creation for Mexicans was sidelined.

The current government of Mexico, led by Andres Manuel Lopez Obrador, is applying a strategy to fight corruption and influence peddling from the highest spheres of power. It seeks to adequately regulate both foreign and domestic private investment for the benefit of the most disadvantaged sectors—without tolerating the abuses, looting, and transgressions that were previously covered up by the government.

With a policy focused on transparency and anti-corruption, Lopez Obrador's government uncovered rigged contracts in hydrocarbons and clean energies, which illicitly benefited politicians and businessmen. Above all, President Lopez Obrador put a stop to the abuses that several foreign energy companies, such as the Spanish company Iberdrola, were committing in Mexico, still viewing Mexico as a land of conquest and plunder, almost as the Spanish Crown did in the best years of New Spain.

There is no doubt that if the energy reform had been carried out correctly and legally—and if it had remained faithful to its original principles—Mexico would be on the way to prosperity. Then, as Jose Lopez Portillo said, the country would be ready to manage abundance. Instead, what was obtained was vile plundering. But as the saying goes: would have, should have, could have. The important thing is that Mexico is in a process of structural change and renovation. The deterioration of PEMEX has stopped. And the company still has an important role to play, not for the world, because its role was never there, but in the domestic market. The salvation of PEMEX will help Mexico for a hundred years. Mexico will not only be self-sufficient in fuels but will be exporting gasoline to all of Latin America, whose countries will be renewing their vehicle fleets at a slower rate than the United States, the European Union or the Asian giants. Mexico is still in a process of structural change and renovation, with a perspective of the current government to recover the energy sovereignty for which Lázaro Cárdenas fought so hard, and of which one would think that the general would be very proud.

Chapter 12

Made in China

China's Trade with the Americas

A popular belief dictates that better figures of the Virgin of Guadalupe are made in China than in Mexico. The influence of the Asian giant extends to Latin America, Europe and even Africa, where China has become an important investor and trading partner, with its sights set on mineral, energy, fishing, and agricultural resources. China is forcing the United States to avoid political and economic hegemony in the world. Curious History: The relationship between Mexico and China is older than the ties between China and the United States; and yet, the United States has benefited more from its relationship with China than Mexico. Here's a look at how the two eagles have related to the greatest power in common: China.

Trade relations between China and Mexico date back to colonial times, when maritime routes between the two countries were established. Under the European empire, products from New Spain made their way to other continents. During the Qing dynasty, Mexico was just one more destination in China's economic agenda.

Before the beginning of the Qing dynasty in 1644, China did not allow trade relations with other cultures. Its first commercial contacts were with Central Asia and the Middle East, followed by later contact with Africa.

Let's follow this history with a Chinese merchant family. What the patriarch does for a living is not considered important; he is not a writer or involved in philosophy. He is regarded as a parasite, and his family is degraded by their lower social status, losing privileges and quality of life. After decades, at the end of the eighteenth century, Europe opened its market to Chinese products. This was followed by a series of treaties—such as the one following the Opium War of

1839 to 1842 and during the 1890s with Japan—laying the economic bases for China's trade.

The relationship between New Spain and China was by imperial order. The Spanish viceroyalty existed under the laws of the Catholic religion, the *encomienda* (a Spanish labor system that rewarded conquerors with the labor of particular groups of non-Christian people), slavery, tribute, and a caste system. The economic policy is geared toward monopolies. In its social hierarchy, both natives and mestizos are the Spanish Crown's minions. The accumulation of precious metals is paramount and fueled by intense mining activity. At first, the Spanish Crown prohibited trade in silver, but they soon had a change of heart.

In 1565, the Philippines was added to the Spanish Empire. That same year, the Manila Galleon, better known as "La Nao de China," began making the voyage between New Spain and China via the Acapulco-Philippines route. At that time, the Spanish Empire allowed informal trade relations with China. The Philippines figured as the anchor of trade between the two, and silver, highly valued in Asia, was exported from New Spain to the East.

There were two Manila galleon routes; the first is the "Carrera de Indias," which was the trade route between Spain and its colonies in the Americas. A secondary route is the "Carrera de las Islas de Poniente," i.e., the Philippines, smaller in volume and centered on the Acapulco-to-Manila relationship. Trade between Acapulco and Manila lasted, uninterrupted, for 250 years.

The so-called route of the Orient, along which the Nao de China sailed, ended in the port of Acapulco. On certain specific runs, it went as far as Peru. Mining provided the most lucrative cargo for these commercial voyages.

Once the merchandise was unloaded in the port of Acapulco, it was transported to the capital of New Spain, with a stop at the Royal Customs house in Patzcuaro to pay the corresponding taxes. At that time, this was the viceroyalty's most profitable trade route.

The Port of Acapulco and the Manila Galleon

The most important strategic and commercial port in the viceroyalty of New Spain until Acapulco came into being was La Navidad, located in the province of Nueva Galicia, now the municipality of Cihuatlan, Jalisco. Most maritime functions were concentrated there, including a shipyard for the construction of expeditionary ships.

Then, in 1565, Andres de Urdaneta discovered and documented a travel route through the Pacific Ocean from the Philippines to Acapulco, which became known as Urdaneta's route or the *tornaviaje* (the Return Voyage). Eventually, the warehouses of La Navidad were dismantled and moved to Acapulco, although "the jewel of the Pacific" would continue to receive merchandise from China, such as spices, crockery, and cloth. Compelling reasons for replacing La Navidad as the main port include its location in a disease-prone area and lack of forests to supply wood for shipbuilding. In addition, the arduous shipping route for transporting artillery, weapons, ammunition, and iron pieces from the port of Veracruz had to involve the Coatzacoalcos River. These factors gave Acapulco the advantage.

The presence of an Asian population in New Spain dates back to 1540 with a slave and cook under the tutelage of Brother Juan de Zumarraga, first bishop of the viceroyalty. When the *tornaviaje* between the Philippines and Acapulco was established as a main route, it is estimated that anywhere from 40,000 to 120,000 people of Asian origin were brought to the Americas between 1565 and 1815.

A member of our protagonist family decides to board the Nao de China. His idea is to settle in the Americas where, like many Asian travelers, he would join a guild in Mexico City or Puebla de los Angeles. The colonial government changed its regulations to allow them to stay.

At the beginning of the eighteenth century, products from Asia and elsewhere were offered in different trading centers, such as the Acapulco Fair (a celebration and commercial event that took place on arrival of the Manila galleon) and the Parian market in Mexico City's main square. They also supplied the markets of Puebla and Jalapa or were distributed to the mining centers or main cities in the Bajio and Oaxaca. Asian products were considered luxury items. Only well-to-do families could acquire them and show them off; figures made of porcelain adorned the most luxurious mansions in the city. Our protagonist family will prosper thanks to the porcelain trade.

After 1815, during the War of Independence, trade between New Spain and the Philippines was suspended. Asian goods—fans, screens, table sets, porcelain, and silk—no longer arrived. Other trading also stopped, including some unique and controversial examples such as fighting cocks, a practice that dates back some 2,500 years in Asia.

Decades go by, and trade between the two countries, China and Mexico, was sporadic and insignificant. The descendants of our Asian family are still active in trade, although now they export products for industrial use as well as discs, wooden articles, bags, wigs, and toys. In the middle of the twentieth century, around 1965, the shipment of Asian cotton begins, with an annual flow worth more than 30 million pesos; a year later, demand for cut opals from Asia increases, with trade reportedly worth around 50,000 pesos per year. In 1971, the export of cotton increased to an annual amount of 54 million pesos.

Despite this, trade relations between Mexico and China failed to take off in the 1970s, even with the official reopening of trade in 1972. Among the contributing factors are differences in productivity between the two economies, low demand for products, and unprofitable prices.

This changed toward the end of the 1970s and beginning of the 1980s, when bilateral trade reached unprecedented growth. Both nations set out to develop their economies under a new model that included sustained trade. China and Mexico enter the global market, with specific roles from a labor perspective. Mexico's economy is situated in the intermediate and final stages of the product chain; China is also positioned in this sector as well as other countries in Asia and the Americas.

Their participation in the World Trade Organization and the Asia-Pacific Economic Cooperation Forum (APEC) is aimed at achieving the economic and commercial balance that will allow them to compete on a regional level. They are committed to strengthening the region given the growing interdependence of the region's economies. This scenario includes the flow of trade and capital from direct foreign investment and the outlook for GDP, balance of payments, and technological exchange—in addition to expected job creation and better environmental conditions.

In 1982, the Mexican government faces a deep internal crisis (once more) under the presidency of Miguel de la Madrid, which delays the nation's trade development plan. Conversely, since 1979, the Chinese government officially steered its economy toward a new model, eliminating semi-autarkic production based on heavy industry. Its perspective on the international market is progressive.

As a result, China uses a moderate and intelligent process; the overall objective is to safeguard the interests of the nation. In this way, it positions itself for success in the free market. Mexico applies an open, neoliberal economic model with a lack of unification. It adheres blindly to the macroeconomic rules of the International Monetary Fund and the World Bank, also obeying the guidelines of the Washington Consensus of 1989 in the area of taxation.

After three decades in the communist bloc, China opts for an arrangement that enables better development prospects for the nation. It is worth noting that in China, the state decides on each market, unlike Mexico, which is open to an assigned market.

As we can see, the bilateral history between China and Mexico is as long as a dragon. Let's now turn to an emblematic product that generates generous dividends for both countries: porcelain.

Once again, we take a step back in time with our protagonist family, to the years when porcelain was exclusive to China, which enjoyed a monopoly both in Europe and the Americas. This family and others involved in the sector prospered until the beginning of the seventeenth century, when porcelain manufacturing was greatly reduced. Seeing the ongoing external demand for this product, Japan said, "Get out of the way—I'm coming in." The Japanese entered the market, but they did not have the same credentials as China, who enjoyed trade relations with other countries, including Mexico. Japan turned to China to be its intermediary. While the strategy is correct, Mexico was already manufacturing a substitute for porcelain. This was *talavera*, a kind of glazed ceramic that is now very popular in central Mexico. At first, its design imitated Asian work, but it later integrated the identity of Mexican culture with original designs. This product is now known as *talavera poblana*.

Mexico and China Enter the WTO

During the first quarter of the twentieth century, growing nationalism emerged in Europe, leading up to the First World War. Nations were busy implementing protectionist measures against international trade on a scale that had never been seen before. Once war broke out, protectionist policies were sidelined in favor of a struggle to divide the world into distinct zones of influence.

After the Great War, around the 1929 economic crisis, countries adopted new guidelines to safeguard their industries, imposing a series of limitations on products coming from abroad. In the midst of the economic depression, in the 1930s, countries applied trade barriers as a means of safeguarding their industries, such as the example of casual imports and raising tariffs. With the advent of World War II, the risk of such restrictive measures on trade between nations became evident.

Multilateral reciprocity is not restored once the conflict is over. Only the industrialized countries are able to raise their tariffs through quotas and exchange control mechanisms. At the end of World War II, the role of the Allied countries, led by the United States, was decisive in establishing a new world economic system and international economic law.

On August 4, 1994, through the Decree Approving the Final Act (DOF), the Uruguay Round published multilateral trade agreements. That same year, on December 30, the agreements approved by the

World Trade Organization went into effect, accrediting Mexico as a founding member.

The Uruguay Round established a significant reduction in tariffs—a tariff being the official rate that determines the fee to be paid in various branches, such as rail transport or customs. As a result, the developed countries reduced tariffs by 40 percent while the rest, including Mexico, by an average of 30 percent. A grace period of five years is granted for industrial products, while in the agricultural sector, it is six years for developed countries and ten years for developing countries.

The Uruguay Round applies to nations bound by the General Agreement on Tariffs and Trade (GATT). These types of tariffs are known as bound tariffs—specific commitments made by individual governments and WTO members. Mexico's bound tariff is around 50 percent, although its tariffs are not tied to GATT because they are lower. Mexico is committed to reducing its bound tariff from 50 percent to 35 percent; so far, Mexico has not modified its tariffs and maintains reciprocity in accordance with its recent trade liberalization.

China began moving from a socialist economy, under state administration, to a socialist market economic model. This shift enabled it to enter a multilateral trade system. It is worth noting that China was among the twenty-three original GATT nations in 1947. However, when the People's Republic of China (PRC) was created around October 1, 1949, its participation in international affairs was paused. Disregarding the advantages of participating in the GATT, China was in no hurry to regain its place in the WTO, having rejected its own membership.

By 1978, under the leadership of Deng Xiaoping (in power from 1978 to 1989) and with a renewed geopolitical position, China sought to join the principal international organizations—the World Bank, the International Monetary Fund (IMF), and the GATT. In the early 1980s, it joined the World Bank and IMF. In 1982, it was granted observer status in the GATT; in 1986, it became a GATT Contracting Party and resumed its membership. On March 4, 1987, it began participating officially. During an appearance at one session,

China's representatives presented their plan to the GATT. China accepted GATT's request for reforms to its socialist market economic model and committed to a policy of openness at the international level, aimed at strengthening economic and trade relations with the rest of the GATT's members.

Deng Xiaoping skillfully presented China as a developing country, thereby protecting the country's agricultural and other sectors with the vision of better planning and political stability. The agreement between both parties—China and the GATT—is based on the following principles: expansion of companies with international trading rights; self-determination of costs (limited price controls); and implementation of a foreign exchange system that eliminates anti-export bias on the real exchange rate.

Finally, such mechanisms condition China's acceptance of conventional trade guidelines, i.e. tariffs and nontariff barriers.

The Opium Wars and the First Commercial Treaty of the United States with China

Opium cultivation originated in India, where the British Empire exploited its commercialization. In fact, it was a British company that agreed to pay for silk, porcelain figurines, and Chinese tea imports with opium. In the 1830s, England sent an average of 1,400 tons of opium to China per year, to the satisfaction of thousands of Asian users. But the joy would not last long. In 1839, Emperor Daoguang prohibited the opium trade within Chinese territory due to the Chinese population's growing addiction.

This prohibitionist measure affected the British economy since the opium business in China represented enormous profits. The British Crown decided to attack China in retaliation. Unable to defend against the large British fleet, the Chinese emperor announced his surrender in 1842, with the Treaty of Nanking. This agreement between the British Empire and the Qing dynasty stipulated the following: the opening of five ports for international trade; the free marketing of opium; the elimination of taxes on foreigners for domestic trade; and the cession of Hong Kong Island to the British government.

On July 3, 1844, the Qing dynasty signs the Treaty of Wanghia— also known as the Treaty of Wangxia—which is presented as a peace, friendship, and trade agreement, with tariffs, between the United States and China. President John Tyler (1841–1845) ratified the agreement on January 17, 1845. Its clauses are similar to those of the Treaty of Nanking, although more specific. It is the first trade agreement between the two countries.

However, these treaties did not bring peace to the Chinese empire. In 1856, another conflict with England broke out. The British accused the Chinese Coast Guard of having interfered with a British ship for no reason, and they demanded the release of its crew members. The conflict escalates with the British fleet opening fire on the city of Canton. Using the logic of European imperialism, the British government asks for help from its allies and anyone else with an interest in China. France responded and supported the British. In 1860, the battle of Palikao was fought, ending in defeat for China for the second time against England and its allies.

Sanctions imposed by the new treaty were more severe and excessive. China was obliged to indemnify France and England for the war; it must also allow the migration of labor to the United States, and of course, the legalization and sale of opium was added too.

Other world powers joined in; the United States, France, and Russia forced China into this unequal treaty. Their hands tied by the agreement, the Chinese open up eleven new ports destined for foreign trade.

China was required to send local labor to the United States to work on the construction of railroad lines. The Chinese workers arrived in California, where the US government was planning to build a railroad tunnel. The construction site is located high in the state's snowcapped mountains. It took between ten thousand to twenty thousand Chinese workers to perform the heavy task of crushing stone and building a tunnel. The conditions were deplorable, and the pay was even worse. Essentially the Chinese had to do work that the Americans did not want to do.

This was a period of time when the state of California was experiencing the gold rush. Americans concentrated on mining while the Chinese worked on the railroads, although a few did get jobs in the gold mines. The exploitation of Chinese labor was key to construction of the first transcontinental railroad by the Central Pacific Rail Company.

Later, as a result of Asian immigration to the United States, Chinatowns emerged. These communities began to prosper due to their discipline and work ethic. Envious locals start rumors that the Chinatowns are places of low morals, and they accuse the Chinese of operating brothels and opium dens.

Anti-Chinese sentiment grows. In 1882, President Chester Arthur (1881–1885) signed the Chinese Exclusion Act that banned Chinese immigration for a set period of ten years. In 1902, this law became permanent.

In 1943, the law was finally repealed under President Franklin D. Roosevelt. This gesture was a step toward improving relations with China, which had become a US ally during WWII and whose help was needed in the Pacific.

Richard Nixon Opens to China

Today, the world follows China with great interest. This Asian giant, prosperous and territorially vast, has a complex history that is worth recalling. Its imperial order comes from the so-called dynasties that predate our era. The last dynasty in a long succession of imperial families is the Qing dynasty, which was overthrown after ruling for 250 years. In 1912, the Republic of China was officially founded, although this did not ensure that the country was unified.

Divisions existed between the China that welcomed regime change and the China that wanted to prosper through foreign trade. In this rivalry, the so-called warlords play a major role; one side wants to focus the country's course on trade and development, and the other tries to overthrow it and rule their own way. Later, the intervention of several foreign nations leaves the country divided between the Republic of China and the People's Republic of China.

The United States stayed away and limited trade activity with this part of Asia. Not until the dissolution of the Soviet Union, which catapulted the United States to the top as a world power, did bilateral relations improved. The Chinese and Soviets were enemies at that time, and despite sharing a critical border, they could not stand the sight of each other.

After the Second World War, the United States began positioning itself on the world stage while other nations were barely catching their breath. China was badly damaged due to recent wars and internal divisions. World War II was officially declared in 1939, although China, always ahead of the curve, had already been at war with Japan since 1931. World War II ends in 1945, but China does not encounter a period of peace. It undergoes a civil war that ended with the communist victory. Its leader, Mao Zedong, gloriously assumes the office of chairman of the People's Republic of China.

Although the People's Republic of China held the majority power, there was still opposition from the Republic of China in alliance with other nations. It is here that the United States—whose embassy is located in the Republic of China—intervenes with a plan of action that later evolves.

Around 1972, US President Richard Nixon travels to China for the first time to strengthen bilateral relations; this could be called being a fair-weather friend. The visit is a historic event in which a far-right president visited a far-left counterpart. The idea that opposites attract is probably true. Their agenda focuses on solving differences to map out future relations. The outcome of this visit is that the US changes its isolationist policy toward China in order to better focus its energy against the Soviet Union. Richard Nixon succeeds in greatly improving trade and overall relations with China. China does not oppose US growth; in return, the United States prefers a strategic ally to an enemy.

By 1979, the United States recognizes the People's Republic of China, and the Republic of China takes on an international identification as Taiwan. A bilateral trade agreement is completed, and the two nations establish their embassies in each other's capitals on March 1, 1979.

Disagreements arise again during Jimmy Carter's presidency, when China opposes US arms sales to Taiwan, but in the end, a diplomatic solution is reached.

In the 1980s, the United States supports Most Favored Nation (MFN) status for China, giving it a huge market advantage. Bilateral ties between the nations were strengthened when the Asian giant joined the WTO on December 11, 2001, after fifteen years of unsuccessful attempts. For China, this is an invaluable vote of confidence with other nations.

China Becomes America's Factory

China's entry into the WTO comes as a shock to many because the attack on the Twin Towers on September 11, 2001, are still top of mind. Many had expected the US to suspend trade agreements with countries suspected of wrongdoing. China shrewdly acts quickly and fully supports the US position in its fight against terrorism.

The connection between these nations is logical. The United States is known for its excessive consumerism, and China has been producing and exporting products since ancient times. This explains why, since joining the WTO, its economy has grown to become the second largest in the world, behind only the United States. However, although trade and diplomatic relations between the two countries have become stronger since the Cold War, another cold war is now on the horizon between the two countries themselves.

This may seem an absurdity taking into account their mutual cooperation to strengthen political and economic ties. To get to the heart of the matter, it is useful to go back to the moment of China's entry into the WTO.

When granted MFN status, China has benefits given only to developing countries. Like Mexico, China must lower tariffs on various products in addition to opening its market in the services sector. China can then export textiles without having to pay the respective quotas under the protection of MFN and WTO entitlements.

In turn, transnational companies take the opportunity to enter the Asian market through China. This opens up sectors that were previously limited or off-limits to foreigners. In a domino effect, foreign investment increases significantly. China promises transparency to its investors, although its biggest incentive is the reduction of the average tariff from 24.6 percent to 9.4 percent, plus an import license and the elimination of quotas.

In the face of China's spectacular growth, the position of the United States and the WTO is no longer the same. They now view China through more suspicious eyes.

The United States has been a founding member of the WTO since 1995, and it has great influence over it. It accepts China's profile as an economic and political partner until 2018, when President Donald Trump accuses the Asian country of unfair practices, such as dumping and intellectual property theft. Dumping is a commercial practice that involves the sale of a product below its normal price or production cost as a strategy to dominate competition in the market.

Donald Trump announced the application of tariffs on Chinese products. His counterpart, Xi Jinping, applying the logic of an eye for an eye, has been imposing the same measure on American products since 2013.

A trade war begins between the two nations and escalates. Diplomatic representatives begin to dialogue, without much progress. On August 23, 2018, the United States imposes a 25 percent tariff on Chinese products; China responds with retaliatory tariffs in the same percentage. China appeals to the WTO without success. The United States goes for a third round of tariffs, and history repeats itself.

These nations have a meeting scheduled for September 2018, which China decides to suspend. Not until November do trade

300

negotiations resume, via telephone and between their respective presidents. At the G20 summit, they reached a temporary truce, agreeing not to impose more tariffs or increase existing ones.

Although a more favorable and friendly outlook for both nations is predicted for 2019, global technology mega-companies, such as Google and Huawei, enter the fray. This is ignited by President Donald Trump adding Huawei to a list of companies not accredited for business dealings with US companies. At that point, Huawei was outselling industry leaders Apple and Google. What starts as a trade disagreement veers into a war for control of new technologies, including AI and 5G.

The trade wars between the United States and China have compromised aluminum and plastic production and even agriculture. At issue here is leadership in the technology market. Today, bilateral negotiations are at a standstill because the United States is still dependent on China for 5G technology.

Mexico: Trump's Option Instead of China

Over the past thirty years, and since its entry into the WTO, China has opened up its trade capacity at an unprecedented rate. It has positioned itself as an exporter, excelling in both the domestic and foreign markets. As part of this plan, it minimizes international competition. As a superpower, China has repositioned its status in the WTO, mainly because it has gone from being a developing country to a global player.

In this upward swing, China has become the main supplier to the United States, surpassing Mexico in 2003, despite the tariff advantages that the latter enjoys under NAFTA. In terms of trade relations, Mexico and China have achieved a growing dynamic, highlighting imports from Asia to the Americas.

Among the products exchanged between the two nations, China mainly imports primary goods such as minerals, salts, and chemicals. At present, in the products exchange, the intermediate goods outstand, being used as inputs in, for example, the assembly of screens, HF, TV, and FM signal installations, or antenna adjustments; in addition, automated machines for data processing, digitalization, and portable equipment, such as cell phones. Mexico also sends minerals such as copper and concentrates, crude oil, bituminous mineral, lead, and concentrates.

In terms of the current trade agreement, China obtains greater profits. Although Mexico has a deficit in terms of the balance of trade, its numbers indicate growth. The trade openness policy of both countries is based on a system with a priority role for the state in economic activity. In particular, China combines its socialist economy with a capitalist strategy, resulting in a socialist market model. As for Mexico, its economic development model is based on the principles of a mixed economy, where different sectors interact, such as the public and private sectors.

In the Chinese model, priority is given to the domestic market, with marked indicators of poverty reduction and social progress. As for Mexico, its model has the opposite effect, given current poverty and social underdevelopment.

A stumbling block between the two countries, beyond their political will, is the crisis caused by COVID-19. While this pandemic kept the world on alert during the first half of 2022, bilateral support was strong for keeping trade relations moving forward.

In 2016, Mexico suffered a diplomatic crisis with the new Donald Trump administration. Faced with the refusal to finance a border wall between the two countries, Trump threatened to impose high import tariffs on Mexican products, such as avocados, which would greatly affect both economies. Some voices pointed out that it was in Mexico's best interest to divest from its main trading partner and turn its attention to China. Instead of two eagles, better an eagle and a dragon.

There is a political crisis in the United States. That is undeniable. The crisis began with George W. Bush and has continued to this day. The weakening of U.S. governments has coincided with the exponential rise of China. The great dragon, which for centuries was absent from the global map, will occupy its rightful place as the cradle of much of humanity's progress. The country has already decided to act and stop looking at its gigantic navel. The dragon has the world feeling the flames of its breath.

It is true that Mexico's relationship with China is older than the U.S. relationship with China. However, it is not stronger than Mexico's relationship with the United States. Mexico and China are neighbors by sea, and this allows for an important trade relationship. Despite this, the link between Mexico and the United States is stronger, closer and longer than that with China, making it impossible for the Asian giant to one day replace the United States in Mexico's favor. Likewise, the United States has become aware of the importance of its southern neighbor and has displaced Chinese products in several industries to make room for Mexican products. Otherwise, it would have lost competitiveness.

On July 6, 2020, President Andrés Manuel López Obrador was holding one of his many morning conferences. I was at his side, as I had been assigned to report, as I do every Monday, on who's who in fuel prices. The president was talking about the good relationship with the U.S. government and with then President Trump, given that he would be traveling to Washington D.C. the following day. That would be the first meeting between the two presidents. President López Obrador was mentioning the advantages of the new treaty between Mexico, the United States and Canada regarding the automotive industry, and it occurred to me, perhaps because I had my leg crossed, that my shoes represented very well the commercial integration of the three countries that signed the USMCA. In the middle of the conference, I told the president that my shoes have elements from all three countries: the sole of a U.S. bull, deer skin raised in Canada, tanned in Leon, and assembled in Mexico, precisely in Manuel Doblado, Guanajuato. Family-owned companies from the three countries are involved in the manufacture of the shoe thanks to USMCA. The president invited me to present my idea in front of the reporters. At the end, the president said with great humor that I had corrected him, and that made us all laugh.

The pandemic forced a huge substitution of imports from China, and Mexico is benefiting from this change. A clear example is the Mexican shoe industry, which almost came to extinction due to the onslaught of Chinese products, since a cheap and well-made shoe made it impossible to compete with Mexican products. A compensatory tariff was imposed on Chinese footwear and that helped the Mexican shoe not to die. Then came the pandemic. The huge U.S. market, which made possible the supremacy of Chinese shoes in Mexico, quickly replaced imports into Mexico.

Mexico was the main supplier of footwear to the United States during World War I and World War II. That is where the Mexican footwear industry was really born. Afterwards, China took that position and Mexico focused on its domestic market. Now, with the crisis between China and the United States, and with imports from China becoming more expensive because of the pandemic, Mexico has become competitive. It is a resurgence of the footwear industry that has not been seen since the end of World War II. The same thing that is happening with footwear can also be seen in the more economically important automotive industry. Both assembly industries (automobiles and shoes) reflect China's exit from this trade equation between Mexico, the United States and Canada, and are the best thermometer to measure, in the North American market, the substitution of Chinese for Mexican.

Carlos Slim, Mexico's most successful businessman, has stated that: "the need for the United States and Canada to produce domestically is great, but the possibility of having the costs they have with China is not more likely than with Mexico". The United States and Canada do not need China if they have Mexico. It is in North America's interest to keep its industry in the region. It is safer from any eventuality, as was seen with the COVID 19 pandemic or the war between Russia and Ukraine. What used to be manufactured in China will be made in Mexico in the coming years. Therefore, the two eagles stand together and so will face the dragon. After all, all three also fly.

General Lazaro Cardenas and Mao
Zedong in China 1959.

President Richard Nixon and Mao
Zedong in China 1972.

Chapter 13

Organized Crime and Corruption

Hooked on Drugs

An eagle flies over its desert domain. From high above, he can detect prey—such as mice or rattlesnakes—emerging from hiding places in the sand. For a moment, he thinks he spots his next meal, but his sharp vision has fooled him; it turns out to be the skeleton of a hare. He easily takes flight again, confident that sooner rather than later, some prey will be caught in his talons. Sparse clouds and thin air allow the clear blue sky to glow as if it had just been painted. The eagle is unaware that he is flying over the wasteland that divides two countries. The bird pays no attention to territorial divisions, laws, flags, or square kilometers. From the air, he only observes what lies ahead, which is more desert and silence, a slight breeze, and three or four cacti.

A noise catches the eagle's attention. He looks down as a large, old truck rolls by, leaving behind a cloud of brown dust. It is not the first time this eagle has seen these vehicles in the desert; some were heading north and others south, sometimes during the day, sometimes in the early morning.

The truck stops; it seems its tires are stuck in the dirt. The eagle flies overhead, keeping his distance, and watches as dozens of people jump from the truck, desperate for air to breathe. A little girl looks around, and all she can see is nothingness and the bird flying above her.

The eagle knows that if he waits long enough, these people can also serve as food, when the sun, thirst, oblivion, and other animals finish them off. Suddenly, three patrol cars surround the stranded truck. The eagle had already detected them from above, when people could still flee, but there was no way he could have warned them.

Sirens blare, and people run in panic even deeper into the desert. Others kneel down and cross their hands behind their backs, thinking of the failure of their journey, of the lost illusion, of how much it will cost them to try again. The arrests proceed, and the eagle leaves the area before the officers also demand to see his immigration papers.

Up ahead, the eagle spots another movement. This time, several trucks in a convoy are heading south. They stop not because of a malfunction but because a patrol car is blocking their way. The curious eagle approaches, probably thinking that there is food inside those vehicles. Out of the corner of his eye, he observes an officer getting out of the car. On his second pass, he sees the same officer speaking to a man as the first truck's cargo bed opens. On his third pass, the eagle sees that the inside of the truck is full of weapons. Noticing that there is no food there, the eagle resumes his journey, but not before watching as a man hands the officer a yellow envelope before the line of trucks resumes its march.

Finally, the eagle looks for a place where he can rest for a while. Before the sun goes down, the bird finds a scene of horror. He perches on top of a cactus to assess the human corpses, the burning vans full of holes. Also scattered on the ground the eagle looks at several objects similar to those that were inside the truck. One of the men lying on the ground is still breathing. The eagle will stare at him until he stops moving. Other scavenger birds circle above the trail of bodies. As the wind blows about some green bills and broken bags with white powder, the eagle, with the same unperturbed gaze, thinks about how strange the desert has become in recent years.

The problem of drug trafficking unites Mexico and the United States more intimately than the clandestine tunnels crossing under the shared border. It is a painful phenomenon that has hurt both countries. The suffering is not equal though; Mexico bears the brunt of this maelstrom.

It is commonly said that Mexico provides the drugs and the dead, and the United States provides the consumption, the weapons, and the money. The reality is that this issue is often more complex than it appears, a complexity that is difficult to explain in television series, soap operas, or *corridos*. The imagery of drug trafficking is full of mythology, clichés, and beliefs alien to the truth; the images are usually about a conflict between bad hit men against good cops or brave capos who wear fancy clothes and live in tasteless mansions accompanied by beautiful and exotic women. In the real world, the illicit drug business is quite different. Instead of the false glamour portrayed in some TV series, what we have are thousands of murdered and disappeared people, territories taken over by and in the hands of organized crime, shootings in the streets, a weak rule of law, and a heightened perception of insecurity. Now Mexico, which was once considered only a transshipment point for drugs that would end up in the United States, has become a drug consumer coupled with violence caused by the cartels' quest for territorial control.

The consumption of toxic substances is not something unfamiliar to either country; its use has been around as long as coffee. In the Americas, the original peoples ingested hallucinogenic substances for spiritual purposes, for healing in rites and religious ceremonies; its meaning was shamanic. During the times of colonization, and even after independence, both countries were free of the problems related to drug consumption, except for tobacco and alcohol. The drug trafficking mess was not unleashed until the twentieth century, when drug supply and demand and the prohibition of consumption by governments combine in a deadly cocktail.

As time went on, and with the evolution of the chemical industry, demand and consumption of synthetic drugs moved in a completely different direction from the consumption of enervating drugs by the original peoples. The production and distribution of drugs now involves cartels, firearms, money laundering, drug lords, executions, and the corruption of institutions, plus a system marked by violence and crime that is becoming more and more widespread every day.

At present, both in Mexico and in the United States, the consumption of chemical substances generally speaking is illegal, although the legalization of marijuana has been recognized in several US states. On the streets of New York, stalls and trucks selling products made with marijuana—such as candy, lollipops, gummies, ice cream, and magic brownies, in addition to the classic joint—can already be found. This business turns over millions of dollars, completely legal. It is estimated that the sale of cannabis in the United States generates profits of $150 billion, and several risk-rating agencies such as Standard & Poor's predict that this will be one of the top industries in the future.

On the other hand, the decriminalization of cannabis consumption in Mexico has been rolled out slowly and without much momentum. The congress has approved regulations allowing a person to carry up to five grams of cannabis—any more, and they could be charged with selling drugs. Supporters of the legalization of all drugs claim that this would take significant profits away from drug traffickers and strip them of their power and economic capacity to buy weapons and corrupt police, politicians, and institutions.

Neither are Americans bad for buying and using drugs, nor are Mexicans bad for selling drugs. In the United States, some politicians claim that Mexico is killing American citizens because of the drugs they export. This accusation is not valid. The truth is that drugs are bought and sold on both sides of the border. Indiscriminate drug use in the United States costs lives in hospitals, while in Mexico the cost of lives is on the streets. Drug trafficking moves globally; it is a transnational business, with outstanding dividends. Consequently, in all nations legal statutes are created and modified to curb this business. Unfortunately, this has not happened equally.

A little more than a century ago, Mexico and the United States had similar levels of violence and crime. There were bandits on both sides, the occasional gold wagon was stolen, and the occasional beagle was hanged. In the 20th century, crime became more sophisticated. The United States knew how to control (and manage) its criminality. Mexico was unable to keep it at bay. Today, that violence represents a heavy social, political, and economic cost for Mexico. We have a systemic problem.

In the case of Mexico, in the 1970s the government implemented actions to address a problem that was moderate back then compared to the savagery we see today. Following international guidelines,

Mexico focuses on development and implementation of laws to regulate the use and sale of drugs.

At the same time, the country established strategic collaboration agreements with other nations, notably the United States, where there was a high demand for synthetic drugs. When President Lyndon B. Johnson complained that the Mexican government was tolerating the trafficking of drugs to the United States, then-President Gustavo Diaz Ordaz replied, "Mexico is the trampoline for drugs to the United States; close your pool and the trampoline will end." The fact is that despite combined efforts, neither the resources allocated nor the bloodshed has reduced the demand for drugs.

Drug trafficking is a thorny issue between Mexico and the United States. This is all the more understandable if we consider that this business makes use of corruption at all levels and operates as a kind of autonomous entity. In various regions of Mexico, criminal groups are in charge, deciding on the lives of the local inhabitants. The intervention of drug traffickers in local electoral processes has also been documented, where they have imposed mayors or assassinated candidates who oppose their interests. Likewise, several criminals, in their infinite brazenness, have competed in elections hand in hand with all political parties.

Because of situations such as these, it is often mistakenly believed that only in Mexico does the problem of corruption abound as an unsolvable and persistent evil. Corruption in Mexico is a cultural issue. Former President Enrique Peña Nieto went so far as to say so. Indeed, during his administration, whether for cultural reasons or not, there were too many cases of corruption. However, on the other side, things are no better. The United States also has its corruption scandals, although the truth is that they have been able to hide them better than the Mexicans.

At the beginning of his novel *Conversation in the Cathedral*, Mario Vargas Llosa asks himself, "At what point did Peru get screwed?" In the same vein, we could also ask, "At what point did drug trafficking and corruption screw up Mexico? How much of that can be blamed on the United States?" Let's take a look at the past to find the answer.

During the nineteenth century, President-elect Rutherford B. Hayes, who governed from 1877 to 1881, went against the custom of clientelism or the exchange of quid pro quo by apportioning public offices, which is quite well-known in Mexico. Decades later, President Warren G. Harding enabled corruption by his own friends and associates—the so-called Ohio Gang, because they were born in that state, like the president. The most notorious cases of bribery during his administration had to do with oil concessions.

Another U.S. corruption case is the famous Watergate affair. Richard Nixon was president of the United States and had just won re-election. In 1972, five people entered the Democratic compound at the Watergate Hotel in Washington, D.C., with the intention of removing documents from the site. A guard at the complex noticed that something unusual was going on; after ascertaining that the strange activity was not the result of ghosts or paranormal occurrences, he alerted the police, and the intruders were arrested. After an investigation, it was learned that those people were trying to steal documents from the Democratic Party to favor Nixon in the elections. Then the scandal broke. The president ordered the investigation to be buried and it backfired. Before the world, Nixon looked like a liar, a cheat who abused his power.

With no possibility of appeal and on the ropes, Richard Nixon resigned from office after giving a final speech from the Oval Office. It is the first time in history that a U.S. president has resigned from office.

In another, more recent scandal, Donald Trump was the protagonist. Russian hackers had allegedly intervened in internet forums and social networks, such as Facebook, during the 2016 elections to tilt public opinion toward the Republican candidate. However, this was never proven, despite accusations by the Democrats and media coverage.

This scandal can be summarized as a series of allegations against the Republicans based on a cyberattack that affected Hilary Clinton's 2016 presidential campaign. Russian hackers, calling themselves "The Dukes," stole confidential information from the Democratic

National Committee. Hilary Clinton herself claims that she lost the election because of that hacking. Trump denied all charges against the Republican Party. However, he never rules out that the hacking may have come from the Russians. With no evidence either way, Donald Trump won the presidency under the suspicion that he got help from the Kremlin.

The Stench of Corruption in Mexican Politics

The names of former presidents Enrique Peña Nieto and Carlos Salinas de Gortari are linked, whether they like it or not, to corruption. This does not mean that Mexico was clean and a global example of political honesty before their presidential terms. There are many sayings in Mexico that portray corruption: "He who doesn't cheat never gets ahead," "There is plenty for the taking when the government is paying," and "In a lame-duck government, only a fool doesn't take as much as they can." It is worthwhile to take stock of the leaders who have occupied the presidential chair to serve themselves rather than benefiting the citizens. This will allow us to understand the root of such an unhealthy and deep-seated practice.

Following the transition from Agustin de Iturbide to Porfirio Diaz and after the Revolution of 1910, dictatorships and corruption were thought to be a thing of the past. This was not the case. There was a change of generations in which corrupt leaders from the old guard left—and new ones took over. It was as simple as that.

This is the case of Miguel Aleman Valdes (1946–1952), whose father was a revolutionary general. Throughout his life, he used politics for his personal gain. During his presidential campaign, he wasted huge amounts of money to sweep away his opponents. Once in office, facing the first protest by PEMEX workers, he turned to the Mexican Army to repress them. His administration focused on privatization of companies and supporting foreign investment in which he directly and indirectly took part. His personal wealth was greatly enriched by his presidency.

Luis Echeverria Alvarez (1970–1976) headed a government replete with sociopolitical scandals. Before taking office, he was already being harshly criticized for his participation in the 1968 Tlatelolco student massacre. Echeverria was serving as secretary of the interior when the shooting at the Plaza de las Tres Culturas took place. In 1971, civil groups began demanding answers and an end to impunity for this tragic event. The government's response was the so-called "Halconazo," also known as the Corpus Christi Massacre, resulting in the death of seventeen protestors (other figures speak of 225 dead); the exact number of wounded is not known.

On June 10, 1971, student demonstrators hit the streets of Mexico City. A government-trained paramilitary group—Los Halcones—violently repressed the students, this barely three years after the tragedy in Tlatelolco. Luis Echeverria washed his hands of the Corpus Christi Massacre, saying he had nothing to do with the incident, although he did little to bring those responsible to justice. Later, the government waged a dirty war against the civil movements related to Tlatelolco, kidnapping and executing leftist sympathizers, political opponents, and guerrilla fighters who believed that armed resistance was the only way to change corruption in the Mexican political system.

During Echeverria's government, the so-called death flights were constant, a method of extermination so characteristic of dictatorships, which used airplanes and helicopters to throw people into the harsh solitude of the sea. This dark period is known as the Dirty War. To date, it is unknown how many people disappeared during the Dirty War in Mexico during the 1970s. The government of Andres Manuel Lopez Obrador has decided to create a *Comision para el Acceso a la Verdad de la Guerra Sucia* (Commission for Truth on the Dirty War), which seeks to clarify the crimes and human rights violations committed by the Mexican state during those infamous years.

Following this period was Jose Lopez Portillo (1976–1982), a controversial character who showed obvious favoritism during his government and oversaw a series of corrupt acts that he tried to justify as necessary to rescue the nation's currency. With open social disapproval due to crisis the nation was going through, his administration nationalized the banking system and established across-the-board exchange controls. When faced with the dreadful devaluation of the Mexican peso, Lopez Portillo went so far as to say, "I am responsible for the helm, not the storm,"

The promised abundance from oil was poorly exploited, unleashing instead the demons of corruption everywhere. With wastefulness and excessive spending, Lopez Portillo ended up putting the country deeper into debt than it already was. However, during his last state of the union report, the Mexican president apologized to the nation and announced the expropriation of all private banks: "It is now or never, they have already looted us, they will not loot us again." As he read his rousing speech, his voice began to crack as he dedicated a few words to the dispossessed and marginalized of Mexico: "To those who six years ago I asked for forgiveness, which I have been carrying along as a personal responsibility." He pounded his fist as his eyes teared up, and Congress wrapped him in unanimous applause. Lopez Portillo lamented that he could not have done things better, "More I could not do," he said before wiping a tear from his eye. History still does not know whether it was genuine or fake.

Carlos Salinas de Gortari (1988–1994) assumed the presidency under a cloud of suspicion about his victory. During the vote count, the system indicated a percentage in favor of his opponent, Cuauhtemoc Cardenas Solorzano, a leftist politician and son of former President Lazaro Cardenas del Rio. However, mysteriously, the tabulating system crashed, or went silent, in the middle of the night. When it was reactivated, Carlos Salinas was ahead in the vote count. This provoked widespread displeasure to the point that opposition legislators demonstrated against Carlos Salinas assuming the constitutional presidency, alleging that Cardenas was the victim of fraud. Nothing and nobody could stop Salinas de Gortari. Once in power, the president ordered the arrest of petroleum union leader Joaquin Hernandez Galicia—La Quina—to show that his government would not tolerate corruption. He also assembled an administration worthy of leading a nation; it was a government of graduates from the best universities in the United States, and they became known as technocrats.

With an economic policy pointed toward privatization, the Salinas administration granted over-budget compensation to the banks nationalized by Lopez Portillo in addition to exempting them from paying taxes. At the same time, he auctioned off the national telephone system, Telmex, to businessman Carlos Slim, who became the richest man in Mexico. Although the Salinas presidency has been accused of many instances of corruption, these have not been possible to prove. His government remained indebted to his promises to the nation.

However, Carlos Salinas ably took advantage of long-standing mechanisms for resources allowed by the political system. This is the case of the so-called *partida secreta* (secret appropriation), an official account created in 1917 and protected by Article 74 of the Constitution, which allows the president to use this resource at his discretion with no accountability.

Carlos Salinas is accused of plundering half of that allocation. This accusation does not come from the opposition or his enemies but from people close to him who occupied high positions. Former President Miguel de la Madrid, who preceded him in power and was a member of the same political party (the PRI), acknowledged that the amount taken was half of the account. In an interview with journalist Carmen Aristegui and in what can be considered a true misstep by de la Madrid, he suggests what happened. He also accused the former president's brother, Raul Salinas de Gortari, of having had links with drug trafficking and of outrageously enriching himself thanks to obtaining contracts from his brother's government. The former president's words provoked a national scandal.

It was the first time a former president of Mexico had expressed a negative opinion about his successor. It also broke an unwritten law in the PRI system that former presidents of Mexico should keep silent, a kind of *Omertá,* and keep a low profile once their term of office was over. Later, suspiciously, former President de la Madrid disavowed his accusations, justifying his own words as a slip of the tongue due to his state of health and advanced age. It was the last interview Miguel de la Madrid would give, and he would die of pulmonary emphysema a few months later. Could it be true what the poet Gabriel Celaya said when he wrote, "When the reckless clear eyes of death look straight ahead, truths are told?"

The issue caused a stir again when Luis Tellez, who served as undersecretary of agriculture during the Salinas administration, corroborated the theft of half of the secret appropriation by the president. He also stated that this act was in addition to many others that hurt the country. The statement came from an illegal recording of Tellez. The media soon broadcast his words. Luis Tellez backtracked and publicly declared that his comments took place during an informal lunch with friends, recorded without his authorization. "The recording is real, although the statement about Salinas is improper." Like former President de la Madrid, Luis Tellez distanced himself from his accusations against Salinas de Gortari, claiming to have no evidence on his part about the former president's illicit actions.

The fate of Raul Salinas is the other side of the coin from a give-and-take in which each accusation lacks support and evidence. Without the same capacity for retaliation, he was accused of illicit enrichment and influence peddling, among other charges, during Ernesto Zedillo's administration (1994–2000). His luck came crashing down when he was accused of being the mastermind behind the murder of his brother-in-law Jose Francisco Ruiz Massieu, secretary general of the PRI, on September 28, 1994. Carlos Salinas de Gortari was cleared of suspicion of corruption and illicit activities, but his close associates, including his brother, paid for his transgressions. While Carlos Salinas lived in exile in Europe, Raul Salinas spent ten years in the maximum-security prison of Almoloya.

Another character who cannot escape these exposés is Enrique Peña Nieto, protagonist of several corruption and influence-peddling scandals, which to this day continue to come to light.

In 2014, Carmen Aristegui's investigative team revealed that President Peña Nieto's wife, a former soap opera actress, owned a mansion worth approximately $8 million. The matter became even more complicated when it became known that a government contractor had gifted the house. The conflict of interest was evident. Angelica Rivera, Peña Nieto's wife, published a video explaining the origin of what the media was already calling "Peña Nieto's white house," although very few people believed those explanations. After his wife was thrown into the lion's den, Enrique Peña Nieto apologized to the nation, stating that the troubled mansion no longer belonged to Angelica Rivera or anyone in her family.

In 2016, representatives of the construction company Odebrecht were accused by US authorities of paying $10.5 million in bribes to officials of a government-controlled company in the state of Mexico, Peña Nieto's home state. The disbursements happened between 2013 and 2014 to secure and obtain contracts for public works and infrastructure. When the identities of the Mexican company and the officials involved in the bribery were revealed, the name of Emilio Lozoya, former director of PEMEX, came as a surprise.

The case escalated in the media. After the testimony of several officials, Odebrecht was banned and fined up to 1.2 billion pesos. Despite this, Peña Nieto's government did not show much interest in cleaning up its own corruption scandals, hoping that public opinion would eventually forget about the issue.

When Lopez Obrador took office in 2018, the case was taken up again. A year later, the head of the Attorney General's Office (FGR, for the acronym in Spanish), Alejandro Gertz Manero, decided to dive into the case. Emilio Lozoya was arrested in Spain and extradited to Mexico in 2020 after being a fugitive from justice for several months. His status was that of a protected witness, since Lozoya sought to avoid going to jail in exchange for his testimony. This would have meant valuable information to go after other higher-ranking public officials involved in the case, including members of Peña Nieto's close circle such as former treasury secretary Luis Videgaray. However, when the former director of PEMEX did not provide the valuable evidence he claimed to have, leaving the prosecutor waiting like a village bride, the Attorney General's Office lost patience. Everything blew up when photographs were taken of Emilio Lozoya dining in a luxury restaurant when he was supposed to be under house arrest. Lozoya's frivolity infuriated the prosecutor, Gertz Manero, and it was not long before the former PEMEX director began sleeping in jail at last, from where he continues his trial. Today, the courts are still resolving this case.

Another corruption scandal during the Peña Nieto administration was the so-called Estafa Maestra (Master Swindle; the name of a journalistic investigation by a Mexico news portal). It is alleged that at least ten federal agencies diverted public funds in an amount of around $400 million.

Government agencies such as the Ministry of Social Development (Sedesol, for the acronym in Spanish), PEMEX, and the Ministry of Agrarian and Urban Development (Sedatu, for the acronym in Spanish) were involved, among many others. These institutions made agreements with public institutions and universities, which in turn made agreements with other companies, and so on. In this sort of chain, the money trail passed from hand to hand and was very well hidden. Up to ten companies were involved in a single agreement, to give an idea of the extent of corruption, looting, and embezzlement of public resources.

In this game, the universities were intermediaries and received their payments. The misconduct surfaces when it is discovered that there is an irregularity both in the fiscal domiciles of the companies and of their owners. The companies exist on paper, but their addresses are vacant lots or houses; the owners are homemakers or fronts who knew nothing about the illegalities. In addition, the heads of the government agencies never signed any of the agreements; mid-level officials signed them.

So far, only Rosario Robles, former head of Sedesol and Sedatu, was in jail due to her direct involvement in the *Estafa Maestra*. The rest of the officials are suspended, and only a few face criminal proceedings.

To this gallery of dishonor, we can add the case of Ayotzinapa. This incident provoked nationwide outrage because of governmental impunity. On September 26, 2014, in the small town of Iguala, Guerrero, municipal police kidnapped a group of students from the Isidro Burgos Normal School, as it was believed the students had plans to ruin an event featuring the mayor's wife, who had ties to criminal groups. It is said that the police themselves handed the students over to hit men from a local drug cartel and that they caused the Ayotzinapa students' disappearance by burning their remains in the Cocula landfill. Despite the seriousness of the case, the Peña Nieto government was unable to find out what had happened and where the missing students were. The entire country demanded to know their whereabouts, yet an investigation full of contradictions, irregularities, and even torture was carried out, which has affected the due process of hundreds of people detained for this case. To this day, it has not been possible to learn the truth or find the remains of all the students, to bring some sense of closure to their families.

Finally, Enrique Peña Nieto is accused of being part of the Atlacomulco Group, whose great heretic is the politician Carlos Hank Gonzalez. In what is the height of cynicism, Carlos Hank Gonzalez has confirmed corruption in the country, declaring, "A poor (bad) politician is a poor (broke) politician." From his wisdom, we can also rescue the following phrase: "Morality is a tree that bears no fruit." Although its own members deny the existence of the group, it is said to be made up of Mexican politicians who are members of the PRI in the state of Mexico.

In light of these recent accounts of corruption and impunity, the government of Mexico has a responsibility and an enormous challenge to shape a new image for the country—and to completely banish, once and for all, the damned corruption.

American Crime

The subject of crime in the United States is often related to serial killers, largely because of film and television. Just look at how much content has been made about Charles Manson, Ted Bundy, or the

Zodiac Killer. Serial killers attract audiences eager for scary movies and strong emotions, their names becoming almost as familiar as instant soups, although it is not known if they are just as dangerous. However, for now, we will focus on crimes in the United States committed for the purpose of getting rich. Our starting point will be the New York Mafia, which reached its peak during Prohibition and then diversified its business to stay in power.

The term *Mafia* refers to any criminal organization that achieves a monopoly on activities in a given locality. Its methods include violence and crime. The difference between cartel and Mafia is simply the name. In Mexico and South America, organized crime groups dedicated mainly to drug trafficking are known as cartels, but in the rest of the world, they are called Mafias. You can find the Italian Mafia in Europe, the Chinese Triads in Asia, the Yakuza in Japan, and the Mara Salvatrucha in Central America, and many others around the world. The Mafia, like the cartels, engages in illegal activities from which they acquire profits. The Mafia is known for trying to do "legitimate" business with dirty money; lately, the cartels are trying to copy this model, which we will see below.

The New York Mafia is the most successful criminal organization in the United States. The backbone of its foundation was based on five families: Genovese, Colombo, Gambino, Lucchese, and Bonano. It is worth taking a step back in history.

During the last decades of the nineteenth century, thousands of immigrants from Europe arrived on the shores of New York. Among them were members of these five families, who dreamed of their illicit business prospering in the United States. Once they saw how things worked, they understood that there was a difference with Italy. Let's not forget that these families come from Sicily, where the Mafia was known as the Cosa Nostra.

Of course, there was already crime in the United States before the arrival of the Mafia, mostly robberies, murders, and extortion. Famous criminals were Jesse James, an outlaw of the Old West and member of the James-Younger gang, compared to the fictional Robin Hood, murdered after a betrayal. Or Kate Barker—known as

Ma Barker—a legendary criminal from the so-called public enemy era, when the press followed the exploits of Midwestern gangs.

Once the Italian Mafia gets settled in the United States, it progresses from small local crimes to a larger scale. Later, it sets up an organizational system in which its members see themselves as entrepreneurs and businessmen. They can operate openly in Italy, but in the United States, they do not have that same freedom. Consequently, they diversify their business. They begin by offering protection to their own compatriots, recently arrived in the port city; the paradox is that this protection is against their own selves. To put it another way: "Pay me to protect you from me."

As the Mafia's economic position and reputation grows in Little Italy—a neighborhood in the south of Manhattan where most of the Italian community settles—it begins its territorial expansion. This forces them to add more members to be able to control their domain. The Italian Mafia ends up dominating a large percentage of the activities carried out in New York.

Let's take a look at their activities. They are involved in everything from garbage collection to charging commissions for construction of public works. They are so involved in local business that if anyone wishes to carry out any economic activity, successfully and unopposed, they must first go to the Mafia and pay the corresponding fee.

These Mafia families have judges, policemen, detectives, politicians, and all kinds of public workers in their pockets. If any of their members are jailed, they continue their criminal activities from prison without any problems. Of course, witnesses who appear in court are pressured to keep their mouths shut. That's the equation: going against the Mafia means signing your own death warrant.

When Prohibition goes into effect in the United States on January 17, 1920, following an amendment to the country's Constitution, the Mafia families exploit this opportunity by selling liquor illegally. These are the Mafia's best years, especially for Al Capone, the infamous American gangster. Capone did not belong to any of the founding families of the Italian Mafia in New York, but he still became the most important bootlegger in the whole country during Prohibition.

The profitability of this business preceded the sale of drugs, which would later trigger a phenomenon of addiction in the country. But let's follow Al Capone's dirty business, up to the moment of his arrest and death.

Unlike the immigrants and founders of the Italian American Mafia, Al Capone was born in Brooklyn in 1899 of Italian parents. This gives him an advantage; he knows how both the US market and the Mafia system operates. We are with Al Capone when Prohibition goes into effect. He is a young man of barely twenty-one, ambitious, with a singular astuteness that will help him shine in the world of crime.

Shortly before the enactment of Prohibition, his first steps as a criminal begin in Brooklyn. An opportunity presents itself to him, and he doesn't waste it. Everything will change when the boss of his gang entrusts him with his business in the city of Chicago. Here begins the legend of Al Capone.

Skilled at mingling in diverse social circles, Al Capone presents himself as an honorable and successful businessman. Charismatic and smiling, we are with this mobster as he hands out his business cards at an elegant cocktail party attended by actors and singers. Journalists take pictures of him, which later appear on the covers of magazines. Such a socially engaging demeanor makes him one of the in crowd.

But Capone's smile would not remain fixed forever. When the new mayor of Chicago takes office, he reveals that his intention is to put an end to the Mafia and gangs in the city. Al Capone, once again, demonstrates his criminal prowess as he moves his center of operations to the outskirts of the city. It doesn't stop there. Once again, we witness Capone in action, but this time, it is not at a gala cocktail party. The Mafia leader is mourning the death of his brother, resulting from violent clashes his organization is having with the police. Subsequently, Al Capone unleashes terror on the city, turning it into a war zone. Under the maxim "shoot first and ask questions later," the violence reaches its peak with the St. Valentine's Day

Massacre. On February 14, 1929, Al Capone, instead of spending the day with his sweetheart, ordered the execution of five members of the rival North Side Gang. Al Capone's men, disguised as policemen, faked a raid in which they placed their enemies against the wall and then executed them with their tommy guns.

The St. Valentine's Day Massacre caused furor and outrage across the entire country as Al Capone took over the city through crime and terror. His notorious reputation grabbed the spotlight, and he became wanted by the US government. President Herbert Hoover himself ordered the secretary of the treasury, Eliot Ness, to put an end to Capone's reign.

A determined Eliot Ness begins his mission and immediately faces several obstacles. Chief among these is corruption in Chicago. Al Capone has most of the city's police officers, judges, and detectives in his pocket. Consequently, Ness assembles an incorruptible team, which will become known as the Untouchables.

Eliot Ness and the Untouchables look for any pretext to catch Capone. They have a hard time apprehending him in spite of multiple crimes including murder, bribery, and illegal liquor sales. Without any documents linking his name to his earnings, they cannot prove his guilt. And unlike some Mexican police, the Untouchables dare not plant false evidence on Al Capone to incriminate him. Ironically, the long-awaited arrest will be for a token crime. Again, we accompany Al Capone at the moment he is arrested for carrying an unregistered gun; his time in prison is brief, but the blow has been struck.

In 1931, officials seized more than half of his clandestine merchandise; they also shut down many of his places of business. Worse, the Untouchables and the IRS discovered Capone's Achilles' heel: tax evasion. Only then could they catch him. On October 17, 1931, a jury found Al Capone guilty of the crimes charged, and he was sentenced to eleven years in prison. Unfortunately, the mass killings he ordered, his extortions and robberies, and so many other crimes he committed remained unpunished. After spending some time in Alcatraz prison, Al Capone was released in 1939 for health reasons since he was suffering from dementia caused by untreated syphilis. Sick, ruined, and without the power that his empire in Chicago once had, he died in Miami, Florida, on January 21, 1947, from pneumonia. His death was an exception in the underworld; the notorious gangster did not die by gunfire, despite having killed with a gun numerous times.

With the repeal of Prohibition, Joseph P. Kennedy (1888–1969) acquired the rights to import Scotch whiskey, thus creating a vast network of multimillion-dollar investments. As for Al Capone's conviction of income tax evasion through money laundering, this is a charge leveled in an infinite number of cases both in Mexico and in the United States. With respect to Mexico, many of its politicians are accused of this illicit practice, but the law is applied to few because of the difficulty in following the trail of their operations.

As for the United States, although it cannot be described as a tax haven, unethical investors can still use the system to gain benefits, guarantees, and rewards. For example, if a drug trafficker or criminal wishes to acquire goods or businesses legally, but without proving the origin of their income, the solution is in the real estate market. An ethical and honest person could face obstacles and complications to investing their "clean" money.

Let's go to Miami, where the real estate market has grown exponentially overnight. Tourists, including many foreigners, arrive, enjoy the sun and beaches, and then return home. In this city of pleasure, some foreigners, not all, hide an illegal agenda for business in their travel plans. They land in Miami, their wallets stuffed with cash that cannot be used to purchase large houses or exotic cars in their own countries. The magic formula, a simple but effective tax strategy, is to launder money by using funds for real estate projects. Once these projects are completed, each investor makes a hefty profit. In return, the profit is clean money with no problem to use. Such is the success of this method that it is still as popular as buying and selling gold.

On this point, we take a short detour. The gold business proceeds as follows: a group of illegal mines, mainly from Peru, send their gold production to companies in the United States. These are usually fronts, which then offer it to the highest bidder. The transaction results in millions of dollars of profit even though the illegal gold is paid well below market value. The chain continues. After the sale to companies, and even to the US government, legal money is obtained, cleaner than the air after a good rain.

In 2017, controversy broke out among a group of businessmen who used the gold method to launder millions of dollars. Samer Barrage and Juan Granda, both in their thirties, went a little too far and laundered $3.6 billion that came from selling gold extracted from illegal mines in Peru. This dirty gold was sold in Miami using front companies to make the operations look legitimate. The US government intervened in the matter since illegally extracted gold still belongs to the country of origin—in this case Peru, although other South American countries were also victims of this plunder. The money earned from the sale of the gold was used to finance drug traffickers.

Some of the legal proceedings against the criminal groups involved in this type of illicit activity have already concluded, and others are still awaiting a slap on the wrist from justice. Whether they are Mafia families, gangsters, or capos, they make their fortune and increase it in the United States through illegal means—either partially or totally—but don't tell anyone that I told you all this.

Drug Traffic in Mexico

Every human being has cancer cells, and the organism oversees eliminating them every day. A healthy country is like a healthy human being that is destroying its cancers. The terrible thing is when the cancerous cells do not fight each other and join, forming a malignant tumor. The drug trafficking tumor first emerged in the United States, which has had several throughout its history. It has managed to remove some and survive. The opposite is true for its southern neighbor. Drug trafficking and violence have formed the cancer that has most damaged Mexico.

Mexico has not been spared from suffering the scourge of the war on drugs. Over the past two decades, drug trafficking has become one of the biggest problems for both government and society. The trafficking of illegal drugs in Mexico brings with it myriad other illicit activities, including fuel theft, human trafficking, migrant smuggling, extortion, and kidnapping. The growth of criminal groups poses challenges that both the US and Mexico share since organized drug crime crosses borders and is linked to circles of power and connected with decision makers across the social spectrum—politicians, military, and businesspeople.

Drug cartels have great economic capacity and territorial positioning, and they grow and dispute control of the different states where they operate. Unfortunately, this happens through truly horrifying violence. Tabloid journalism has exploited this violence in its daily circulation. For now, we leave this aside to focus on the history of this gigantic drug trafficking network, its system of operation, and the pacts of impunity cartels have enjoyed to date.

Arms trafficking and drug distribution and consumption go hand in hand. It is an activity carried out in the shadows, given that it is illegal and returns billions of dollars in profits every year. Among the areas most affected by this activity is Central America, which serves as a bridge between the two front lines of drug trafficking: on the one hand, production in South America and, on the other, its link to consumption in North America. It is a corridor in which Mexico is well positioned, but the United States holds the unenviable first place in global drug consumption.

Let's jump back to the 1970s, when cocaine moved through the Caribbean to the United States. Back then, the dismemberment of the drug cartels in the south took place. This empowered and converted Mexico into the main platform for the production, introduction, and distribution of drugs, filling demand in the United States. Mexico's cartels are quick to implement a plan of action for a multimillion-dollar business involving everything from police chiefs, military zone commanders, and corrupt judges to show business figures.

Marijuana, cocaine, amphetamines, heroin, and other substances are the protagonists of their empowerment.

The horrible nightmare of thousands of murders, kidnappings, robberies, and human rights violations wormed its way into the government itself. In the 1970s, the intersection of the Dirty War and the rise of organized crime involved and helped numerous political and business careers. Many could attest to this, such as the then-governors of Sinaloa, Guerrero, and the state of Mexico.

The worm was left intact, sheltered by corruption and impunity. By 2000, narcos already had the capacity to put the government in check. Although its gestation took place during PRI governments, it was precisely at this time that the PAN took the presidency. But this ideal moment to unravel the origins of organized crime—to break its networks with politicians, security forces, and rulers—was wasted. The frivolity and incapacity of Vicente Fox, who ignored the issue during his six-year term, added to the complex circumstances that his successor, Felipe Calderon, created, worsening even more the country's stability.

During the presidency of Felipe Calderon (2006–2012), his administration confronted cartels that were already in charge of important areas of the country. Drug trafficking was taking place across wide swaths of the country, particularly on the US border. His plan did not work, exposing the general distrust of society toward the government.

Felipe Calderon's strategy against organized crime has been questioned because his war unleashed a wave of savagery that did not exist before. It is a recurrent metaphor that Calderon unconsciously hit a hornet's nest—without thinking that the wasps would defend themselves with fury and violence. More preoccupied with reporting on killings and arrests of cartel members as if they were success figures, Calderon also sought legitimacy following the closest and most questioned presidential election in recent times. With the suspicion of electoral fraud hanging over him, success against the cartels would give him the legitimacy he craved. Unfortunately for

Mexico, this plunged the country into a war from which, a decade later, it has not been able to emerge.

Corruption has permeated every six-year presidential term. Government leaders and high-ranking officials have taken advantage of their brief stays in power to benefit themselves, with no regard for society. The diversion of public funds to personal interests overrides any agenda priorities—such as national security—and ends up helping organized crime.

While we follow the shared history between Mexico and the United States, the topic of the cartels brings us to a singular figure: the subject of numerous films, songs, and television series.

Terrorist, drug trafficker, politician, and businessman, Pablo Escobar was born into a campesino family in Rionegro, and from an early age, he demonstrates his other abilities. Determined and aggressive in purpose, Pablo Escobar founds the Medellin Cartel, skilled in the production, distribution, and sale of cocaine to the international market. His business thrives like no other. We look in on him as he makes a toast to his henchmen—a team of experienced criminal professionals, just as bloodthirsty as their boss—and to the successful Medellin Cartel that supplies cocaine to the Mexican and US markets; its distribution network operates in 80 percent of the world.

While most capos kept a low profile for their own survival, Pablo Escobar opted for the public stage and the spotlight, reminiscent of the gangster Al Capone. When he was powerfully positioned in Colombia, he decided to enter politics and run for Congress, with resounding failure. But this setback did not stop the immense fortune that the drug trafficker amassed thanks to cocaine.

The Colombian government decides to confront him head-on. The war between Colombia and the Medellin Cartel is unleashed. An extremely astute man, Pablo Escobar surrenders to the authorities to calm the waters in exchange for not being extradited to the United States. The small detail is that the prison is completely his. He had it built himself. Instead of serving his sentence in a state-run prison, Pablo Escobar is confined to "La Catedral," where he enjoys parties, women, and other privileges and freely operates his criminal business. So many excesses inside La Catedral do not go unnoticed, and instead of being considered a maximum-security prison, it became known as a maximum-comfort prison.

After staying there for a year, Escobar learns that he is to be transferred to a real prison, and he decides to escape from La Catedral along with some of his lieutenants. The government once again launches a manhunt for him—with the support of the Colombian National Police Special Operations. Finally, after a long time on the run, living hand to mouth and unable to use his millions of dollars, Pablo Escobar was killed at the hands of the Colombian justice system on December 2, 1993—dead without honor or glory on one of the many rooftops of Medellin.

Colombia and the world celebrated the fall of Pablo Escobar. One less capo. But if the drug business proves anything, it's that it is a hydra that regenerates the heads that are cut off. The king is dead; long live the king. Miguel Angel Felix Gallardo, who was born in 1946 in Culiacan, Sinaloa, proves this. This man worked as a policeman, but he found meaning to his life in drug trafficking. With great organizational abilities, he manages to unite the cartels that control the drug business in Mexico. In return, he is baptized "El Jefe de Jefes" (the Boss of Bosses). His fame and recognition earn him a *corrido*, popularized by the group Los Tigres del Norte, which is a hit nationwide.

Demonstrating his skills in the marijuana business, Felix Gallardo is the first to lead what becomes called a drug cartel. Under his leadership, the main drug distributors in the country apply to join. He decides to base himself in the capital of the state of Jalisco, with his Guadalajara Cartel. From there, he coordinates the operations of a criminal group that includes high-caliber capos such as Rafael Caro Quintero, Ernesto Fonseca, Amado Carrillo Fuentes—better known as El Señor de los Cielos (the Lord of the Skies)—and Joaquin "El Chapo" Guzman.

Although his operations began with marijuana, the Boss of Bosses later shifted to distributing the drugs that Pablo Escobar and other cartels shipped from Colombia. In order to disguise his illicit trade network, he diversifies his income and expands into legal businesses.

Among the narcos who collaborate with him is Rafael Caro Quintero, a native of Badiraguato, Sinaloa, born in 1952, also known as the "Narco of Narcos." Together with Felix Gallardo and Ernesto Fonseca, he founded the Guadalajara Cartel. Caro Quintero's trajectory is characterized by drug cultivation (he was a farmer before becoming involved in crime) and a crucial murder attributed to him, which accelerated his downfall.

The crime in question is the murder of Enrique Camarena, a DEA agent working in Mexico. In the United States, this affront was unforgivable and provoked a diplomatic crisis between the two countries. In the DEA's logic, the corruption of the Mexican political system allowed someone like Rafael Caro Quintero to torture and kill the U.S. agent in retaliation for the destruction of thousands of marijuana fields at the El Búfalo ranch. As a result, the DEA placed Rafael Caro Quintero among the most wanted criminals. This brought problems to his cartel.

The DEA launched Operation Leyenda. Since they did not trust the Mexican authorities, they undertook the illegal arrest of several suspects. The first was Dr. Humberto Alvarez Machain, who was in charge of keeping Enrique Camarena alive so that his executioners could continue torturing him. The doctor was arrested and taken to El Paso, Texas, prompting the Mexican government to accuse the United States of kidnapping and violating extradition treaties. Rubén Zuno Arce, brother-in-law of former President Luis Echeverría, was also arrested. Zuno Arce was accused of owning the house where Camarena died. Not even all the influence of former President Echeverría was enough to get his brother-in-law out of jail. Sentenced to life imprisonment, Zuno Arce was imprisoned for 23 years in the United States, and died behind bars always claiming his presumed innocence.

Caro Quintero was arrested, although he was never extradited to the United States. In yet another example of the corruption unleashed by drug trafficking, on August 9, 2013, Rafael Caro Quintero was suspiciously released by a judge after obtaining an injunction from the federal justice system. The longtime drug trafficker walked out of prison on his own two feet, and when authorities tried to remedy the mistake and arrest him again, Caro Quintero had already disappeared, ready to resume the criminal business he had left pending.

And as the saying goes, there is no deadline that is not met and no debt that is not paid. Almost four decades after Camarena's death, Caro Quintero fell again. Long gone were the days when Caro Quintero offered to pay the national foreign debt in exchange for his freedom. Located in the tangled Sinaloa highlands, the Mexican Navy went after the drug trafficker. Among so many thickets, Caro Quintero was located thanks to a Navy-trained dog, which sniffed out his guilt from a great distance. The second arrest of Rafael Caro Quintero was a much-applauded triumph for the government of Andrés Manuel López Obrador. Sadly, it was not all celebration. During the operation, a Navy helicopter crashed, killing fourteen soldiers who had participated in the capture of the so-called "Narco of narcos", who is now in prison, awaiting his possible extradition to the United States.

And history repeats itself: one falls, but another one comes along, equally or more qualified for the job. Amado Carrillo Fuentes, Don Neto's nephew, is known as the "Lord of the Skies" because he pilots and manages a fleet of airplanes, including a Boeing 727. Drugs are his only cargo; he even moves his cargo on commercial airplanes. He is initiated into the business under the supervision of his uncle Don Neto, but he later earns his own position and even surpasses his tutor. The Señor de los Cielos becomes the leader of the Juarez Cartel after overthrowing his boss, Rafa A. Guajardo. After the fall of his uncle and the imprisonment of Caro Quintero and Felix Gallardo, luck is on his side—as well as the countless clouds that accompany him on his clandestine airplane trips.

With the drug operation in his hands, Carrillo Fuentes partners with Pablo Escobar to get merchandise to the United States. Later, after the fall of the Colombian drug lord, the Señor de los Cielos will become the most wanted criminal in Argentina, Colombia, the United States, and Mexico.

With an appropriation exclusively for bribes to high-level officials, it is estimated that the Señor de los Cielos had a modest annual income of $25 billion. Unlike the Colombian capo, Amado Carrillo avoids the public spotlight and is discreet. He undergoes plastic surgery in an attempt to change his facial physiognomy and go incognito for the rest of his days. But there's many a slip twixt the cup and the lip. El Señor de los Cielos dies in the operating room, under suspicious circumstances, at the age of forty-one.

Joaquin "El Chapo" Guzman is probably the most famous Mexican drug trafficker. He was extradited to the United States in 2017, after escaping twice from maximum-security prisons in Mexico. He is currently serving a life sentence in the dreaded ADX Florence Penitentiary in Colorado. Joaquin Guzman Loera was born, like other capos, in Badiraguato, Sinaloa, in 1954. He was the leader of the Sinaloa Cartel along with Ismael El Mayo Zambada.

Unlike the Señor de los Cielos, El Chapo trafficked his merchandise through clandestine tunnels to the United States. His area of influence included the northern and southern border areas of Mexico. In 1993, he was imprisoned in Guatemala after being wanted for the accidental death of Cardinal Juan Jesus Posadas at the Guadalajara airport. Once captured, El Chapo was handed over to the Mexican government. He escaped from Puente Grande prison in 2001, and it has been speculated that some public officials intervened in his favor due to the simplicity of the escape since El Chapo apparently escaped from Puente Grande hiding in a laundry cart. Once free, Joaquin Guzman became the most powerful drug lord in the country, with worldwide recognition. Like many other criminals in the business, his wallet bought the silence of politicians in exchange for his well-being.

El Chapo Guzman had virtually no competition in Mexico. He set up his center of operations in Sinaloa, where the people appreciate him. When a reward is offered to anyone who informs on his whereabouts, the appeal is in vain. After the death of Osama

Bin Laden in 2011, El Chapo Guzman became number one on the FBI's most-wanted list. For many, there is no reward worth handing over Mexico's drug kingpin.

In 2014, an elite group of Mexican marines conducted a raid on an apartment building in Mazatlan, Sinaloa. Stealthily, the marines positioned themselves outside Guzman Loera's door during the early hours of the morning, and without waking the neighbors, they managed to arrest the most-wanted man in the world without firing a single shot. El Chapo Guzman was transferred to a maximum-security prison in the state of Mexico, the Almoloya prison, which was presumed to be the most secure and impenetrable penitentiary in the country. The Peña Nieto government's celebration of his capture lasted only a year. The capo, once again mocking the justice system, escaped from Almoloya through a tunnel a kilometer long that led from his own cell, which his people had built without anyone realizing.

The government of Enrique Peña Nieto admits its ineptitude in complete humiliation. In an interview given to journalist Leon Krauze months before the escape, President Peña Nieto had recognized that an eventual escape by Guzman Loera would be an unforgivable affront. But in addition to errors, it was evident that corruption existed in the upper echelons of power, making it easier for the drug trafficker to flee.

Months passed, and the priority of Mexican security agencies was to find El Chapo. In 2016, for the third time, his recapture was announced, but this time, there was no peaceful arrest. Navy Special Forces confronted El Chapo's hit men at a house in Los Mochis, Sinaloa, sparking a heavy shootout. El Chapo managed to escape from the house, again using a tunnel built under a bathtub. Guzman Loera ran through the city's sewage system until he emerged through a manhole.

Together with one of his lieutenants, they robbed a woman's car at gunpoint and fled in panic. But as Ruben Blades sings: "Life gives you surprises—surprises give you life." The lady reported the theft of her vehicle, and a federal police patrol car stopped them on the highway, unaware that the officers were detaining Chapo Guzman himself. The security forces had already given him up for lost when they received the miraculous call.

Mexico's president again celebrated the recapture, hoping that the embarrassment of the escape from Almoloya would be forgotten. Given Guzman's history of prison escapes, he was promptly approved for extradition to the United States, where charges awaited him in seven states. The trial against the kingpin was held in November 2018, in Brooklyn Federal Court. He was found guilty of all charges and sentenced to spend life in prison in the middle of the Colorado desert, with no privileges, no sunlight, no dreams, and no power. And with the king dead, long live the king; Chapo Guzman was succeeded by his sons to control the Sinaloa Cartel.

At this point, it is important to identify the presence of cartels during each six-year presidential term of government. During the period of Vicente Fox, the Sinaloa and Gulf criminal group dominated. During Felipe Calderon's turn in office, a new cartel called Los Zetas, based in the northern part of the country, was on top. Before the emergence of this crime group, its members had been part of the Gulf Cartel. The founding members of Los Zetas were former elite military personnel belonging to the Special Forces Airmobile Group, the GAFES (for the acronym in Spanish). After deserting from the Mexican military, they sold their loyalty, knowledge, and violence to the Gulf Cartel as bodyguards to its then-leader, Osiel Cardenas Guillen. When they decided to go their own way, Los Zetas applied unprecedented methods of cruelty, such as beheading enemies and dismembering bodies, causing violence to reach levels never seen before during the six-year term of Felipe Calderon.

The situation becomes even more complicated when a breakaway group from Los Zetas relocates to Michoacan, President Calderon's home state, and a turf war breaks out. Los Zetas changed the traditional business scheme of the cartels. In addition to the sale and distribution of drugs, they expanded their range of activities to other criminal pursuits, drawing attention to the authorities' incompetence, corruption, and lack of control. During the Calderon administration, Nuevo Leon, Tamaulipas, and Coahuila became true war zones, in addition to Michoacan.

Los Zetas did not hesitate to apply the policy of terror, without differentiating between rivals, government, and civilian population. They migrated from drugs to kidnapping, plus the collection of extortion fees from businesses, with a high dose of violence. Because of the training they possessed and their scheme of action, Los Zetas was a criminal group with a penchant for handling high caliber weapons, which they did not hesitate to prove their potency to the Mexican Army and Navy. But being the most violent cartel in Mexico brought consequences to Los Zetas, as they became a priority target of the government for liquidation, if not extermination. They gradually lost power, resources, and presence in states, since in addition to confronting the government, they had to fight for "plazas" with other rival organizations. Today it can be said that Los Zetas as such have disappeared. All their founding members are dead or in prison, and their unworthy place has been taken by other equally or more violent groups, such as the Cartel Jalisco Nueva Generación.

As already mentioned, drug trafficking is a business that can hardly prosper without the participation or complicity of political power. All these drug lords and organizations have counted on the help of some authorities and officials to evade justice in exchange for large sums of money. Such complicities between drug traffickers and members of the government have reached the highest level.

On December 10, 2019, former President Felipe Calderón became suspiciously silent on his social networks. Genaro García Luna, his public security secretary, architect of the war against drug trafficking, had been arrested in the United States, accused of receiving bribes from the Sinaloa Cartel.

Imagine that. After the president, the top security official in the country accused by the United States of being on the payroll of a criminal organization. Apparently, neither Felipe Calderón nor the DEA ever found out about their little angel's antics. And Garcia Luna is not only accused of taking bribes to turn a blind eye, but apparently also conspired to traffic large quantities of cocaine into the United States. There could be no hope for the pacification of the country if the man in charge of fighting criminals was on the enemy's side. The head of Mexico's security apparatus from 2006 to 2012 looking out for the interests of drug traffickers.

The Genaro Garcia Luna trial was held in New York City in the same federal court where El Chapo was tried. In February, 2023, Garcia Luna was found guilty by a jury of all charges he was accused of, and he will probably face a life sentence in an American prison. Many have already put on their raincoats and umbrellas, ready to receive everything that the fan that will be the trial against Genaro García Luna will throw at them.

Mexico is no worse off given that the United States is suffering from a political crisis and rampant fentanyl consumption, which has led to thousands of deaths from overdoses of the substance. Sadly, our numbers of drug addicts are not so disparate in proportion. Mexico first sold drugs to the United States and then developed its domestic market. There is still a long way to go before the problem is completely eradicated, but as Thomas Fuller said, "the darkest hour of the night comes before the dawn". Organized crime violence is the main challenge for Mexico in the coming decades. The United States cannot turn a blind eye to this problem. Both nations buy, sell, and consume the same drugs. Neither the United States is Superman guarding Metropolis nor Mexico is full of Midwestern outlaws. Neither bad Mexicans nor bad Americans. Still, in the solution to this barbarism, the United States has a 30-year head start on Mexico (as on other issues). Their model has been more effective, and if the United States could remove its malignant tumors, so can Mexico.

Arms Trafficking and the Fast and Furious Fiasco

Multinational efforts to curb the production, distribution, and consumption of synthetic drugs is unfinished business, further complicated by the profitability now enjoyed from arms trafficking.

Both drug and arms trafficking are illegal businesses that represent a risk to society in every sense of the word.

On the US–Mexico border, the arms trade proceeds through a criminal network that flows between the two countries. Of all the weapons seized in Mexico, 70 percent come from the United States.

In the United States, the right to easily possess a firearm—be it a pistol or an assault rifle—facilitates their transfer to Mexico. It is a very profitable business in dollars, but at the same time, it negatively impacts society. The figures do not lie. Homicides by long and short weapons have grown 5.2 percent, a trend that started in 2015 and has continued as 2020 figures show. According to the executive secretary of the National Public Security System, 70 percent of the murders committed in Mexico in 2020 will be committed with firearms.

The border between the US and Mexico is rife with corruption and complicity that enables criminal business to prosper. This reveals the government's inability to control a serious problem of illicit trade that has a direct impact on the security of its citizens.

We can appreciate the high demand for weapons from the power struggle among criminal organizations themselves. This is not a peaceful competition; the level of violence demands increasingly powerful weapons to defend territories, eliminate opponents, confront the authorities, control the members of the organization, shoot in the air, show off on social networks, and ensure the fulfillment of transactions.

In clandestine arms trafficking, we have individuals, gangs, human trafficking organizations, and other criminal groups. So far, Mexican authorities have not identified an organization that deals exclusively in arms trafficking in the country, although intermediaries that supply the cartels have been identified.

However, the transfer of arms is not exclusive to the drug cartels. In 1994, a large arsenal entered Mexico, the same year the Zapatista Popular Revolutionary Army of National Liberation (EZLN, for the acronym in Spanish) emerged. The exact number of weapons that entered the country between 1994 and 1996 is unknown, although a statistic from 2007 indicates the seizure of twenty thousand firearms at roadside checkpoints. Mexico is a lucrative market for arms trafficking. Of course, organized crime exploits this business.

According to federal authorities, around fifteen million illegal weapons circulate in the thirty-two Mexican states. All come from the United States and are in the hands of criminals, kidnappers, petty assailants, hit men, and drug traffickers. The manufacturers include Browning, Maju, Ruger, and Smith & Wesson.

Of this group, Smith & Wesson is the leader. It handles more than sixty different types with a range of calibers, models, barrel lengths, and armor alloy—not taking into account the finish since this depends on the needs and requirements of the buyer. Colt, on the other hand, produces around thirty-five versions that meet demand from the law enforcement and security sector.

Ruger is the number-four company in the US weapons industry. It focuses on the manufacture of rifles, shotguns, pistols, silencers, and revolvers. Between 1984 and 2004, it produced more than twenty million firearms. Today, they offer models for sport hunting, target shooting, self-defense, and law enforcement.

Browning designs weapons, cartridges, and mechanisms—as well as automatic and semiautomatic weapons—and it produced the first gas-operated machine gun.

The United States produces weapons, and Mexico consumes them, just as Mexico produces drugs that are consumed in the United States. Give and take. While the US leads global trade in weapons and its laws facilitate their manufacture, Mexican laws are strict on the subject. In spite of the black market in weapons, Mexico actually has a completely legal path to gun ownership. The acquisition of a pistol requires a series of checks as well as documentation from the Ministry of National Defense, which authorizes and validates the carrying of the acquired weapon. Pistols are the most in demand; if the weapon is approved for protection and personal defense purposes, the law allows up to two weapons per household. However, on many occasions, the buyer will opt for an illicit weapon, not so much to skirt the law but because fulfilling the requirements to own are laborious and time-consuming.

Let's go back to 2005. The US government is on alert due to the growing wave of insecurity and violence along its shared border with Mexico. The US Bureau of Alcohol, Tobacco, Firearms, and Explosives (ATF) launched the Gunrunner Initiative. This agency focuses on the investigation and prevention of federal crimes as well as the illegal use, manufacture, or possession of firearms and explosives.

The Gunrunner Initiative led to Operation Fast and Furious, which lasted from 2009 until 2011. The strategy was to introduce traceable or marked weapons of all calibers into Mexican territory, to be sold to Mexican cartels, with the aim of locating mass buyers or leaders of organized crime. At that time, there was no military involved the fight between the Zetas, Gulf, and Sinaloa Cartels.

The Merida Initiative, a US security cooperation program to combat drug trafficking in Mexico, was also part of the effort. Operation Fast and Furious boils down to the arms trade, from Arizona to Mexico, through a controlled crossing; its success involves the identification of networks of links, buyers, and distributors of weapons.

The name Fast and Furious comes from the fact that the buyers are car racers and prefer desert areas, a reference to the successful movie saga. The operation is undertaken without the authorization or knowledge of the Mexican government. Unfortunately for the ATF, man proposes, God disposes, and then the devil comes along and messes everything up. At the end of the day, no criminal networks were identified, and violence on the border was not reduced. Instead, the cartels increased their firepower with the new weaponry; the level of violence, death, and instability in Mexico increased.

More than two thousand weapons were illegally transported and purchased in Mexico because of this failed operation. The scandal only erupted when it was discovered that two assault rifles that had entered Mexico thanks to Fast and Furious were used to assassinate Brian Terry, a US border agent. Both Mexico and the United States promised to apply the full weight of the law and to punish those

340

responsible for this failed operation. As you can imagine, it all came to nothing.

Fast and Furious is a failure that sets a precedent for future strategies, which should not be delayed. One mistake should not discourage action when citizen security is at stake.

If the cartels have achieved greater firepower and are better armed than federal officers or any other police force in Mexico, this must be countered with congruent initiatives that attack the root of the evil, to achieve the longed-for dismantling of organized crime.

It is often said that he who kills the cow is just as guilty as he who catches its leg. U.S. arms manufacturers are not free of sin. It has been proven that millions of weapons are smuggled into Mexico through frontmen, which often end up in the hands of organized crime. Mexico has waged a legal battle against several U.S. gun shops, accusing U.S. arms producers of engaging in practices that facilitate the illegal trafficking of weapons into Mexico. On the other hand, U.S. courts have argued that its gun industry is shielded from the misuse of weapons. Lawsuits have been unsuccessful because of this shielding. Despite this setback, the Mexican Foreign Ministry remains determined to go to court against the gun companies, which of course share responsibility for the crisis of violence in Mexico. The pain and violence that afflict the southern neighbor of the United States must stop.

Joaquín Guzmán Loera, a.k.a. El Chapo.

Alphonse Gabriel Capone, a.k.a. Al Capone.

Chapter 14

Migration: Plurality in Unity

The United States, The World's Melting Pot

I am the son of an American son of Italian and German and English, and of a Mexican with Spanish and French ancestry. The melting pot, or cultural melting pot, is everywhere. In Mexico it occurred on a smaller scale, compared to the United States, which has received millions of Europeans, Indians, and Asians. Mexico received a few thousand people of a few nationalities. The United States received people from all over the planet. If someone stands at the top of the Statue of Liberty, at the very torch, and shouts: Raise your hand if you come from such and such a country, chances are that no nation mentioned will be left without a raised arm.

The United States reflects like no other the melting pot of the entire world. There is no nationality, no country, no ethnic group that has not ended up in the American Union. Mexico had a more limited melting pot, made up of Japan, China, Lebanon, Spain, France, Colombia, Chile, Cuba, Venezuela, and so on. Another difference with its northern neighbor is that in Mexico, immigrants take a long time to take root in their new land. I dare say that, even after many years, few succeed. One reason is that in Mexico there is no Mexican way of life. Nor is there a state policy of forced integration.

In the United States, on the other hand, the newcomer quickly must learn to speak English, sing the national anthem, learn about George Washington's life and get a taste for hamburgers in order to integrate into the American way of life as soon as possible. Not even a decade goes by when they are already part of it. The United States has no official language, and yet not speaking English means giving up the key to opportunities. No matter where you come from, the

344

American way of life is one and everyone must adhere to its mantle, its unwritten rules. First you are American and then all the other nationalities you want. Integration is not full, to the detriment of minorities such as Latinos, Asians, or Africans. By mixing in the melting pot, newcomers contribute to the whole, but are left with little.

Immigrants entering the United States leave behind their foreign status. You can be Russian, but by naturalizing, speaking English and following the American way of life, Russia is left behind to put the United States and its way of life first. Only in this way, under this model, could someone like Arnold Schwarzenegger, born in Austria, become the governor of California years later. Only in this way the son of a Kenyan can be president of the United States.

Naturally, over the years, a melting pot of people of different races and cultures began to develop in the country. What is known as melting pot comes into play, where a heterogeneous society, made up of a mosaic of individuals, becomes over time a homogeneous society, in which cultural differences dissipate and similarities and common characteristics begin to be seen.

African migration, although forced, cruel, and violent, is part of the cultural mix of the United States. It is part of its very essence. Although the term *melting pot* refers to a harmonious and peaceful integration of diverse cultures; in the United States, this process has not been without difficulties. Its biggest problem is the racism that still prevails in a considerable part of the white population, which feels that the arrival of people from different countries around the world endangers the American way of life. For them, so much diversity nullifies the homogeneity that characterized the United States, forgetting that this very diversity—and the willingness to receive it—was what made the country great. That is why the United States was known worldwide as the melting pot *par excellence*; anyone could become a US citizen regardless of their origin, and that mixture of so many races and cultures would form an even stronger identity. The melting pot seeks to be the opposite of racial segregation or the formation of ghettos that separate people by nationalities or skin color. The curious thing is that the same history of the United States has belied the good intentions of its American melting pot; in its territory, there are still ghettos, Chinese, Italian, and Latino neighborhoods, and racism that refuse to disappear. Interracial marriage between whites and African Americans was frowned upon in the United States, even being illegal in several states until 1967.

Mexico has also received migratory flows that have shaped its essence as a nation. If it were a recipe, Mexico is mainly Spanish, with a lot of mixture of various indigenous peoples, a bit of Sephardic, a touch of Lebanese, some Chinese, and a small pinch of Japanese. It also received African influence coming from slaves who arrived centuries ago. As mentioned in a previous chapter, the areas of greatest Afro-Mexican influence are the Costa Chica, in Guerrero, and Jamiltepec, located on the coast of Oaxaca. Afro-Mexicans represent approximately 2 percent of the population, so they do not weigh as much in the Mexican melting pot of cultures. Despite this melting pot, Mexico is not homogeneous. It cannot be said that there is only one Mexico, and this diversity of people is the result of migratory flows that have been received with open arms. Mexico's immense gastronomic variety is the best proof of how the mosaic of cultures arrived to enrich what already existed.

Tijuana and San Diego are the great melting pot of Mexico and the United States. There are even people, gringos, and Mexicans, ochops and pochos, who live and have homes on both sides. In these enormous border cities, the two nationalities mix and create new artistic currents. It is the capital of the Ochop and its culture. Julieta Venegas, one of the most important Mexican singers and songwriters on the world scene, was born there. Born in Long Beach, California, but raised in Tijuana, Julieta Venegas knew how to take the best of the rhythms and sounds of both nations to create her music. Juan Gabriel, Mexico's great idol, lived most of his life in the United States, between Florida and Texas, and passed away on a sad day in August 2016 in Santa Monica, California, during a concert tour in the United States. Although he was born in Parácuaro, Michoacán, and was formed in Ciudad Juárez with hits such as El Noa Noa, Juan

Gabriel found much of his inspiration on the other side of the Rio Bravo. After all, sadness and tenderness also exist there. Other cities where interesting cultural mixtures are being formed are El Paso and Ciudad Juarez, reflected in Tex–Mex. Food, music, language, painting, writing, ideas, and beliefs are mixed. They are no longer pochos, gringos, or Mexicans. Perhaps, without knowing it, they identify themselves as ochops.

The family of one of my uncles is named Katula and they come from Iraq, but they emigrated to Lebanon and from there they came to Mexico. From Mexico, half of the Katula family moved to California, the other half stayed in the states of San Luis Potosi and Guanajuato. Despite arriving in Mexico, the family split up to stay in two neighboring countries. There are thousands of similar stories, involving people from all over the world, where half of the family is in Mexico and the other half in the United States. For example, during World War II, Mexico received many exiles from Poland, and of those many, very few Poles stayed in Mexico.

The United States was key in my birth but not in my education. Thanks to my father, I got to know the culture and history of that country since I was a child. My parents sent me there several times to attend summer camps, where I took courses in magic, acting, tap and jazz. Although I was young, I knew a lot about the history of Mexico and the United States. Many ideas swirled around in my head. Instead of behaving like a normal child, I questioned myself about the disparity between Mexico and the United States, if between the Thirteen Colonies and New Spain there was not such a difference during the colonial era. I understood that it was normal for the two countries to eventually become unequal, but why was the disproportion so great? I compared the National Palace with what was the White House, or downtown Mexico City with downtown Dallas, and I wondered what had happened. I read and researched. And instead of finding answers, I had more and more doubts.

In Mexico I am a Mexican who looks like an American, and in the United States I am a Mexican who was born in California. Because of this condition, on a few occasions I felt discriminated. In Mexico

I was called a *gringuito* and a CIA spy, even though I knew the history of the country better and I was more polite than my slanderers. In the United States, at summer camps, the same thing happened, even though my last name sounded un-Mexican. My performance was not homogeneous to the American way of life because I was not raised that way, even though I had an American father. They told me: "You are a foreigner, but I don't know where you come from". They didn't like my accent, and when they identified me as Mexican, they discriminated me, although I was as *güero* as they were.

My first experiences in the United States were not very pleasant. And for a change, even in the summer camps I suffered discrimination. Where do I fit in, I asked myself, where do I fit in? I didn't identify with the Latino, the Mexican American or pocho, nor with the redneck American, and despite living with diverse people who were part of the cultural melting pot, I didn't have a full identity with any group. It took me more than forty years to realize that what I am is an ochop, a pocho in reverse.

Then came the culturalization of the world, which makes people's place of origin less evident and important in the 21st century. What is valuable is no longer where you come from, but where you are going. But in 1970, this question was important. In Leon, Guanajuato, there were very few foreigners and binationals. In the United States, migrants were found in the countryside, not so much in the cities or in the circles where we lived.

The summer camps in the United States were the melting pot, and in that pot, I stayed with a Japanese classmate who spoke little English and no Spanish. We practically became friends on a first-name basis. Even so, within the segregation I identified more with that Japanese boy than with my American and Latino classmates. For some I was too Mexican, for others I was not very American.

Slavery was abolished in the United States in 1865, but this does not mean the disappearance of racial problems in the nation. The United States is the result of an integration of cultures from all over the world, of people who came to the promised land seeking to build, to contribute, to excel, to create something better. Would the slave traders have imagined that from some group of people kidnapped in Africa, there would be the ancestry of the first black president of the United States? Would the child who on the boat constantly asked his mother about his destiny, in the middle of the loneliness of the ocean, have imagined it? Barack Obama, son of a Kenyan economist and an American anthropologist, is an excellent example of the wonders of the melting pot.

Chinese: The First Migration Flow Stopped by the United States

In 1850, California was annexed to the United States. After overstepping its boundaries with Mexico and taking away a good part of its territory, the US was beginning to dominate in the international arena. After their first trade treaty with China, the United States turned around and backed the British Empire in the Second Opium War. In exchange, the US obtained cheap labor to build one of the nation's most ambitious projects: a transcontinental railroad linking to California. Forced by defeat, the Qing dynasty sent poor farmers, who were paid a pittance, to work as laborers. This triggered the mass migration of Chinese to the United States. Also, as a consequence of the opium wars, the Chinese Empire handed over Hong Kong to Great Britain.

By 1779, the population of China had reached 275 million inhabitants; by 1850, it had grown to 430 million. This increase was accompanied by a shortage of rice in densely populated provinces, such as Fujian and Guangdong. The Qing dynasty was weakened by the opium wars against England and its allies. Between 1850 and 1864, it also faced the Taiping rebellion, which was brought on by internal social strife.

In accordance with their religious principles, the Taiping people demanded the acceptance of puritanical norms of conduct, equal distribution as a result of effort, and communal work of the land. In this state of crisis, with migration and trade already open with the West, Asians began to leave, attracted by California gold fever, which started around 1848.

California enters the Union as a free state, free of slavery. It needs workers for its mines; after the first influx of labor thanks to the opium deal, the mining companies hire migrants from Asia, conditioned on loans that pay for their relocation. Repayment is from the earnings obtained in the United States. Under these arrangements, workers have no annual contracts. Chinese merchant associations in San Francisco and charitable associations mediate the agreements. In exchange for the workers' safe conduct, their wages are administered by employers or accountants, and they withhold their salaries to pay back the loans. Any worker who wishes to return to China needs a certificate that corroborates that the debt has been repaid. This is the responsibility of the Pacific Steam and Mail Company, which has a monopoly on passenger transportation from Asia.

Most of the Chinese who arrived by ship to California are faced with a reality different from what they expected; the California mountain of gold is an illusion. Mining production is not stable. The gold mines are full of disappointed prospectors, work is very scarce, and newly arrived immigrants barely make enough to eat. In the urban areas, hostility toward foreigners is evident. Inside the mines, the discontent translates to violence. White workers want to expel the Asians, and they do so in Yuba County in Northern California and Columbia County, in the state's south. Under these circumstances, during the 1860s, the Chinese community grows slowly. According to the national census, there were thirty-five thousand Chinese, although some estimates say there were forty-seven thousand.

The situation is one of six of one, half a dozen of the other. The Asian community in California finds new opportunities in the cotton and wheat fields of Alameda, Fresno, Sacramento, and Santa Clara—as well as in the shoe, tobacco, cotton, and cigar industries. Their activity expands into commerce, laundry service, and domestic work. Their excellent cuisine earns the respect of even those who despise them, which gives them an additional advantage.

With an ability to adapt and survive, Chinese communities settle in California and soon make their presence felt in Chicago and New York. Initially concentrated on the outskirts of the mining districts, they later become established in specific urban areas, which eventually come to be called Chinatowns. These areas embody their culture; they preserve their language and replicate their business activities, enabling them to cope with discrimination. During this period, communities are mainly comprised of men who have left their families behind in China.

During the nineteenth century, the Chinese community aimed for economic prosperity in the United States. At the same time, unfortunately, animosity toward them in the mining regions grew. It was even said, somewhat absurdly, that because the Chinese accepted the humiliation of being exploited in undignified working conditions, they should be excluded from the country.

October 1871 was an infamous date in the history of racial discrimination in the United States. A crowd of approximately five hundred whites and Hispanics entered Chinatown in Los Angeles and murdered and robbed its residents. The death toll was somewhere between seventeen and twenty Chinese immigrants. Some were hanged, and others are shot; one report details the mutilation of a finger to steal a diamond ring. After the attack, the police arrest ten people. Eight are convicted of involuntary manslaughter, but the convictions are later overturned.

Problems continue. Jesus Bilderrain, a Los Angeles policeman, is making his rounds in an area called Negro Alley, when he responds to a shootout that results in an injury. Bilderrain signals a warning and calls for backup by blowing his police whistle. Civilians arrive; a local rancher, Robert Thompson, attempts to intervene and chases a Chinese man to the door of a house near a drugstore. The neighbors fend off Thompson with gunfire and kill him. The chaos grows, and the city marshal, Francis Baker, rushes to the scene. News reaches the mayor, Cristobal Aguilar, and then spreads throughout the city. Thompson's murder gives rise to rumors that the Chinese in Negro Alley are killing whites, increasing hatred toward them.

The Burlingame–Seward treaty, signed in 1868, regulates and permits immigration from Asia to secure US economic interests. But in light of increasing anti-Chinese incidents in the country, this treaty is annulled. President Ulysses S. Grant expresses approval for anti-Chinese legislation in 1874. However, because of Congress's ineffectiveness, Grant focuses on only a series of recommendations to address Chinese prostitution. It should be noted that Asian women are stereotyped as prostitutes; indeed, the first women to migrate from Asia are hired as such. From the depths of racist ignorance, the Chinese start to be labeled as the "yellow peril."

Around 1875, the US Congress passed a law—known as the Page Act—prohibiting the entry of Chinese women who supposedly engaged in prostitution, which was considered immoral. This effectively led to blocking Chinese immigrants, which California celebrated with a holiday and public demonstrations against the Asian population.

In 1882, a law is enacted to curb the influx of Chinese laborers to the United States; it is the first time a federal law forbids the entry of a certain ethnic working group. The restriction is also aimed at women. Although the entry of small groups of students and businessmen is allowed, the latter are not allowed to travel with their families. Only the wives of US-born Chinese or certain businessmen are allowed to enter.

These measures set out a pattern for other nations to follow in the immigration issue. Although the United States legitimized immigration in terms of freedom of opportunities, in the nineteenth century, it legitimized racism as a national policy.

The country entered an economic depression in 1873 and 1877, but the concern for safeguarding white labor continued. By 1888, the Scott Act applied restrictions on the reentry of Chinese workers who had left the United States—even with the legal certificate authorizing them to do so, as stipulated in Section 6 of the Chinese Exclusion Act of 1882.

In 1889, Chae Chan Ping, a worker who had traveled to China and boarded a ship in Hong Kong to return to the United States through the port of San Francisco, was denied reentry. The authorities at the time argued that, based on an act of Congress approved on October 1, 1888, and supplemented by the laws of 1882 and 1884 restricting immigration, the certificate was annulled, and his right to land in the United States was rescinded. Chae Chan Ping appealed, taking his case to court under the Scott Act, without success.

The Naturalization Act was another matter that hurt the Chinese community. In 1790, guidelines were stipulated for the naturalization of white foreigners in search of their freedom. By 1870, Charles Summer, a senator from Massachusetts, petitioned Congress for any foreigner to have the opportunity to become a naturalized American, regardless of their place of birth. Congressional representatives from the Western states were opposed because they considered such a provision to be favorable to citizens from Asia. They only agreed to a modification that applied to foreigners who were natives of Africa or of African descent.

As a final appeal in support of the Chinese, it is argued that the term *white* is not established or determined in the act, thereby allowing an interpretation to include a person of Chinese ancestry. The federal courts then define white race as corresponding to the Caucasian race, while the Mongolian race corresponds to the Chinese.

Racism toward the Chinese is so strong that attempts are made to deny citizenship to their children born in the US, for the purpose of deporting them. A case worth reviewing is that of Wong Kim Ark.

In 1898, the US Supreme Court made a landmark decision on this case. Wong Kim Ark was denied reentry to the US after a trip to China. He was born in San Francisco when a law existed denying citizenship for Asians born on US soil. The Supreme Court rules on citizenship status based on the Fourteenth Amendment as to the circumstances of birth: a child born in the United States to parents of Chinese ancestry, permanently residing in the United States, engaged in local business, with no diplomatic position or employment or under the command of the Emperor of China, is therefore a citizen of the US.

Congress can take no action to repeal such a provision. This is an important precedent because in the twentieth century, the world changed its perspective in a radical way. When the United States entered the Second World War, its position was in support of racial, religious, and cultural diversity, which it spread throughout the world. This explains the repeal of the 1882 law that excluded Chinese from the right to become naturalized US citizens. China allied with the United States during the world conflict, and they fought against the Japanese Empire together, emerging victorious in 1945. Later, strategic cooperation with Asia is on the horizon.

During the Cold War, and with the Immigration Act of 1952, the discriminatory exclusion of the Asian population came to an end. Nevertheless, a system according to racial criteria prevailed, under the establishment of quotas based on origin. Finally, through the Immigration Act of 1965, any impediment or obstacle to the presence of Chinese in the United States was eliminated.

Photo by Maria Sheffield, 2021.

Ricardo Sheffield

From Within We Are the World

In 1965, the Immigration and Nationality Act of the United States was passed. The law facilitated the entry of skilled immigrants from India between 1968 and 1992. The law also contained a clause regarding family reunification for highly qualified and educated professionals with a good command of English.

With such an incentive, around 1975, the United States began to welcome doctors, engineers, university professors, physical education teachers, scientists, and intellectuals. This signified a real brain drain for India. By the mid-1980s, approximately twenty thousand people had entered the US under the limits set by the Immigration Act. During this period, Indian citizens who had become naturalized US citizens sponsored an increasing number of immigrants from their home country.

Their presence rose to one-third of all immigrants to the US, but by the 1980s, this flow decreased. From 1990 onward, immigration laws were passed that once again prioritized skilled human capital, with restrictive clauses regarding temporary workers. This was a period of significant labor demand in the US market.

It is noteworthy that the Indian population migrates to developed countries, availing themselves of academic education and vocational training. The US Institute of International Education says that between 2004 and 2006, applications from Indian students to institutions of higher education increased, particularly in the areas of health and cybernetics, surpassing even Canada, China, Korea, Japan, and Taiwan. These students, once they have completed their university studies, prefer to stay in the US and work rather than return to their countries of origin. In the long run, they end up becoming global ambassadors.

Another group that formed its own migratory history in the United States is the Irish. Going back to the nineteenth century, let's look at the life of a typical Irish family. Potato farming supplies their daily diet; the wealthy class controls the trade of meat and other supplies. Around 1845, heavy rains damage the potato crop throughout the island, and the community to which this family belongs faces a serious epidemic.

This crisis is one of the most disastrous human catastrophes of nineteenth-century Europe. At the beginning of the 1840s, the Irish population fluctuates around 8.5 million; by 1850, more than three million have died. A similar number manages to emigrate to Australia, Canada, the United States, and the United Kingdom.

The Irish people were devoutly Catholic for the most part, for which they faced discrimination. Today though, Americans with Irish ancestry celebrate their roots and accept that they are descendants of immigrants, and the Irish are assimilated into most of the political forces that govern the United States.

Italian immigration to the United States is another separate chapter. From the 1820s onward, they started arriving from Sicily and southern Italy. Years later, between 1890 and 1900, around 656,000 migrants arrived in North America; the majority were men, two-thirds of the total.

If the Irish are driven by terrible famine, the Italians are driven by economic poverty, particularly in the southern regions of Italy. The neighborhoods where they settle down are known as Little Italy. As with the Chinese neighborhoods, the Italians in these neighborhoods coexist and maintain and develop their own culture and culinary traditions; here, they will never be deprived of pasta or meatballs. But conditions do not change overnight for the Italians. Arriving in the United States with little money and no education, the only work they can find is hard labor.

The situation is terrible: overcrowded with poor hygienic conditions, and tuberculosis abounds. They also suffer discrimination from anti-Catholic groups and those who rail against migrants, even to the point of lynchings.

Italian immigration peaked between 1900 and 1914. From the onset of the First World War to its conclusion, the number of arrivals took a turn. In 1921, the US Congress imposed regulations to establish how many persons could enter the country; later, in 1924, another similar provision tried to restrict the entry of people from southern and northern Europe. About two hundred thousand Italians had entered the country annually in the first decade of the twentieth century; after restrictive immigration legislation, only four thousand per year are allowed.

Let's take a look at the history of the Jews in the United States. The first recorded Jewish immigration—twenty-three refugees from Recife, Brazil, who disembarked in New Amsterdam, today New York—dates from 1654. Their relocation was due to the loss of Dutch territory in South America to Portugal. New Amsterdam, under the Dutch Crown, offered them refuge, although Governor Peter Stuyvesant did not want their presence.

Around 1776, about two thousand Jews, mostly Sephardic, are living in the United States and contribute to the victorious War of Independence, mainly in South Carolina and Charleston. One man, Jaim Solomon, generously (or naively) lent $200,000 to the independence cause, money that was never returned to him. Poor Solomon forgot the wise saying: "You scratch my back, and I'll scratch yours." Although George Washington acknowledged that without Solomon's help it would have been difficult to win the war against the British, the good man died bankrupt, perhaps waiting for a payment that never came.

Another Jew, Francis Salvador, is victim of the first murder in the state of Georgia. The Jewish community also participated in the independence of Texas in 1836; one of its members, Dr. Albert Levy, was a physician for the Texas Volunteer Army. The Jewish presence is also notable during the Civil War, in which some three thousand individuals fought with the Confederates and seven thousand with the Union. On the Union side, twenty-nine-year-old Brigadier General Edward Solomon served in the cavalry, and there was a regiment of German Jews from Philadelphia, known as the Cameron Dragoons. Colonel Abraham Charles Myers, a West Point graduate, served on the Confederate side.

During the 1830s, the largest immigrant community was the Jews, who settled in the northern part of the United States. In the 1850s, German Jews, whose vocation was trade and textile manufacturing, entered the United States and settled in different cities around the country, building many Reform synagogues. They are also active in the banking sector in New York City.

The Ashkenazi Jews, who are Eastern Yiddish speakers, entered the United States between 1880 and 1914 and settled in New York; this community practices an Orthodox or Conservative religion. They are the founders of the Zionist movement in the US and are mostly involved in the textile industry. This community became drawn to the political sphere; many joined the Democratic Party coalition in the 1930s.

According to statistics, the Jewish population in the 1790s is only around two thousand and is mostly made up of English and Dutch Sephardic Jews. By 1840, it climbs to fifteen thousand and to 250,000 by 1880. At the start of the First World War, approximately two million Jews leave Eastern Europe; they are Ashkenazi Jews who speak Yiddish and come from Byelorussia, Lithuania, Moldavia, Poland, Russia, and Ukraine. The Polish Jews are concentrated in New York, involved in the textile industry as suppliers to a nationwide chain of stores and organized into well-run unions.

At the start the Great Depression in 1929, the situation for Jews in Europe worsens with the rise of Nazi Germany. During World War II, some five hundred thousand Jews—their ages ranging from eighteen to fifty years old—enlisted in the army that formed part of the Allied forces. After the end of the conflict, the Jewish community works to recover economically. Quotas established in the Immigration Quota Act of 1924 are eliminated in the Immigration and Naturalization Act of 1965, allowing expanded immigration.

Jews begin to settle in greater Miami and Los Angeles and take advantage of the educational benefits offered by the country. Marriages between Jews and non-Jews take place, and this population grows in the United States.

Starting in the nineteenth century, both Reform and Conservative Judaism are active and present in the United States. Jews create their own schools, like the Polonies Talmud Torah, founded in New York in 1806. By 1970, some four million Jews live in the US, and two million live in New York alone.

Now to review the history of migration from Latin America, a source of great controversy in the US. According to the census, by 2000, Latin American immigrants numbered 14.5 million, up from one million individuals in 1960. The number does not include persons who are in the country illegally.

In view of this phenomenon, it is important to take a look at the 1960s, when immigration to the United States was no longer relevant for Europeans. The US was at the height of economic expansion and needed migrants to fill the labor gap. The previously mentioned immigration law of 1965 ends up facilitating family reunification as well as allowing a system of temporary visas for agricultural workers. This makes conditions favorable for a steady and growing flow of Latinos who plan to stay in the US.

Mexicans are a large percentage of this group. In 2017, 44.5 million immigrants were documented, according to estimates from the Migration Policy Institute, a Washington-based think tank specializing in migration issues. There are ebbs and flows in the migratory pattern. For example, there is a continual increase until migration reaches its highest point in 2007, with 12.8 million; during 2014, the flow decreases to 11.7 million immigrants. This is due to a slow recovery after the world economic crisis of 2008, which saw many Mexicans return home.

According to the Migration Policy Institute, Mexicans who have recently entered the United States are better educated with better English skills. This makes for better employment opportunities than previous generations had—and better possibilities for advancement. Cultural roots unite the Mexican community, but recently, immigration laws are being debated, now focused on Latinos.

Despite the United States being a multiracial society, more and more of its citizens do not identify with any one origin. Their roots are multicultural, which positions them as true citizens of the world.

In Mexico: Not Many, But Hardworking

In Mexico, migration took place during different significant phases. The Spanish Crown was responsible for the flow of slaves from Africa; it was a system that was endorsed and quite profitable for the empires of that time. During the period of Mexican independence, in the nineteenth century, Europeans and Asians entered the country. In the twentieth century, immigration to postrevolutionary Mexico takes on a distinctive note as the nation receives political refugees from all over the world, especially those citizens fleeing dictatorships in Latin America. The welcome given to Spaniards escaping from Franco's regime, sponsored by General Lazaro Cardenas, is a chapter by itself.

Since the 1990s, under the banner of globalization and NAFTA, Mexico has been a permanent route for migrants from Central America. Some choose to remain in Mexico; others continue their journey north to the United States.

Going back in history to the period of New Spain, soldiers and sailors arrived by sea from Andalusia, Extremadura, and La Mancha. Later, the flow includes people from Aragon, Catalonia, Madrid, Leon, and Valencia—and then from France, Portugal, and the Flemish countries. The so-called Llovidos—Jews, Moors, and Gypsies—arrive, altering their documentation to circumvent the Spanish Crown's restrictions for entering New Spain and avoid migratory controls.

The result is a motley crew of immigrants arriving to colonial America, made up of religious devotees, aristocrats, marquises, and counts as well as illiterates and truants, in addition to the slave trade.

The impact on the native population in New Spain is appalling. The community is decimated due to epidemics brought by European immigrants; measles and smallpox claim 70 percent of the victims. The final blow is the precarious living conditions they must endure.

By the eighteenth century, Spaniards originating from the peninsula were no more than 1 percent of the total population; Spaniards born in New Spain, called Creoles, made up 10 percent. It is worthwhile to look at the arrival of groups that complement the population in a particular way to understand their integration into Mexican culture.

As already mentioned, the native population is decimated by overexploitation; the demand for hard forced labor in the mines is solved by the arrival of slaves from Africa. Most of them came from the Yoruba or Mandingo ethnic group. The municipality of Yanga was founded in the current state of Veracruz; it was the first African slave community to rebel against the Spanish Crown, led by the black leader, Yanga, in 1609. African slaves also settled in the region known today as the Costa Chica as well as in Oaxaca and Guerrero.

Over time, the population of African descent reaches 1.5 million. Their impact on Mexican culture in both music and dance is evident in the fandangos and sones and in the appropriation of the marimba in Chiapas. Religious syncretism of African gods occurs; a striking example is the devotion to Santa Muerte, an icon with Afro-Cuban and Catholic influences.

Apart from the presence of Spaniards due to the conquest, there was a flow of other Europeans to Mexico. During the Second Mexican Empire, with the presence of Maximilian of Habsburg, the French arrived, although many leave after the overthrow of the emperor. Their communities remain, however, in the cities of Monterrey and Guadalajara.

More Europeans arrive to work in the manufacturing sector, mainly Germans, French, Irish, Italians, and Russians. At the beginning of the twentieth century, the English settle in the Veracruz port area, which is where British companies are exploiting Mexican oil.

We move along in history to the time of the Spanish Civil War, which lasted from 1936 to 1939. President Lazaro Cardenas decided to offer asylum to a population persecuted by the dictatorship of Francisco Franco. Between 1939 and 1942, around twenty-two thousand to twenty-five thousand refugees arrived, including prominent intellectuals and scientists.

Jews also arrived. The first Jewish community in Mexico dates from the late nineteenth and early twentieth centuries. Its members came from the Middle East, mainly Syria and Lebanon, as well as the Balkans and Eastern Europe. Attracted by President Porfirio Diaz's policy of encouraging foreign investment, they also sought a place where anti-Semitism was not rampant. In 1912, they founded the Sociedad de Beneficencia Alianza Monte Sinai (Mount Sinai Benevolent Alliance), which focused on helping their own community. In 1914, in Mexico City, they built the first Jewish cemetery: Mount Sinai Pantheon.

Years go by, and the world enters a crisis. National socialism arises in Europe, and with it, the persecution of the Jewish population in Europe as never before. In 1938, after the Ley General de la Poblacion (General Population Law) limits the entry of Jews into the country, a central committee is created for refugees. Years later, an Israeli court is created to fight anti-Semitism; today, this institution represents the entire Jewish community in Mexico.

Toward the middle of the twentieth century, the Centro Deportivo Israelita (Israelite Sports Center), the largest intercommunity institution for the Mexican Jewish community, was established. A Conservative congregation, Beth Israel, began operating in 1957; its members are Anglo-Saxon, and the Hispanic version dates back to 1961.

The Asian population in Mexico has been around since the arrival of the Nao de China, although this results from the trade relationship and not migration per se. At the end of the nineteenth century, a group of immigrants arrive in Mexico, wanting to cross the border to the United States through the Baja California Peninsula. They fail in their venture, so a large number of Chinese settle in Mexicali; their settlement in the center of this city is known as La Chinesca. Like the Russians, groups of Chinese settle in the Guadalupe Valley, in particular, in the municipality of Ensenada. Others land in the states of Colima, Guerrero, Jalisco, Nayarit, Puebla, Sinaloa, and Tamaulipas.

In the early twentieth century, ships from Canton and Hong Kong unload goods in the ports of Guaymas, Ensenada, and Mazatlan. On board are immigrants willing to work on the expansion of railroads in the southwestern United States and Mexico. Most of them are men; they are hired to lay rails and build railroad stations.

With this rough and poorly paid work experience, the Chinese became pioneers in the construction of rail transportation. In 1902, the Colorado River Land Company was founded in the Mexicali Valley, opening its doors to Chinese who wished to work in the desert zone.

As the nineteenth century ends and the twentieth century begins, the United States is no longer willing to accept Chinese workers, given that the railroad construction project is complete. In addition, the 1882 law effectively prohibits the entry of Chinese to the US. This coincides with an agricultural boom in Mexicali that could not be sustained with Mexican workers alone. So, between 1910 and 1920, the Chinese were allowed to work in this land—so far from God and so close to the United States.

Unfortunately, as happened in the United States, discrimination and death also occurred in Mexico. On May 15, 1911, near Torreon, Coahuila, 303 Chinese were murdered after the city was overrun by the Maderista revolutionaries (Maderismo was the first of the movements that made up the Mexican Revolution, led by Francisco I. Madero). Curiously, popular folklore assigns responsibility for the massacre to Pancho Villa's soldiers, calling the incident a "sudden outbreak of violence" and not a cruel act of xenophobia and intolerance in which even children were murdered. The novelist and poet Julian Herbert has written a splendid book about this terrible event, *La Casa del Dolor Ajeno* (*The House of Other People's Pain*). Likewise, in the penitentiary of Hermosillo, Sonora, three hundred Chinese individuals were unjustly imprisoned; they were tortured with the consent of the postrevolutionary government in a lamentable display of racism. This Chinese population was stereotyped and discriminated against—without taking into account their invaluable contributions to the nation's economic development.

Japanese immigrants first arrived in Mexico on May 10, 1887. A group of thirty-five migrants established the Enomoto neighborhood in Acacoyagua, Chiapas, where they cultivated coffee. This was one of the first Japanese exoduses to Latin America and sets an important precedent for later. After World War II, Japanese interest in Mexico continued. As a result of the war and the boom in the automotive industry, the migratory phenomenon took on a new dimension.

Today, most of the Japanese community is focused on creating private companies with diverse business lines. Mexicans of Japanese origin are outstanding citizens, thirty thousand strong, with a notable presence in various cities in Nuevo Leon and Yucatán.

Another group whose presence dates back to the viceroyalty is the Arabs. They entered Spain as Muslims and converted to Catholicism. Doing so allows them to travel to New Spain. However, the greatest migration occurs during the twentieth century when there is an exodus of Iraqis, Lebanese, Palestinians, and Syrians in search of asylum. At the end of World War I, after the dissolution of the Ottoman Empire in 1923, Mexico accepted those with Ottoman papers. They were not considered Arabs and were also confused with European or Anatolian Turks.

After the crisis between Israel and Arabia, the flow of political refugees, mostly Lebanese, increased, reaching approximately one million. Between 1860 and 1914, around five hundred thousand individuals entered the country. Today, the Arab community participates actively in the economy, with multiple professional and business activities. Whether they are Muslims converted to Catholicism or Maronites (Christian ethnoreligious group native to the Levant region of the Middle East), their ancestry is European, mainly Turkish. The largest number of Arab descendants lives in Acapulco, Aguascalientes, Cancun, Ciudad Juarez, Mexico City, Cuernavaca, Guadalajara, Leon, Mexicali, Monterrey, Puebla, Queretaro, San Luis Potosi, Tijuana, Torreon, and Veracruz.

Mennonites settled in Mexico in 1922. This community maintains its cultural identity, whose origins date back to the pacifist wing of the Anabaptist movement, which began in Zurich, Switzerland, in 1522. They are recognized for their cultivation of citrus and fruits, sale of livestock, and production of milk and animal feed. Their well-known Mennonite cheese is now an essential part of Mexican cuisine.

Other migrants, such as the Molokan Russians and Catalans, focus on the wine industry for which they have received international recognition. Another successful community is the Italian community of Chipilo, Puebla. Famous for producing milk and raising cattle, they have also been quite innovative and successful with several franchise schemes, most notably the Italian Coffee Company, which is positioned nationwide.

With all this history, it might seem that the laws in Mexico encourage immigration, but that's not the case. Not until recently, in 1998, was dual nationality accepted. In the following paragraphs, we will focus on migration between the nations of the Americas and Mexico.

There are one million US citizens living in Mexico, some of whom are senior citizens enjoying their retirement. In the US, Mexicans account for 75 percent of the total number of migrants.

During the 1970s and 1980s, a wave of individuals starts seeking political asylum. Mexico accepts an influx of Argentines, Chileans, Colombians, Peruvians, Uruguayans, and Venezuelans seeking new lives, pushed by crises in their countries of origin, some of them governed at the time under terrible military dictatorships. Most reside in Mexico City and Leon. This group includes citizens with an interest in education; when they migrate, their intention is to obtain scholarships that will allow them to specialize through further studies.

In Mexico, there are communities of Cubans, Dominicans, Haitians, Jamaicans, and Puerto Ricans; many Puerto Ricans settle in Guadalajara, and many Cubans settle in in Leon.

Today, Mexico is among the most attractive destinations for foreign investors. It maintains trade relations with all corners of the world, enabling businesses to diversify. In addition, the economic relationship Mexico has with the United States contributes to migrants' interest in investment and positioning.

In the United States, the melting pot has a lot of everything, and the jumble is forced, without losing the basis of the American way of life. Mexico has few immigrants from few countries, and their integration comes late because there are no policies that promote the Mexicanization of newcomers. The melting pot is good or bad depending on the eyes that look at it. For the United

States, this process has worked to become the most prosperous and powerful nation on Earth. It has also worked for Mexico, because the country's great capital comes from these Lebanese, Spanish and Italian immigrants. The seeds of Mexico's richest families originated in distant lands. These families took time to assimilate to the new customs, but when they do, they became a very important part of the national dynamic. Despite their foreign origin, these families are now fully Mexican. They arrived against the tide with a culture of sacrifice and work, knowledge, and something very important: they arrived hungry. That is the key.

We begin with Daniel Servitje Montull, who was born in Mexico City in 1959. A descendant of Spanish immigrants and owner of one-third of the shares of Grupo Bimbo, a food company the produces bread, cookies, candies, and pastries. Its worldwide footprint reaches more than thirty-three countries. The idea of starting a bakery company with the name of Bimbo was born in 1943; Italians usually call their children "bimbo," a contraction of the word "bambino." The company's logo, a friendly, affectionate teddy bear with a chef's hat, came about in 1945, when white, brown, and toasted bread products were first wrapped in cellophane.

Lorenzo Servitje (Mexico City, 1918), whose father was an immigrant from Catalonia, Spain, started working in the family bakery at the age of sixteen. With his father's support, he studied public accounting at the UNAM. At the age of thirty, he opened his own bakery, El Molino, in partnership with two others. In 1937, he took over the family business when his father died unexpectedly, and he was in charge until 1945.

Bimbo was created thanks to the association of five partners, including Lorenzo Servitje. He served as its first manager until 1963, when he became CEO and president until his resignation in 1981. On February 3, 2017, he passed away at the age of ninety-eight in Mexico City.

In the 1980s, Bimbo began exporting its bread to the United States with great success, and at the same time, it began trading on the Mexican Stock Exchange. In 1997, Bimbo was taken over by

Lorenzo's son, Daniel Servitje Montull. Under his leadership, by the end of the 1990s, the company had expanded to thirty-three countries on four continents. At this rate, one day Martians will probably want Bimbo to put a little shop on Mars too. In 2021, the company had revenues of $17.4 billion, with a net profit of $1.7 billion.

Our review continues with Pablo Diez Fernandez (Vegaquemada, Leon, Spain, 1884), a Spanish philanthropist who arrived in Mexico at the turn of the twentieth century. With a special talent for business management, he was one of the first shareholders of Cerveceria Modelo, where he served as CEO starting in the 1930s. When Pablo Diez announced his retirement, he retained the position of honorary president of Grupo Modelo. He died in Mexico City in November 1972.

During his tenure, he improves the group's infrastructure, expanding facilities and constructing plants. The company grows into a modern production facility, unmatched in Mexico. Its first brands become firmly entrenched with Mexican consumers: Modelo, Corona, and Negra Modelo beer. Corona beer can now be found even in the most remote places in the world, helping to establish Mexico as one of the most important beer exporters today. The consortium also acquired Cerveceria la Estrella, Cerveceria la Laguna, and Cerveceria del Pacifico. And since Mexico always has "a thirst for danger" (an advertising slogan for the brand in Mexico), Grupo Modelo dominates the market with a 57 percent share. Despite having to suspend production due to the COVID-19 pandemic, Grupo Modelo did well, in part thanks to e-commerce during the shutdown.

Another figure linked to this business group is Felix Aramburuzabala Lazcano-Iturburu (Eskoriatza, Spain, 1886), who migrated to Latin America to escape poverty. He had an exemplary career at the head of Cerveceria Modelo, serving as its second president. His heirs are successful Mexican businessmen, and his granddaughter is Maria Asuncion Aramburuzabala, a businesswoman considered the richest woman in Mexico.

Venancio Vazquez Alvarez was born in Galicia in 1900. Accompanied by his wife, Maria Raña, he arrived in Mexico City in 1928. His commercial venture begins with a small business offering household products, located in the Guerrero neighborhood. The couple lived on the second floor of the building, where they instilled a strong work ethic in their six children. Olegario Vazquez Raña learned from his father's teachings, becoming the director of some of the most important business holdings in Mexico, including hotels and hospitals, fast-food restaurants, department stores, media outlets, and airport-management companies.

Among these businesses, Grupo Empresarial Angeles is a leader in the private health care sector; thousands of people are treated in its thirteen hospitals. The Camino Real hotel chain also belongs to this group, with a total of twenty-one properties and more than four thousand rooms throughout the country. Grupo Imagen and the newspaper *Excelsior* are a protagonist in the Mexican media; more than twenty-two thousand people are employed in its radio and television divisions.

We continue with the Lebanese community and their exemplary performance in the country, beginning with Carlos Slim Helu (Mexico City, 1940), a Mexican businessman and engineer. He is among the wealthiest men in the world (in 2008, he reached first place), and his assets amount to $80.6 billion. The Carlos Slim Foundation supports projects focused on education, environment, art, and health. Patriarch of Grupo Carso, Slim remains the richest man in Mexico. This important conglomerate owns several companies, including Sanborns, Miniso, and Saks Fifth Avenue in Mexico as well as the Soumaya Museum. Another company in the group, America Movil, counts the telecommunications company Telmex among its subsidiaries, with presence in almost the entire American continent.

A beloved figure in the state of Oaxaca, Alfredo Harp Helu (Mexico City, 1944) illustrates his Lebanese ancestry and professional dedication with the motto: "the best investment is in Mexico." A public accountant graduated from UNAM, he is a founding partner of the brokerage firm Acciones y Valores de Mexico. In 1991, he joined the group that acquired Banco Nacional de Mexico (Banamex). Since 2000, the foundation that bears his name has been carrying out philanthropic works with an impact nationally.

Finally, we have Lazaro Chedraui Chaya, who left his native Lebanon to settle in Xalapa, Veracruz. Around 1920, he founded a haberdashery in Xalapa with the support of his wife, Ana Caram. The business was named El Puerto de Beirut, but by 1927, it adopted the name Casa Chedraui: La Unica de Confianza. Today, it is a supermarket chain that employs thousands of Mexicans nationwide.

Over the years I have talked to many important entrepreneurs in Mexico and the United States about how they built their fortunes and their businesses. The stories are often the same, but the circumstances in each country are different. It would have been difficult for U.S. entrepreneurs to repeat their success story living in the Mexican environment.

The United States did not lack any people or ethnicity, it had everyone, the entire globe was there. The Mexican melting pot is made up of only a few countries. The jumble of nations, cultures, customs, ideas, and idiosyncrasies adds, not subtracts. It is impossible to ignore the benefits of migration. Although the U.S. has enhanced it to a superlative degree, to the point that it has taken the shine off its position as a melting pot of the world and a multicultural nation, Mexico is a place of opportunities that always welcomes with open arms anyone who is willing to reciprocate.

Chapter 15

From the Economic Strength of the Land to Innovation

Shipyards Made America Great

It is impossible to imagine the American continent developing without a maritime connection. Merchandise was transported on great ships, in good weather or bad, in calm waters or rough seas. As part of this constant back-and-forth, mainly between Europe and America, shipyards played a decisive role in the fate of the future independent nations.

Let's think about a master shipbuilder from that time. His work consists of making and repairing ships that can cross the ocean in calm weather or in storms on the scale of the universal flood. It makes no difference whether he is a great English or Spanish master; what matters is that he builds a noble and sturdy vessel, an indomitable wooden leviathan that cannot be intimidated by the fearsome gods of the sea. This kind of work has existed throughout the ages, dating back to the great masters of navigation: Phoenicians, Egyptians, Romans, and Vikings. During the Middle Ages, maritime activities dominate; both kingdoms and small seafaring communities poked their noses beyond their borders thanks to ships, mainly on the waterways of Africa, Asia, and Europe.

During the fifteenth and sixteenth centuries, shipbuilders started to use some manufacturing processes to meet the demands of military, commercial—of both goods and slaves—and passenger transportation. These activities became so all-important to the Catholic monarchies that they granted tax breaks to certain companies involved in trading operations.

Faster and lighter ships eventually replaced the galleon, a ship of great tonnage used for military or commercial purposes and suitable for the American gold trade. The newer ships could travel longer distances and carry more cargo.

For royalty of this period, particularly Felipe IV of Spain, who ruled from 1605 to 1665, launching this type of vessel was a priority. The shipyard guilds worked for days on end without rest—even on holidays—to meet this priority. During this period, the demand for ships exceeded production, driving up the cost of each ship.

However, the Crown, both in Spain and England, would only consider increasing the number of expeditions to remote places with a return cargo of goods to underwrite the risk. When the economy began to shrink, private shipyards proved to be the best option.

Once the Genoese explorer Christopher Columbus succeeded in his voyage to the edge of the Americas on October 12, 1492, the appetite for unknown lands would not abate until they were conquered and colonized.

Once the conquest was complete, the Spanish Crown reinforced its naval fleet. Its priorities were total control of the colonies and secure transoceanic trade. The fleet had to deal with attacks from European pirates. In 1522, only one year after the fall of Tenochtitlan, Hernan Cortes ordered the construction of four ships to explore the coasts of the territory already under Spanish rule. Shipyards were built in Coatzacoalcos and San Blas, located on the coasts of the Gulf of Mexico and the Pacific Ocean, respectively, although their capacity and profitability were short-lived. The Spanish Crown preferred to use shipyards operating in Spain; by the eighteenth century, they had chosen to concentrate their workshops in the Philippines instead of Mesoamerica.

The port of Veracruz became the center of operations for the Spanish Crown. Decades and centuries come and go. Shipbuilding techniques are transferred from generation to generation, with inevitable technological advances. Surprisingly, in spite of the country's enormous maritime potential, the first shipyard in independent Mexico only dates back to 1929. On the initiative of an officer named Ignacio Garcia Jurado, who was in charge of the vessels, a small military shipyard was built in the fortress of San Juan de Ulua. In 1935, a dry dock was built for ship maintenance and repairs. A few years later, in 1943, the secretary of the navy constructed another, solidifying the country's shipyard industry. At the same time, steel production was booming, and steel was fully involved in the manufacture and assembly of ships.

In 1956, at the behest of Admiral Antonio Vazquez del Mercado, construction began on Mexico's first steel ship. In 1958, with the ceremonial breaking of a bottle across its bow, this vessel, christened the *Mexico*, began sailing proudly in the waters of the Gulf of Mexico.

Let's witness that important day for Mexican navigation. After 150 years of shipbuilding inactivity, the country was once again putting a colossal vessel in the water. As shipyard workers operated the first steel ship, those responsible for the project looked on nervously, including the project manager, an Italian engineer named Alberto Farina. Expectation was growing among the witnesses as the *Mexico* slowly made its way to the sea. The steel ship, weighing five hundred tons and measuring fifty-two meters long, stayed afloat, surviving the deceptive firmness of the water. Even the seagulls in the sky were in an uproar with the celebrations.

The history of shipyards in the United States took a very different path. Their administration became a priority for a government that was focused on military and trade. The history starts in 1767 with the Gosport Shipyard in Virginia, which was destroyed by a fire in 1779. By 1794, the newly independent government included it under the jurisdiction of Norfolk. In 1799, they launched the nation's first military ship. Military production lasted until the end of the Civil War, and then it turned to commercial transport.

Toward World War II, while Mexico's shipyards were advancing slowly, the United States exploited its potential to the hilt. A parenthesis is in order here because at the beginning of the twentieth century, the US already owned the largest shipyards in the world, based in New York. Its return to military production during World War II included a menu of aircraft carriers, battleships, and submarines. At the same time, the construction of small ferries and large-tonnage ocean liners for civilian use continued.

Following the Allied victory in Europe, trade became more significant, drawing on naval technology along with an expansion of ports. For Mexico, this meant foreign investment. The Maryland Drydock Company shipyards began operating in Veracruz, mostly for the construction of fishing boats and ship repair.

In the 1970s, the shipyards continued to grow in Mexico. President Luis Echeverria ordered the creation of a state-owned company, Astilleros Unidos S.A., to manage the nation's shipyards and supply patrol boats to the Mexican Navy. Meanwhile, the steel industry continued expanding in the United States. Gigantic ships for exporting goods to other continents began to be produced.

But nothing lasts forever, and what goes up must come down. The golden age of shipyards declined at the end of the twentieth century. As the demand for naval warships fell, so did the large-scale production of previous decades. Although most of the world's flotillas had been built by 1985, production went from seventy commercial ships to only four by 1990. Even though the production in 2000 rose slightly to more than ten, there is no comparison with the glorious past.

Mexico's shipyards are focused on small construction projects and repair of cargo ships as well as tankers for transporting oil and gas. Consequently, the sector does not suffer to the same degree as in the United States.

The US Navy still operates its own shipyards, a total of 115 in 2021, with production dropping as previously noted. From being a leader in shipbuilding, the United States dropped to nineteenth position. Government subsidies for shipyard manufacturing decreased under the argument of being unable to compete with foreign shipyards.

Development at the Speed of Locomotion

From movement by sea, we now take a look at movement by land. Trains represent many things. For some, they are a getaway, the opportunity to reach the promised land. They can represent an escape, movement, or progress. The arrival of a train at the station can mean joy for someone waiting for a passenger. The departure of a train is sadness for someone who does not want to say goodbye. Trains can be used for wonderful things, such as moving goods, or they can also be instruments for terrible acts as happened during the Holocaust. Through railroads, both Mexico and the United States modernized. During his long tenure in office, Porfirio Diaz planned to incentivize the country's development through railroads. Meanwhile, the United States built the largest railroad network in the world, with more than 250,000 kilometers of track.

Let's go back in time to the beginnings of this impressive means of transportation. Before the United States' independence, in 1720, the French were already using a small railroad for the construction of their fortress in Louisburg, in what is now Canada. Later, in the middle of the eighteenth century, when the British Empire still dominated New England, a railroad was built around the Niagara River and served as a border between Ontario, Canada, and New York.

At the turn of the nineteenth century, the US began to analyze English railroads; they thoroughly studied geographic conditions as well as the trains' steam-powered propulsion, just as they had with ships. First came the freight railroads. Then, around 1830, the first steam passenger train began to run in Massachusetts. Small private companies also appeared, laying tracks near ports and mines. During this period, Cornelius Vanderbilt began to make his fortune thanks to ships and railroads.

Those early railroads had a number of weaknesses. When their return journey involved an uphill climb, additional power was needed to get them moving—even pack animals were used. Before the passenger railroad was launched, the government employed the best engineers to add a cable return track, which was powered by steam. A bidirectional engine was added, allowing the train to easily travel back and forth. This vehicle operated continuously for more than a century, hauling goods. Eventually, it would be used primarily for tourism.

As for Mexico, although Porfirio Diaz fully exploited this means of transportation, we have to take a few steps back before his time. The arrival of the railroad in Mexico was a long and exhausting process, delayed for a number of reasons, including lack of budget, constant changes of government, and the reluctance of some politicians. In 1837, President Anastasio Bustamante granted a concession to the former minister of finance, Francisco Arriaga, to begin construction of a railroad line between the port of Veracruz and the country's capital. Although the cost of the project would have been six million pesos back then, the plan was not implemented. The project was resumed in 1842, unsuccessfully, during the presidency of Antonio Lopez de Santa Anna.

Around this time, a French company led by Hippolyte du Pasquier de Dommartin obtained authorization to begin the construction of an interoceanic line in Chihuahua. At first, Santa Anna was opposed to this project, claiming that it fell under federal jurisdiction. However, after a lot of begging, he finally gave in. Around the same time, though, the *Treaty of La Mesilla* was signed on December 30, 1853, which affected the Mexican government's jurisdiction over the territory earmarked for the railroad. Once again, the project was abandoned.

In 1850, thirteen kilometers from the port of Veracruz to El Molino were finally inaugurated. A month later, the public was expectantly boarding the train. The Escandon family, who fervently promoted the railroad in Mexico, entered the scene. One of its members, Manuel Escandon, declared in 1856, "Ever since there were railroads in Europe, the idea of building one in Mexico has been a kind of an obsession of mine." In 1858, the Reform War between Conservatives and Liberals broke out, and the project went dormant. After Maximilian was shot at Cerro de las Campanas, construction of the railroad went forward. A year later, in 1872, President Sebastian Lerdo de Tejada had the privilege of traveling by railroad for the first time from the capital to Veracruz.

Mexico had forty kilometers of railroad tracks by 1860, while the United States could boast of more than fourteen thousand kilometers in 1850. By 1860, railroads were already linking the most important US cities of the time; in addition, the construction of the first transcontinental railroad began that same year. From then on, the railroad would become an important and indisputable piece in the economic ascent of the United States. This means of transportation could reduce the cost of transporting goods and expand the market's range. At the same time, it stimulated the growth of the coal, iron, and oil industries.

In 1880, a concession was granted in Mexico to the owners of the Atchison & Topeka Railroad Company in Kansas to build the central railway line linking Chihuahua to Mexico City. It is worth noting that US companies seemed to be favored by the Mexican government in these types of contracts.

The construction of the Mexican Central Railway happened quickly. Unlike its predecessor, which connected Mexico City with Veracruz and was built at a rheumatic snail's pace, the Mexican Central Railway was completed in only four years. In 1884, the 1,970 kilometers of railroad connecting the capital with the northern border were ready. It stimulated the country's economy by reducing transportation times and costs. A journey by other means, such as carriage, horse, or donkey, between Chihuahua and the capital city required nine days of travel—if the adventurous traveler was lucky. The traveler was also exposed to constant assaults perpetrated by groups of bandits or the unpredictable temperament of nature. That is why they said that the road can't be trusted. The strenuous travel time was reduced to nine hours by train, including greater safety for the passenger.

At the beginning of the twentieth century, when railroads were at their peak, problems started to arise. Users in the United States began to complain about high fares, which resulted from the monopolies that controlled transportation in a number of states. Consequently, the US government implemented laws to prevent these companies from continuing to abuse prices.

Unrest targeting the railroad industry spread to Mexico, and workers complained about excessive workloads. To prevent problems from escalating, Porfirio Diaz decided to create Ferrocarriles Nacionales de Mexico in 1909, which would assume financial responsibilities and handle railroad-related matters.

In 1910, at the start of the Mexican Revolution, there were more than twenty thousand kilometers of railways operating in the country. During the armed conflict, the railroad industry suffered a series of setbacks. Most of the foreigners who worked and had interests in the railroads decided to return to their home countries, and revolutionary groups repeatedly blocked routes to prevent the Mexican army from obtaining military equipment or to keep cities incommunicado without access to supplies and ammunition. The always-astute Pancho Villa used the railroad to surprise his enemies, packing the cars with fierce machine gunners who ambushed the orderly cavalry ranks that were loyal to the government.

During the Mexican Revolution, trains transported soldiers and were useful to both the government and the revolutionary forces. There are several famous photographs that reflect the importance of railroads in the conflict. One of them shows a female soldier, known as "Adelita," leaning on a train ladder, her hands holding onto two bars. Her face is an enigma. We do not know if the woman is looking at a battle, a burning town, the deserted prairie, a train station, death, or simply the victory that can be seen up ahead. Behind her, other women share her journey, waiting for the moment when the train stops so they can continue contributing to the armed movement. This photograph pays homage to the Mexican Revolution's *soldaderas* (women who participated in the conflict), and it inspired a classic Mexican song, "La Adelita," in which the railroad is a protagonist: *"Y si Adelita se fuera con otro, la seguiría por tierra y por mar, si es por mar en un buque de guerra, si es por tierra en un tren military"* (And if Adelita were to leave with another, I would follow her by land and by sea, if by sea on a warship, if by land on a military train).

Following the revolution, Mexico's railroad infrastructure was in very poor condition—as were almost all the towns, roads, and cities where battles took place. The sector required heavy investment in order to rescue long-distance transportation of goods. In 1937, a year before the nationalization of oil, President Lazaro Cardenas ordered the expropriation of Ferrocarriles Nacionales de Mexico as well as most of the railroads.

Everything was looking good for the Mexican railroad industry to take off again. In 1940, another railroad was built in Chihuahua with eleven tunnels. By 1959, the country had more than seventy tunnels and thousands of kilometers of railroad tracks. At the same time, economic expansion attracted large-scale investment. However, due to unfortunate government planning, lack of labor discipline, and the indifference of workers to the affairs of a company, which in theory belonged to them, the railroad industry again went into a tailspin.

Another strike broke out in 1959 when leftist leaders Demetrio Vallejo and Valentin Campa demanded better wages and benefits for railroad workers from the government of Adolfo Ruiz Cortines. The wage increase they demanded was a mere 350 pesos, but they also sought to expel all the corrupt leaders from the union, who were as plentiful as coal in engines. The railroad movement, unlike other popular organizations such as the CTM (Confederation of Mexican Workers), was not in cahoots with the PRI; it was identified with the left. Vallejo himself had joined the illegal Mexican Communist Party when he was only twenty-four years old. In order to improve their working conditions, the railroad workers were not afraid to fight tooth and nail against the full power of the state. The conflict lasted until the government of Adolfo Lopez Mateos, and he proved not to be very patient in resolving this inherited problem. In the absence of any agreement, the government severely repressed the striking workers, violently destroying their camps and firing and imprisoning thousands of workers, including Demetrio Vallejo and Valentin Campa. Paradoxically, those who truly were corrupt accused the union of corruption, and the strike leaders were unjustly imprisoned for ten years in the Lecumberri prison. One of the demands of the student movement that shook Mexico in 1968 was the release of Vallejo, Campa, and many other political prisoners.

In 1995, during the presidency of Ernesto Zedillo, Ferrocarriles Nacionales de Mexico was privatized, throwing aside the legacy of

General Lazaro Cardenas. Six years later, in 2001, the dissolution of Ferrocarriles Nacionales was announced. The railroad is currently used for the transportation of goods; only three tourist routes operate, including the famous *Chepe,* which runs through the beautiful landscape of Chihuahua. Of the thousands of railways that the country once had, not even the vestiges of their tracks remain now. Almost all of it was sold and privatized, which is a shame, since during the Porfiriato, the country had an extensive and well-defined railroad infrastructure. While several European countries were betting on the train as their primary means of communication and development, in Mexico, neoliberalism decided to dismantle the railroads and sell them for scrap.

After another period of stagnation, the twenty-first century has witnessed President Andres Manuel Lopez Obrador bringing back the railroad industry in Mexico. With the help of the armed forces, the Mayan Train is under construction, which will have commercial and tourist routes to Palenque, Chiapas, crossing the states of Campeche, Yucatan, and Quintana Roo. Likewise, Lopez Obrador decided to continue with the construction of the Mexico-Toluca train, which the administration of Enrique Peña Nieto left unfinished due to mismanagement and embezzlement.

As for the United States, passenger lines have a similar end. After the advent of the automobile and affordable air travel, the passenger railroad market is gradually declining. It is difficult to compete against commercial airlines, which reduce travel times and have a more attractive ticket cost. Even so, the railroads continue to be a force in the transportation of goods, moving more than 25 percent of the nation's products per year. We can conclude that while Mexico has failed to catch the train several times in its history, is has yet to happen to the United States.

American Inventiveness

Throughout its history, the United States has sought to go over and above, looking for solutions to the problems of everyday life, creating technology that facilitates human existence, improving on inventions of the past, or simply seeking to demonstrate that nothing is impossible. And if anyone doubts that man can step on the moon and plant a flag, American inventiveness shows that through hard work, innovation, intelligence, ambition, and resources, they can prove the skeptics wrong. As Mark Twain said, "And since they did not know it was impossible, they did it."

Although there has been a lot of talk lately about the decline of the American empire, about the crisis of values and identity in the United States, this apparently has not affected its technological innovation. Its system encourages development and production. Moreover, its melting pot is so large that it stirs up ideas from all over the world, providing fertile ground for innovation. The country maintains its global dominance through large corporations, and the day has not yet come when Chinese tech companies will succeed in overtaking US companies—even though they are working tirelessly to do so. In the meantime, the world continues to consume inventions from the United States.

Innovation is synonymous with patents. The race to create new inventions never rests for a single day. That's how it is; the more you know, the more you grow. The United States, with its technological leadership, is the nation with the largest registry of patents and inventions in the world.

In *Estados Unidos: En la intimidad y a la distancia* (Debate, 2020, *America through Foreign Eyes*, Oxford University Press), Jorge G. Castañeda points out that the patent scheme in the United States, along with the tax code, contributed to monetizing inventions. This resulted in several billionaires—including the Carnegies, Fords, and Rockefellers—donating money to philanthropy and becoming patrons of the arts and academia. As Castañeda points out, "If an inventor can become a tycoon, and the latter can be recognized and appreciated as a pillar of the noblest segments of society, the circle is closed. The inventor becomes an idol, a hero, a great man and woman, whom others seek to emulate ... In the United States, there is enormous social recognition and praise for great inventors."

During the nineteenth century, patent wars were commonplace. Whoever was fortunate enough to register a never-before-seen product got all the credit and financial gain that went with the creation. For example, Alexander Graham Bell is considered the inventor of the telephone. Bell was under the enormous shadow of the Italian Antonio Meucci, who twenty years earlier built the *teletrofono*—a telephone-like device that was capable of transmitting acoustic signals through electricity. Due to economic problems, Meucci did not obtain his patent, a circumstance that Bell took advantage of, creating the Bell Telephone Company in 1876, which is better known today as AT&T. But justice always comes, even if it's sometimes a little delayed along the way. In 2002, the US Congress passed a resolution recognizing Meucci as the true inventor of the telephone.

And we cannot talk about the telephone without mentioning Samuel Morse, an American painter and inventor, creator of the Morse telegraph, which was the preferred system of communications during both of the twentieth century's world wars. Samuel Morse introduced a system to transmit messages by means of electronic pulses. The first telegraph line operated between Baltimore and Washington.

Another controversial case is the war of electrical currents between Thomas Alva Edison and Nikola Tesla. Edison, who patented 1,093 inventions, also founded the General Electric Company, which is still in existence today. To him, we owe the supply of electric power and all the benefits it brings. In 1887, he created an industrial research laboratory for product innovation, and a qualified team of mechanics and technicians helped him patent around four hundred inventions. He was undoubtedly a capable and astute man. He is credited with inventing the incandescent lamp, although it is now known that he only perfected it. In the 1880s, the US government began to invest in lighting in public spaces. Edison was awarded a contract to operate Menlo Park's lighting and power supply system, consisting of fifty-three light bulbs.

In the middle of the twentieth century, also called the century of inventions, Edison became an example to follow for migrants who wished to fulfill the American dream. His counterpart is Nicolas Tesla, a Serbian-American who is credited with inventing the radio as well as the use of alternating current to send electricity at high voltage. This genius went on to patent around seven hundred innovations. Among his world-changing inventions, apart from the radio, are X-rays, the electric motor, neon lamps, and wireless telecommunications. He was part of Edison's laboratory, but there was some friction between them because he did not feel that he was being adequately compensated for his talent. If any benefit came out of that rivalry, it is that the competition between Edison and Tesla meant the creation of countless inventions that improved the world—even if some were only done to one-up the other.

The internet began in the United States as a project led by the Massachusetts Institute of Technology (MIT) to connect terminals to each other. In 1962, Joseph Carl Robnett Licklider, known as JCR or Lick, worked on a system to protect government-owned computers from a possible nuclear attack by interconnecting them. In 1981, IBM—a company founded in New York in 1911—launched a personal computer for the business market. Called the IBM PC, it was as big as a prehistoric egg. Although the computer is not entirely a US invention, we cannot deny that Americans perfected it on a far-reaching scale. Visionaries Steve Jobs, Steve Wozniak, and Ronald Wayne founded Apple Computer in 1976. They began by creating personal computers and achieved success with the innovative Macintosh. Their iPod revolutionized the way we store and listen to music, sending the compact disc market to the dustbin. The influence of Apple products on modern society is huge. It is difficult to find someone who does not take pictures with their smartphone, write manuscripts on their MacBook, read the news on their iPad, or listen to music with their AirPods. Its flagship product, the iPhone, is the best-selling smartphone in the world, and every year, a new model appears with multiple improvements over the previous one.

In January 1996, Larry Page and Sergey Brin, graduate students at Stanford, were working on a university project to organize all the information on the internet. From this modest assignment, Google was born. The giant company now owns the most widely used search engine in the world, as well as Google Drive, Gmail, Google Maps, and YouTube.

Another influential name in history is Henry Ford, and he is erroneously credited with creating the moving assembly line. He was not its inventor, although he did perfect it. To fulfill his dream of having affordably priced vehicles circulating throughout the country, Henry Ford installed an assembly line for the Ford Model T, and that mass production scheme is still profitable today. Another pioneer in the field, Ransom Olds, patented an assembly line for Oldsmobile, a company that was later absorbed by General Motors.

There are other patents that we would consider improbable, but their impacts move the worldwide economy. Such is the case of the toilet paper roll, which was registered by Seth Wheeler in 1891. Another patent commonly used and indispensable today, although more sophisticated, is that of the airplane. The Wright brothers, after several failed attempts, flew the first airplane in 1903.

Let's move on to other inventions almost as complex as those already mentioned. The first industrial robot, Unimation, was patented by George Devol and was used for the first time in a General Motors assembly line in 1953. The Missile Launch System, patented in 1965 by Timothy Eddins, is a system used by NASA that allowed man's first trip to the moon. Neil Armstrong stepped onto the lunar surface and declared that it was a small step for man but a giant leap for mankind. This system was also used for the launch of the *Saturn 5* rocket.

Among the key inventions in our times is the 3D printer, created and patented by Chuck Hull, founder of 3D Systems. Its technology has applications for the food industry, human anatomy, and surgical purposes. It can print virtually any object, including prostheses, mock-ups, firearms, toys, and even human organs.

However, not all disruptive inventions came from the United States. Mexico, although on a smaller scale, also has examples to highlight. The color television was created thanks to the engineer Guillermo Gonzalez Camarena, founder of Mexico's Channel 5 television network. In 1940, he invented what is known as the Sequential Trichromatic Field Sequential System—STSC—to transmit television programs in color and remove color blindness from the images seen on the screen. Gonzalez Camarena also invented the simplified two-color system, which would later be used by NASA for its space television transmissions. On February 17, his birthday, Inventor's Day is celebrated in Mexico in honor of this renowned scientist.

Another example of controversial patents is the contraceptive pill, a contribution of Mexican scientist Luis Miramontes Cardenas. The first oral contraceptive, created in 1951, started the sexual revolution by separating sex and reproduction and effectively giving women the power of choice. Although he was not credited with the discovery at the time (the credit was first given to Carl Dejarassi), the twenty-six-year-old Mexican's legacy was later acknowledged. Nevertheless, the company headed by Carl Dejarassi patented the pill, and recognition and money were shared with Dejarassi's business partner. The pill went on the market in 1961 under the label of Syntex, which at that time was a Mexican company. Due to bureaucratic negligence, Syntex ended up becoming a US company. Finally, the multinational firm Roche absorbed Syntex and since then has been distributing the contraceptive pill around the world.

The list of patents that have revolutionized the world is extensive. Regardless of their controversial history, as we have seen, it is all about human inventiveness and creativity to transform the world from a positive perspective. Nothing new emerges from conventionality. Technological advancement and progress come when someone disagrees with the status quo and works to change it. For two hundred years, the United States has looked at the world with the intention of selling its wonders. Mexico, on the other hand, has always looked first to the domestic market, and only then has it dared to go out into the world. As we have seen, the developed US system motivates innovation, which Mexico, due to its limitations, has not achieved. But there would be something in the way of innovation at which Mexico would excel: a creative, cultural, and artistic element whose richness goes back to its origins.

Artistic Innovation

The Mexican Revolution culminated in the enactment of the 1917 Constitution, the subsequent assassination of the principal revolutionary leaders, and the rise to power of Plutarco Elías Calles in 1924. Mexico underwent several social changes once the rifles and cannons were silenced and calm returned to the desolate battlefields. The new political class prioritized institutions over bullets. The Mexican political system ceased to defer to one man indefinitely, as happened during the Porfiriato, and instead changed to a system in which one man would be unconditionally deferred to for a four-year (and later, six-year) term.

After a century of civil wars in which Mexico barely stopped to catch its breath before engaging in a new conflict, the Mexican Revolution came along; the mother of all of Mexico's civil wars. In the words of Jorge Ibarguengoitia, the same thing happened to the Mexican Revolution as happened to elderly ladies who "acquired a respectability that would never have predicted when younger."

The Mexican Revolution also left another important legacy: artistic innovation that emerged from pain. There are those who believe that artistic creation cannot arise from moments of calm and certainty but instead arises during moments of despair as a response to dark times. From the pain of the Mexican Revolution was born a joy that embraces Mayan, Aztec, and Olmec history and assimilates the suffering of so much upheaval. After the armed revolution, a cultural revolution began to emerge, shaped by writers, painters, sculptors, and architects, and it continues into the twenty-first century.

As for the United States, its economic boom was reflected in several artistic trends. Hand in hand with the economic and military power that the US enjoyed after World War II came an explosion of talent and creativity. Its detonator was the war; after it ended, the glory of cinema, literature, painting, and music was sparked. Since most European cities were devastated, many foreign artists, intellectuals, philosophers, and writers found refuge in the United States. New York became the cultural and artistic capital of the world, and Hollywood established itself as the unsurpassed dream factory. The United States opened its arms to scientists and creators fleeing European devastation and benefitted enormously from their arrival.

The great Mexican artists were the product of the Mexican Revolution and the processing of the pain resulting from that war. After that period of great instability, several artists emerged to elevate Mexico's national identity. Frida Kahlo is probably the most famous Mexican painter in the world. For Chavela Vargas, Frida was a being from another world: "Her eyebrows joined together like a swallow in full flight." She lived in physical pain most of her life, and suffering is a central theme of most of her works. Kahlo moves us with images of a deer with its face and several arrows buried in its skin; herself weeping with a broken spine, steel, lace, and nails preventing her broken soul from vanishing; an unborn fetus, floating sadly like a balloon, tethered to her by a strand of blood. Frida Kahlo captured all her suffering in the paintings she made, although her greatest pain had a name: Diego Rivera.

Frida Kahlo became an iconic character, and the adoration she receives is due more to her persona than to her artistic work. Frida's image follows a path similar to the famous photograph of Ernesto "Che" Guevara taken by photographer Alberto Diaz "Korda" after the Cuban Revolution. The photograph of the Argentine guerrilla became an icon that appears on T-shirts, flags, caps, tennis shoes, mugs, and other consumer items. Frida Kahlo, a communist follower of Marxist ideology, paradoxically has also become a capitalist brand and a feminist banner. She has appeared in American films such as *Frida* (2002), portrayed by Salma Hayek, and *Coco* (2017), from the Pixar animation studio. Even Mattel made a Barbie doll inspired by the long-suffering Mexican painter, but it could not be sold in

Mexico due to a copyright controversy. In 2021, her self-portrait, "Diego and I," in which the image of Diego Rivera with three eyes appears on the artist's tearful face, was auctioned for $34.9 million, making it the most expensive work by a Latin American artist to be sold at auction, far surpassing the record of her husband, the brilliant Diego Rivera.

Diego Rivera, a native of Guanajuato, possessed great artistic talent that put Mexico on the map. Along with Jose Clemente Orozco and David Alfaro Siqueiros, Rivera is the greatest representative of Mexican muralism, an artistic movement that emerged after the Mexican Revolution. Muralism sought to build a new national identity by exalting the indigenous past and class struggles. This movement also aimed to educate the Mexican public and teach them the greatness of their history through art, since at that time, 90 percent of the country's population was illiterate.

Thanks to the support of Jose Vasconcelos, the secretary of public education under President Alvaro Obregon, Diego Rivera painted on the walls of several public buildings, including the National University of Mexico, the Department of Public Education, and the National Palace. Its main staircase features *Epic of the Mexican People,* which portrays five centuries of Mexican history. Another important work of Rivera is his *Sueño de una tarde dominical en la Alameda Central (Dream of a Sunday Afternoon in Alameda Park)* in which historical figures from different periods coexist in Mexico City's Alameda Park. Jose Guadalupe Posada's famous, elegant, and smiling Catrina is at the center of the work.

In 1933, Rivera was hired by tycoon Nelson Rockefeller to paint a mural in the lobby of Rockefeller Center, which is located on New York's Fifth Avenue. The assignment did not go well. Rivera included a portrait of Vladimir Lenin in the mural that adorned no less than the center of world capitalism. Rockefeller felt aggrieved by the Mexican painter's provocation and had the mural, ironically titled *Man, Controller of the Universe*, removed from his wall.

Jose Clemente Orozco became interested in painting when, as a child, he watched Jose Guadalupe Posada work on engravings after returning home from school. This activity, which for many people went unnoticed, awakened in Orozco an enormous artistic talent that might have lain dormant. In the United States, he painted important murals, such as *Prometheus*, at Pomona College in California, and *The Epic of American Civilization*, in the library of Dartmouth College. In Mexico, his powerful art adorns the walls of the University of Guadalajara, Mexico's Supreme Court, and the Palace of Fine Arts. The wars in Mexico and the world always troubled Orozco, and in his works, he harshly criticized the Mexican Revolution, moving away from the idealization that other muralists had of that period. He also portrayed the horrors of the Cristero War, Nazism, and World War II. The characters in Orozco's murals are powerful, energetic, violent, and gigantic. An epic struggle persists in several of them.

In music, Mexico has had great names such as Jose Pablo Moncayo, who composed "Huapango." This extraordinary symphonic work was inspired by the sounds of Veracruz. Moncayo's music sought to exalt Mexican nationalism, highlighting the epic ideals of the Mexican Revolution through his melodies. "Huapango" has been so emblematic for the people of Mexico that it has even been considered a second national anthem.

Manuel M. Ponce is another great of Mexican music to whom we owe the song "Estrellita," one of the most beautiful and popular songs in the history of Mexican music. Ponce did not copyright the song in his name and could not collect the substantial royalties that would have corresponded to him, an omission that he surely regretted in the last days of his life, which he lived in poverty. Juventino Rosas was another Mexican musician and composer. His talent circled the globe with the most danced waltz in history, "Sobre las olas," but he, like Ponce, ended up in total poverty.

Octavio Paz has been the only Mexican to win the Nobel Prize in Literature. This happened in 1990, and the feat has not been repeated. Author of poems such as "Entre la piedra y la flor," "Libertad bajo palabra," and "Piedra de Sol," his most famous book is *The Labyrinth of Solitude*, an essay published in 1950 that explores the behavior of Mexicans, their psychology, their essence, and the origin of their pessimism and apathy. Paz confesses that many of the reflections that give shape to *The Labyrinth of Solitude* emerged during his two-year stay in the United States, when the poet sought to make sense of the American way of life.

In that essay, with his extraordinary lyricism, Octavio Paz explains the differences he found between Mexicans and Americans:

> They are credulous, we are believers; they love fairy tales and detective stories, we love myths and legends. The Mexican tells lies because he delights in fantasy, or because he wants to rise above the sordid facts of life; they do not tell lies but substitute social truth for real truth, which is always disagreeable. We get drunk in order to confess; they get drunk in order to forget (...) Mexicans are distrustful; they are open. We are sorrowful and sarcastic; they are happy and full of jokes. Americans want to understand; we want to contemplate.

Allá en el rancho grande (directed by Fernando de Fuentes, 1936) ushered in the golden age of Mexican cinema. The film made the world look at Mexico's film industry and take it seriously. It helped that the United States and Europe were busy in World War II and didn't have much time to devote to making films. Mexico took advantage of the circumstances and began to film productions with complex, daring themes, far removed from vulgarity.

Let's look back on that Mexico of yesteryear; in the aftermath of the Mexican Revolution, a new national identity was emerging, with an emphasis on ranching and rural life. Packards could be seen on the streets; the president's brother was, in essence, running the country. Instead of cell phones, men carried pistols; people danced to the music of orchestras; and black-and-white movies colored the emotions of their viewers.

These golden years saw the emergence of figures such as the director Emilio "El Indio" Fernandez, Pedro Armendariz, the actress Dolores del Río, and Mario Moreno "Cantinflas," Mexico's most popular comedian. An icon who got his start in vaudeville, Cantinflas later made the big leap to the silver screen. His particular way of speaking even gave name to a verb in Spanish—*cantinflear*—which means to talk a lot and in a convoluted way without saying anything substantial.

Maria Felix—with her unquestionable beauty, enormous theatrical talent, and strong character—conquered the hearts of the whole world. A diva on a par with Marilyn Monroe, Marlene Dietrich, and Elizabeth Taylor, Maria Felix starred in successful films such as *Maria Eugenia* (1943), *Doña Barbara* (1943), *Enamorada* (1946), and *El indio Tizoc* (1956), in which she shared credits with Pedro Infante. Her third marriage was to composer Agustin Lara, and during their honeymoon, he composed "Maria Bonita," a beautiful song that immortalized her in the sentimental memory of Latin America.

Maria Felix and Agustin Lara were considered by the public as Beauty and the Beast. Unfortunately, the marriage did not last, partly due to the poet-musician's uncontrollable jealousy, and Maria Felix went her own successful way. She disdained making movies in the United States, preferring to work in films shot in Mexico or Europe.

Pedro Infante and Jorge Negrete achieved fame at almost the same time. Heartthrobs of cinema and owners of prodigious voices, they both performed in the film *Dos tipos de cuidado* (1953), considered one of the best Mexican comedies. Its most memorable scene (and song) is one where they face off in a singing contest.

The quality of Mexican cinema declined in the following years with sex comedies, low-budget movies, and the absurd, yet classic, films about wrestlers such as El Santo and Blue Demon. Unable to compete against innovative American productions, Mexican cinema became mediocre and repetitive. The advent of television also meant that movie theaters were no longer as popular as they used to be. The Mexican public was left with no superstars. A new boom would come several decades later, in the 1990s, with the arrival of filmmakers such as Alfonso Cuaron, Guillermo del Toro, and Alejandro Gonzalez

Iñarritu, three Mexicans who have won Oscars, raising Mexico's profile high in Hollywood.

Through cinema, the United States has presented its culture to the rest of the world. The influence of American cinema in Mexico is enormous. If anyone has any doubts, they can take a look at the listings of any movie theater and see how many of these productions are Mexican and how many are American. It is no exaggeration to say that people who have never set foot in the United States know the country thanks to its films. The United States sold the idea of the American dream, where everything was possible as long as one worked for it.

American inventiveness took cinema to a higher level than the one started by the Lumiere brothers. They thrilled viewers with the arrival of a train at the station or with a capsule crashing on the face of the moon. American innovation made the world believe that a giant gorilla in love could terrorize New York or that there was a magical and distant land called Oz, besieged by a cruel witch. Hollywood cinema made us dream, laugh, fear, or cry with those artificial representations of reality. Even though there is talk of a crisis in the industry today—and a lack of originality and imagination in its stories—American cinema and television continue to offer great products that immediately become part of popular culture around the world.

Walt Disney, after rejecting many different versions, settled on just three circles to form the head of Mickey Mouse, probably the most famous animated character on the planet. Years later, his company came to dominate the world's entertainment industry. Animated feature films changed forever after movies such as *Snow White and the Seven Dwarfs*, *Pinocchio*, *Dumbo*, and *Bambi*. Disney became a tycoon, building theme parks based on his characters, although he only lived long enough to see the first one built in California. Today, it is hard to find a communications company or intellectual property that is not part of the Walt Disney Company. Not bad for someone who, instead of an empire, only intended to draw a little mouse and his mouse girlfriend.

An heir to the innovative spirit of Walt Disney and Alfred Hitchcock is Steven Spielberg. At a young age, he terrified the world with *Jaws* (1975), his third film, responsible for empty beaches during the summer of its release. Horror sells, and that film was the first to be considered a blockbuster. Spielberg proved that anything that can be imagined could also be filmed. It doesn't matter whether it's about aliens visiting Earth, children flying their bicycles in front of the moon, an island full of dinosaurs, a regiment looking to rescue a soldier during World War II, or the adventures of an archeologist who travels the world searching for treasures before they fall into the hands of the Nazis. Spielberg understood that good cinema could also be great business, that audiences like to be thrilled and moved, and that art and entertainment need not be mutually exclusive. On the contrary, using this seemingly disparate union with talent, Spielberg continues to deliver unforgettable stories.

Many believe that the American novel really emerged with *The Adventures of Huckleberry Finn*. Written by Mark Twain—considered the father of American literature—and published in 1884, the novel is the sequel to *The Adventures of Tom Sawyer*, another classic book. Twain was quite successful during his lifetime, thanks to his humorous writings. He was born around the same time Halley's comet visited Earth and died seventy-four years later, coinciding with its next visit. In his book, Mark Twain portrays an unmistakable link between black and white culture, creating harsh and critical satire about racism of the time.

Many years later, another great American writer, a giant in world literature, recognized Twain's influence on practically all the writers who came after him. In his novel *The Green Hills of Africa*, Ernest Hemingway wrote this famous eulogy: "All modern American literature comes from a book written by Mark Twain called *Huckleberry Finn*. American writing comes from that. There was nothing before. There has been nothing as good since."

Ernest Hemingway was an adventurous writer, one of those who need to live escapades to the limit in order to narrate them in an intense, simple, and honest style. Hemingway was an ambulance driver during World War I and a journalist in the Spanish Civil War, and it is said that he saw the Allies landing in Normandy with his own eyes. His writing shows few details because, like icebergs, what is important is what is not seen with the naked eye. Living in Cuba and inspired by the Caribbean Sea, he wrote his masterpiece *The Old Man and the Sea*, a short novel about an old man who struggles to catch the biggest and strongest marlin the world has ever seen. In 1954, Hemingway received the news that he had won the Nobel Prize for Literature. In the midst of excessive alcohol consumption, depressed and paranoid because of constant monitoring by the FBI, Hemingway committed suicide on July 2, 1961.

The work and style of Ernest Hemingway and William Faulkner, another winner of the Nobel Prize for Literature, greatly influenced the writers of the Latin American Boom: Gabriel Garcia Marquez, Carlos Fuentes, Julio Cortazar, and Mario Vargas Llosa.

Another great artistic contribution of the United States to the world is jazz. Music originating from African, slave, and black rhythms, today it is popular all over the planet. If someone wants to appear more interesting than they really are, they will undoubtedly mention jazz as one of their hobbies. In the vibrant film *La La Land* (Damien Chazelle, 2016), the character played by Ryan Gosling talks about jazz:

> It was born in New Orleans because the people there spoke five languages, and they couldn't talk to each other; their only way to communicate was through jazz ... It's conflict and compromise, it's new all the time and brand-new every night, and it's very exciting.

Jazz is rhythm, swing, improvisation, freshness, stage, melancholy, dance, concentration, tears, life, saxophone, cornet, trombone, clarinet, piano. Its central artists are Ella Fitzgerald, Billie Holiday, Louis Armstrong, Duke Ellington, Nina Simone, and Charlie Parker.

And if there was a king in music to be mentioned, that rank goes to Elvis Presley. Legend has it that, inspired by African-American dances and music, Elvis's sudden hip movements were capable of driving all the women who watched him euphorically crazy. If Bob Dylan innovated with the poetic lyrics of his songs, Elvis did it with nothing less than the restlessness of his body.

In painting, Jackson Pollock led the way in abstract expressionism. His works, valued at millions of dollars, are made up of paint brushstrokes of different colors apparently made without order or sense. They are pure chaos and action and uncontrollable movement. His crazy splashes were influenced by Mexican muralists, especially Siqueiros, and this innovative (and therefore misunderstood) technique has not been without controversy.

The image of a Campbell's soup can and colorful portraits of Marilyn Monroe were works created by Andy Warhol, an icon of pop art and of the frenetic and bohemian nightlife of New York in the 1960s. Known worldwide, Warhol's work represents a critique of the meaninglessness of modern life, mass culture, and consumerism, which was already beginning to emerge as one of the great evils of society. He was quoted as saying that an artist is someone who produces things that people do not need. His famous art studio, The Factory, was a meeting point for artists, singers, celebrities, poets, intellectuals, transsexuals, hookers, and drug addicts. Warhol predicted some of the peculiarities of the current era, such as the unhealthy need for recognition, the pursuit of fame at any cost and for whatever reason, even if you have no talent, as well as the culture of influencers and the selfie. His clairvoyant phrase was this: "In the future, everyone will be world-famous for fifteen minutes." Today, it could be said that, thanks to social networks, anyone can be famous—even if only for fifteen seconds.

American culture was a window through which the world could observe the successes and contradictions of the United States. Its influence on other Western countries extended to cinema, music, dance, literature, painting, and fashion. American culture even showed its vulnerability and solitude, which can be seen in the silent paintings of Edward Hopper. There are many creators who had to go live in the United States in order to succeed; almost everyone consumes Walt Disney movies, Michael Jackson songs, Netflix series, and the lifestyle of the Kardashian family. Today, it is impossible to imagine a more cosmopolitan city than New York. There isn't one, and at this point, the city that will one day replace New York has yet to be invented.

Wealth and Poverty

Wealth and poverty form a never-ending dichotomy for the nations of the world. Balancing wealth and reducing poverty are challenges that define nations. This has often been a historical and social debt for both Mexico and the United States. The persons named below are industrial tycoons who have amassed great fortunes and actually represent a very tiny percentage of the population.

We begin with John D. Rockefeller. Oil brought with it a decisive boom in the economy, with impressive benefits for the United States, and it placed the country on the map of world powers. Rockefeller's wealth was due to his ingenuity in the oil industry, which he monopolized until the US government imposed limits due to the immense power and money he accumulated.

Rockefeller passed away as one of the richest men the world had ever seen. His millions probably helped him reach the age of ninety-seven after enjoying a sublime and privileged lifestyle, but not even all the gold on Earth could prevent his passing. However, his fortune, the one he generated during his lifetime, was inherited as family wealth. To this day, the Rockefeller clan remains among the richest families in the world—with a net worth that exceeds $11 billion.

Another extremely wealthy American family is the Du Pont family. Eleuthere Irenee du Pont de Nemours founded the Du Pont Company in 1802. Of French-American origin, he ventured into the gunpowder business, focusing on chemistry. Today, Du Pont is a worldwide conglomerate. As in the case of Rockefeller, Du Pont was forced to diversify his activities in the twentieth century under pressure from US antitrust laws. Today, the Du Pont assets amount to $14.5 billion, making them the fourth wealthiest family in the country.

In the United States, Jeff Bezos, Bill Gates, and Mark Zuckerberg together have as much wealth as 64 percent of the lowest-income people in their country. In the United States, the great fortunes of the twenty-first century, which place the country at the top of the list of the richest people in the world, are business organizations built on technology. Elon Musk heads the 2022 list with a fortune of $195 billion coming from the online payment system PayPal and the tech company Tesla. Musk is followed by Jeff Bezos, with $124 billion thanks to the titan of e-commerce, Amazon, which started in 1994 as an online bookstore. The company increased its profits during the COVID-19 pandemic thanks to the boom in online shopping. Bill Gates, founder of the software company Microsoft, has $105 billion, and Mark Zuckerberg has $56 billion from developing the social network Facebook. Most of the wealth in the United States is concentrated in their hands, helping to maintain the country's domination of the world economy. Any of them controls a fortune larger than the gross domestic product of several countries.

Year after year, the descendants of these types of families appear in *Forbes*. This happens with many businesspeople from the United States, but it also occurs in Mexico. In Mexico, there are also wealthy families, although, in many cases, mismanagement has wiped out the inheritance. During the Porfirio Diaz government, some families became extremely wealthy thanks to the famous *latifundios* (land tenure system), crony capitalism, or the exploitation of indigenous people who worked the henequen plantations. The Revolution of 1910 and money mismanagement added to their misfortunes. As a result, the wealth of these families, who were so influential during the Don Porfirio era, began to evaporate.

The Garza Sada surname from the city of Monterrey bucks this trend. The name appeared in *Forbes* during the six-year term of President Salinas de Gortari. In 1987, according to *Forbes*, the family's wealth exceeded $1 billion. Their fortune comes from the brewing industry; later they acquired a Coca-Cola bottler and added the successful OXXO chain of stores to their portfolio. Today, the Garza Sada multigenerational wealth is estimated at more than $7 billion, placing them as the fourth richest family in Mexico. Currently, Eva Gonda de Rivera, the widow of Eugenio Garza Laguera, is at the head of this powerful Mexican conglomerate.

Carlos Slim Helu was born in Mexico City in 1940. Between 2010 and 2014, he competed with Bill Gates for the title of richest man in the world. During his youth, he was quite a successful businessman, but his public profile really took off when Mexico nationalized banks and several state-owned companies. Carlos Slim acquired Telefonos de Mexico (Telmex, telephone company) under controversial terms. His business acumen enabled him to establish a telecommunications monopoly in Mexico for a time, and his influence now extends to other countries. Currently, Slim's net worth amounts to $81 billion. He is the richest man in Mexico and the sixteenth richest in the world.

German Larrea Mota Velasco does not like the spotlight and prefers a rather private, low-profile existence. He inherited a fortune from his father, and most of his fortune comes from the construction and mining sectors. Similar to what happened with Carlos Slim, the family business obtained a state-owned mining company that was privatized during the six-year term of Carlos Salinas. His father, Jorge Larrea Ortega, bought it at a much lower price than agreed upon. After completing the acquisition, the mining company—the largest in the country and the third largest copper producer in the world—became part of the Grupo Mexico conglomerate. The Larrea family fortune grew considerably. In 2020, their wealth increased when the mining sector surged by 35 percent, generating growth for the firm of more than 150 percent and a fortune that exceeds $27 billion. Today, he is positioned as the second richest man in Mexico, behind Carlos Slim.

Ricardo Salinas Pliego is the president of Grupo Salinas, a conglomerate of companies in the financial and communications sectors. During the six-year term of Salinas de Gortari, his administration's privatization plan included selling a state-owned television station, Imevision, which Salinas Pliego acquired and turned into TV Azteca. With his entrepreneurial vision, the station became one of the largest in the media sector in Latin America. Salinas Pliego's fortune amounts to $13 billion.

As we pointed out at the beginning, a balance between poverty and wealth is difficult to achieve. Mexico has its billionaires, but the distribution of its wealth is tragically unequal. The fortunes of Slim, Larrea, and Salinas Pliego equal the combined annual income of 78 percent of the lowest earners in Mexico. For perspective, Mexico's richest families account for two-thirds of the country's wealth. This makes for a very visible division between the two sides of the coin: a majority is struggling to make ends meet on a minimum wage, and the richest men in Latin America are Mexicans.

Furthermore, as analyst Viridiana Ríos points out, in Mexico, it is very difficult to become rich if you come from a poor background, and it is almost impossible to become poor if you were born into the cradle of wealth. An example of this inequality can be seen during the COVID-19 pandemic, which did not affect all Mexicans equally. There is evidence that Mexican multimillionaires increased their fortunes during the pandemic by 60 percent, but a majority of the population lost jobs, patrimony, and savings, and they spent what little they had on medicines and hospitals. Not all Mexicans were able to stay locked up in their homes to avoid exposure to the virus. The vast majority had to go out and work. In an article that appeared in *El País*, a woman from Iztapalapa told the reporter: "They ask us to wash our hands frequently so as to not get infected by the virus, but with what water am I going to wash my hands since there has never been any here?"

At this juncture, we take a look at a political figure who is concerned about the neediest social sector of the country. President Andres Manuel Lopez Obrador has traveled throughout the country for twelve years, paying special attention to the most marginalized towns that very few Mexican politicians have noticed. His concern is very clear: he opposes the corruption that made a handful of families in Mexico very wealthy. He proposes that we must put the poor first and separate economic interests from the government. The president never tires of saying that for the good of all, the poor must come first.

President Lopez Obrador signed a decree to limit public officials' salaries to below that of the president; it also eliminated lifetime pensions for former presidents. Lopez Obrador prioritized the generation of economic opportunities previously denied to the most vulnerable sectors. There is no need to look for consent from that generation of politicians focused on personal enrichment. Like Hank Gonzalez bragged at every opportunity, "A poor (bad) politician is a poor (broke) politician."

Both the United States and Mexico have a serious problem with the unequal distribution of wealth. In this respect, the difference between the two countries is minimal. Some time ago, President Lyndon B. Johnson enunciated the phrase "war on poverty" as the banner of his administration. In his speeches, he warned that his administration was focused on combating the nation's poverty rates through direct state intervention. Another precedent is Franklin Roosevelt; his interventionist policy, the New Deal, sought social policies to reduce the terrible ravages of the economic crisis of 1929.

At present, the United States has decided to solve its inequality problem by levying high inheritance taxes and limiting the exercise of patents to twenty years. In 2021, inheritance taxes can reach 40 percent for federal taxes and 16 percent for state taxes; the US levies the highest inheritance taxes in the world. In Mexico, the exploitation of patents is also limited to twenty years, and through social programs, redistribution of wealth and reactivation of the economy is sought. In 2021, the social programs of Lopez Obrador's administration represented 47 percent of the nation's expenditure budget. Each government is looking for the best scheme to reduce the unequal distribution of wealth that puts its social fabric at risk.

Undoubtedly, the social and economic reform of a country begins with effective and fair distribution of resources—and priority is given to the less favored sectors. Another priority of Lopez Obrador is the direct fight against corruption. Corruption must be cleaned like the stairs in a house—from top to bottom. By eliminating corruption from Mexico's political life, the money that went to pay for political campaigns, obscene and superfluous expenses, private airplanes, or trips abroad now goes directly to the people who need it most. President Lopez Obrador says, "There can be no rich government with a poor people."

No country should proudly boast of producing some of the richest people in the world when a large part of its population lives in poverty. For several decades, economic elites have built their fortunes on government benefits; it is time that the priority is on the people who are least able to, those who know the least, those who have the least, and those who have only uncertainty about the future. The inequality between those who have a lot and those who have very little is unsustainable.

The anger in the world against the elites is justified, and it has translated into a popular preference for more authoritarian and dictatorial governments. We must understand that ordinary people care little if the economy grows by 1 percent. As long as they do not feel that effect in their own pockets, nothing will change. Growth figures matter little in the face of a population that has no savings or patrimony and whose purchasing power is decreasing. The poor no longer want to be the buffer for all the misfortunes that befall a country. They do not want preachers or politicians to promise them paradise, eternal life, or good fortune once they are already dead. What a joke. It is about improving existence on Earth here and now.

It is worth dreaming of a different world where one can develop one's talents regardless of whether one was born in a manger or in a silver cradle and societies where no one justifies their privilege by saying that the poor are poor because they want to be. Fortunately, in Mexico and the United States, the narrative about inequality is already beginning to change.

In the seventeenth century, shipyards and their large fleets boosted the trade and economic power of nations. The United States was able to take on a leading role internationally because it fully embraced that

401

model, but Mexico was left on the sidelines when the Spanish Crown gave that role to the Philippines. Later, in the nineteenth century, the railroads became the driver of trade and development. The United States surpassed the entire world in number of trains and kilometers of railroads, but Mexico was caught up in internecine wars. In the twentieth century, the geniuses of the world surprised us with one patent after another—so many that humanity lost its capacity for astonishment. The United States engendered a model that rewarded inventiveness while attracting millions of talented immigrants who embraced their new country because it welcomed and encouraged them for their ingenuity, but Mexico became another country that exported human talent. Finally, in the twenty-first century, where digitalization of knowledge and communication is the engine of development, the United States is the spearhead, and Mexico is a net importer in the rearguard.

This history of lost opportunities on the part of Mexico opened a wider gap with the United States. When the North American Free Trade Agreement was negotiated in the 1990s, the term "asymmetry of the economies" had to be invented to take into account the enormous imbalance between the countries over almost two centuries. It has reached the point where the US economy is several times that of Mexico. In addition, the history of the two nations makes another difference evident: fortunes in the United States were built by taking advantage of their resources—even those that did not belong to the US—developing successful inventions, and creating conglomerates with new products and services. In Mexico, fortunes—in most cases—were achieved on the basis of birthright, perks granted by the government in office, or allowing the exploitation of the Mexican people through de facto monopolies or government grants.

Epilogue

The Eagles Will Keep Flying Together

And just because we're in front of each other
Doesn't mean
We confront each other (how droll)
Our bias doesn't let us see
That from heaven we're side by side
—Kevin Johansen, *Vecino* (*Neighbor*)

When you talk about Mexico and the United States, you probably first think of a soccer match—and then you want to know the final score of the game. Countless academics and intellectuals have studied the relationship between the two neighbors. And yet, in the collective imagination, topics like the disparity—economic, political, and security—between Mexico and the United States still dominate. Likewise, in that imagery, adjectives abound for each country.

In these times of polarization, fake news, and ignorance, for many US citizens, Mexico is a country to the south where anarchy reigns, narcos impose presidents, and the government purposely sends murderers and rapists to its northern neighbor. And for many Mexicans, the United States continues to be a prosperous but war-loving, gun-loving, fast-food-loving country that we do not forgive for the fact that 174 years ago it took away half of our national territory. Despite resentment, grievances, and open wounds, the shared history of Mexico and the United States also includes other precepts, not the usual ones, ones more positive and hopeful.

It is said that former President Sebastian Lerdo de Tejada once said, "Between Mexico and the United States, the desert." Later, Porfirio Diaz coined a famous phrase that is often repeated today—even mentioned by President Lopez Obrador in his first virtual meeting with President Biden: "Poor Mexico, so far from God and so close to the United States." Far from being seen as a benefit, or an opportunity, the proximity to the United States seemed in the eyes of many as a curse. So much to learn from each other! Contrary to what Lerdo de Tejada pointed out, the union between Mexico and the United States goes beyond the desert. These days, the rapprochement between both nations is different. And as President Lopez Obrador said in a meeting with Secretary Antony Blinken, what is being said now is different: "Blessed is Mexico, so close to God and not so far from the United States."

I remember the *"aviso de coco"* (a posted sign warning people that coconuts may fall from a tree) triggered by Donald Trump's candidacy and subsequent electoral victory. Here comes the orange *coco* to destroy Mexico! The world as we know it is coming to an end! This is the worst thing that has happened to Mexico since the fall of Tenochtitlan and the death of Pedro Infante! Trump's reckless statements worried almost the entire planet. In the international media, there was talk of an unprecedented persecution of migrants in the United States, of the debacle of the empire, and the beginning of the Third World War. In Mexico, open television channels organized roundtables where intellectuals called on the government to demand respect from the Republican candidate and make him stop his offenses against the Mexican people. They proposed calls for national unity, retaliation against US companies, and massive pro-dignity marches.

In the end, Trump assumed the presidency of the United States, and the world did not run out of air, rotating in the same way it has done for millions of years. Politics and diplomacy prevailed. And when Donald Trump left office after losing to President Biden, the world kept spinning, there was no tariff increase, no invasion, no nuclear holocaust, no wall paid for by Mexico, and the clocks did not stop ticking. Apart from the appearance of a pandemic, an economic crisis, a change in the educational and labor model, and a global recession, the world remained apparently the same.

It would be difficult to forfeit two hundred years of diplomatic relations just because of one administration. The United States and Mexico are more than their governments and their speeches. They are their people, the millions of shared histories, the communities that communicate in English, in Spanish, and in the mix between them. As I said before, more than a *pocho*, I have the heart of "ochop." I am from here, and I am from there (with Facundo Cabral's permission), and I try to cherish the best virtues of each nation. The sun does not discern where Mexico begins and the United States ends; it shines the same on both sides.

The relationship between Mexico and the United States has survived American expansionism, the independence of Texas, the dispossession of half of Mexican territory, invasions and military interventions, the assault on Columbus, the punitive expedition, the war on drugs, Operation Condor, illegal espionage, migration, Operation Fast and Furious, arms trafficking, coyotes, Donald Trump and his threats, the border wall, the renegotiation of the Free Trade Agreement, and the remoteness of God.

They say that what doesn't kill you makes you stronger—and that people who live in glass houses shouldn't throw stones. These countries have proven to be the exception to the universal decree that dictates that neighbors should always have an adverse relationship. There are no cracks, however deep and old, that are irreparable. So, between Mexico and the United States, the bond.

Before I end, I think of these verses by the poet Mario Benedetti, which may reflect the relationship between Mexico and the United States over two centuries. I look forward to another two hundred years of friendship, cooperation, and understanding. The two eagles will continue to fly close to each other, in the same desert, under the same sky:

> to sum up,
> we are not what we are
> nor less than what we were
> our soul is in disarray
> but it is worth holding
> with our hands / our eyes / our memory

References

Chapter 1

Chablé Mendoza, C. (2010, 19 de agosto). Jacinto Pat y el Levantamiento Maya De 1847. https://quintanaroo.webnode.es/news/jacinto-pat-y-el-levantamiento-maya-de-1847-por-carlos-chable-mendoza-/.

Cozzens, P. (2017). *La Tierra Llora*, Desperta Ferro Ediciones.

González Lezama, R. (s. f.). *La Ley Lerdo: Un Gran Paso Para La Secularización De La Sociedad Mexicana*. Consultado el 24 de agosto de 2022. https://inehrm.gob.mx/es/inehrm/La_ley_Lerdo.

González, D. (2020, 31 de julio). *Las Reservas Indias de Estados Unido, un Estado dentro del Estado*. [Fronteras Blog] https://tinyurl.com/3f4xhhtc.

Madridejos, A. (2017, 11 de julio). El origen de los caballos 'salvajes' de América llega a los tribunales. *El Periódico de Aragón*. https://tinyurl.com/yed3y6yv.

Molina, S. y Rosas, A. (2013). *Érase Una Vez México I: De las cavernas al virreinato*. Editorial Planeta Mexicana.

Mundo Indígena. (2019). *Estados Unidos de América*. IWIA [Online].

Oliver, V. (2015). *Pieles rojas: Encuentros e intercambios con el hombre blanco*. Editorial Edaf.

Valadés, J. (1993). *Breve Historia de la Revolución mexicana (1900–1940)*. Cambio XXI; FCPS/UNAM.

Von Wobeser, G. (coord.) (2010), *Historia de México*, Fondo de Cultura Económica; Secretaría de Educación Pública.

Chapter 2

Camba Ludlow, U. (2019). Persecución y modorra. La Inquisición en la Nueva España, Turner Noema.

Cuevas, M. (1986). *Historia de la nación mexicana* (4a. ed.). Porrúa.

Guevara Paredes, M. (2000). El fenómeno puritano y su influencia en la formación del Estado Inglés de los siglos XVI y XVII. *IUS ET VERITAS*, 10(20), 454–462. https://revistas.pucp.edu.pe/index.php/iusetveritas/article/view/15950

Mckenna, G. (2007). *The Puritan Origins of American Patriotism*. Yale University Press.

Molina, S. y Rosas, A. (2013). *Érase Una Vez México*. MR Ediciones.

Morison, S.E., Steele Commager, H. y Leuchtenburg, W.E. (2017). *Breve Historia de los Estados Unidos*, Fondo de Cultura Económica.

Pérez Memen, F. (1977). *El episcopado y la Independencia de México (1810–1836)*. Jus.

Staples, A. (1976). *La iglesia en la primera república federal mexicana* (A. Lira, trad.) Editorial Sep-Setentas.

The Editors of Encyclopedia Britannica (1998). *King James Version*. (s.e.).

Zavala, S. (2004). *Breves apuntes de historia nacional*. Fondo de Cultura Económica.

Chapter 3

Arnoldsson, S. (1960). La Conquista española de América según el juicio de la posteridad. Vestigios de la Leyenda Negra. Instituto Iberoamericano.

Black, J. (2005). El papel de la monarquía en la Inglaterra del siglo XVIII. *Manuscrits: Revista d'història moderna*, (23), 151–162.

Carreras, A. y Tafunell, J. (coords.) *Estadísticas históricas de España: siglos XIX-XX*. Fundación BBVA

Ciaramitaro, F. El Virrey y su gobierno en Nueva España y Sicilia. Analogías y diferencias entre periferias del Imperio Hispánico. *Estudios de historia novohispana*. (39), 117–154.

Fernández Delgado, M.A. (2012). *El virrey Iturrigaray y el Ayuntamiento de México en 1808*. SEP; INHERM.

Garduño, E. (res.) (2010). La conquista de América el problema del otro. *Culturales*, 12 (6), 181–197.

López de Gómara, F. (1943). *Historia de la conquista de México*. Editorial Pedro Robredo.

Murillo, I. La religión antes y después de las independencias. ¿Fuente de unidad o de conflicto? *Escritos*, 19, (42), 53–77.

Varela Suanzes-Carpenga, J. (2000). El constitucionalismo británico entre dos revoluciones: 1688–1789. *Fundamentos: Cuadernos monográficos de teoría del estado, derecho público e historia constitucional*, (2), 25–96.

Vázquez Gómez, R. (2010). Organización política y cuestión religiosa en las colonias inglesas de Norteamérica: los casos de Virginia y Maryland. *Revista de Estudios Políticos (nueva época)*, (149), 185–220.

Zamora Navia, P. (2012). Reyes y virreyes de la monarquía hispana a la luz de las significaciones políticas del siglo XVII y de la historiografía. *Revista de Humanidades (Santiago)*, (25), 191–208.

Chapter 4

Ferrer Muñoz, M. (1993). La Constitución de Cádiz y su aplicación en la Nueva España. UNAM.

González Lezama, R. (s.f.). La Muerte De Ignacio Zaragoza. https://inehrm.gob.mx/es/inehrm/La_Muerte_de_Ignacio_Zar

M, Brian. (2014, 5 de mayo). *Sinko De Mayo*. [Stuff Happens] https://stuffhappens.us/sinko-de-mayo-12290/

Molina, S. y Rosas, A. (2018). *Érase una vez México 2: Del grito a la Revolución*. Booket.

Morison, S.E., Steele Commager, H. y Leuchtenburg, W.E. (2017). *Breve Historia de los Estados Unidos*, Fondo de Cultura Económica.

Redondo Rodelas, J. (2015). *Presidentes de Estados Unidos: De Washington a Obama, la historia norteamericana a través de los 43 inquilinos de la Casa Blanca*. La Esfera de los Libros.

SEDENA. (2015, 16 de julio). *La Intervención Francesa*. https://www.gob.mx/sedena/documentos/la-intervencion-francesa

Toro, A. (1927). *La Iglesia y el Estado en México*, Talleres Gráficos de la Nación.

Torre Villar, E. (1994) *Estudios de historia jurídica*. UNAM.

Artola Gallego, M. (2005). El constitucionalismo en la historia. Editorial Crítica.

Blanco Valdés, R. L. (2006). *El valor de la Constitución* (3ª ed.).Alianza Editorial.

Constitution of the United States. 1798. (United States of America), Main Page, (Consultado el 21 de agosto de 2011).

Fioravanti, M. (2009). *Costituzionalismo. Percorsi della storia e tendenze attuali*. Laterza.

Tena Ramírez, F. (1988). *Derecho Constitucional Mexicano* (32ª ed.) Porrúa, pág. 65–66.

González de la Vega, G. (2009). La importancia de la presidencia de Barack Obama. *Cuestiones Constitucionales. Revista Mexicana de Derecho Constitucional*, (21), 413–426.

Jiménez Asensio, R. (2003). *El constitucionalismo. Proceso de formación y fundamentos del Derecho constitucional* (2ª ed.). Editorial Marcial Pons.

Schauer, F. (1997). Constitutional Invocations. *Fordham Law Review*, 65 (4), 1295–1312.

Stokes Paulsen, M. et al. (2015). The Constitution: An Introduction, Basic Books.

Arnold, L. (1996). *Política y justicia. La Suprema Corte mexicana* (1824–1855) (Soberanes Fernández, J. y Bunster, J., trad.). Instituto de Investigaciones Jurídicas, UNAM.

Shapiro, M. (2008). Judicial Review Global, En Ferrer Mac-Gregor Poisot, E. y Zaldívar Lelo de Larrea, A. (coords.). *La ciencia del derecho procesal constitucional, teoría general del derecho procesal constitucional. Estudios en homenaje a Héctor Fix-Zamudio en sus cincuenta años como investigador del derecho.* UNAM; Instituto Mexicano de Derecho Procesal Constitucional Marcial Pons.

Cruz Barney, O. (2004). *La codificación en México: 1821–1917. Una aproximación.* Instituto de Investigaciones Jurídicas, UNAM.

Galeana, P. (2013). *El impacto de la Constitución de Cádiz en México.* Instituto de Investigaciones Jurídicas, UNAM.

Frederick, S. (1997). Constitutional Invocations. *Fordham Law Review*, 65. https://ir.lawnet.fordham.edu/flr/vol65/iss4/4

Niemeyer, V. (1990). El Congreso Constituyente norteamericano de 1787 y el Congreso Constituyente de 1916–1917. Comparación y contraste. En Frank Smith, J. (coord.). *Derecho constitucional comparado México-Estados Unidos* (Stebbins, H., trad.). Instituto de Investigaciones Jurídicas, UNAM.

Varela Suanzes-Carpegna, J., (ed.). (1998). *Textos Básicos de la Historia Constitucional Comparada*, CEPC.

Chapter 6

Aguirre Beltrán, G. (1989). La población negra de México. Fondo de Cultura Económica.

Albarrán, R. (2019). *"Cri es Racista."* Presentación del documental HOPPO! Sin rumbo, Guadalajara (FICG).

Alfonso, L. (2016). La conciencia social. (s.e.).

American University. (2020). *American University Black Swing Voter Project*. Fact Sheet. https://www.american.edu/spa/news/upload/bsvp-deck-sf-7-28-2.pdf

Arceo, M. (2008, 10 de julio). Nueva polémica en EU por Memín Pinguín: lo retiran de Wal-Mart. *La Jornada* [Online].

Battiston, G. (2009). Anticipating Obama: An Interview with Zygmunt Bauman. *Thesis Eleven* (98) 141. http://the.sagepub.com

Biosca Azcoiti, J. (2019. 31 de diciembre). Lincoln no era abolicionista, la Proclamación de Emancipación fue una estrategia militar. *El Diario* [Online]

Bobadilla, Roy. (2017, 23 de noviembre). Defiende CONAPRED a Negrito Sandía. *El Deforma* [Online].

Carmona Dávila, D. (s.f.) *Memoria Política de México.* https://www.memoriapoliticademexico.org/

Commager, H. (1964). *Documents of American History*. Prentice-Hall.

Gutiérrez, Rubí. (2009). *El marketing. (s.e.).*

History. (2015). *Barack Obama*. (s.e.).

History. (2020). *Memorias*. (s.e.).

Jornada. (2008). *Nueva Jornada.* (s.e.).

King, M. L. (1958). *Stride Toward Freedom.* (s.e.).

King, M.L. (1968). *Showdown for Nonviolence.* (s.e.).

Knopf, A. (1988). *El proceso de la primera reconstrucción.* (s.e.).

Kolchin, P. (1993). *American Slavery, 1619–1877.* Hill & Wang Pub.

Luján, E. (2019). *El oscuro secreto.* (s.e.).

Martínez Maza, C. (2016): El esclavismo antiguo en los Estados Unidos del periodo "antebellum" (1780–1860), *Gerión. Revista de Historia Antigua,* 34, 383–389. https://doi.org/10.5209/rev_GERI.2016.v34.53748.

Morison, S.E., Steele Commager, H. y Leuchtenburg, W.E. (2017). *Breve Historia de los Estados Unidos,* Fondo de Cultura Económica.

Obama, B. (2020). *A Promised Land,* Penguin Random House.

Van Woodward, C. (1996). *Segregación y Discriminación.* (s.e.).

Chapter 7

Carmona Dávila, D. (s.f.) Memoria Política de México. https://www.memoriapoliticademexico.org/

ECURED. (s.f.). *Intervención estadounidense en México (1846–1848).* https://www.ecured.cu/Intervenci%C3%B3n_estadounidense_en_M%C3%A9xico_(1846–1848) (Consultado el 25 de agosto de 2022).

El Motín de la Acortada. (s.f.). *Historia de México Breve.* https://www.historiademexicobreve.com/2017/10/el-motin-de-la-acordada.html

Fuentes Mares, J. (1956). *Santa Anna: aurora y ocaso de un comediante.* Jus.

Lamadrid, E. (2008). 1845–1846. Notas para la historia de Tampico en la guerra con EU. En Chávez Marín, C. (coord.). *Estudios Militares Mexicanos IV. V Simposio Internacional de Historia Militar. La evolución de las fuerzas armadas.* 263–321.

Molina, S. y Rosas, A. (2018). *Érase una vez México 2: Del grito a la Revolución.* Booket.

Nava, M. (ed.). (2016). *Anexión de Texas a EE.UU.* (1845). https://www.lhistoria.com/estados-unidos/anexion-de-texas#:~:text=Texas%20

a%20EE.-,UU.,la%20Intervenci%C3%B3n%20estadounidense%20
en%20M%C3%A9xico.

Poinsett, J. R. (1825). *Notes on Mexico, Made in the Autumn of 1822.*
London, J. Miller.

SEDENA. (2021, 1 de enero). *24 de agosto de 1821. Tratados de Córdoba.*
https://www.gob.mx/sedena/documentos/24-de-agosto-de-
1821-fueron-firmados-los-tratados-de-cordoba

Taibo II, P.I. (2013). *El Álamo.* Editorial Planeta Mexicana.

Taibo II, P.I. (2006). *Pancho Villa: una biografía narrativa.* Booket. pág.
623, 626.

The Texas Constitution, (s.f.). *Texas Constitutional History.* https://dlc.
dcccd.edu/txgov1-2/texas-constitutional-history

Tratados de Velasco. (1836). En Carmona Dávila, D. (s.f.). *Memoria
Política de México.*https://www.memoriapoliticademexico.org/
Textos/2ImpDictadura/1836TDV.html

Valadés, J. (1947). *Breve Historia de la Guerra con los Estado Unidos.*
Fondo de Cultura Económica.

Valadés, J. (1993). *Breve Historia de la Revolución mexicana (1900–1940).*
Cambio XXI; FCPS, UNAM.

Chapter 8

Cuevas, M. (1986). Historia de la nación mexicana (4a. ed.) Porrúa.

Ferrer Muñoz, M. (1955). *La formación de un Estado nacional en México:
el Imperio y la República federal, 1821–1825.* UNAM.

Herrera Sipriano, F. (2009). *La Revolución en la Montaña de Guerrero.
La lucha zapatista 1910–1918,* México, INAH.

Jiménez, L. y Horcasitas, F. (1974). *De Porfirio Díaz a Zapata. Memoria
náhuatl de Milpa Alta.* UNAM.

Pérez Memen, F. (1977). *El episcopado y la Independencia de México
(1810–1836).* Jus.

Semo, I. (1993).*La transición interrumpida, México 1968–1988,*
Universidad Iberoamericana; Nueva imagen.

Villoro, L. (1953). *La revolución de independencia: ensayo de interpretación
histórica.* UNAM.

Wilkie, J. W. (1978). *La Revolución Mexicana. Gasto federal y cambio social.* Fondo de Cultura Económica.

Womack, J. Jr. (1985). *Zapata y la Revolución Mexicana.* SEP; Siglo XXI.

Zermeño, S. (1978). *México, una democracia utópica: el movimiento estudiantil del 68.* Siglo XXI.

Chapter 9

Castañeda, J. (2014). Amarres Perros. Alfaguara.

Carrasco Picazo, J.P. y López de los Mozos Gómez, R. (s.f.). *La guerra del Golfo.* (s.e.).

Forigua Rojas, E. (2008). Guerras de hoy y de ayer: las guerras de Vietnam e Irak. *Papel Político,* 13(2), 567–614.

Gómez Robledo, A. (1963). *Meditación sobre la Justicia,* Fondo de Cultura Económica.

Gutiérrez Espada, C. y Silvela Díaz-Criado, E. (2006). *El conflicto de Irak I.* Instituto de Estudios Internacionales y Europeos Francisco de Vitoria; Ministerio de Defensa SGT.

Instituto Nacional para el Federalismo y el Desarrollo Municipal. (2019, 18 de marzo). *81 aniversario de la Expropiación Petrolera.* https://www.gob.mx/inafed/es/articulos/81-aniversario-de-la-expropiacion-petrolera?idiom=es

Johnson, P. (2001). *Estados Unidos. La historia.* Ediciones Barcelona.

Lara Martínez, O.R. (s.f.). Historia de la Industria Petrolera en México y la Reforma Energética. *Gestiopolis* [Online].

Martín Maglio, F. (2006, diciembre). *La guerra de Corea.* https://historiauniversal748.files.wordpress.com/2016/12/la-guerra-de-corea.pdf

Roberts, P. (2004). *El fin del petróleo.* Ediciones B.

Sohr, R. (2000). *Las guerras que nos esperan.* Ediciones B.

Van der Brule, A. (2020, 3 de junio). La histórica deuda contraída e impagada de Estados Unidos a España. *El Confidencial* [Online].

Williams, W. A. (1989). *El imperialismo como forma de vida.* Fondo de Cultura Económica.

Chapter 10

Alvarado, M. (1994): La polémica en torno a la idea de universidad en el siglo XIX, CESU-UNAM.

Burton, C. (Ed.) (1992). *The Encyclopedia of Higher Education*. Pergamon Press.

Fell, C. (1989). *José Vasconcelos: los años del águila (1920–1925)*. UNAM

Gómez Oyarzun, G. (1976). *La Universidad: sus orígenes y evolución*. Deslinde; UNAM.

Moreno, R. (2005, 2 de enero). El ferrocarril México Veracruz fue inaugurado con pompa en 1873. *La Crónica* [Online].

O'Gorman, E. (1960). *Justo Sierra y los orígenes de la Universidad de México. 1910*. Universidad Veracruzana.

Pérez-Campuzano, E. y Santos-Cerquera, C. (2016). Entre la pesca y el turismo: cambios económicos y demográficos recientes en la costa mexicana. *Cuadernos Geográficos,* 55(1), 283–308.

Ramírez, C. y Domínguez, R. (1993). *El Rector Ignacio Chávez: La universidad nacional entre la utopía y la realidad*, México. CESU-UNAM.

Rubalcava, R. y Schteingart, M. (2012). *Ciudades divididas: Desigualdad y segregación social en México. El Colegio de México*.

Subirá, J. (2013). Universidades Populares. *Nuestro Tiempo*, (99), 243–244.

Trejo, A. (2013). Las economías de las zonas metropolitanas de México en los albores del siglo XXI. *Estudios Demográficos y Urbanos*, 28 (3), 545–591.

Chapter 11

Álvarez, J., Meyer, L., Brown, J. et al. (2008). Fuentes para la Historia del Petróleo.

Bach, F. y Peña, M. (1938). *México y su petróleo*. Editorial México Nuevo.

Brown, J. (1997). Empresa y política: cómo y por qué se nacionalizó la industria petrolera. En Marichal, C. y Cerutti, M. *Historia de las grandes empresas de México, 1850–1930.* Fondo de Cultura Económica.

Durán, E. (1982). EI petróleo mexicano en la primera guerra mundial. En Meyer, L. et al. *Energía en México. Ensayos sobre el pasado y el presente.* Colmex.

INSP. (s.f.). *Diabetes en México, 9 de Julio del 2020.* https://www.insp. mx/avisos/3652-diabetes-en-mexico.html#:~:text=Desde%20 el%20a%C3%B1o%202000%2C%20la,encuentra%20en%20 un%20nivel%20elevado.

Jorrín Gómez, J. (2019, 27 de agosto). 160 años del primer pozo de petróleo: la locura que creó el mayor negocio del mundo. *El Confidencial* [Online].

Katz, F. (1982). *La guerra secreta en México* (vol. 2), Editorial Era.

Lavín, J. D. (1979). *Petróleo: pasado, presente y futuro de una industria mexicana, México.* FCE.

Oliver, J. (2015, 27 de abril). Necesaria una revolución alimenticia en México. *El Poder del Consumidor* [Online].

Ortuño Arzate, S. (2009). *El mundo del petróleo: Origen, usos y escenarios.* FCE; SEP; CONACYT.

Río García, E. (2009). *La droga que refresca.* Penguin Random House.

Roberts, P. (2004). *El fin del petróleo.* Ediciones B.

Ruz Sosa, M. H. (2001). *Tabasco Histórico: memoria vegetal,* Gobierno del Estado de Tabasco.

Villatoro, M. (2012, 12 de octubre). Fanta, el refresco creado en la Alemania Nazi. *ABC* [Online].

Williamson, H. (1963). *The American Petroleum Industry* (Vol.2). Northwestern University Press.

Chapter 12

Adhikari, R. y Yongzheng, Y. (2002). ¿Qué significará el ingreso en la OMC para China y sus socios comerciales? Finanzas & Desarrollo, 22–25.

Anguiano Roch, E. (2012). Sin sustento político, imposible construir relaciones económicas bilaterales sólidas. En Dussel Peters, E.

(coord.). (2012).*40 años de la relación entre México y China acuerdos, desencuentros y futuro*. Facultad de Economía, UNAM, 37–48.

Cancino, R. (2012). *El ingreso de China a la OMC. Análisis jurídico e implicaciones comerciales para México*. Editorial Novum. pág. 115–116.

Candelas Ramírez, R. (2019, 16 de julio). *El Proyecto del tren Transístmico*. Carpeta Informativa Núm. 119.

Chang, H. (1996). *El papel del Estado en la economía*. Planeta; Facultad de Economía, UNAM.

Dussel Peters, E. (2005). El caso de las estadísticas comerciales entre China y México: para empezar a sobrellevar el desconocimiento bilateral. *Economía Informa*, (335), 50–61.

Gómez Chiñas, C. (2006). Las implicaciones de la adhesión de China a la Organización Mundial de Comercio. En Estrada, J. L. et al. (coord.). (2006). *China en el siglo XXI. Economía, política y sociedad de una potencia emergente*. Universidad Autónoma Metropolitana; Porrúa.

Govaere Vicarioli, V. (2002). *Introducción al Derecho Comercial Internacional*. EUNED.

Hernández, R. (2005). El comercio exterior de China y su relación con México. Una perspectiva histórica. *México y la Cuenca del Pacífico*, 8 (26), 117–129.

Humboldt, A. (1827). *Ensayo político sobre el reino de la Nueva España*. (s.e.).

Leithead, A. (2011, 24 de agosto). China, el pasado ferroviario de California y también el presente. *BBC Mundo* [Online].

Manassero, M. (2008, marzo). China en la OMC: una transformación positiva. *Instituto de Estudios Estratégicos de Buenos Aires*. https://silo.tips/download/china-en-la-omc-una-transformacion-positiva

Mendoza Cota, J. E. (2015). China: Su importancia e impacto en la economía mexicana. *México y la Cuenca del Pacífico*, 4 (12), 65–91.

Morales Castro, J.A. (2003). *Proyectos de Inversión en la Práctica*. Editorial Gasca-Sicco.

Rodríguez, M. (2017, 26 de febrero). Cómo fue la primera gran ley para prohibir la inmigración a EE.UU. 130 años antes de la llegada de Donald Trump al poder. *BBC Mundo* [Online].

Rueda, S. (1998). La Nao de China, riqueza a contracorriente. *Arqueología Mexicana*, 5 (33), 56–63.

UNCTAD (2003), *World Investment Report 2003. FDI Policies for Development: National and International Perspectives*. https://unctad.org/es/node/31014

Chapter 13

Aguayo, S. (2010). Vuelta en U: guía para entender y reactivar la democracia estancada. Taurus.

Gandásegui, M. A. y Castillo, D. (comp.). (2010). *Estados Unidos. La crisis sistémica y las nuevas condiciones de legitimación*. Clacso: Siglo XXI.

Laneydi Martínez, A. (2014) Ciclos económicos y mecanismos de transmisión de shocks desde Estados Unidos hacia América Latina y el Caribe: una breve aproximación. *Revista Temas de Economía Mundial*, (V). (s.p.).

López Betancourt, E. (2011). *Drogas: entre el derecho y el drama*. Editorial Universitaria Ramón Areces. pág. 107–132.

Luna–Fabritius, A. (2015). Modernidad y drogas desde una perspectiva histórica. *Revista Mexicana de Ciencias Políticas y Sociales*, (225) 21–44.

Sánchez Egozcue, J. M. (2009). América Latina en la coyuntura de la crisis financiera internacional. *Revista Pensamiento Propio*, (30), 37–60.

Titelman, D., Pérez-Caldentey, E. y Minzer, R. (2008). Una comparación de la dinámica e impactos de los choques de términos de intercambio y financieros en América Latina 1980-2006. *Serie Financiamiento del Desarrollo*, (203).

Valdés, G. (2013). *Historia del narcotráfico en México*. Aguilar.

Youngers, C. A. (2013). El debate sobre políticas de drogas en América Latina. *Revista Latinoamericana de Seguridad Ciudadana*, (13), 13–25.

Chapter 14

Adams, W. P. (comp.) (1987). Regionalismo, esclavitud, guerra civil y reincorporación del sur, 1815–1877. En Los Estados Unidos de América. Siglo Veintiuno España.

Brading, A. Los españoles en México hacia 1792. *Historia Mexicana. El Colegio de México*, 23 (1), 126–144.

Castañeda, J. (2020). *Estados Unidos: en la intimidad y a la distancia.* Debate.

Eugenio Anguiano Roch, ¨De la dinastía Qing en el siglo XIX hasta el fin de la República de China¨, en *Historia mínima de China*, coord. Flora Botton Beja (México: El Colegio de México, 2012).

González Navarro, M. (1994). *Los extranjeros en México y los mexicanos en el extranjero 1821–1971* (Vol. III). El Colegio de México. p. 133.

González, M. (2021, 23 de enero). Corte ordena inmediata libertad de Florence Cassez. *El Universal*. https://archivo.eluniversal.com.mx/notas/897778.html

Jones, M. A. (1996): *Historia de Estados Unidos*. Ediciones Cátedra.

Khadria, B. (2006). India: migración calificada a los países desarrollados y migración laboral al golfo (Morán Quiroz, L.R., trad.). *Migración y Desarrollo: perspectivas desde el sur*, 87–124.

Martínez, M. (2004). Los gitanos y las Indias antes de la Pragmática de Carlos II (1494–1753), *O Tchatchipen: lil ada trin tchona rodipen romaniI. Revista Trimestral de Investigación Gitana*, (48), 16–23.

Martínez Maza, C. (2016): El esclavismo antiguo en los Estados Unidos del periodo "antebellum" (1780–1860), *Gerión. Revista de Historia Antigua*, 34, 383–389. https://doi.org/10.5209/rev_GERI.2016.v34.53748.

Miranda & Estavillo Abogados. (2011, 28 de junio). *Cambios a la Regulación en Materia Migratoria*. https://studylib.es/doc/5061622/cambios-a-la-regulaci%C3%B3n-en-materia-migratoria

Morgan, K. (2017). *Cuatro siglos de esclavitud trasatlántica* (C. Castells, trad.). Editorial Crítica.

Newsweek México. (2014, 9 de noviembre). Correr en México para sobrevivir a Kenia Archivado el 9 de noviembre. *Wayback Machine*.

Chapter 15

Johnson, L.B. (2017), Un presidente en guerra contra la pobreza, Editorial 50Minutos.es.

López Ayllón, S. y García, A. (s.f.). *Distribución De La Riqueza: El Complejo Equilibrio De La Democracia Constitucional*. Instituto de Investigaciones Jurídicas de la UNAM.

López Obrador, A. (2021). *A la mitad del camino*. Editorial Planeta.

Navarro, R. y Leal, R. G. (2015). *Los ferrocarriles en México*, Editorial Palibrio.

Sáenz, J.L. (2009) Los Astilleros y la Industria Marítima en el Pacífico Americano. *Diálogos Revista Electrónica de Historia*, 10 (1), 47–90.

Wolmar, C. (2013). *The Great Railroad Revolution: The History of Trains in America*. Public Affairs.

Zepeda Patterson, J. (2016). *Los amos de México*, Editorial Planeta.